AF224974

Ballad of Leo's Art

Leo Valenzuela

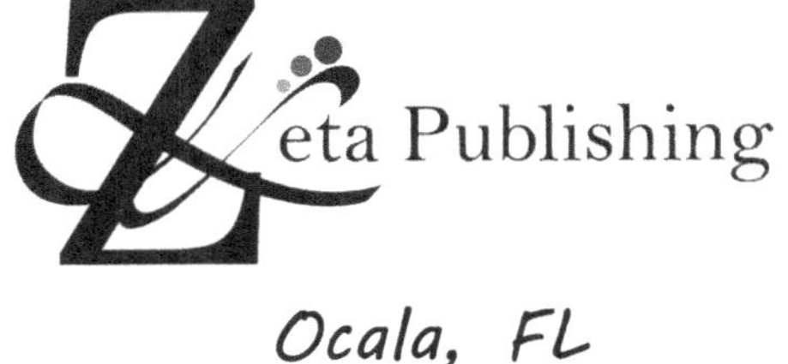

Zeta Publishing

Ocala, FL

Zeta Publishing, Inc
3850 SE 58th Ave
Ocala, FL 34480
www.zetapublishing.com

This is a work of fiction. All of the characters, names, incidents, organizations, and dialogue in this novel are either the products of the author's imagination or are used fictitiously.

Ordering Information:
Quantity sales. Special discounts are available on quantity purchases by corporations, associations, and others. For details, contact the publisher at the address above.
Orders by U.S. trade bookstores and wholesalers. Please contact Zeta Publishing: Tel: (352) 694-2553; Fax: (352) 694-1791 or visit www.zetapublishing.com

ISBN: 978-1-947191-00-6 (sc)

ISBN: 978-1-947191-01-3 (e)

Library of Congress Control Number: 2017941847

Printed in the United States of America

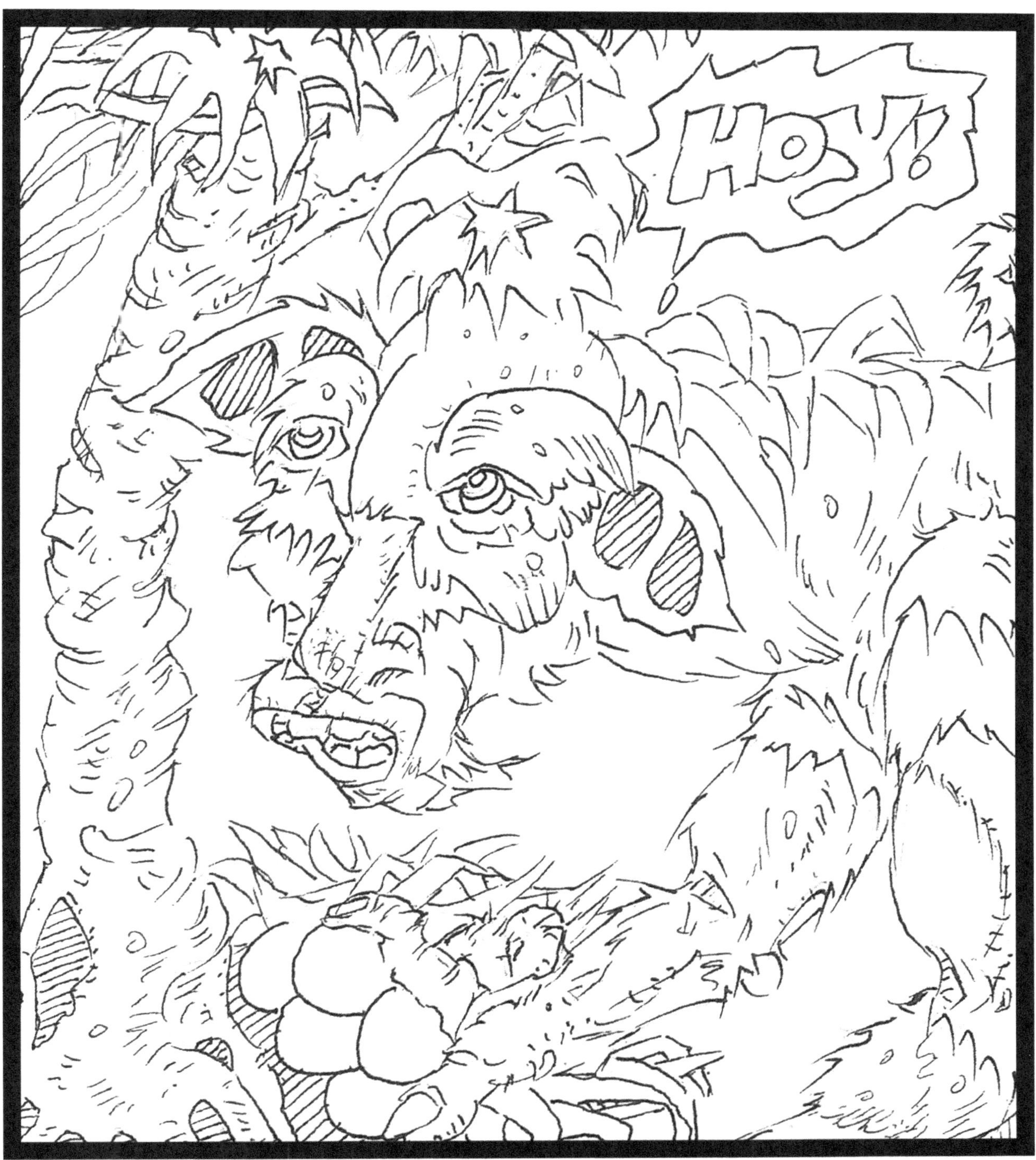

HOY!

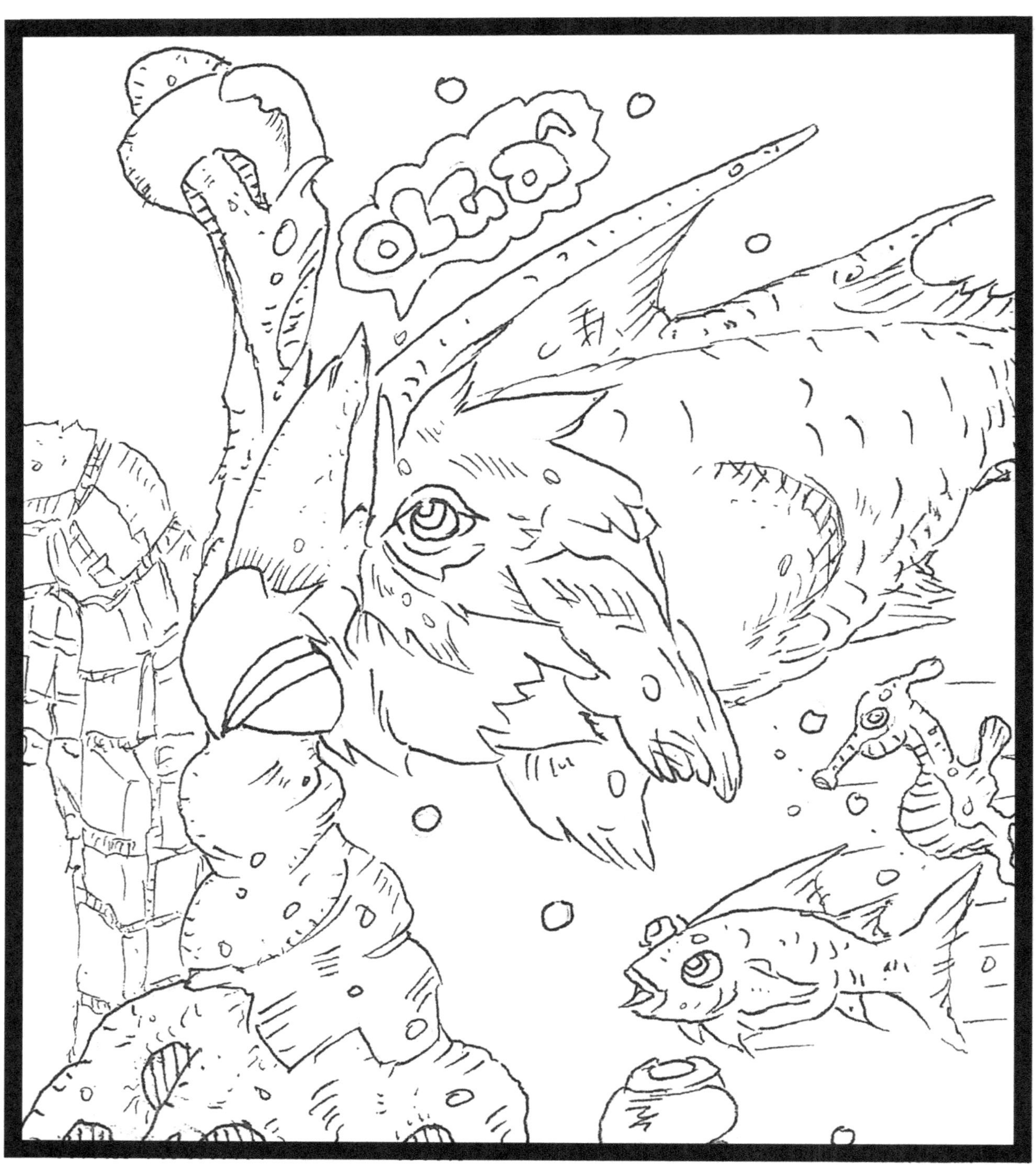

2

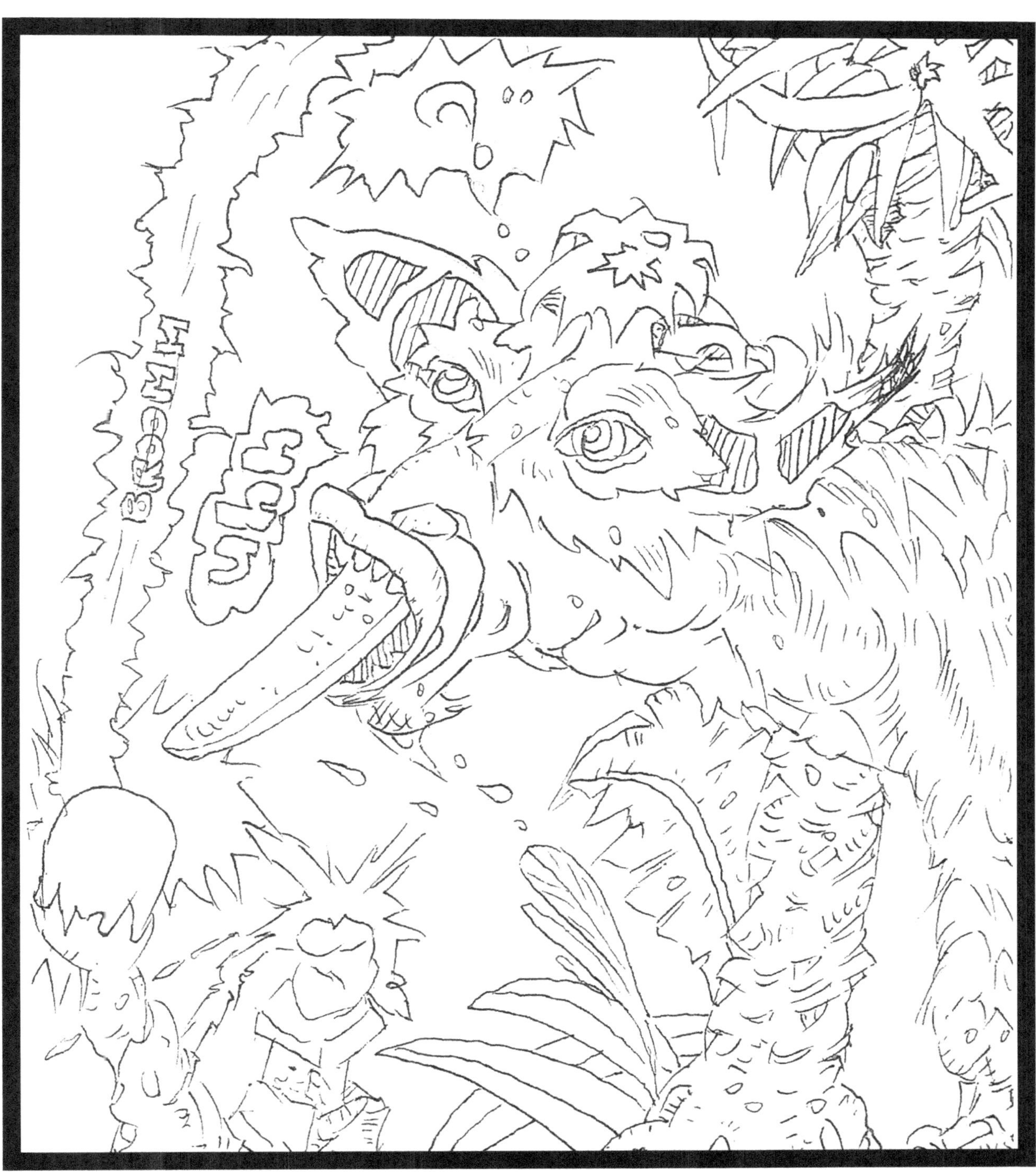

BWEEGH
ubb

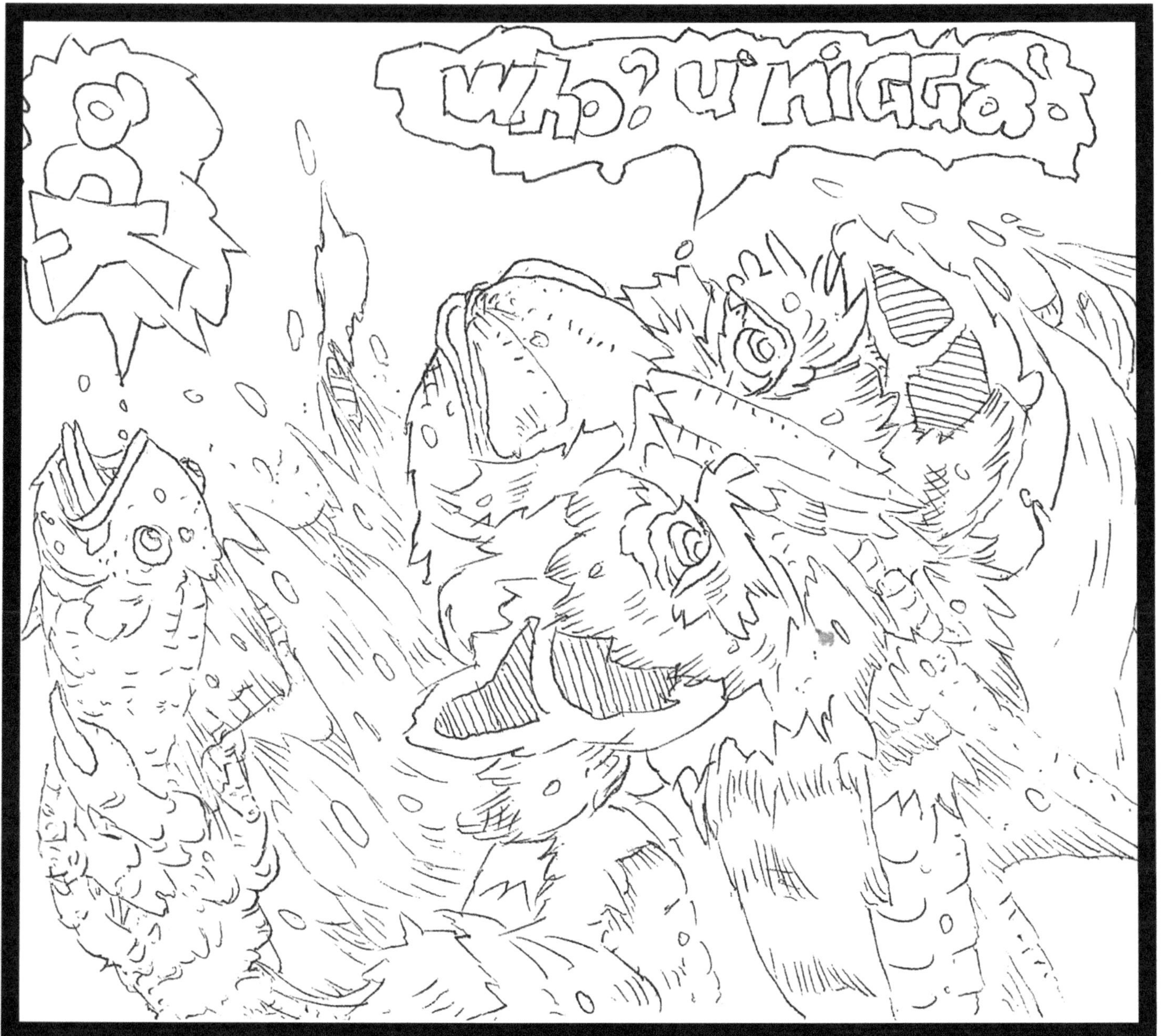
who? u' nigga?
ock

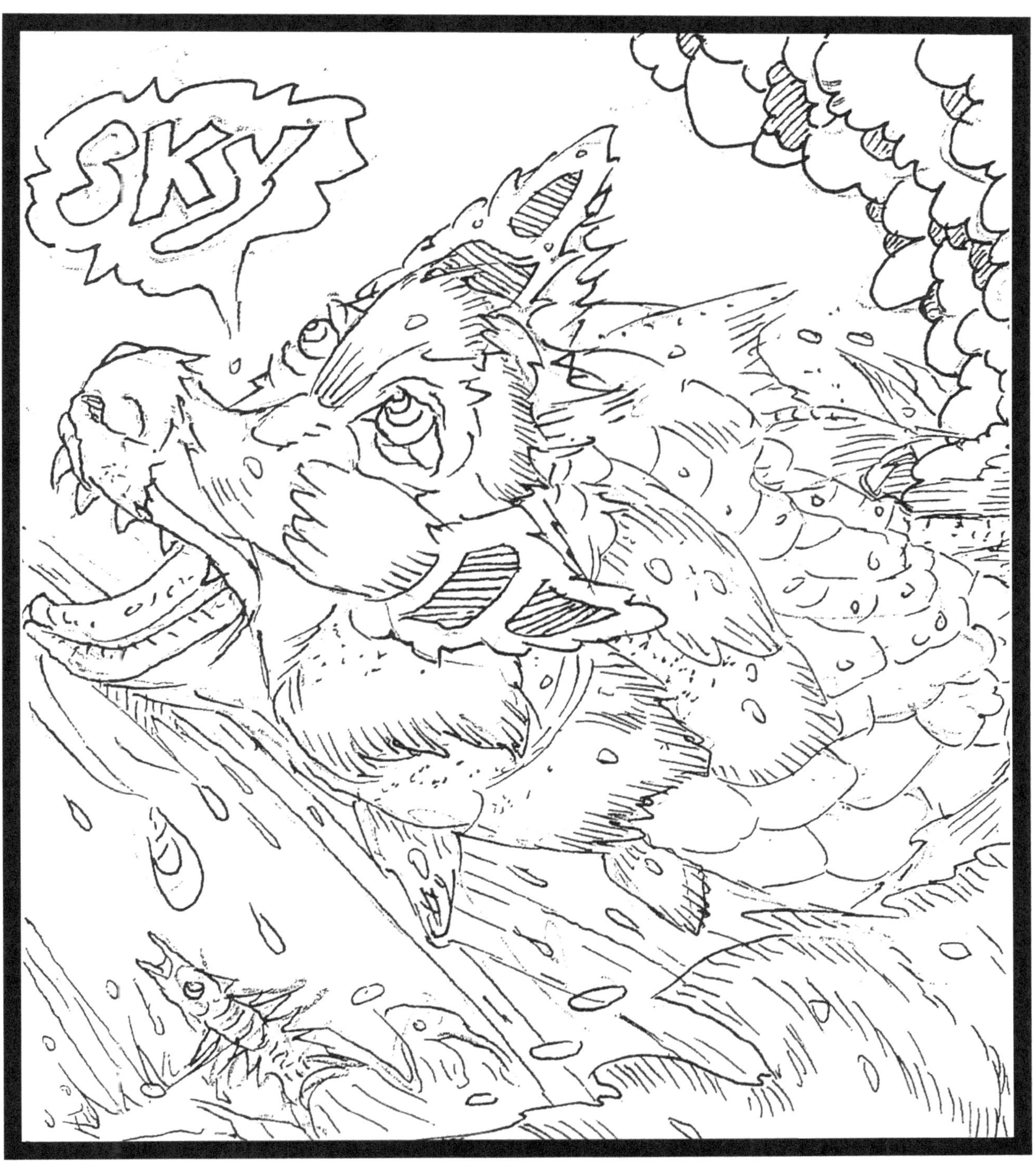

SKY

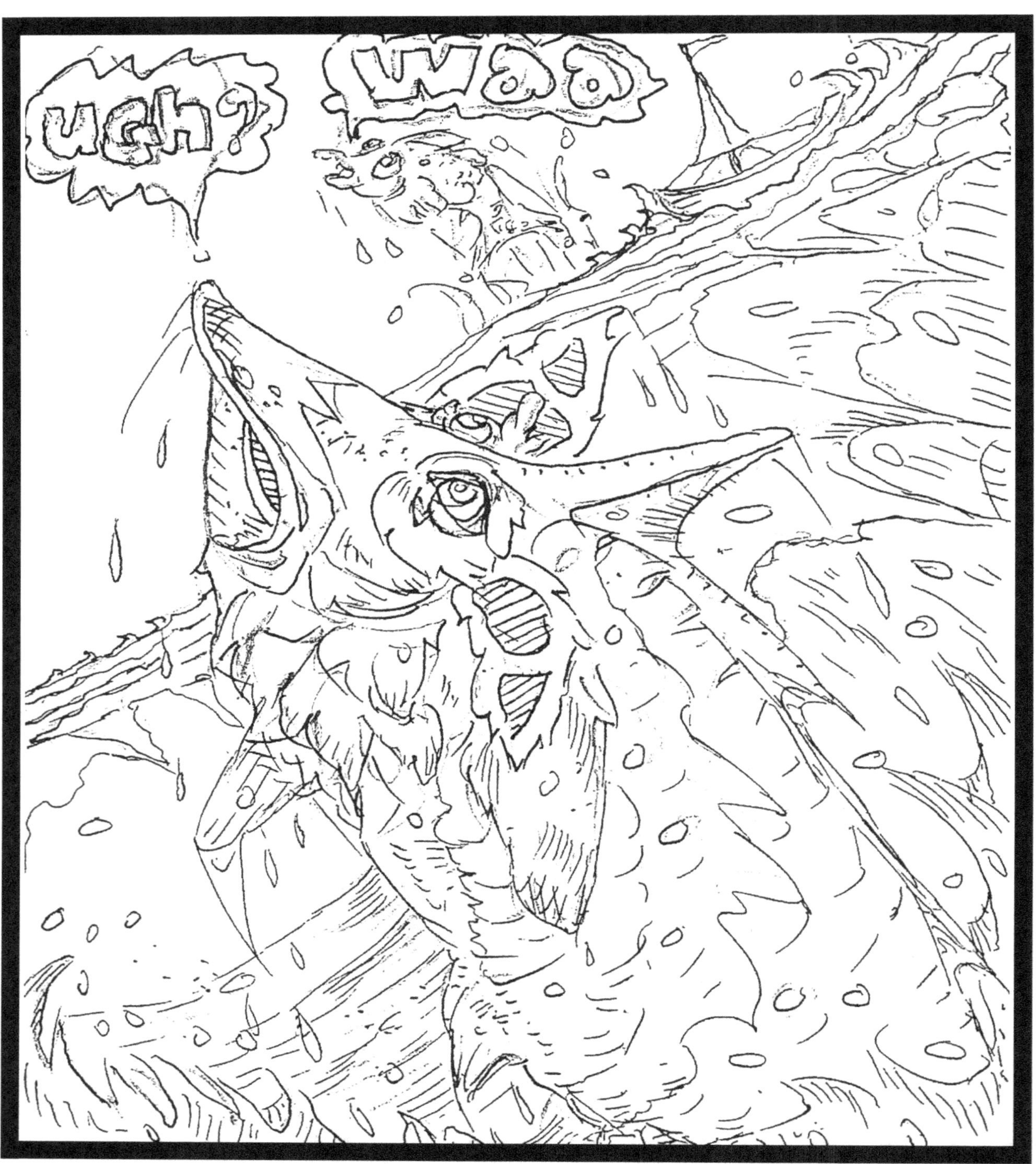

ugh?
waa

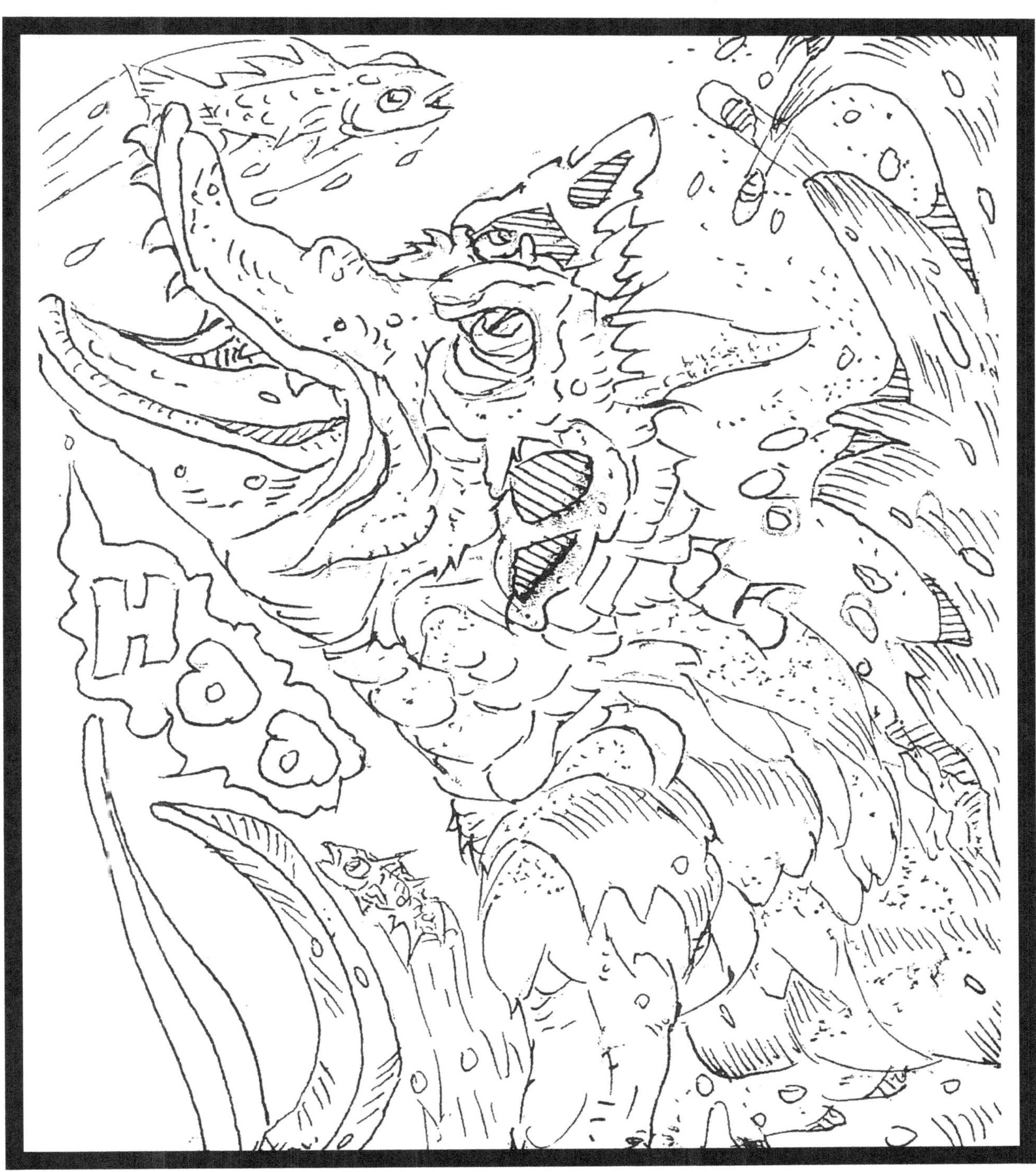

HAA

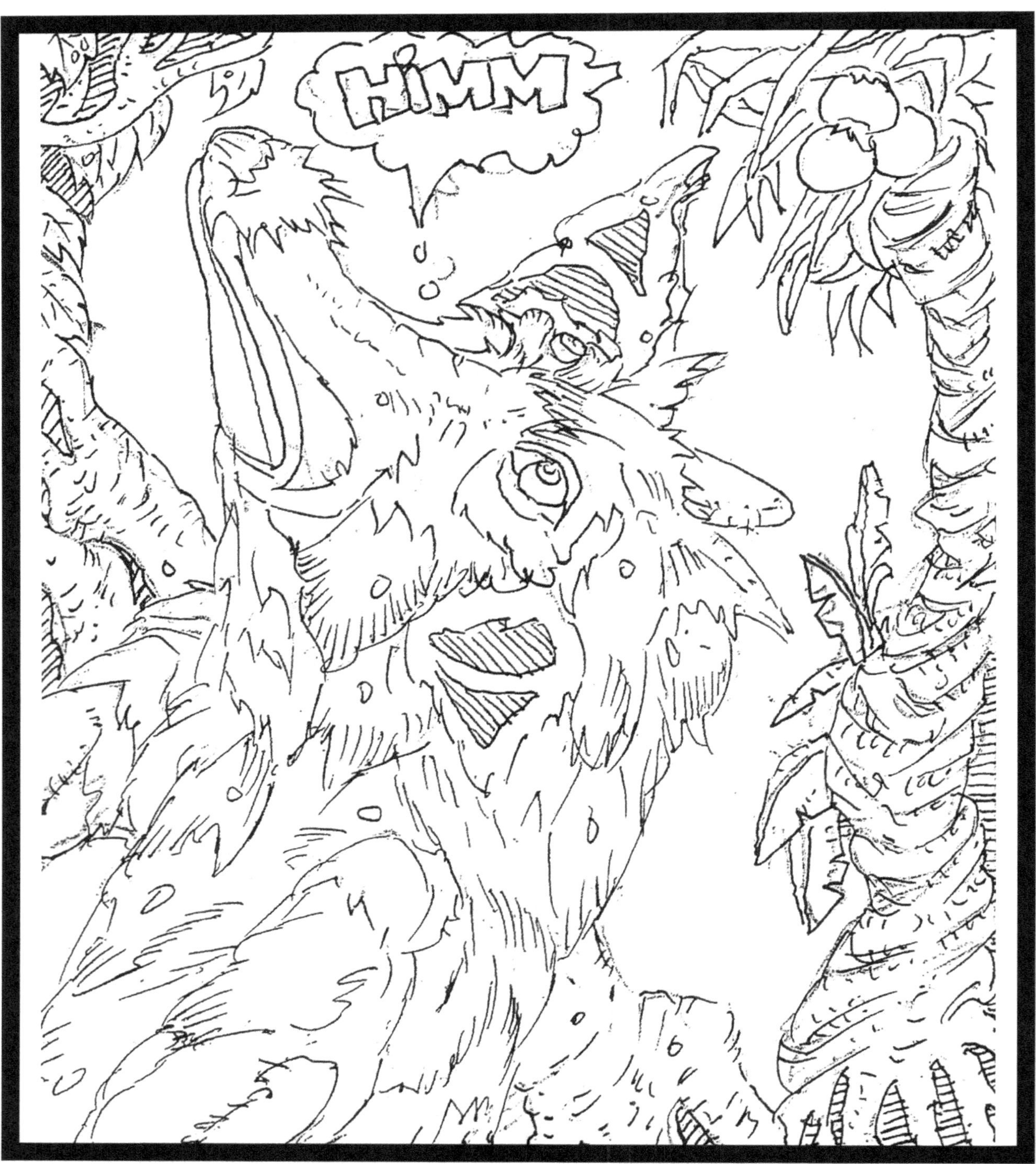
HMM

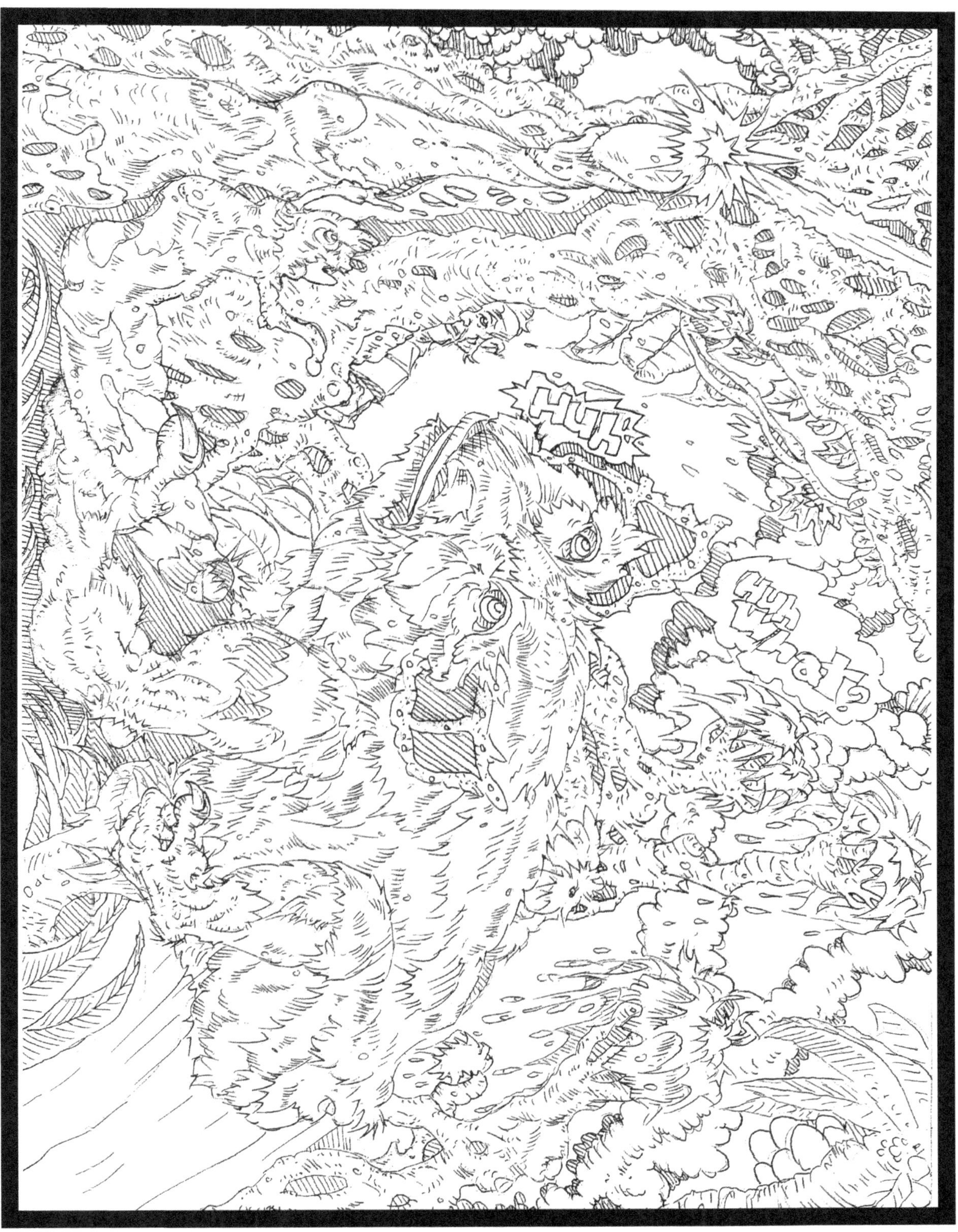

HUH?
HUH WHAT'S

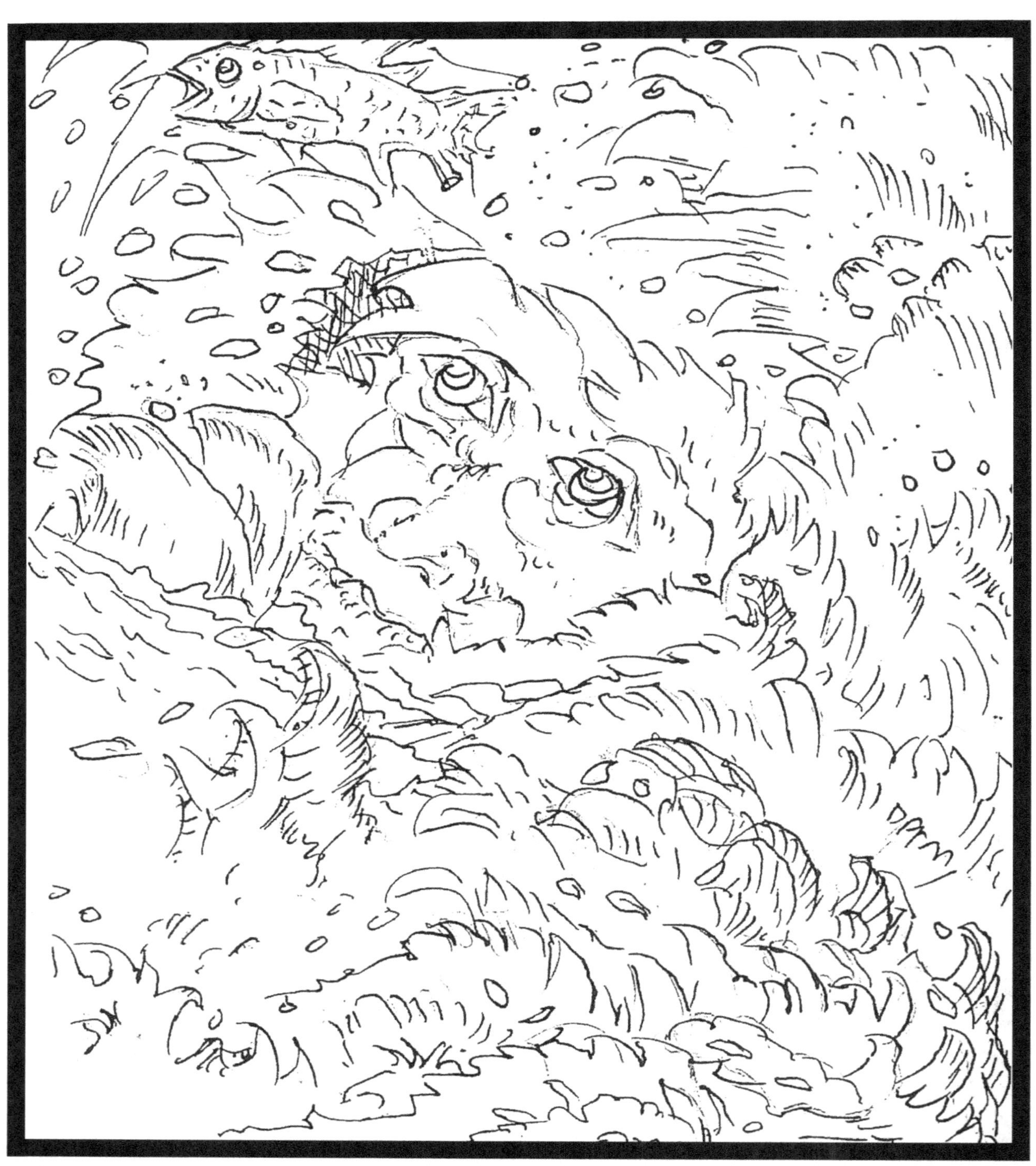

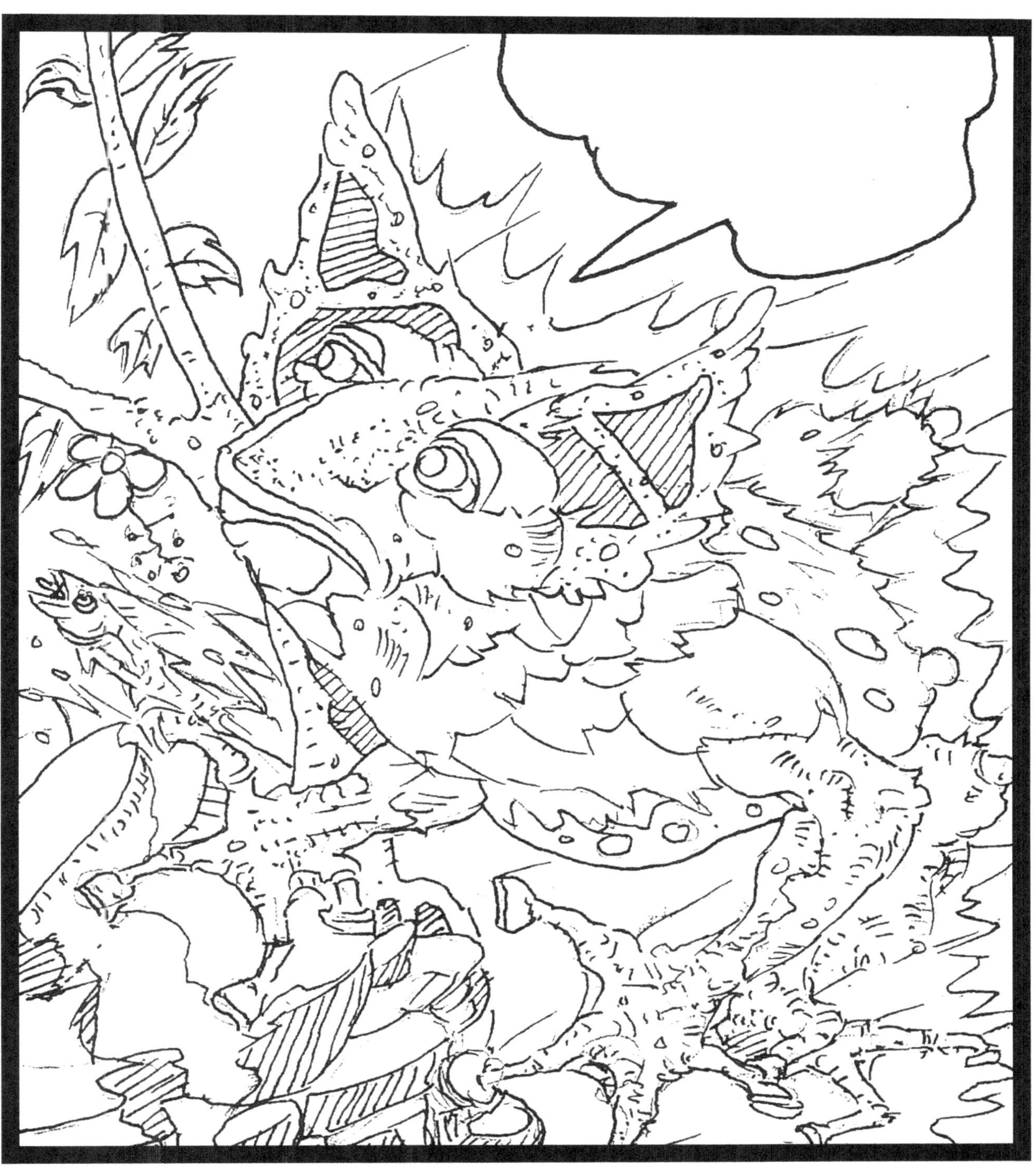

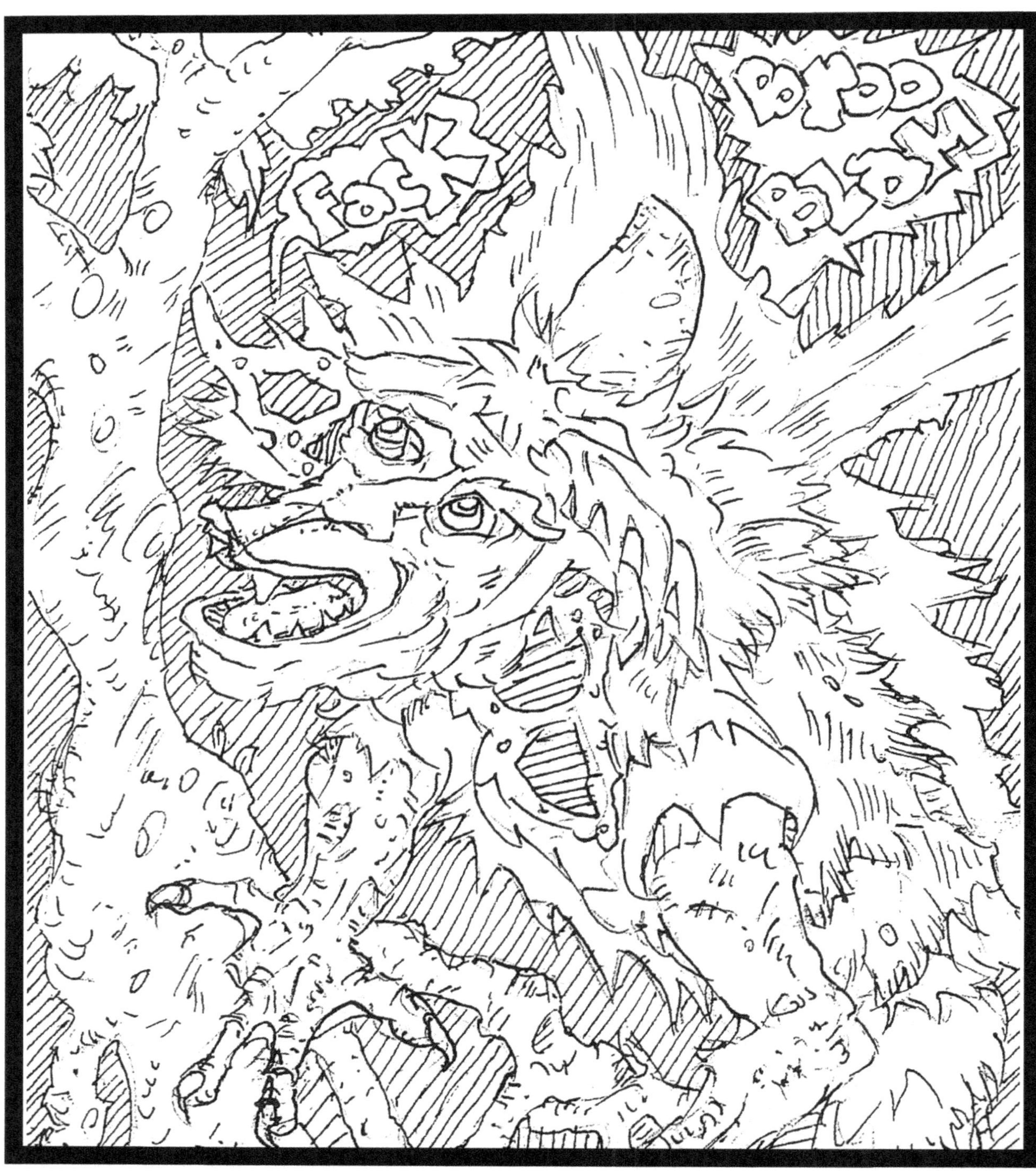
FACK!
BROO
BLAH!

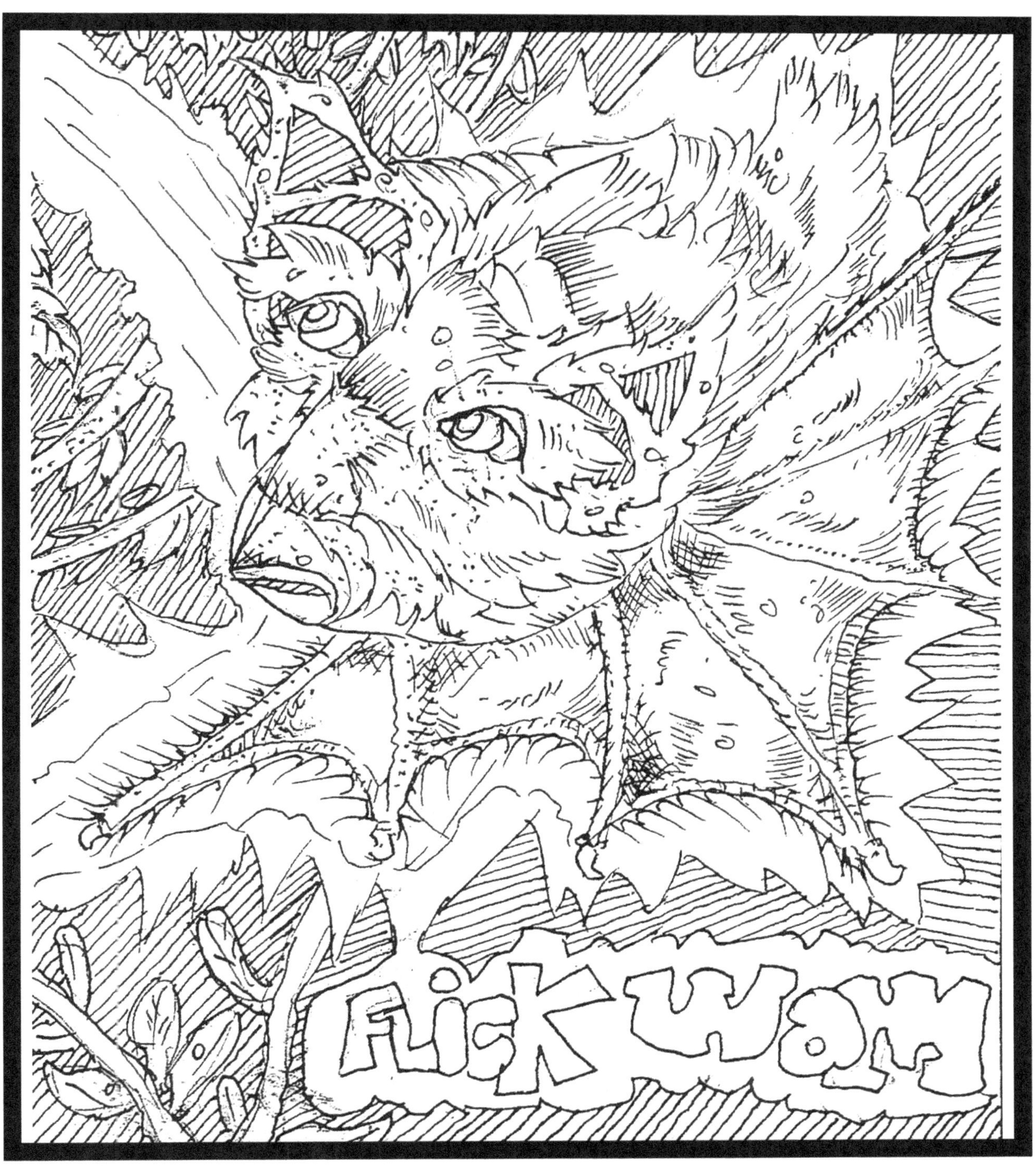

FLICK WALL

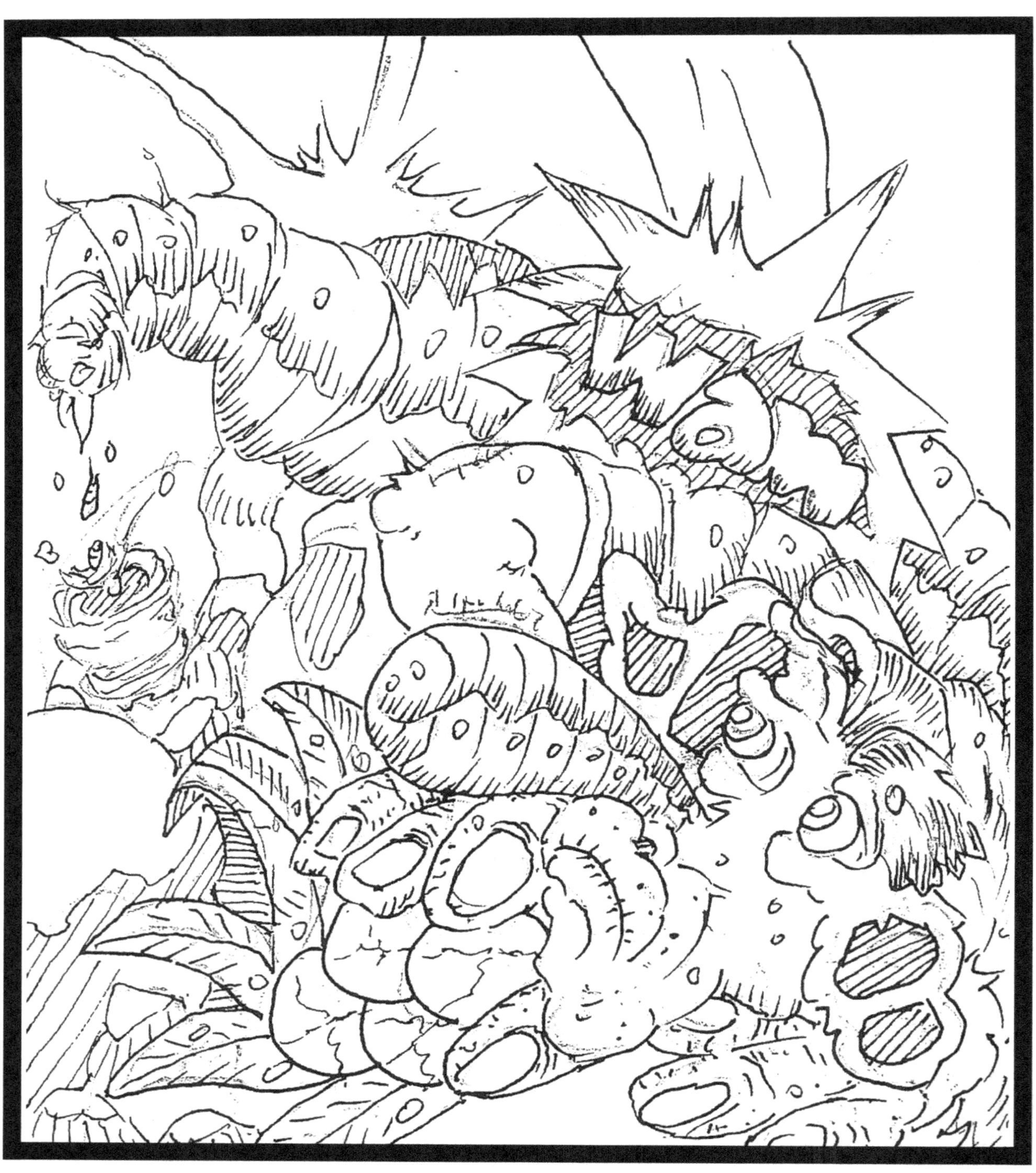

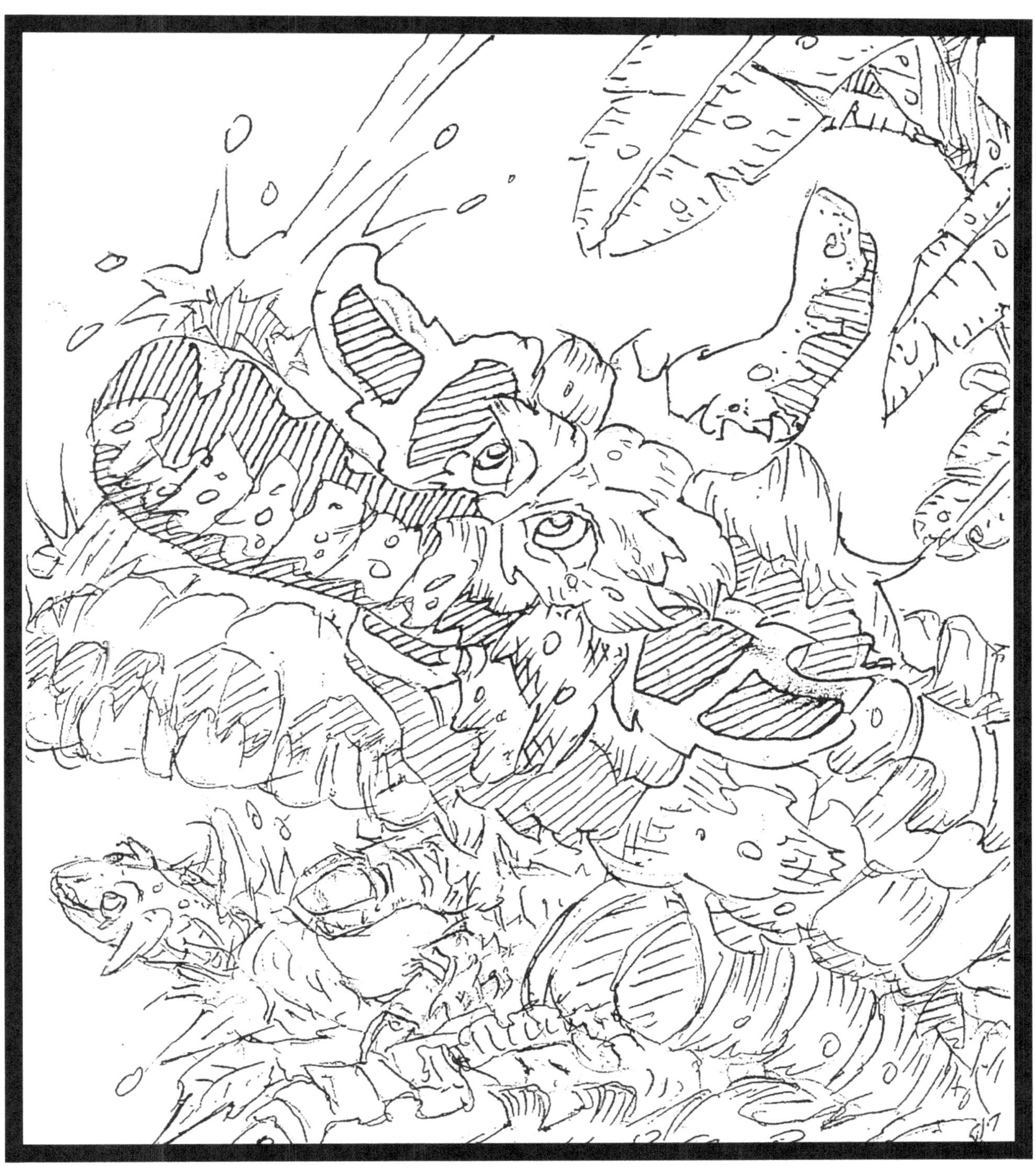

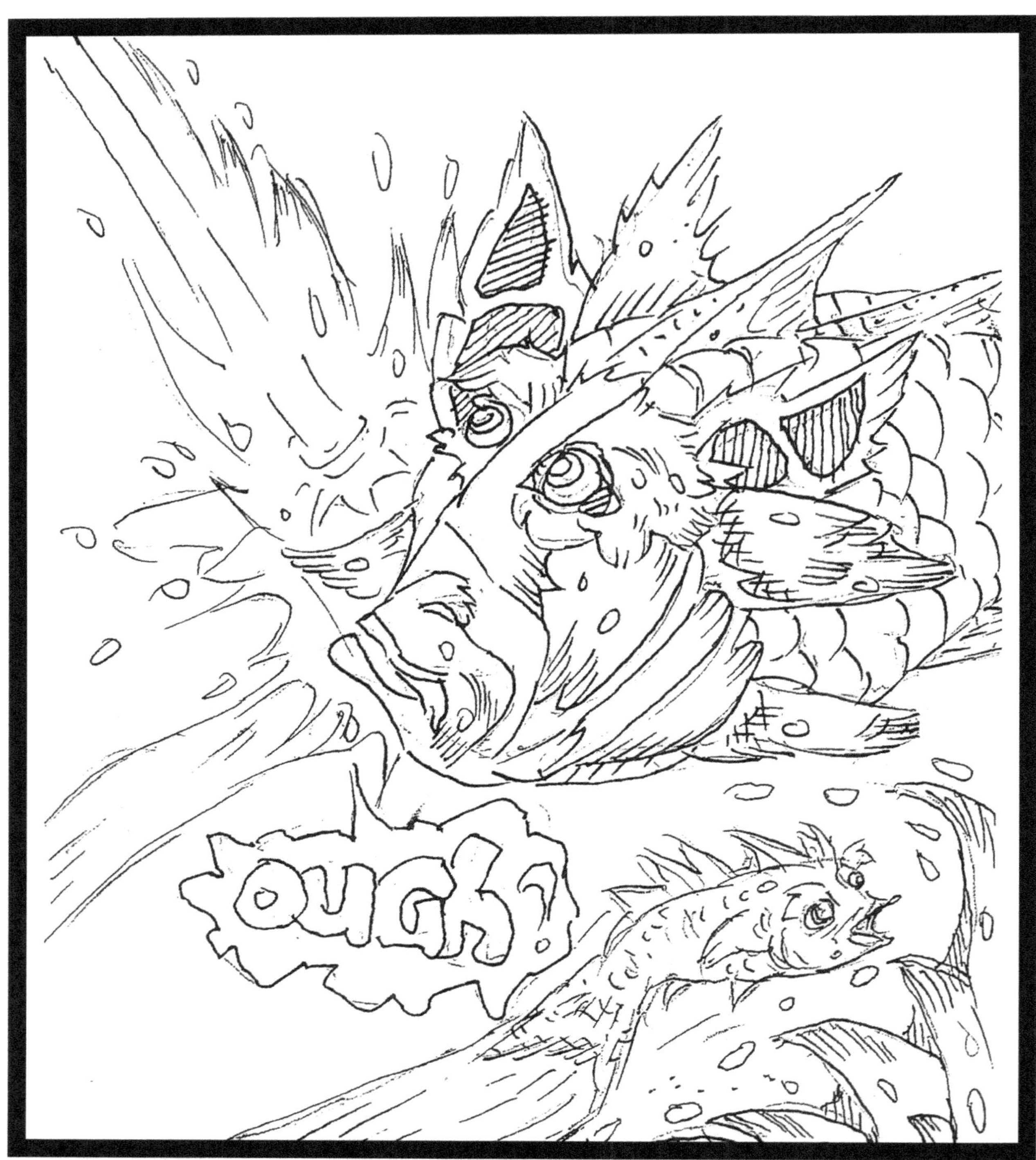
OUGH?

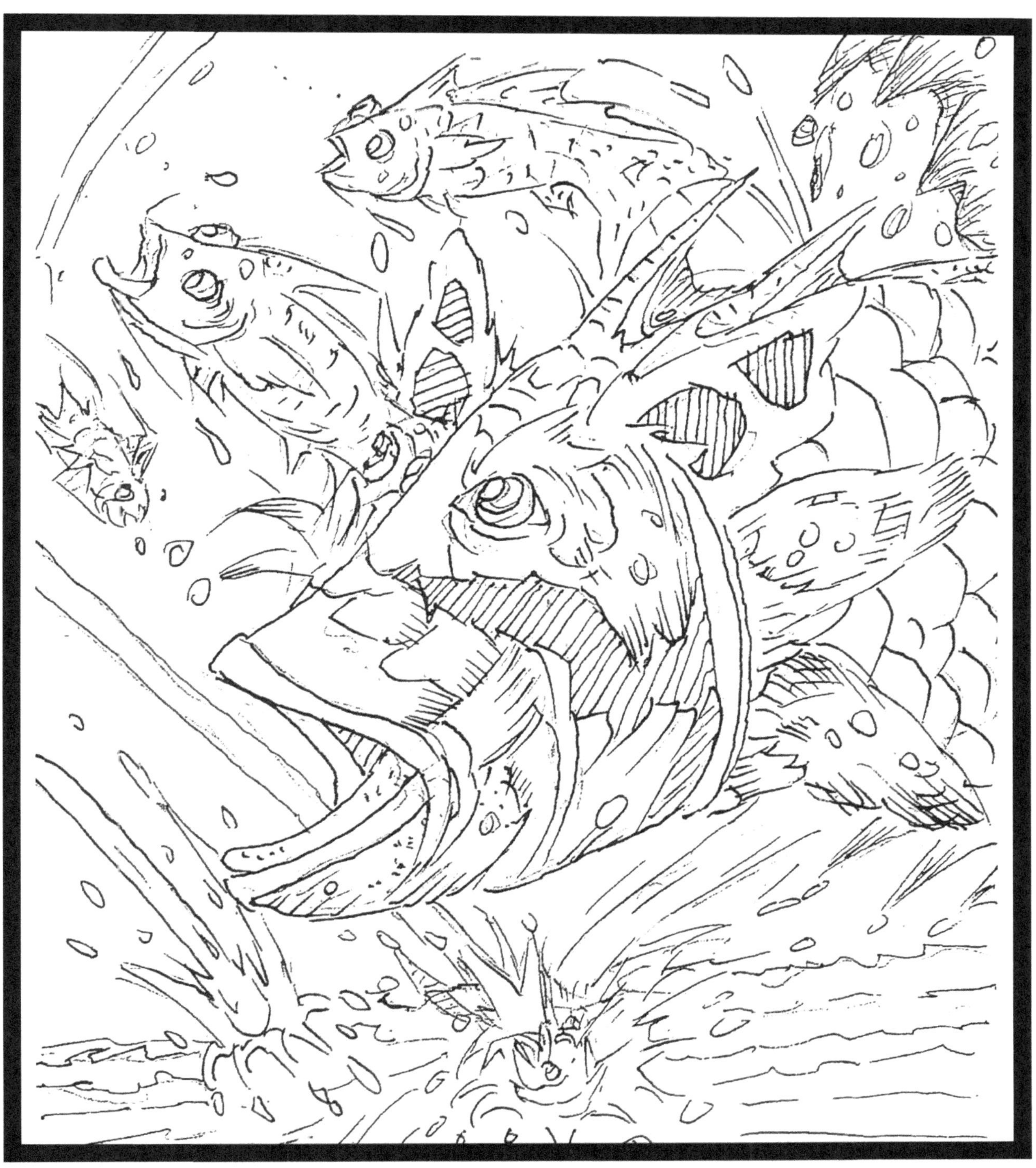

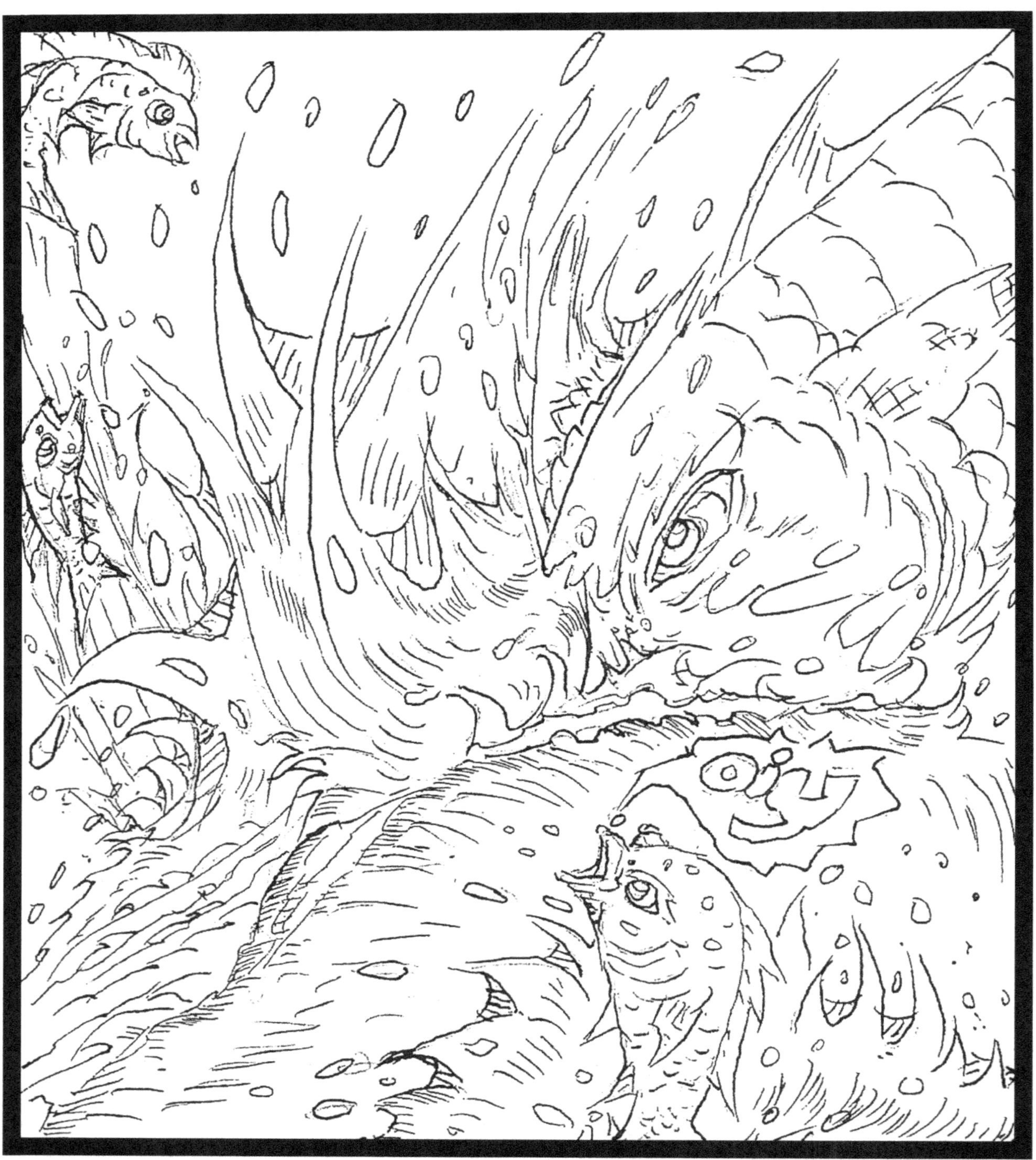

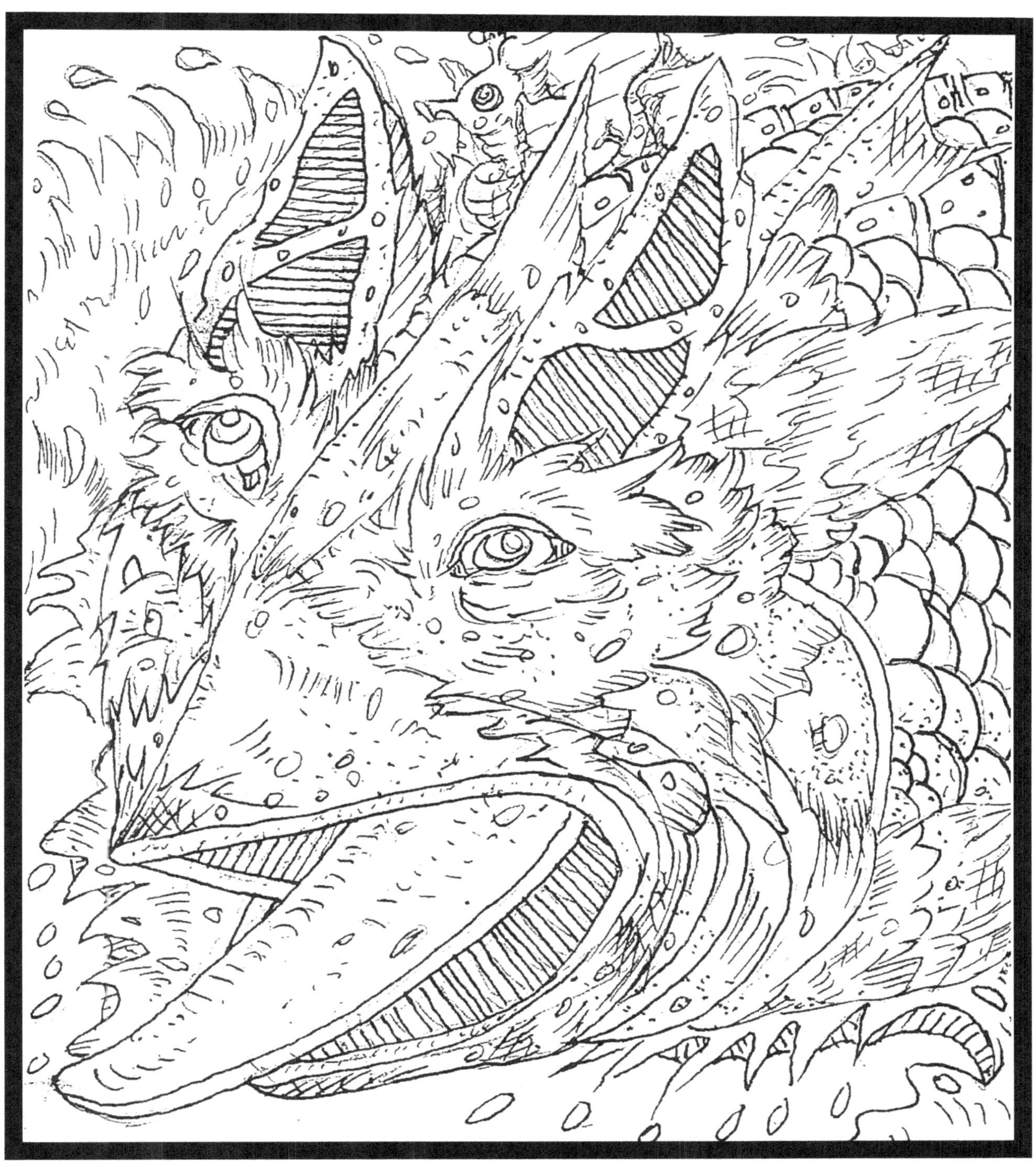

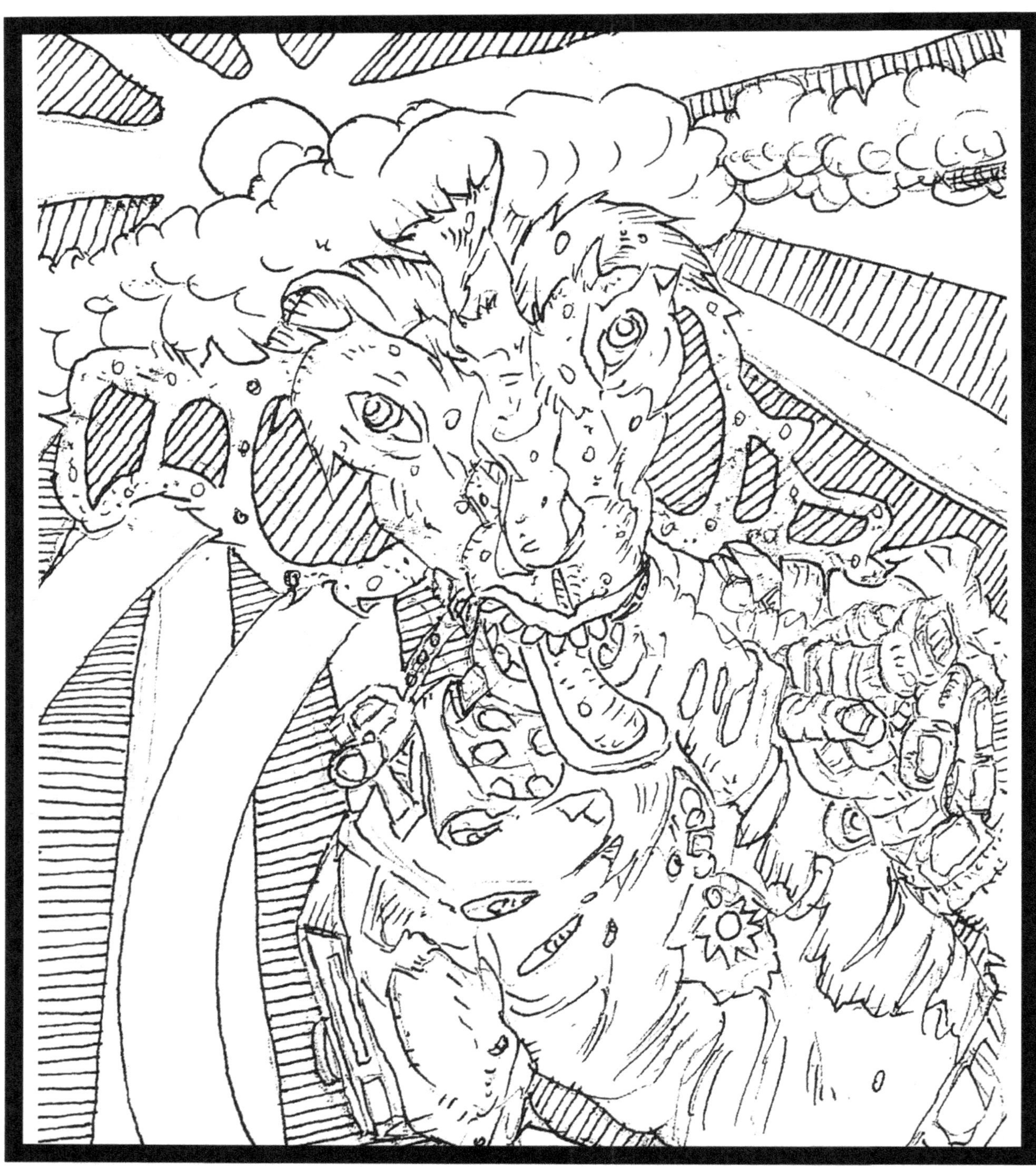

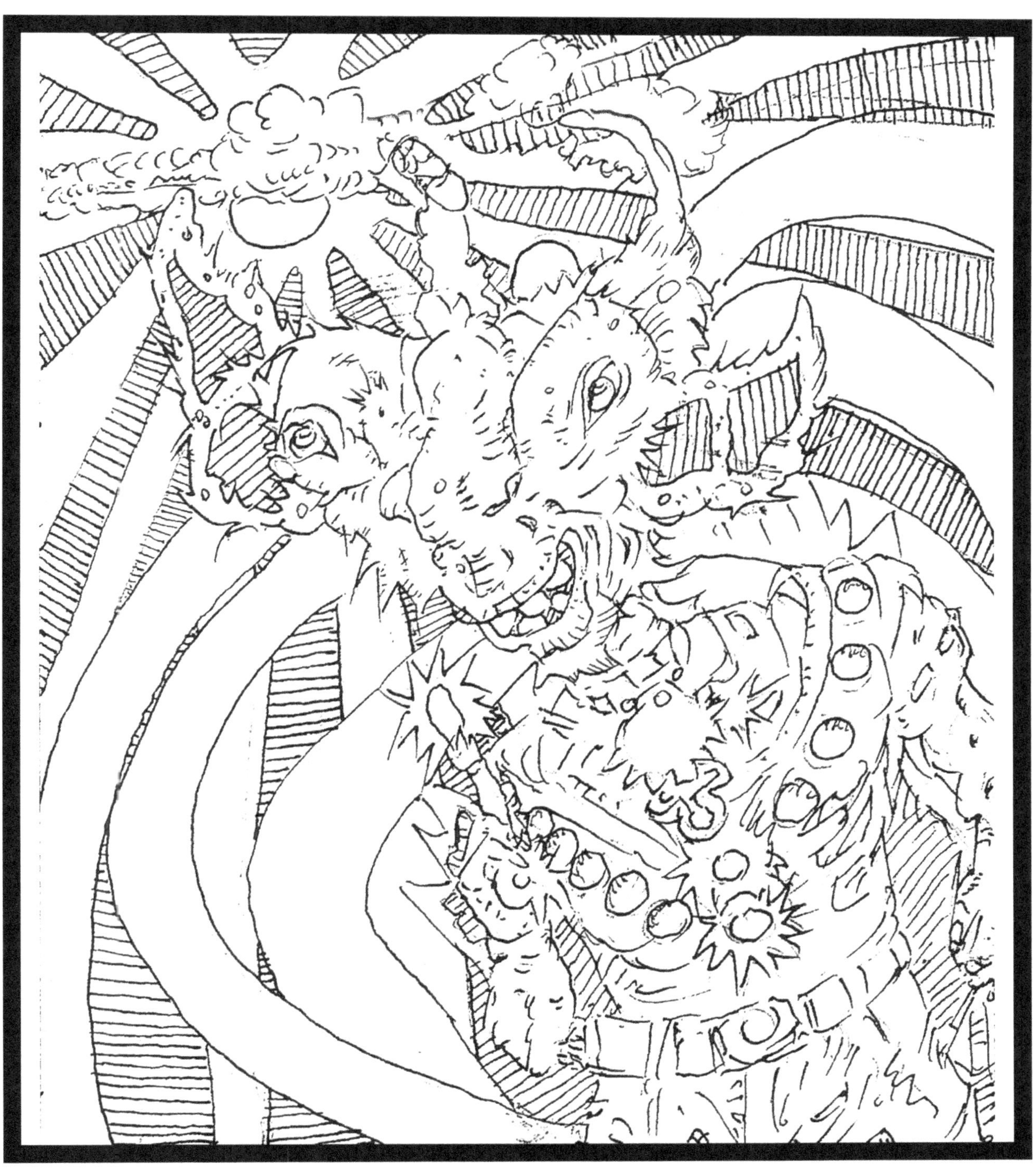

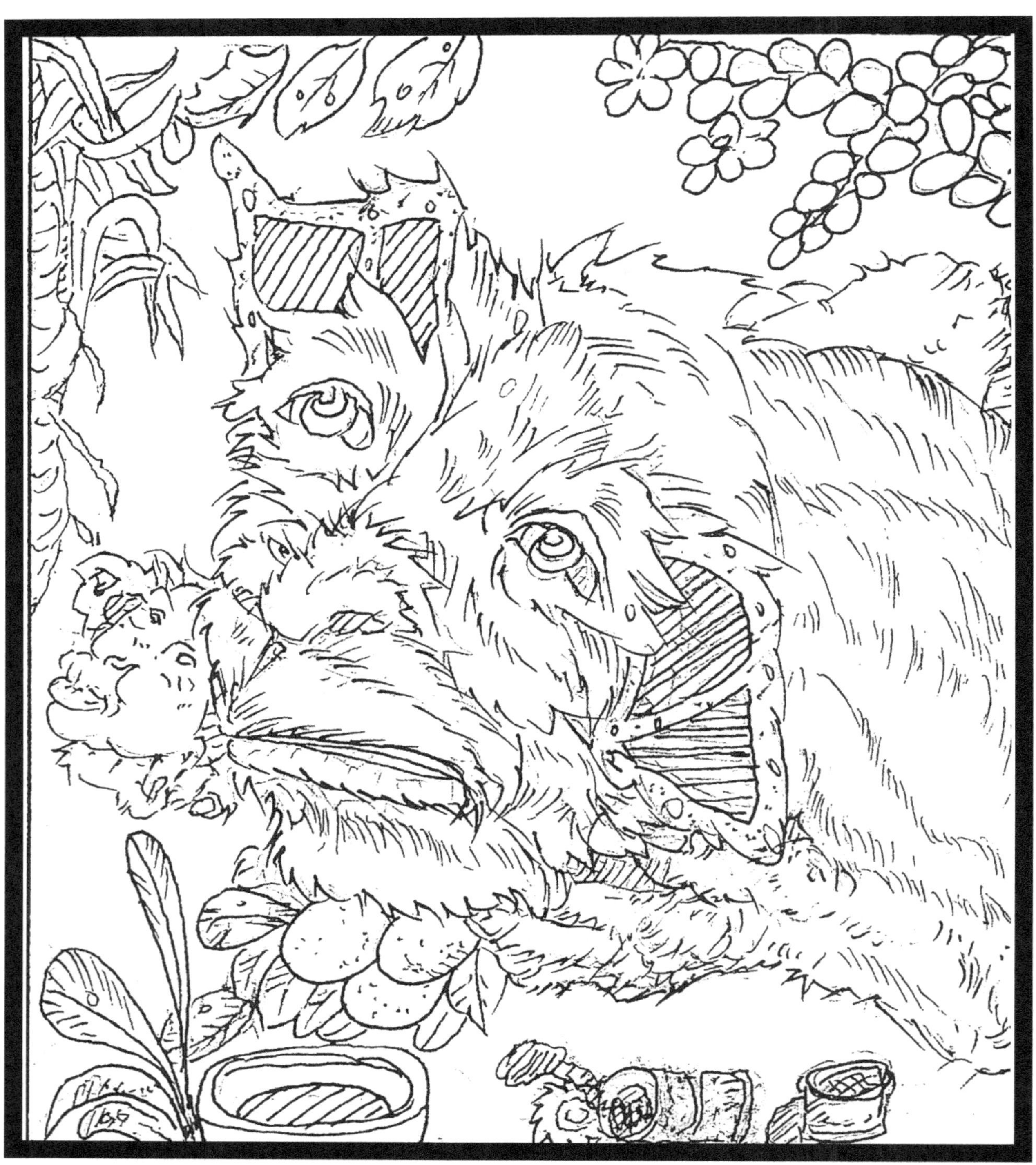

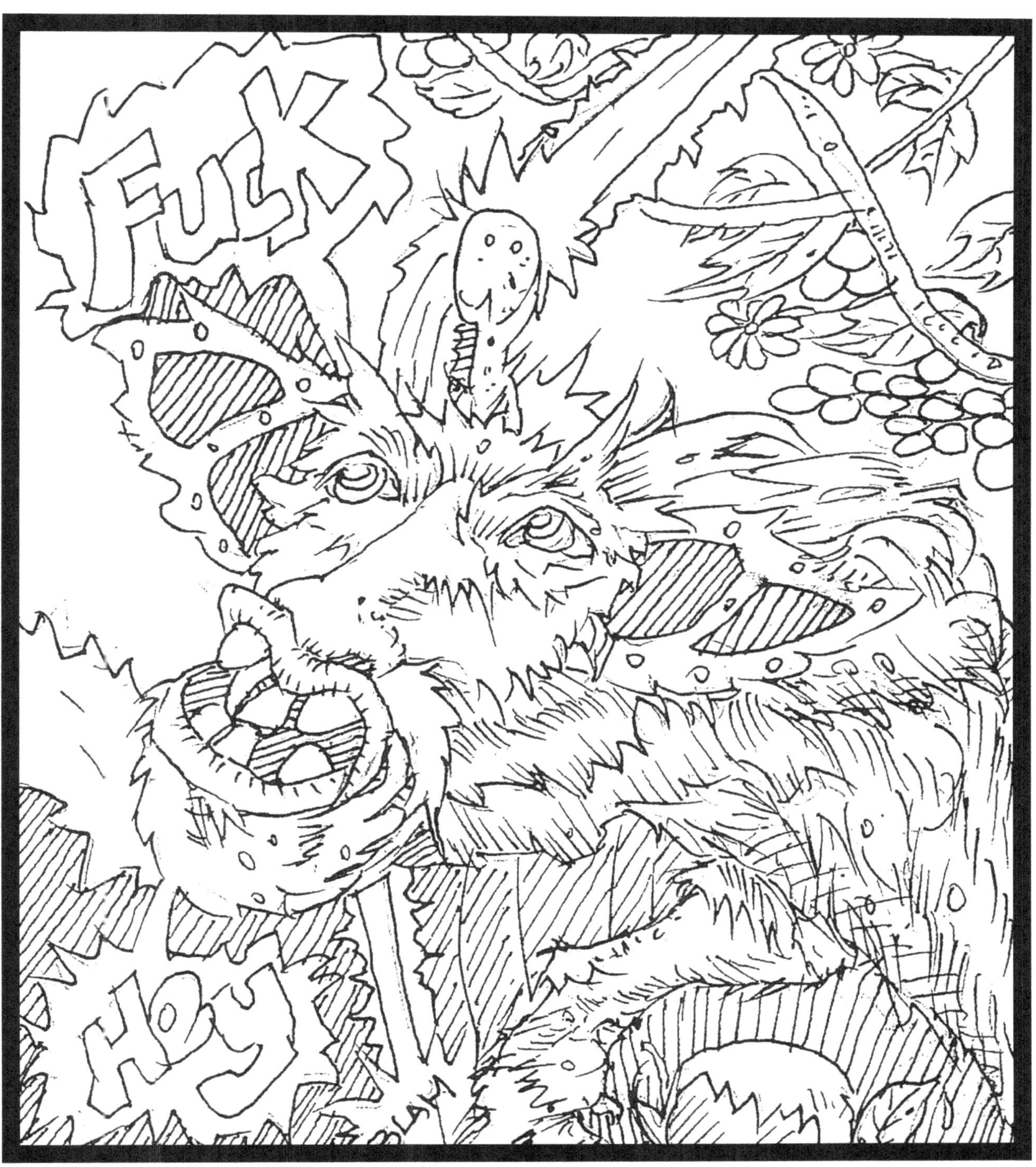
FUCK
Hey!

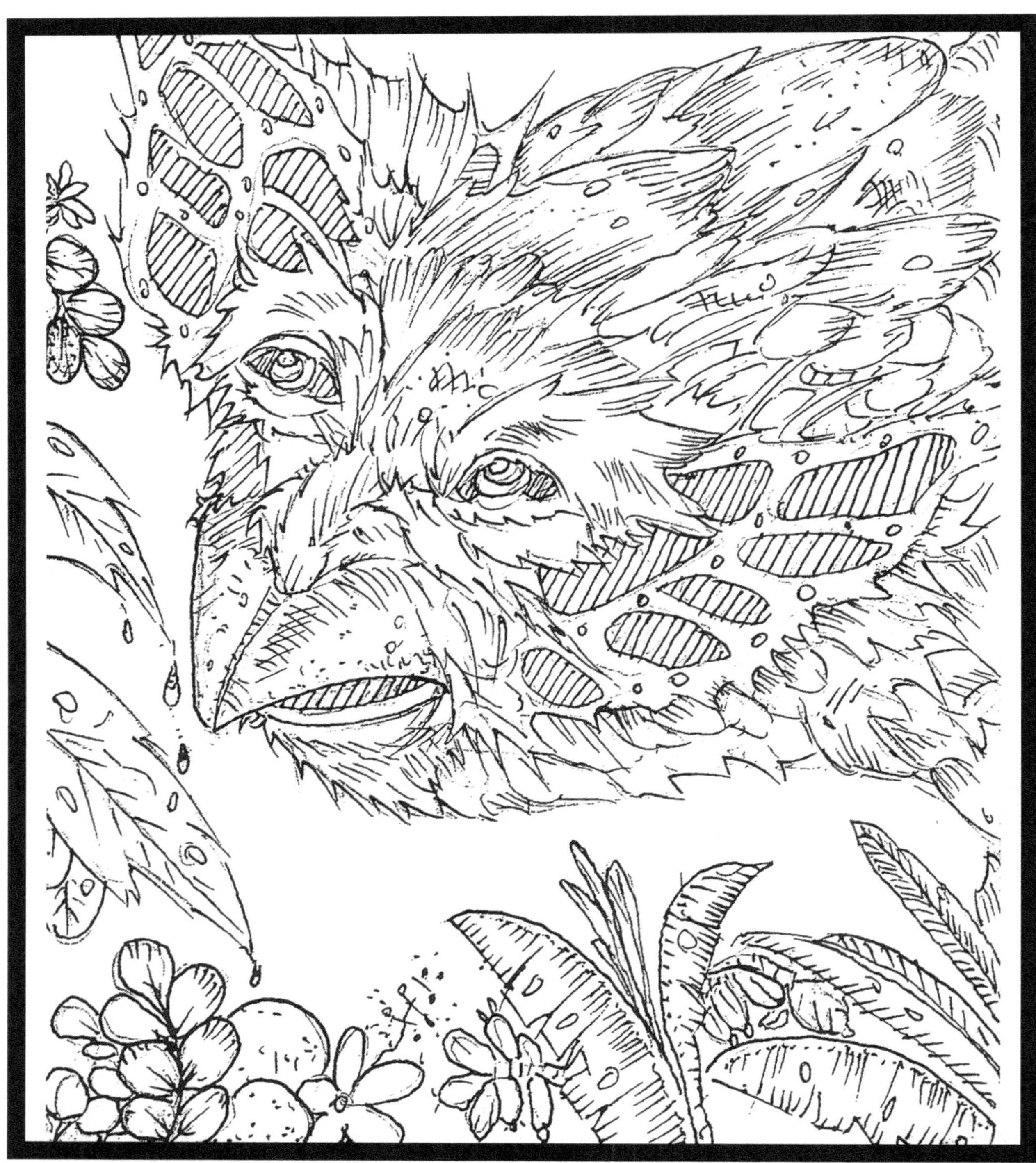

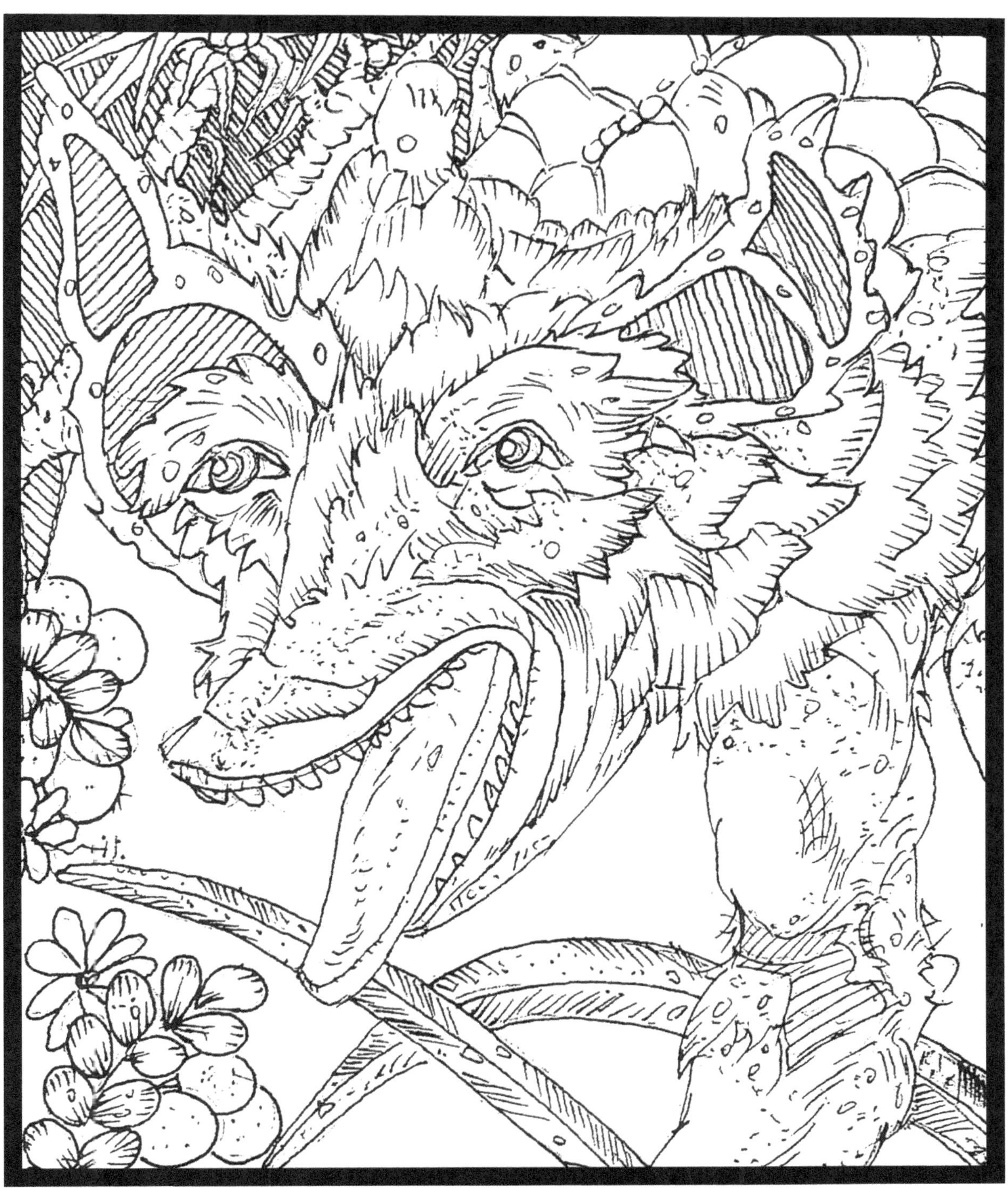

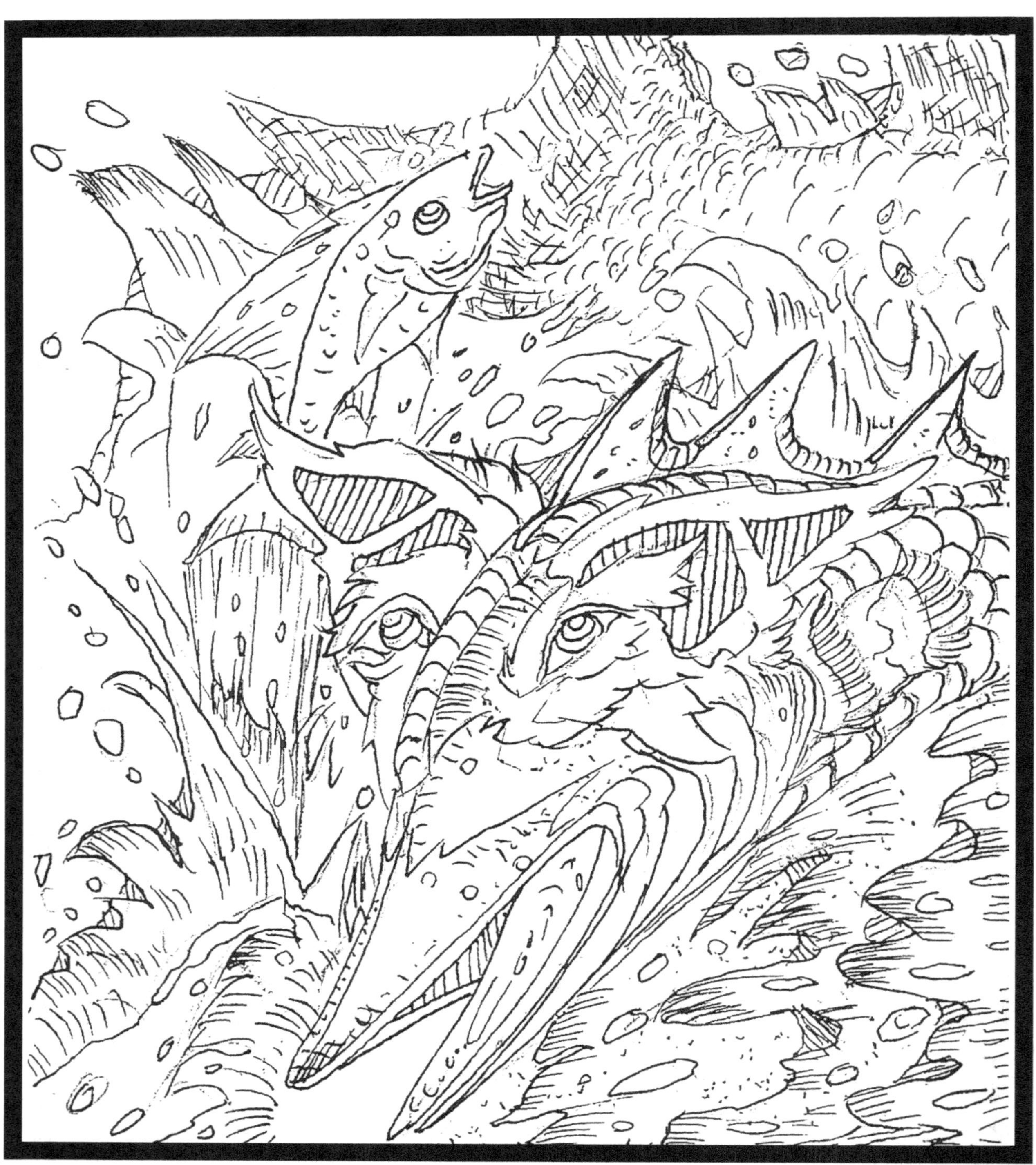

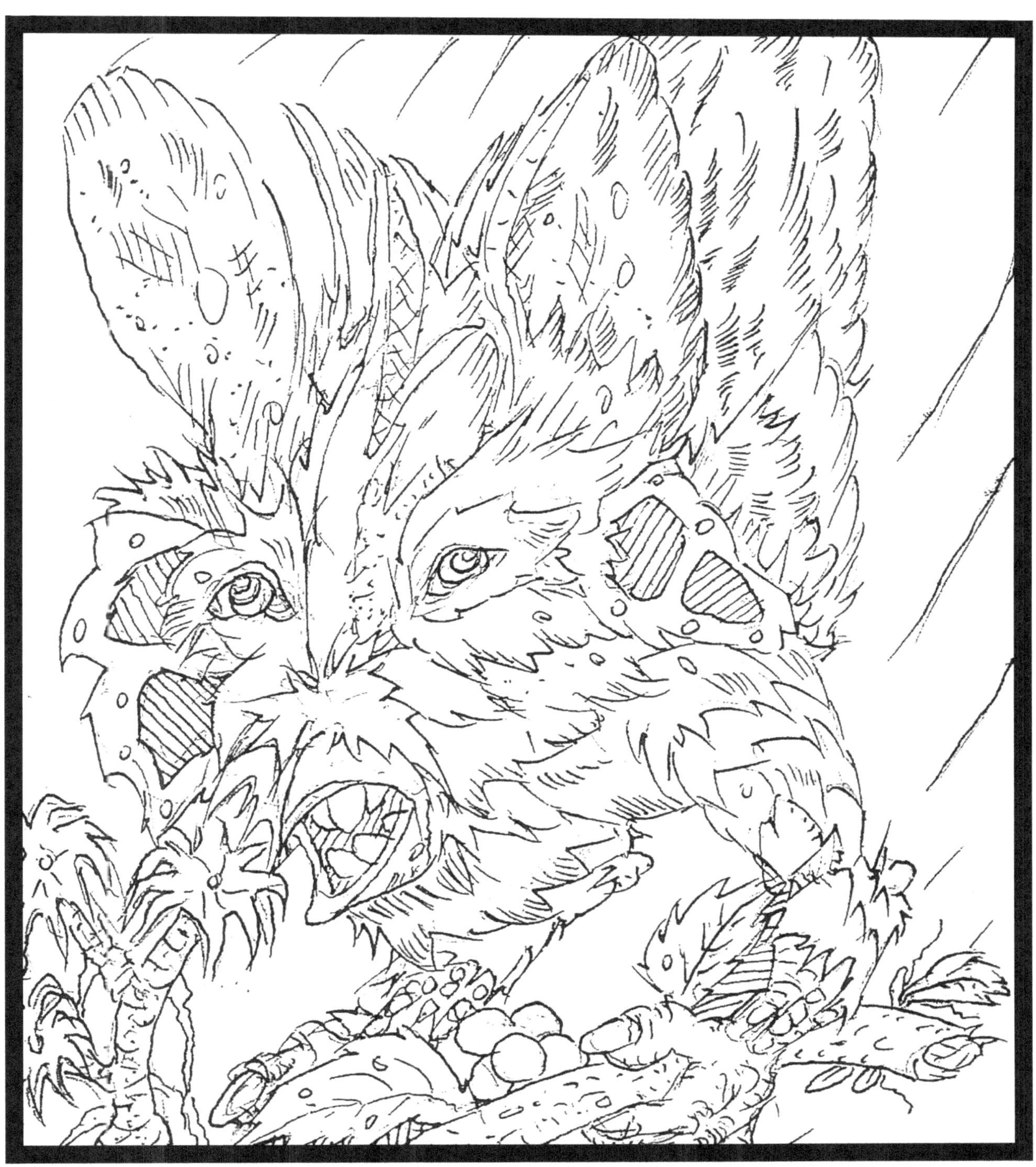

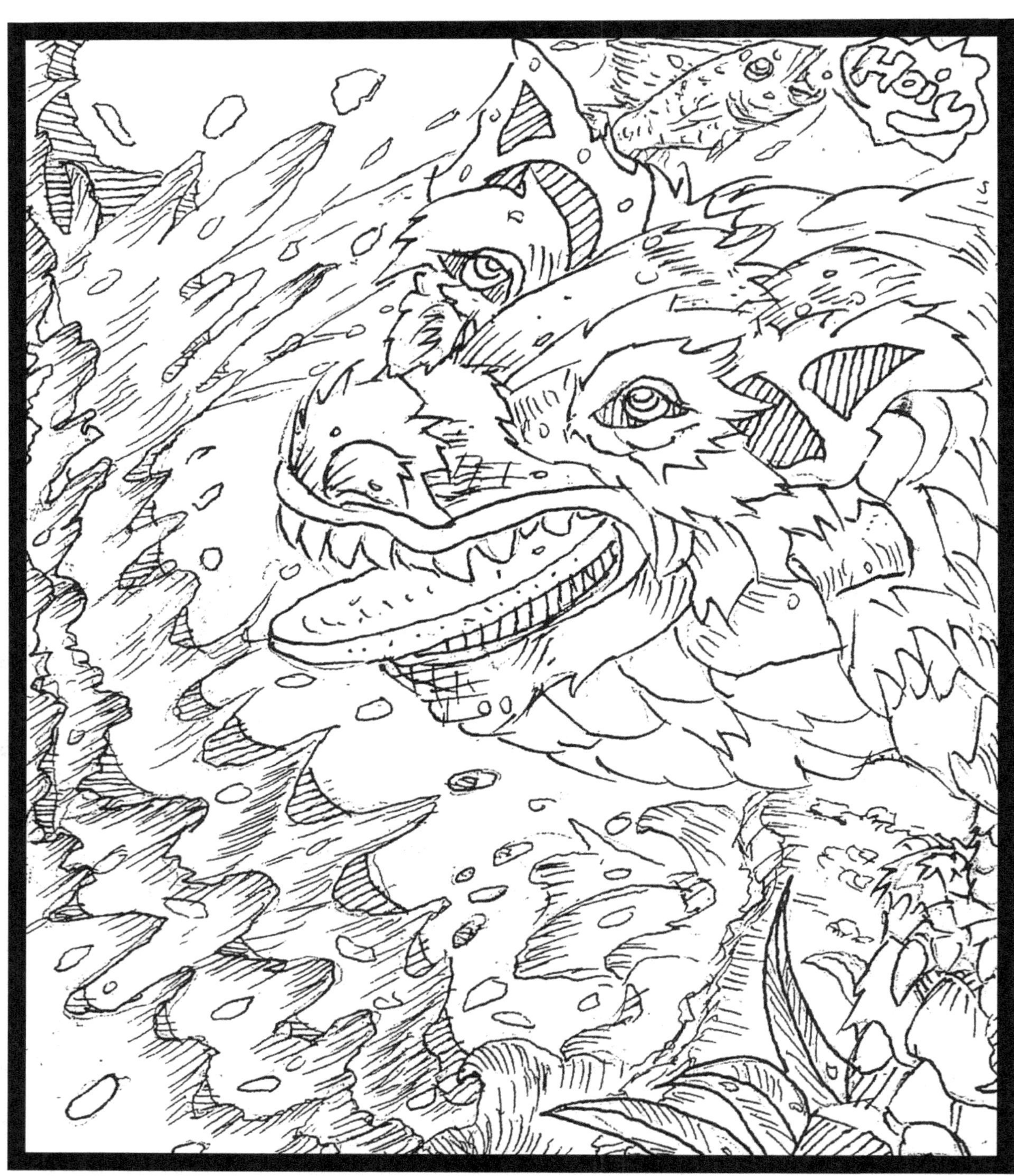
Hoi

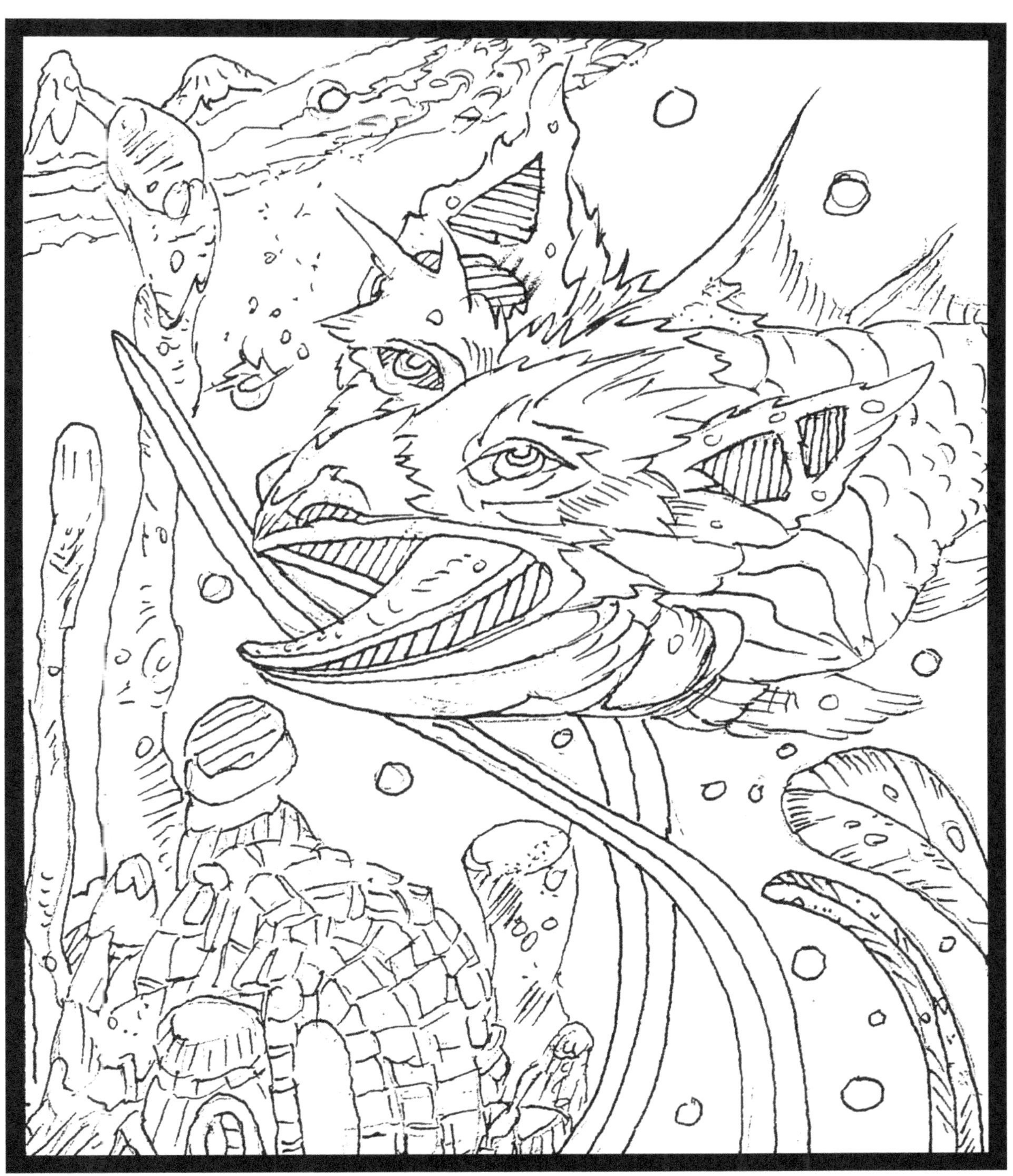

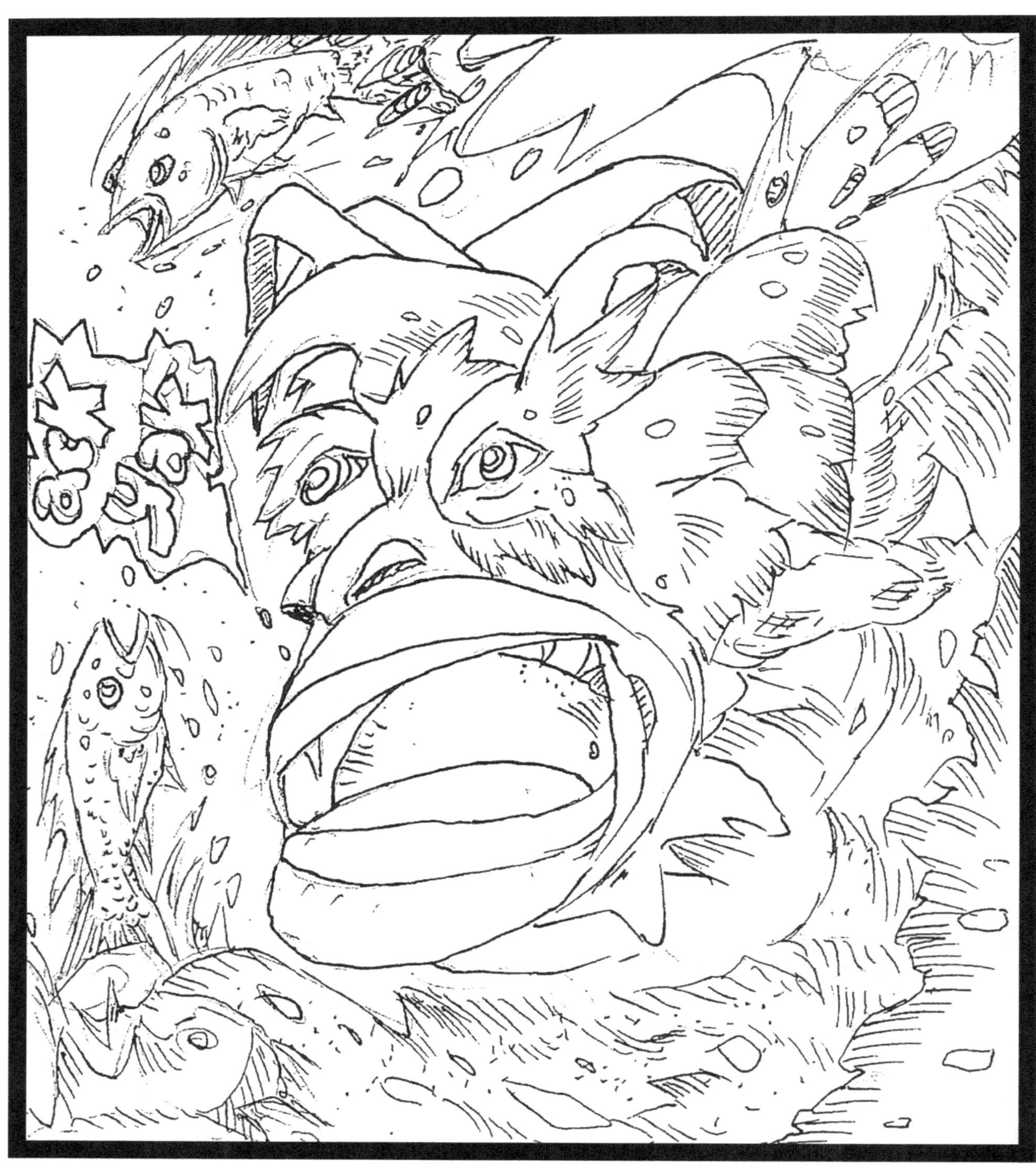

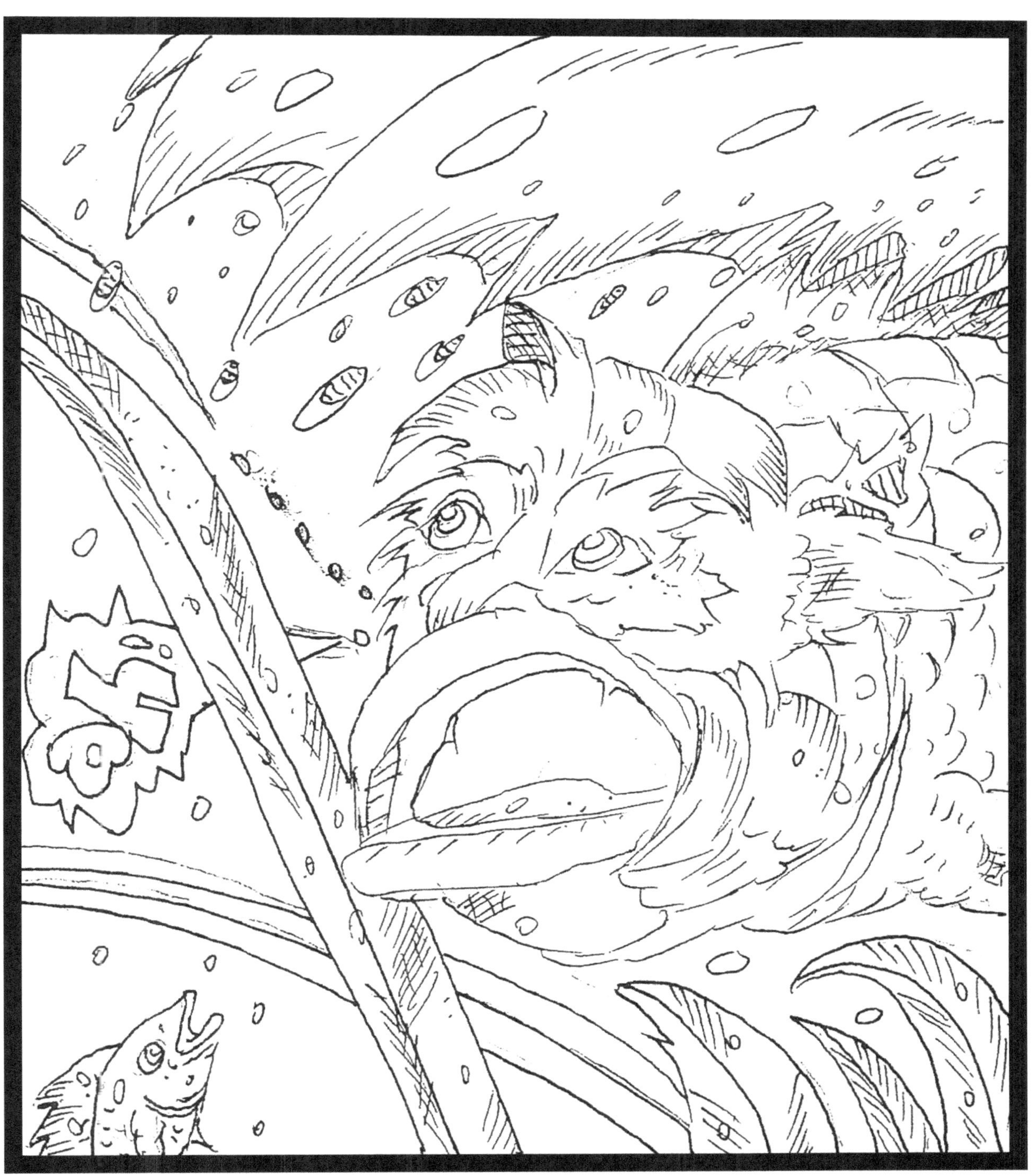

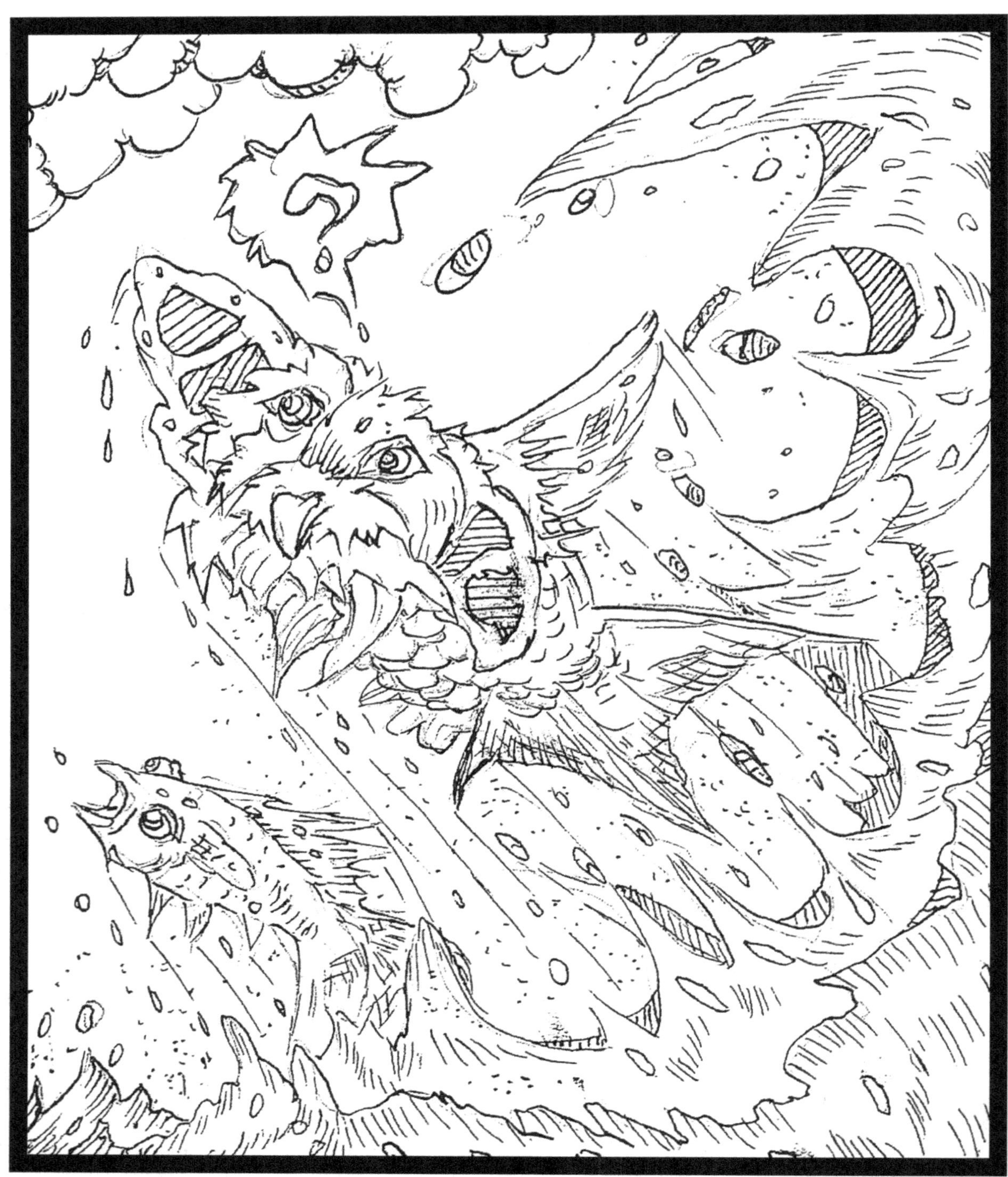

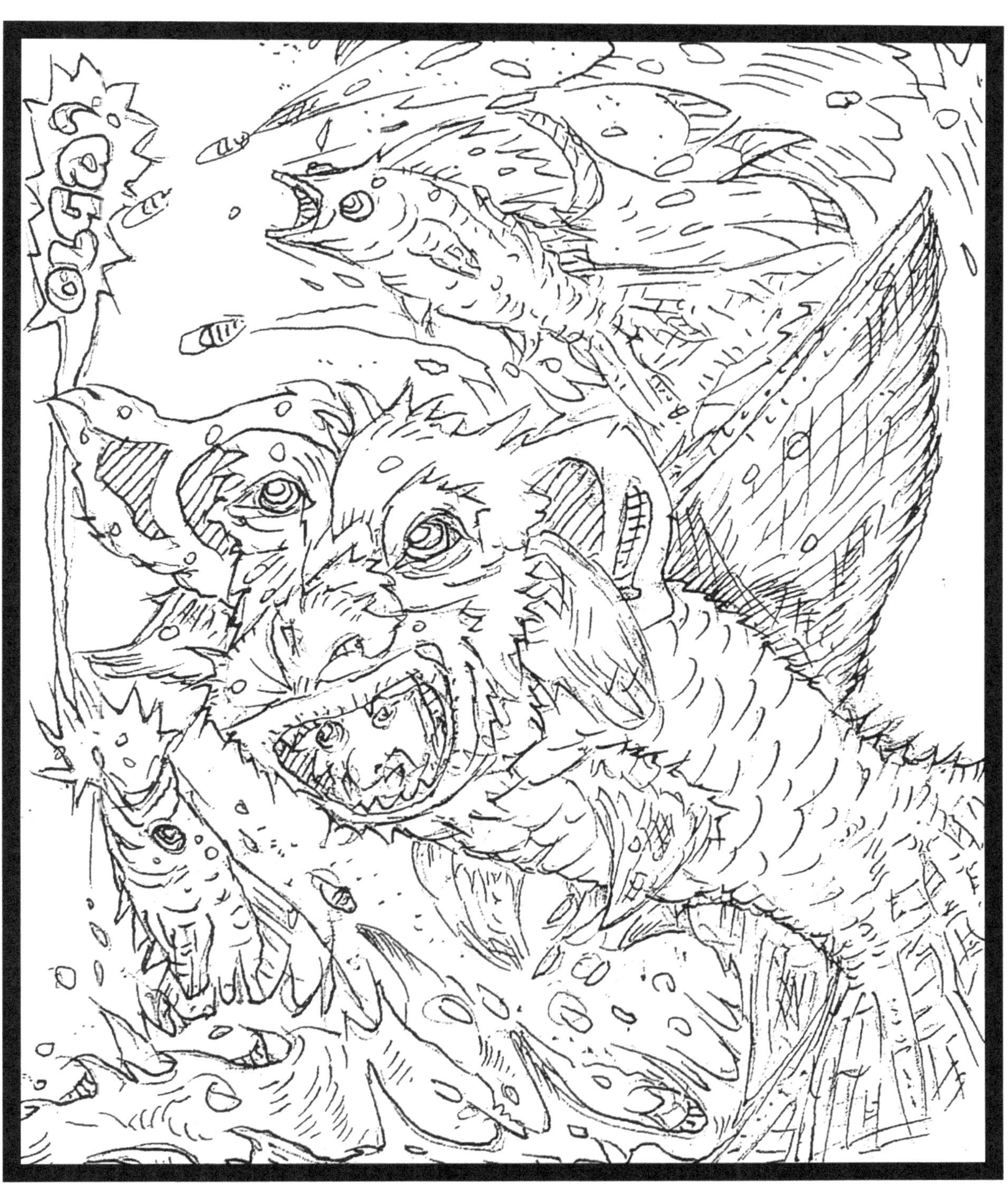

OLGA

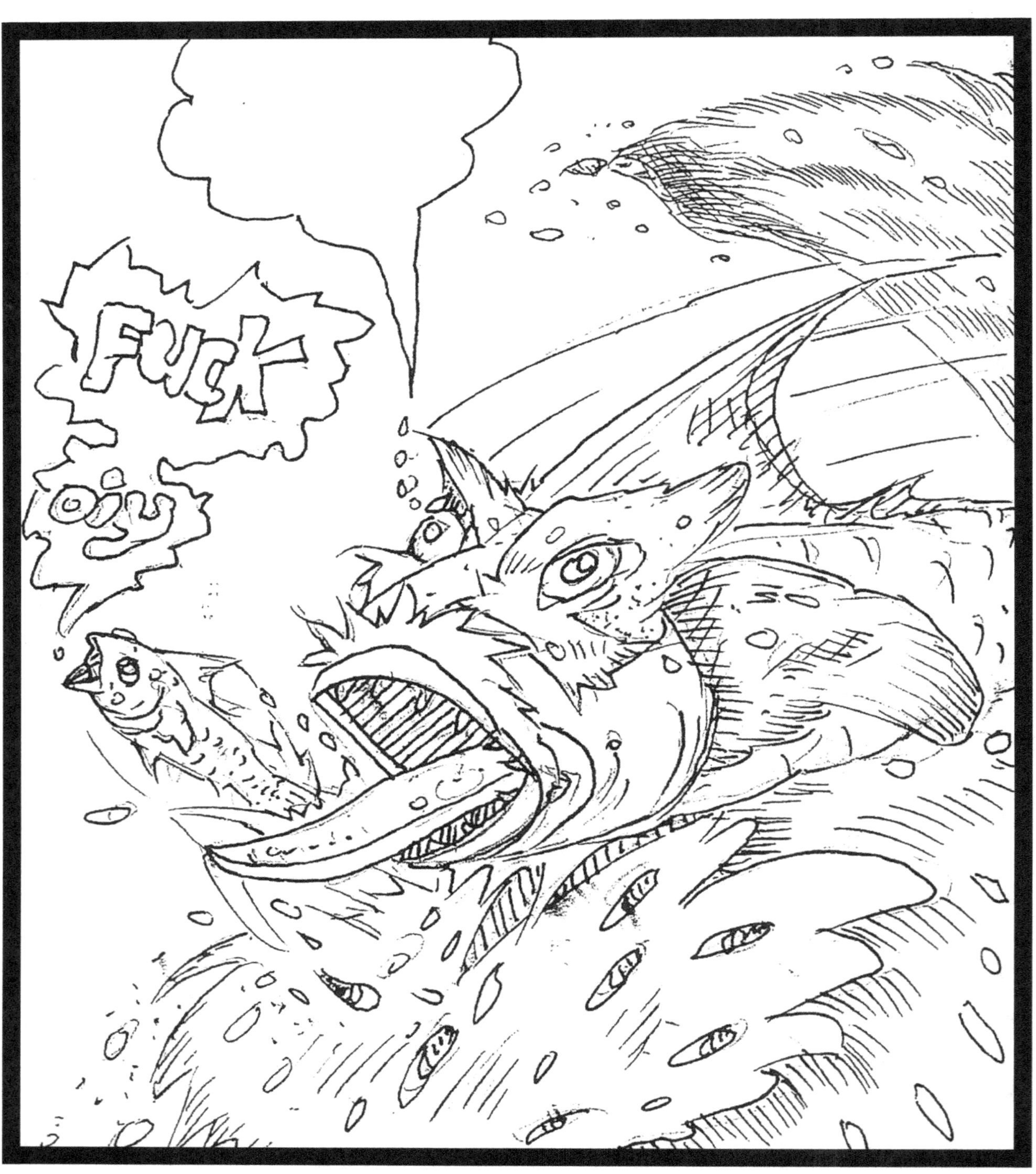

FUCK
OJU

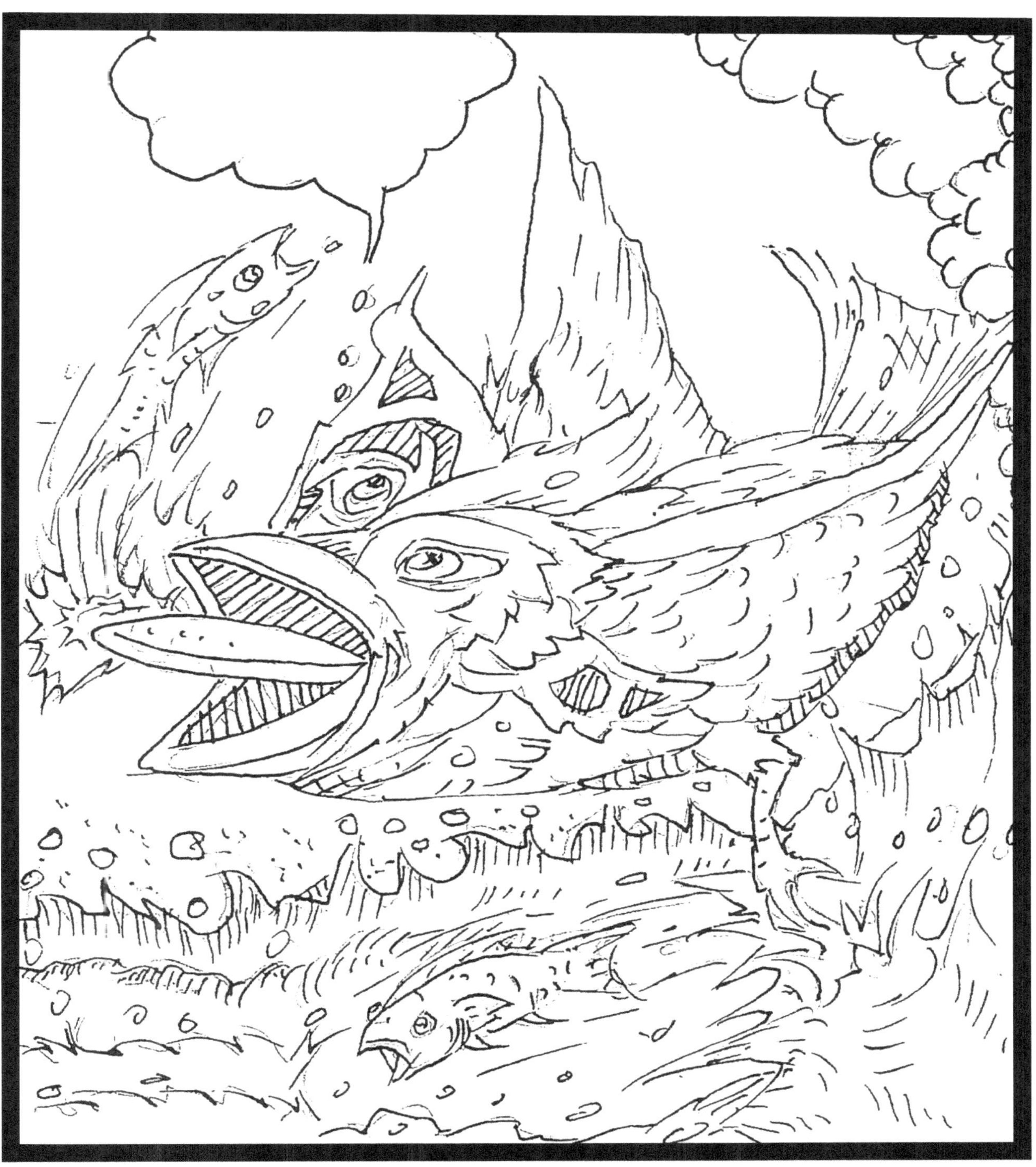

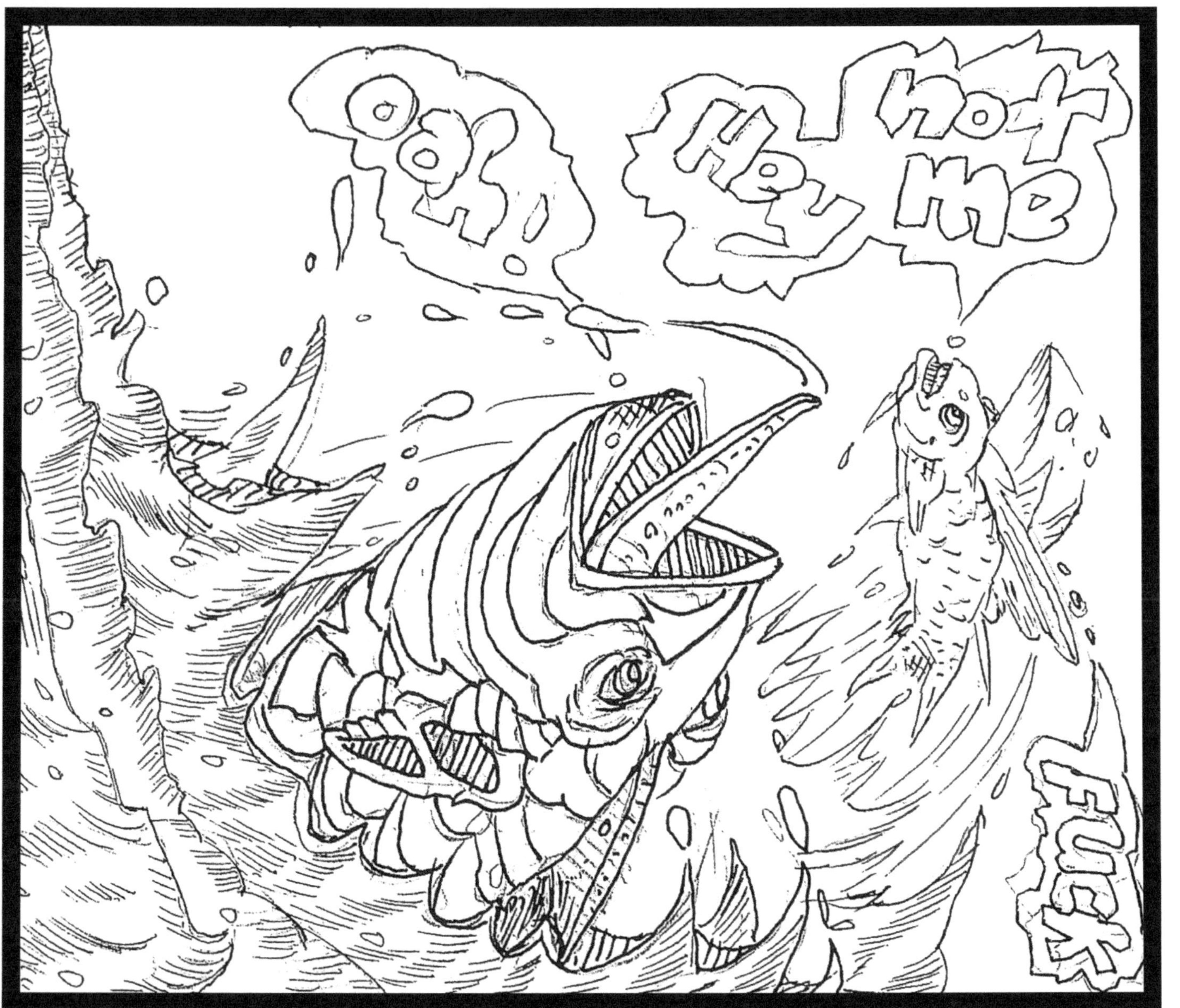

36

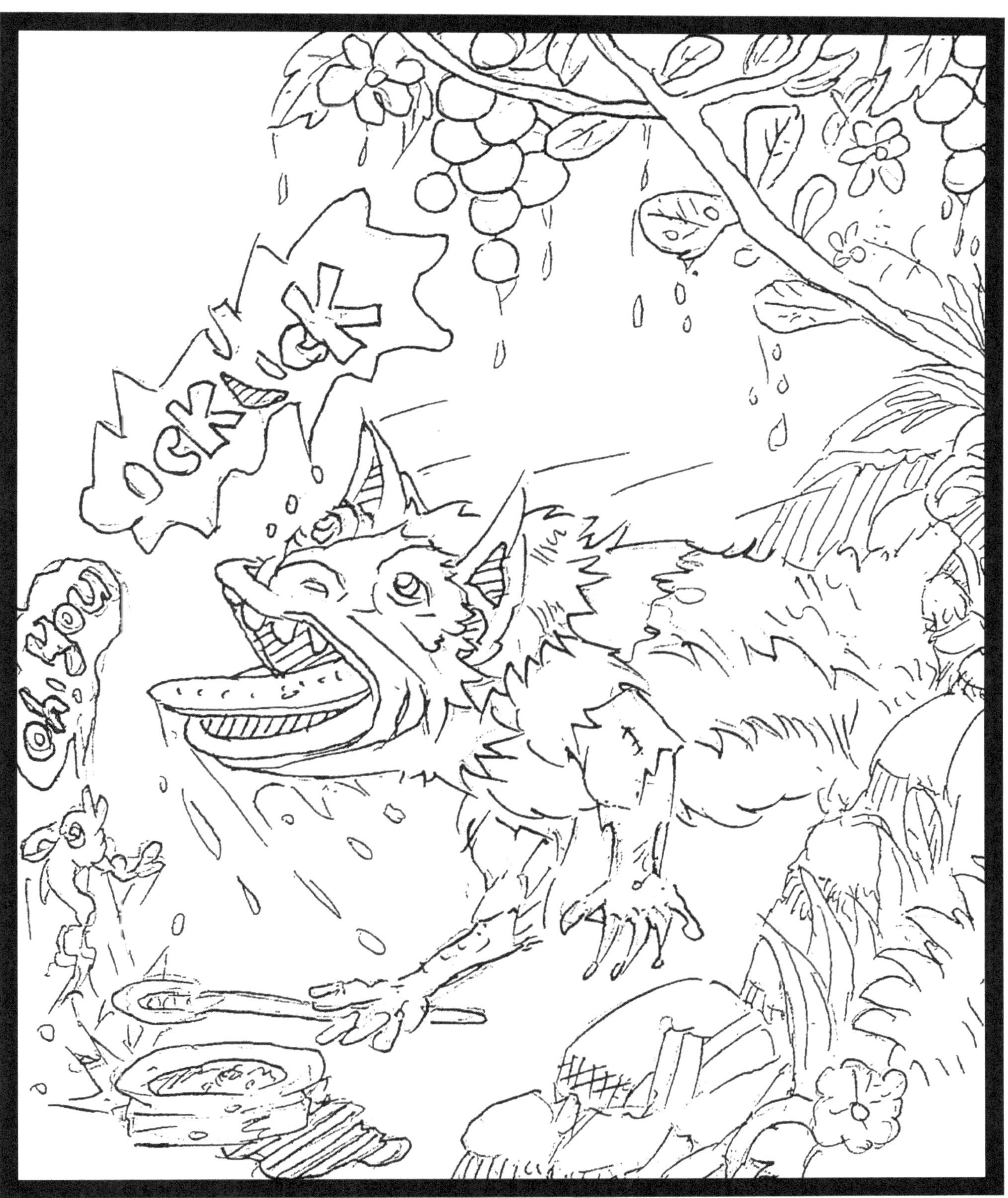

37

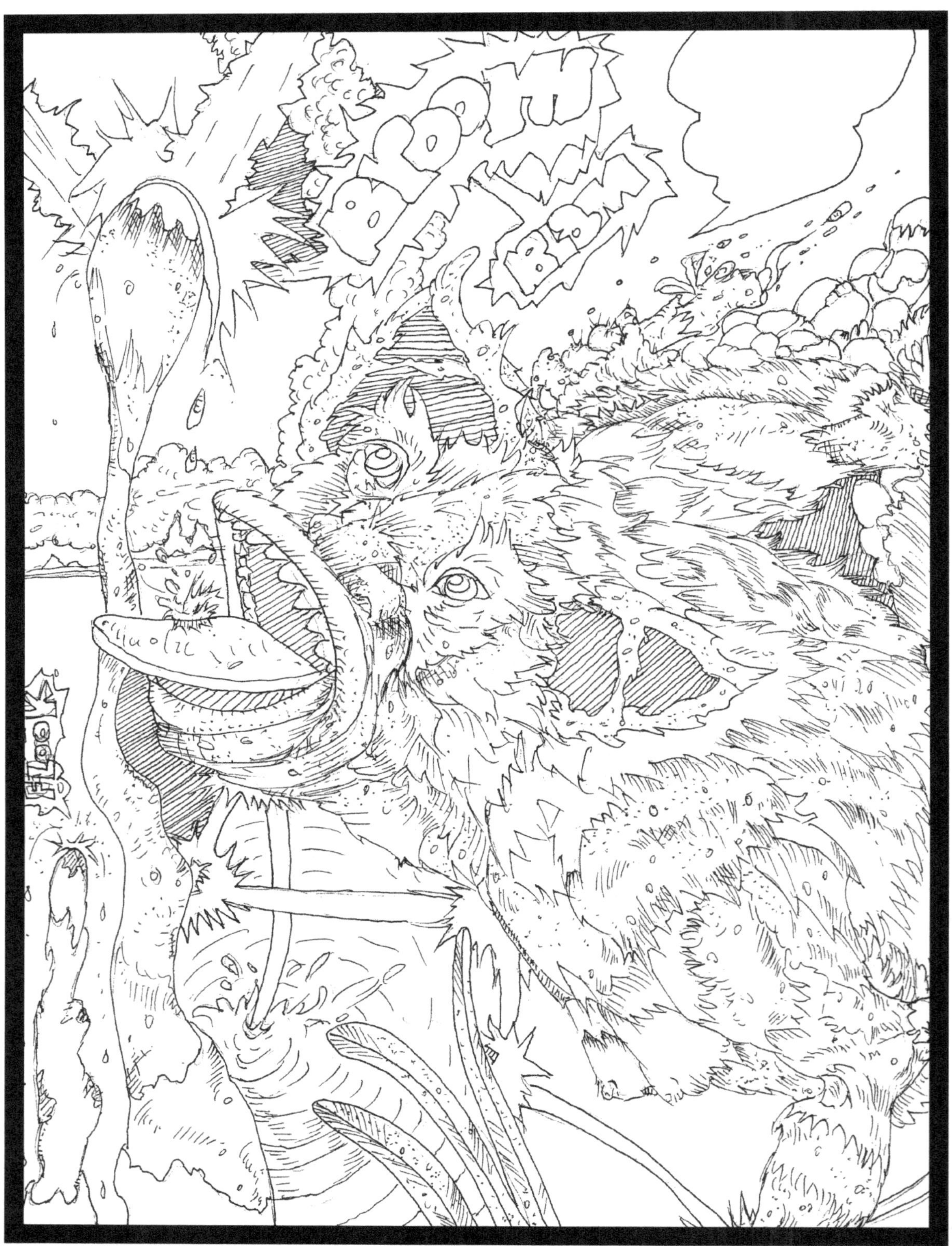
BROOM
BOOM

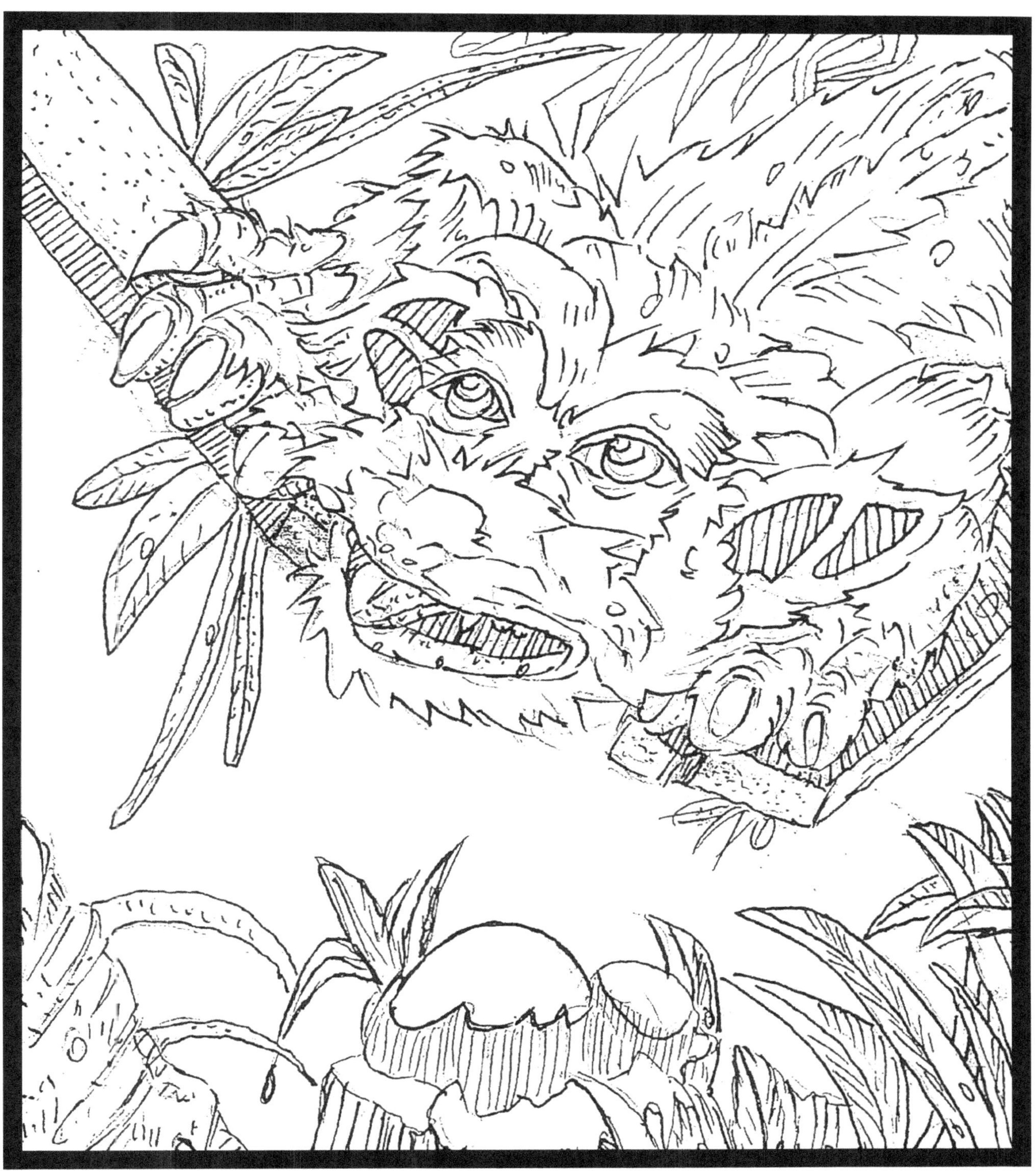

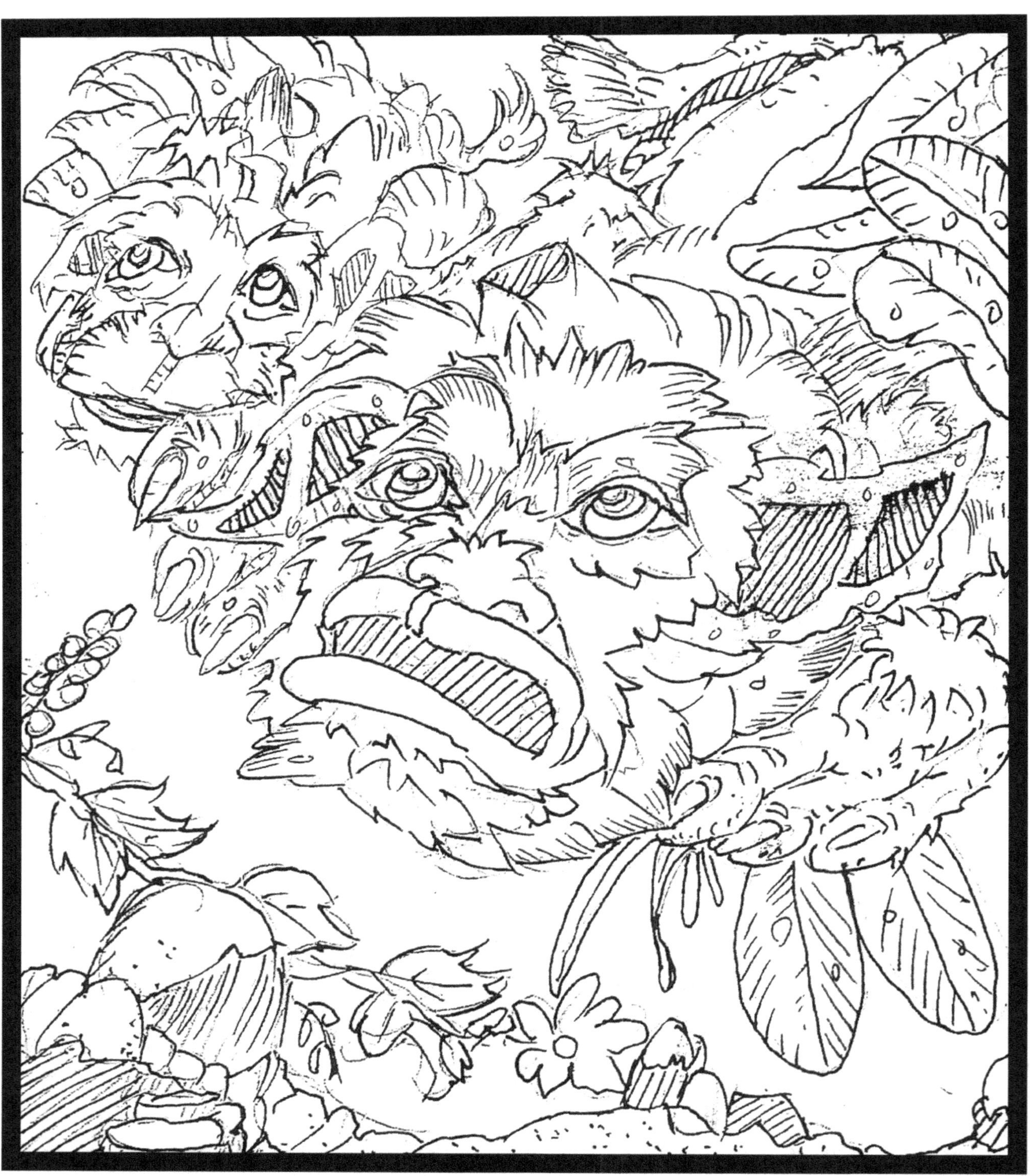

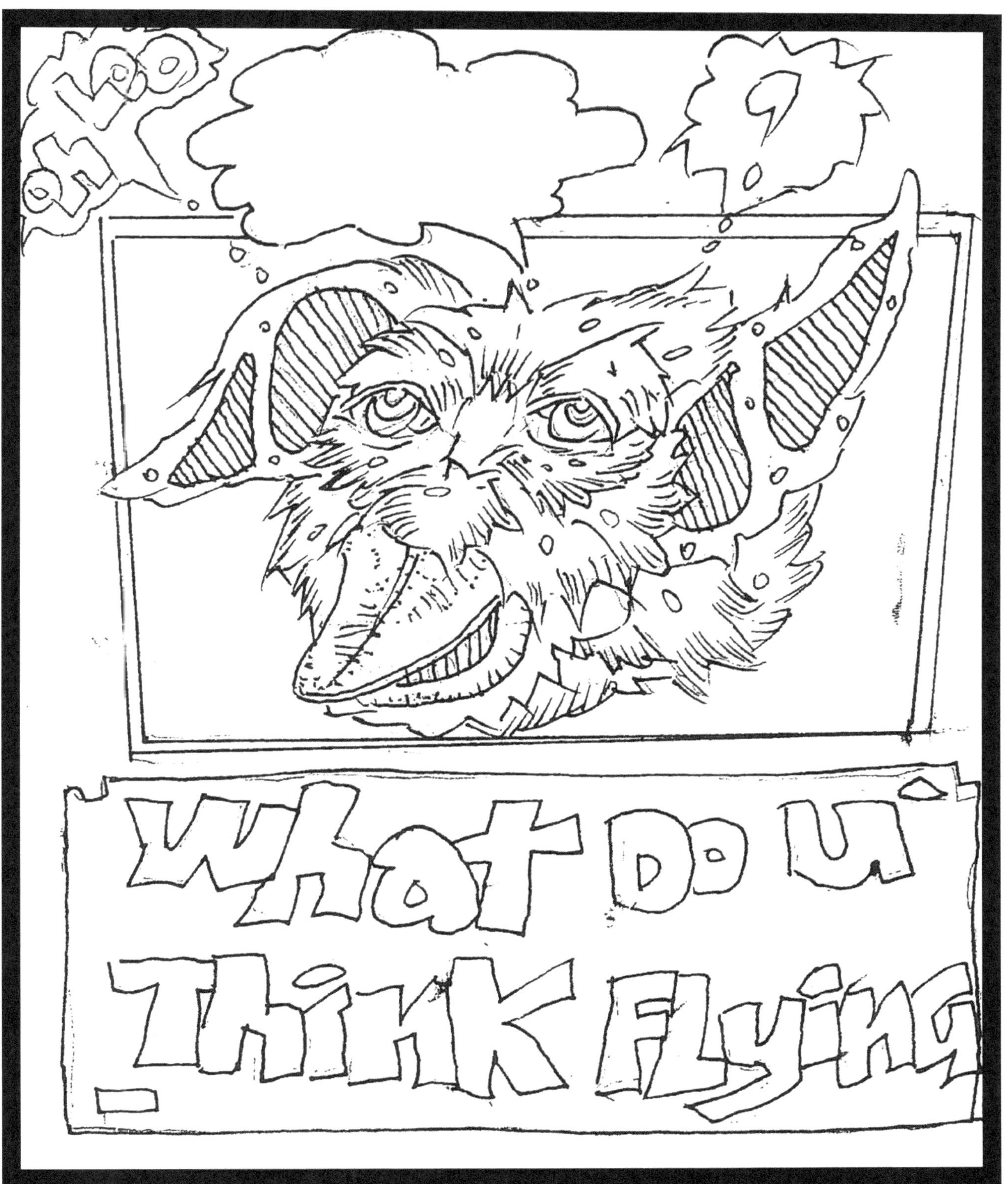
oh no
?
what do u think flying

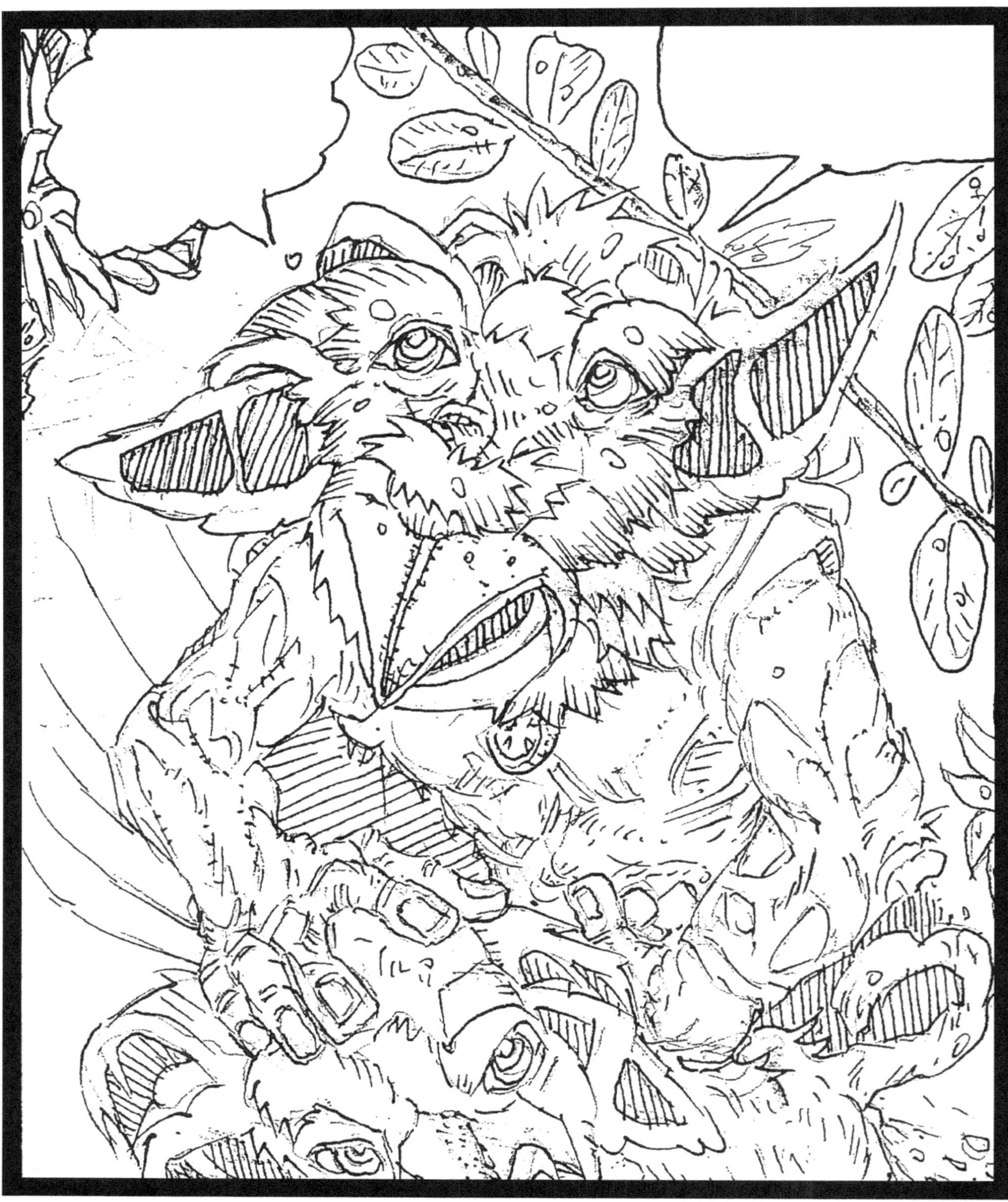

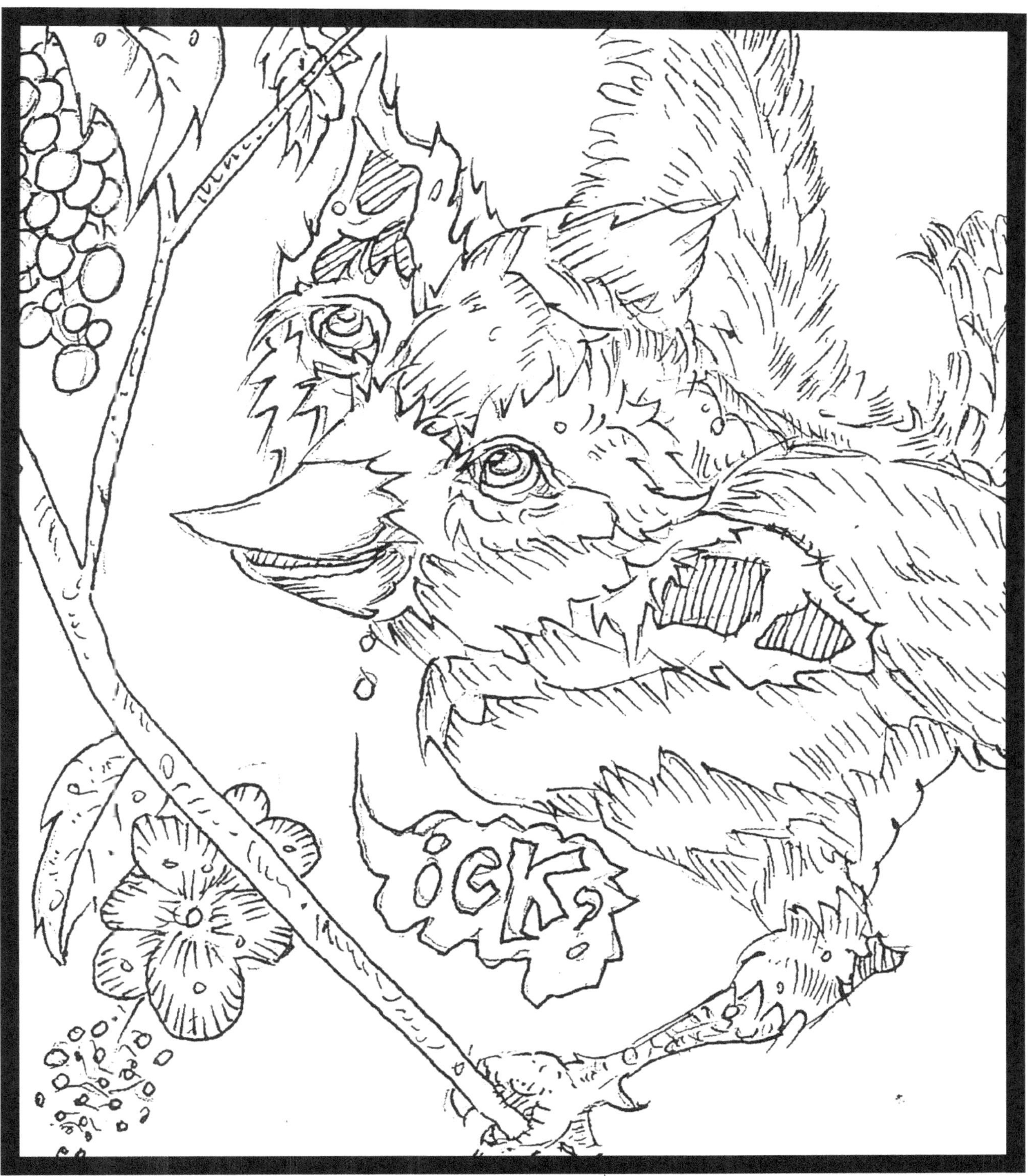
iCK?

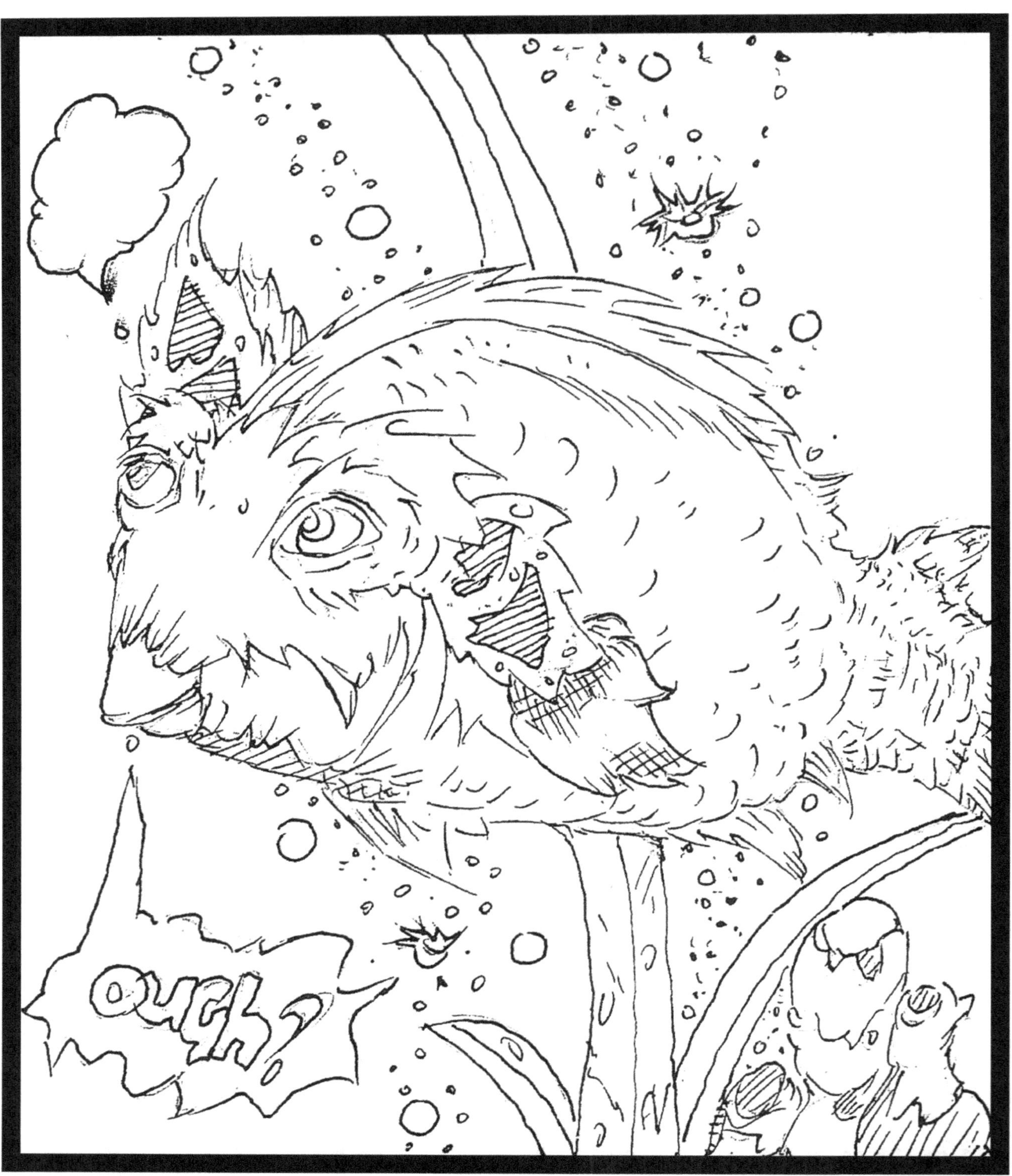

OUGH?

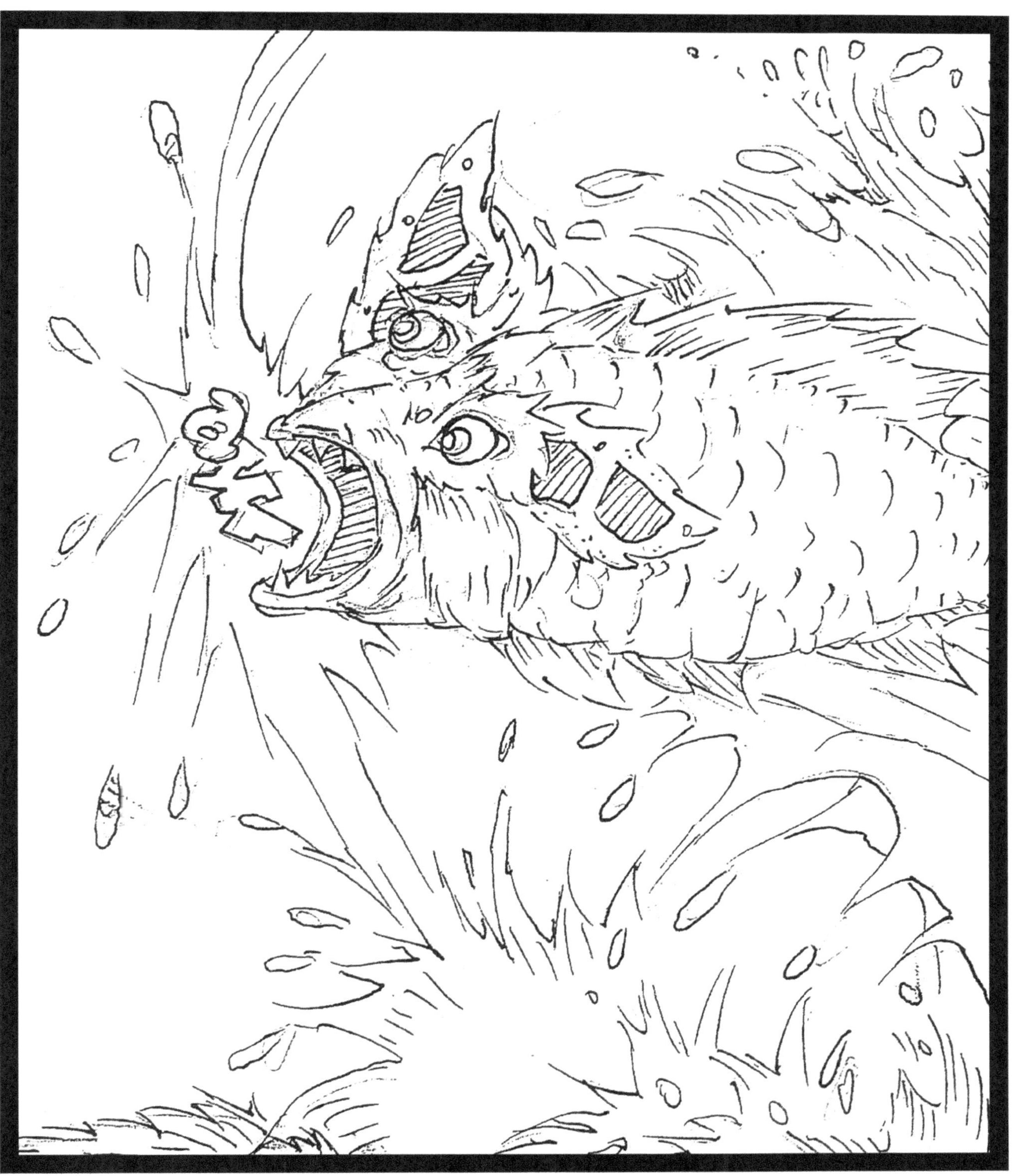

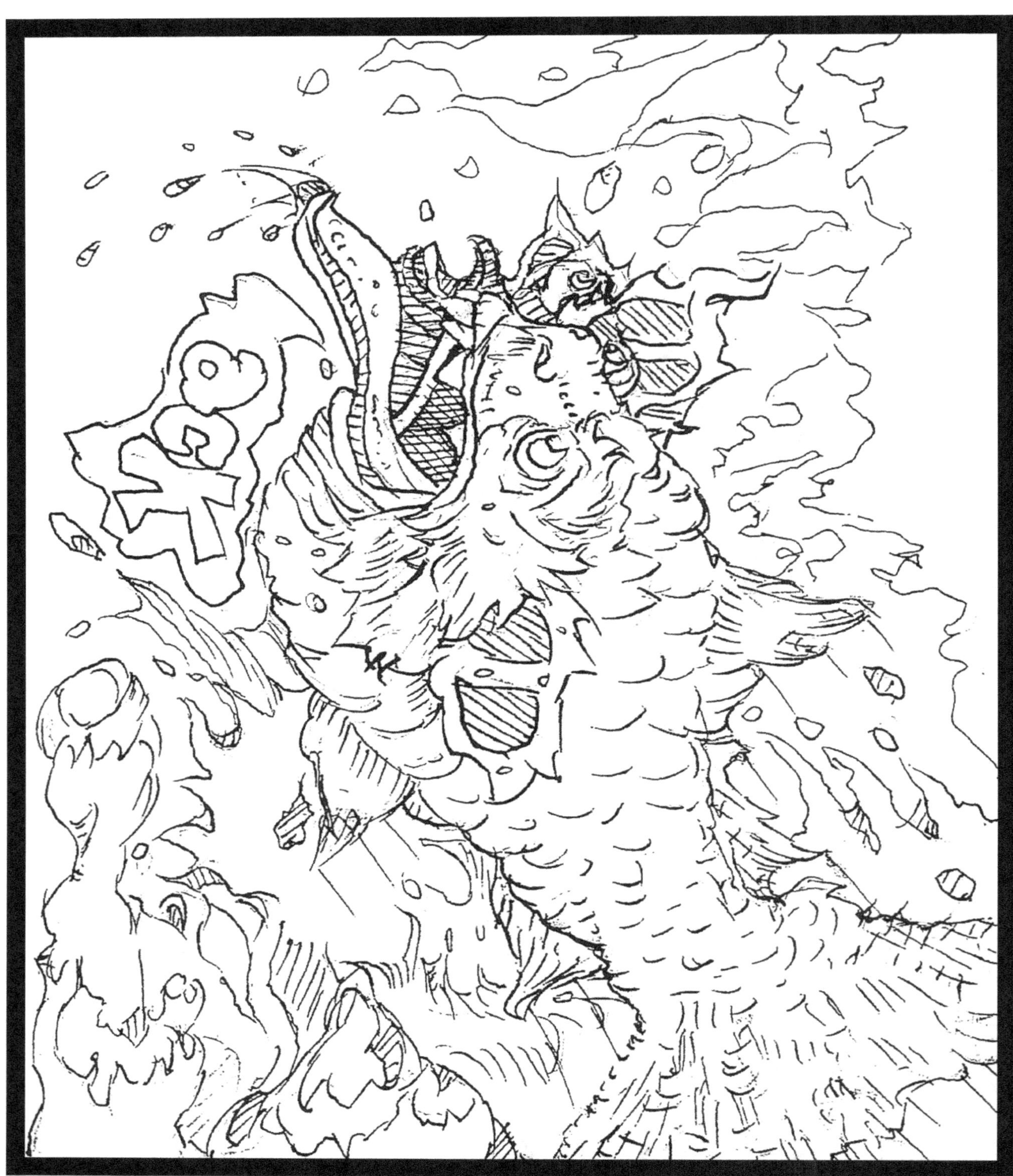

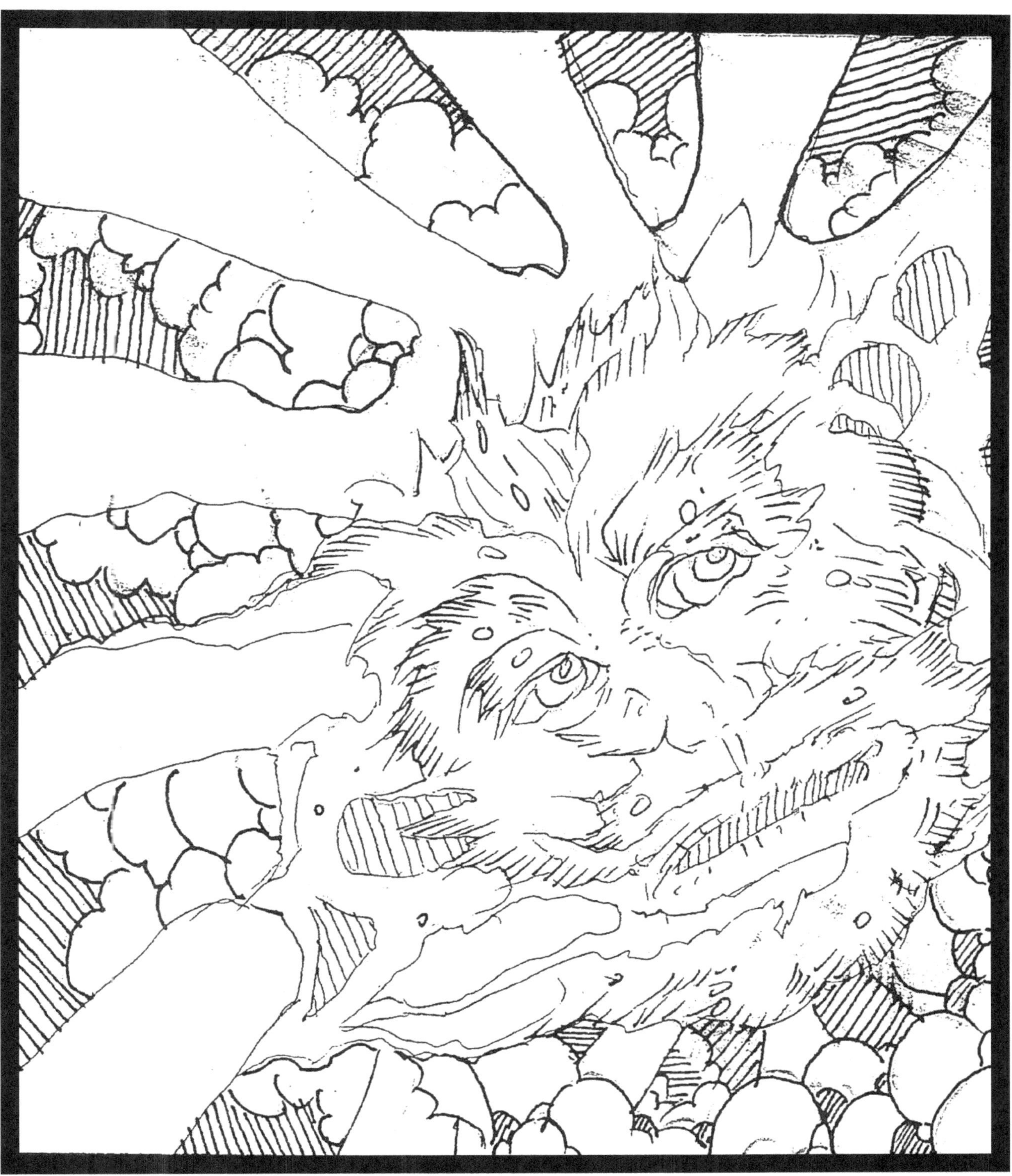

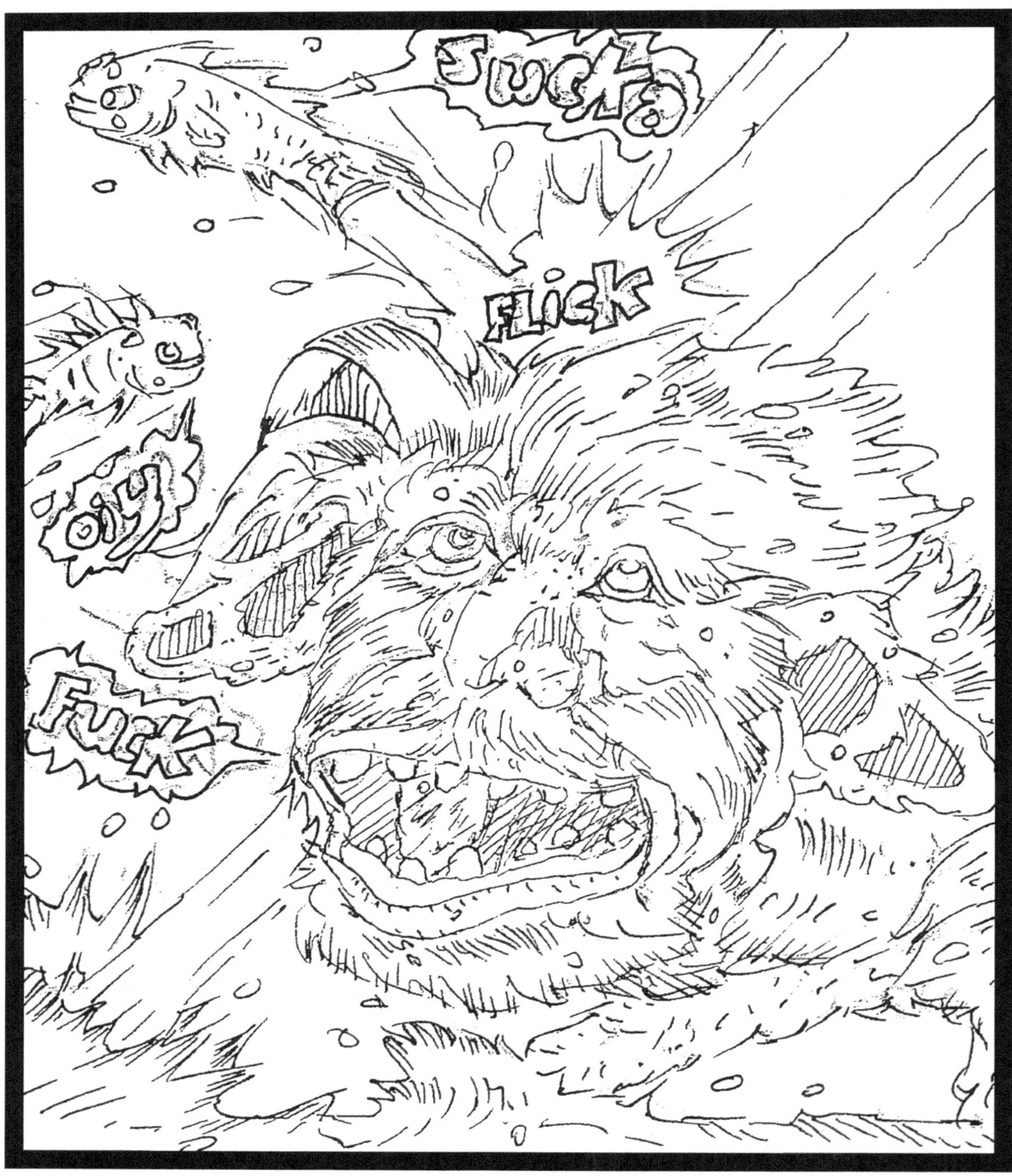

SUCK
FLICK
oiyn
FUCK

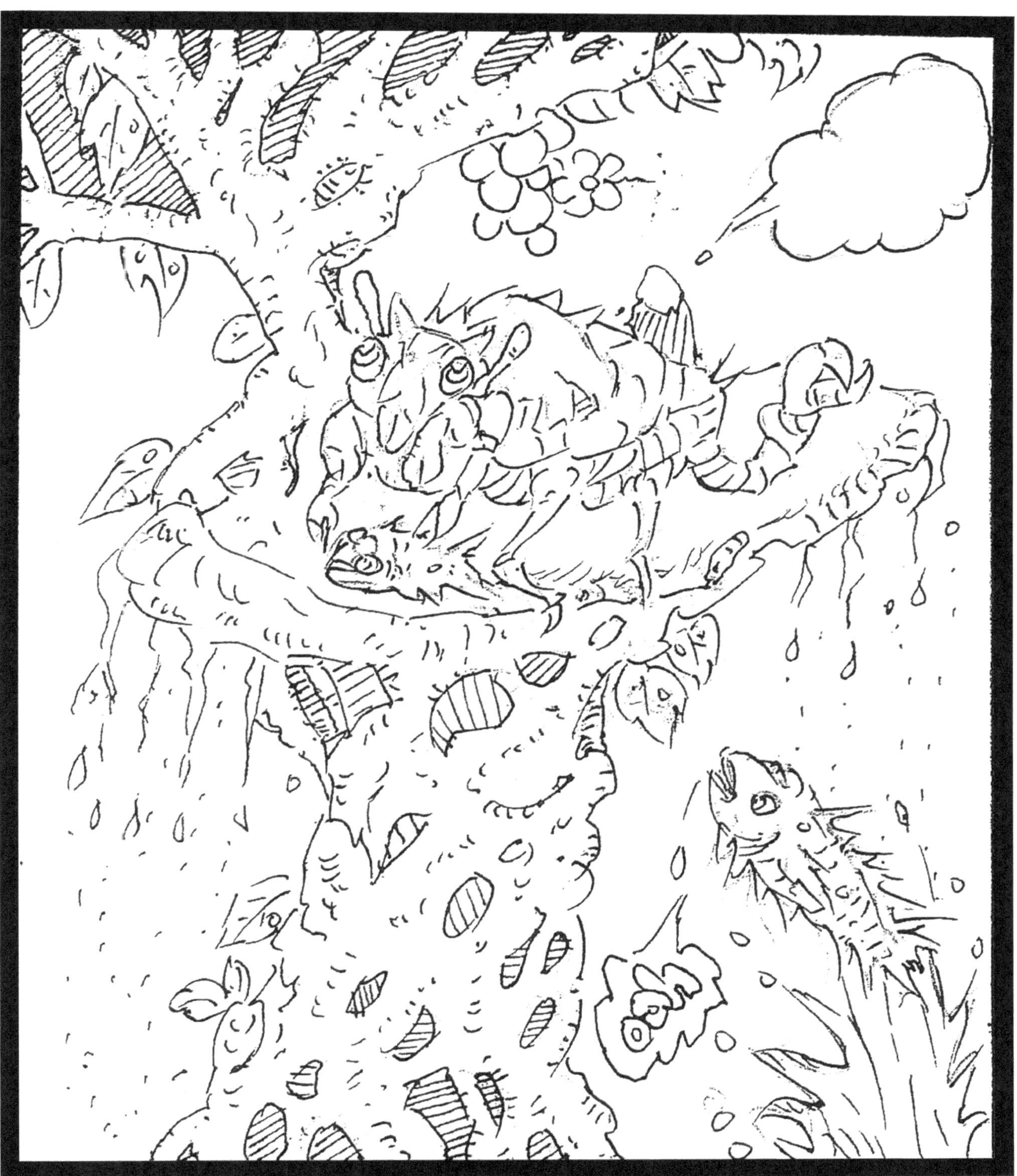

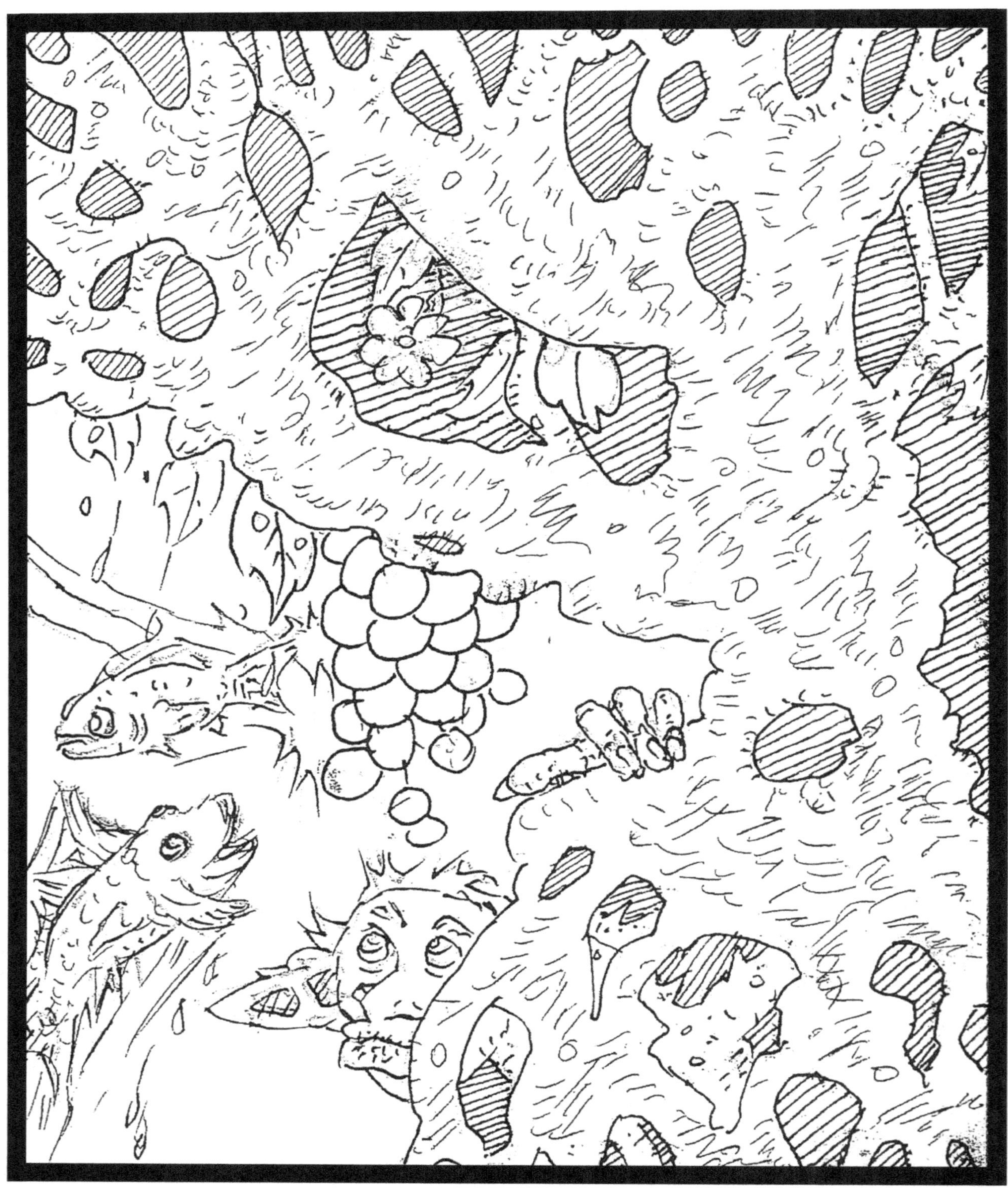

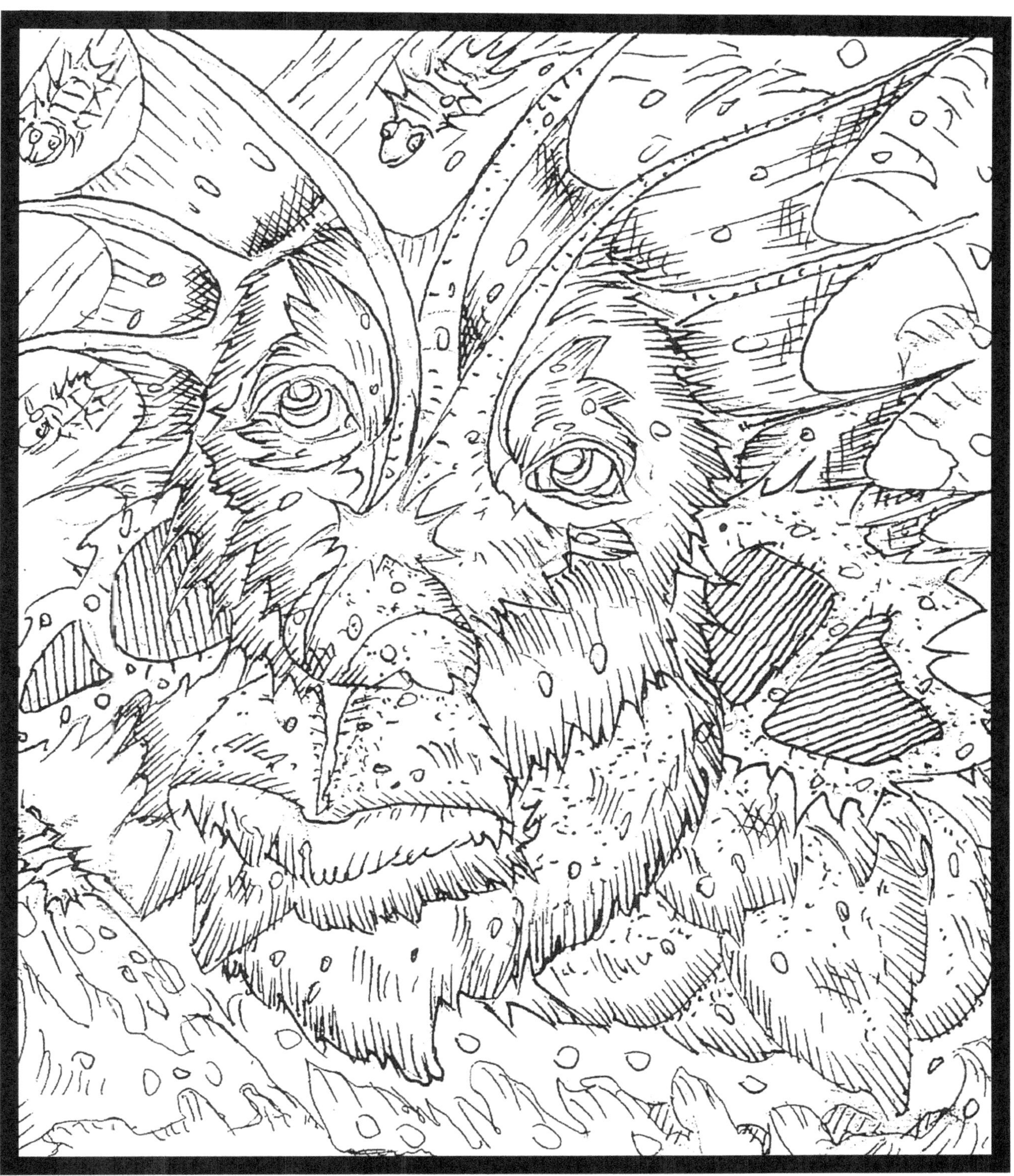

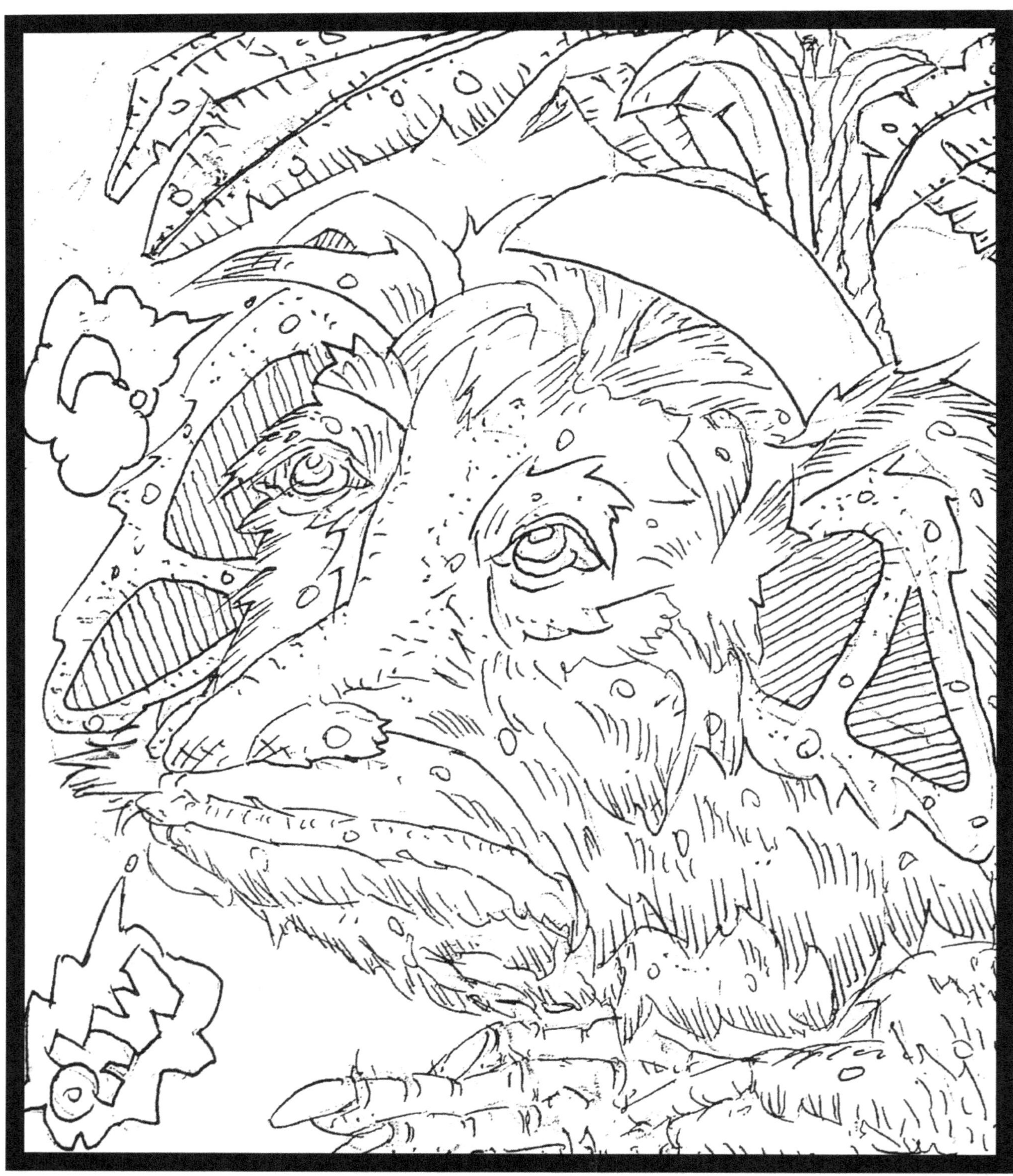

MW

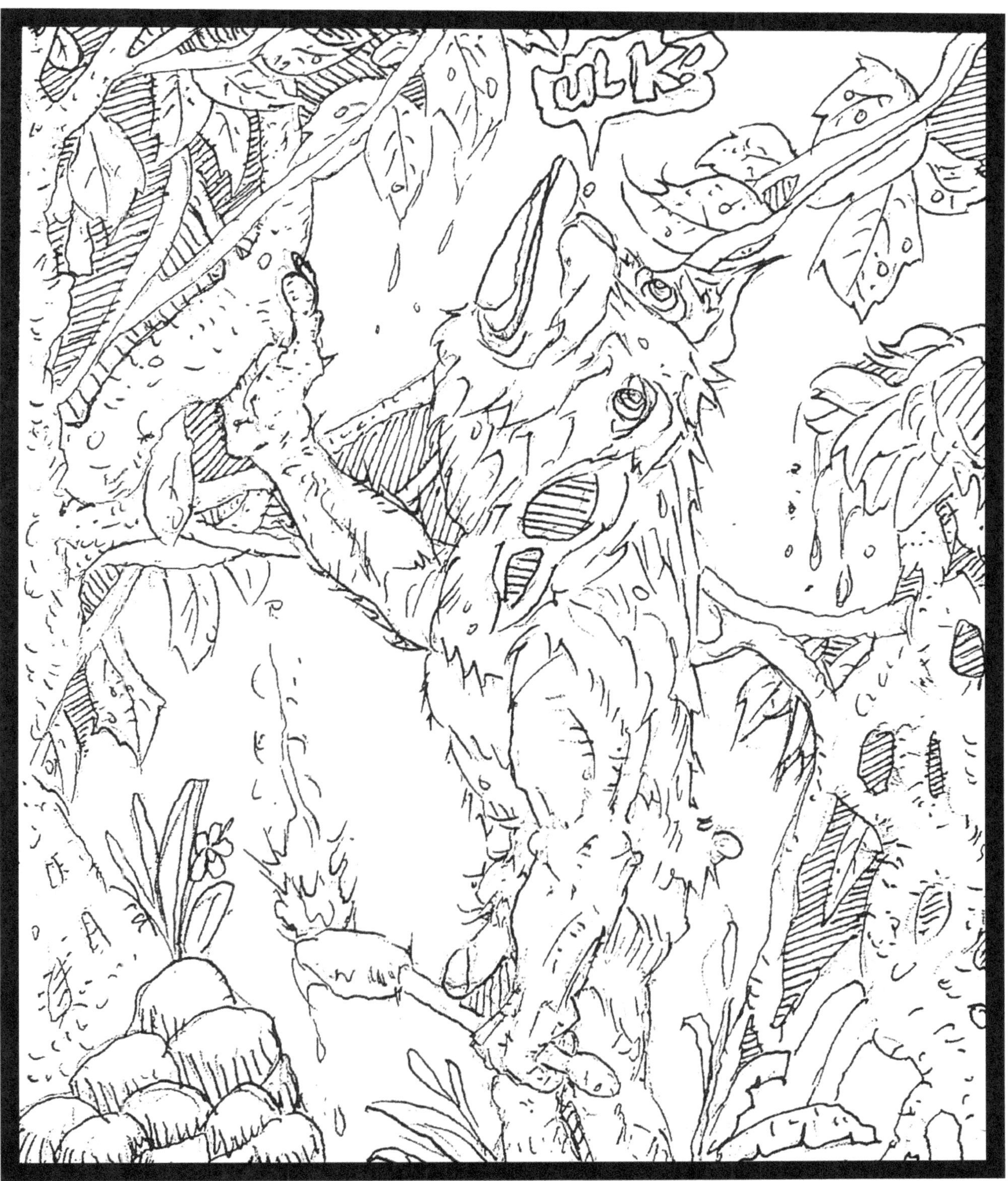

ULK?

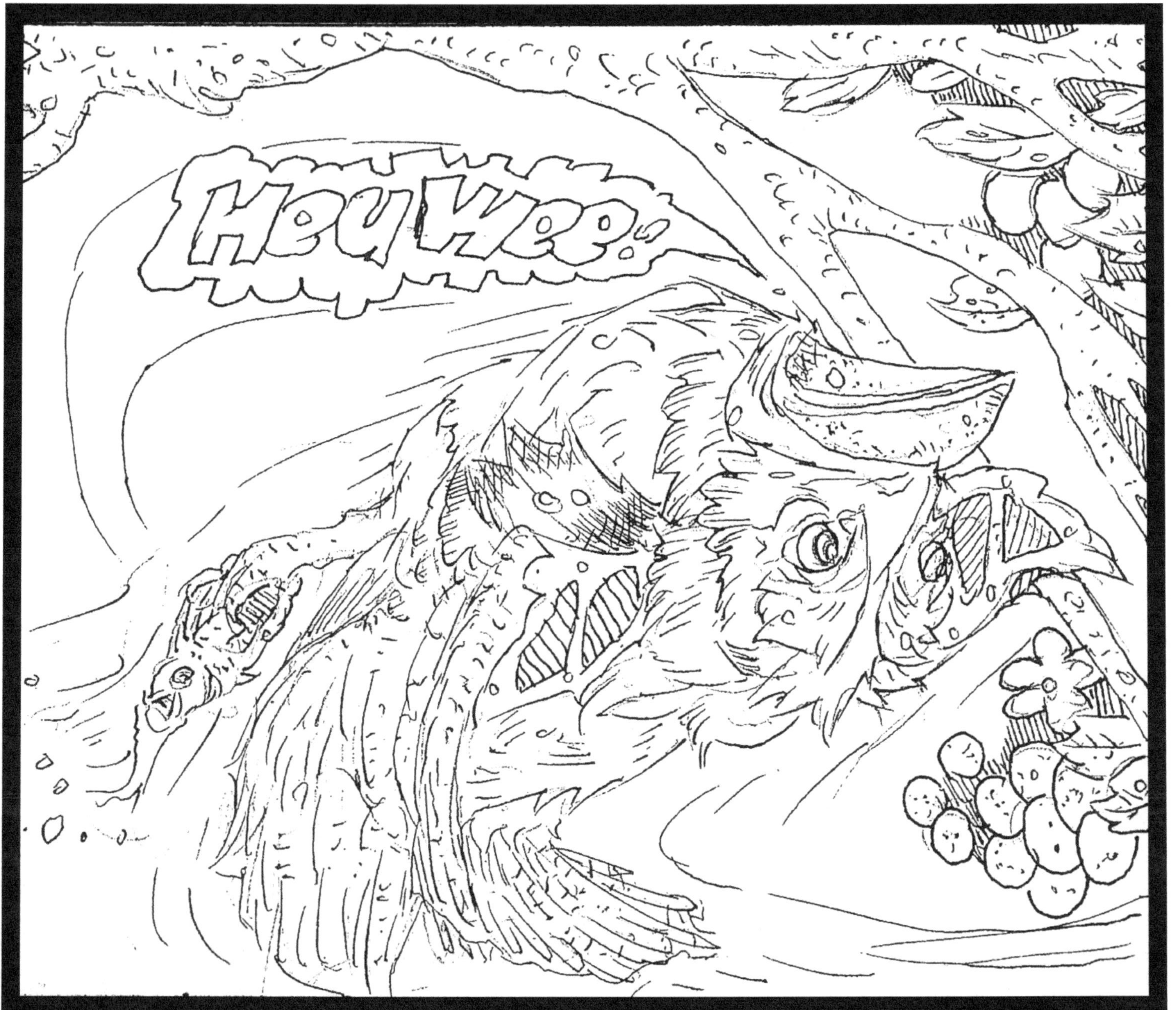

Hey Vee!

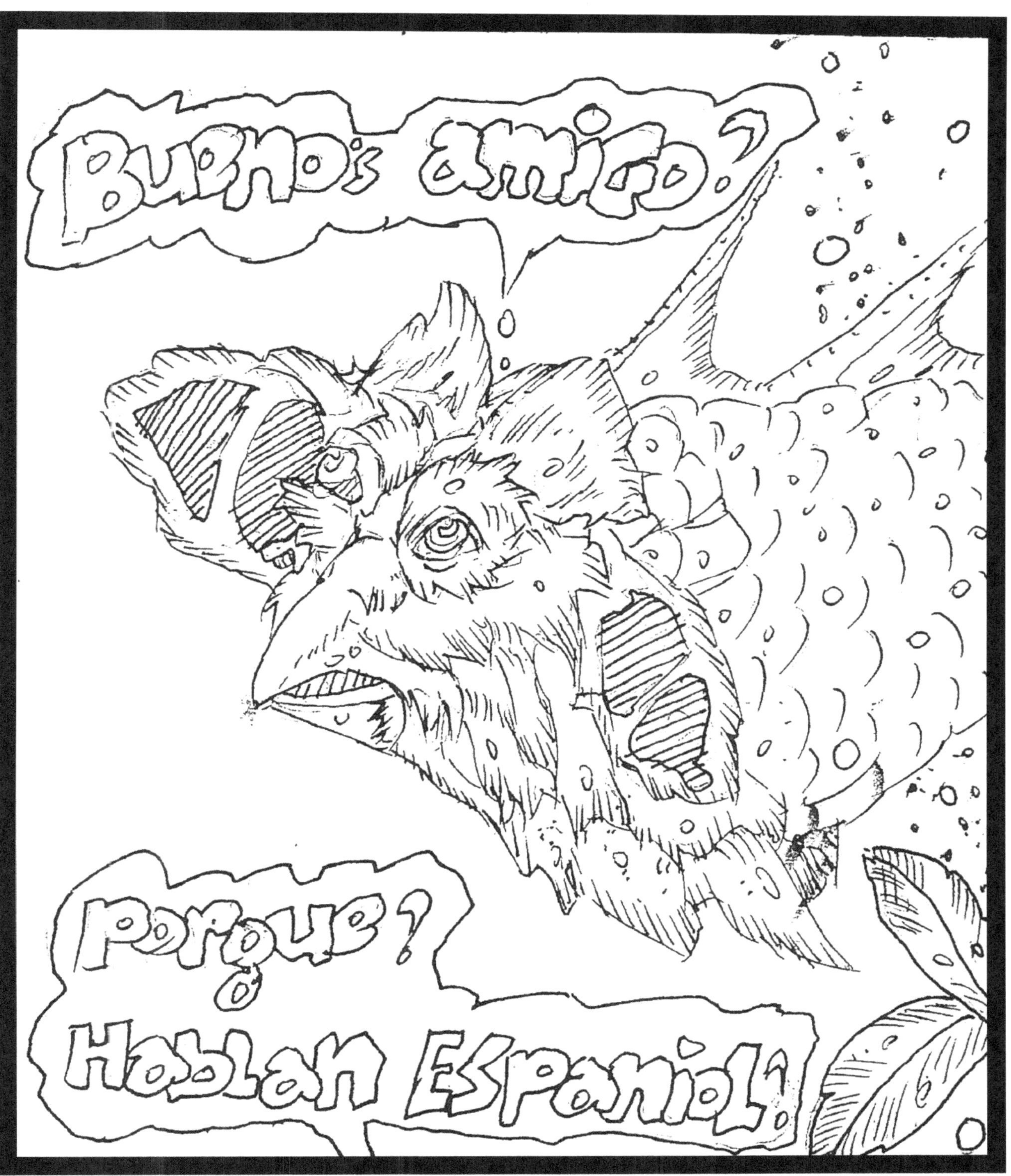

Buenos amigo?
Porque? o
Hablan Espaniol?

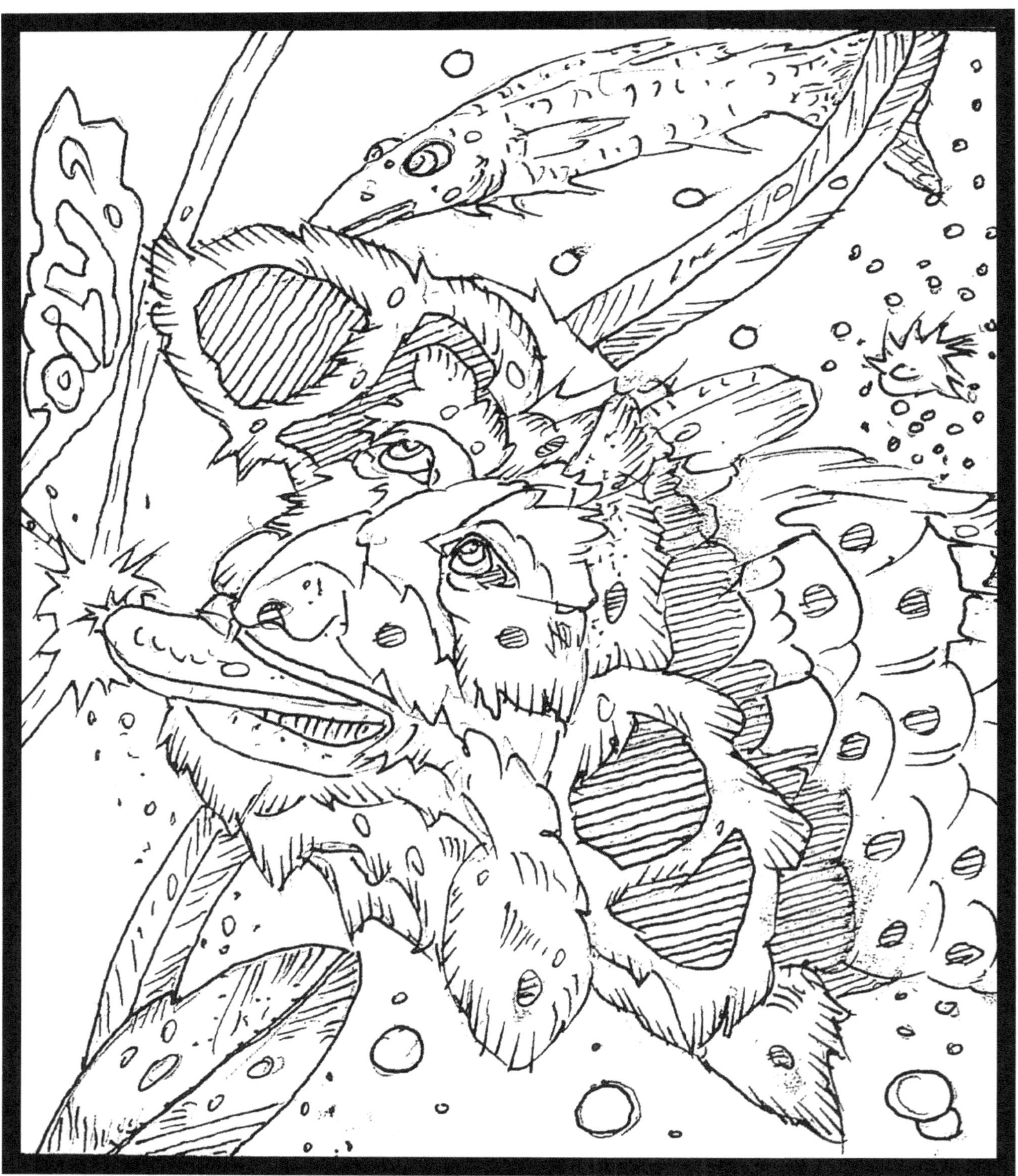

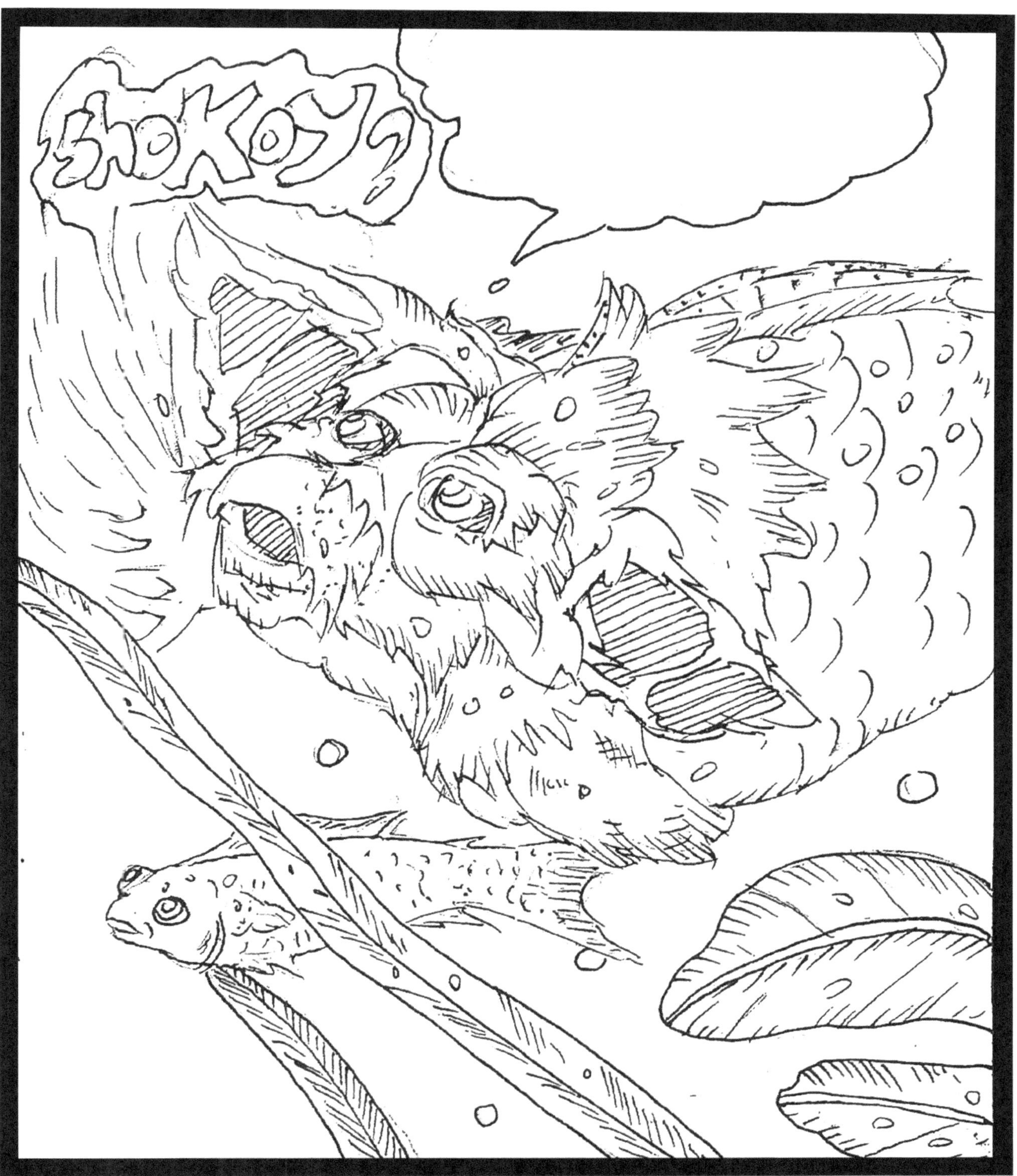

shoKoyo?

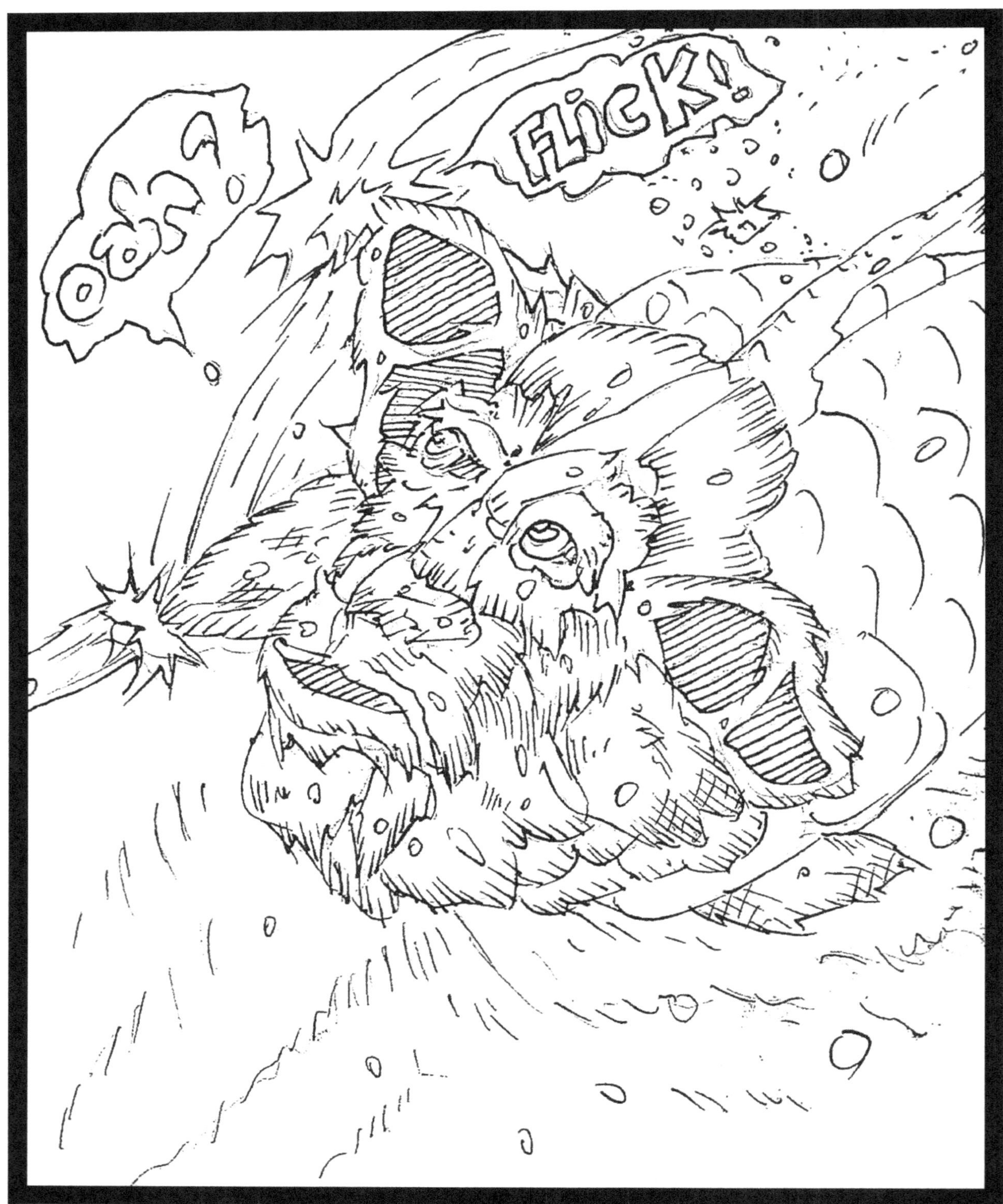
OASP!
FLICK!

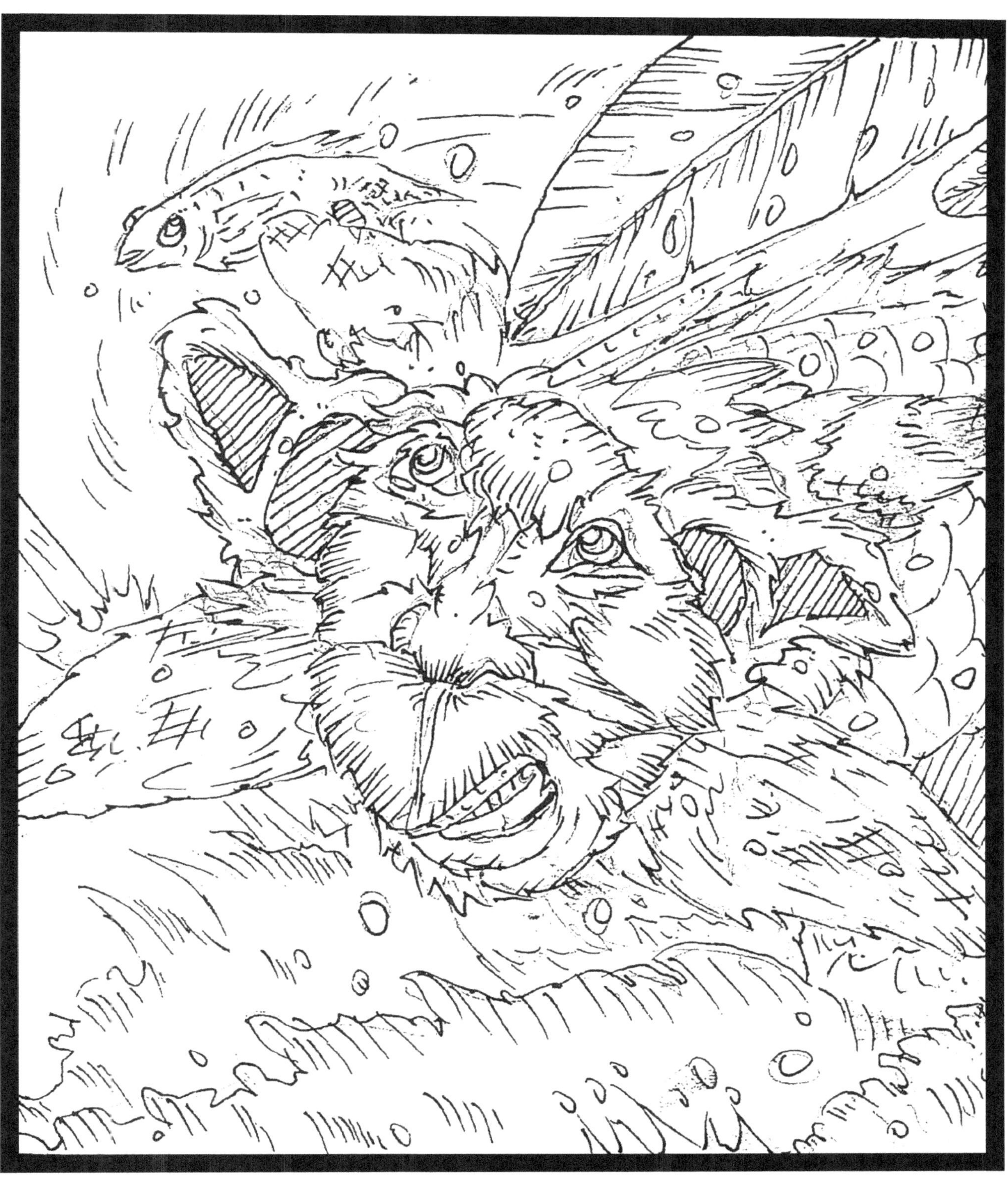

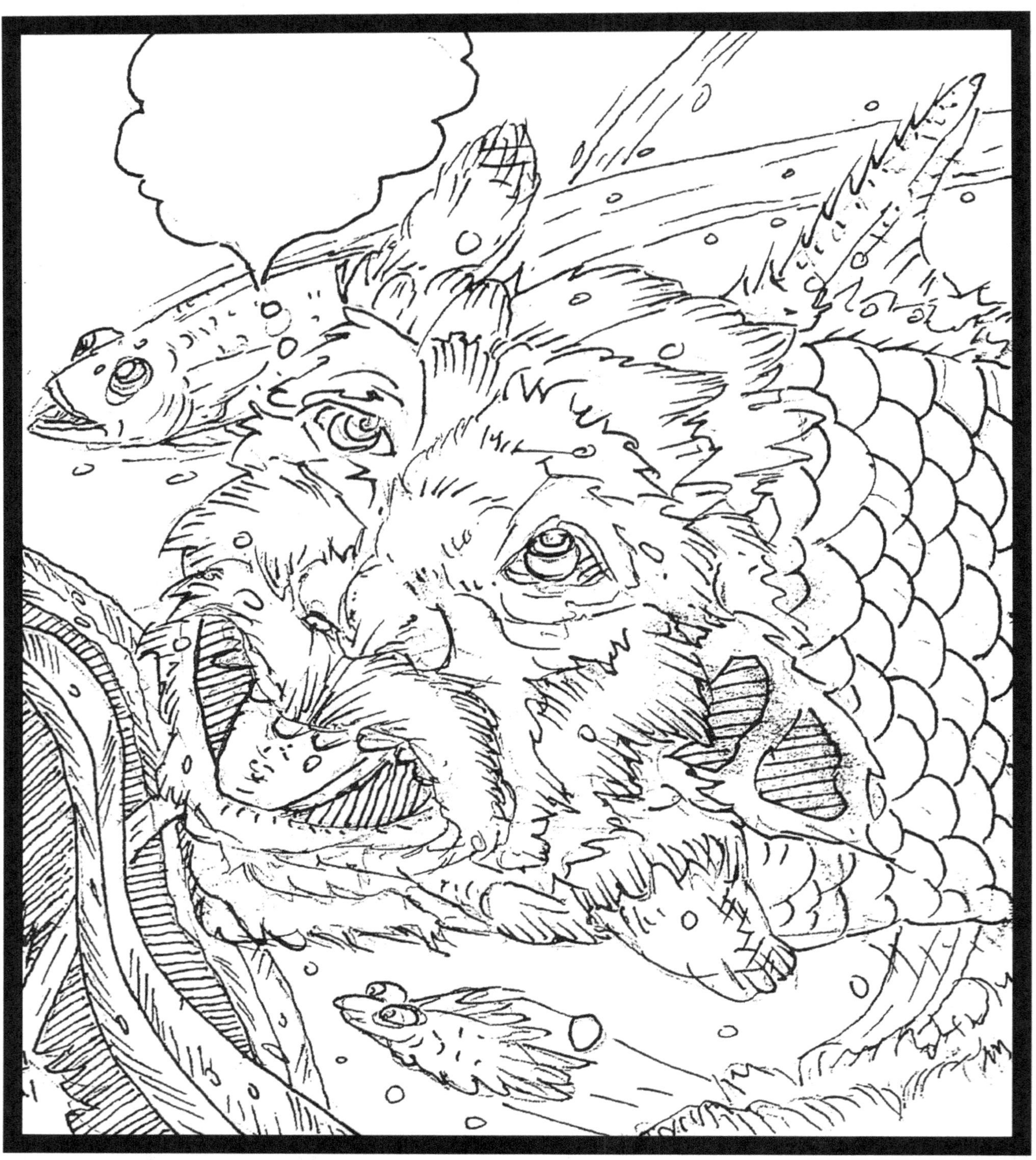

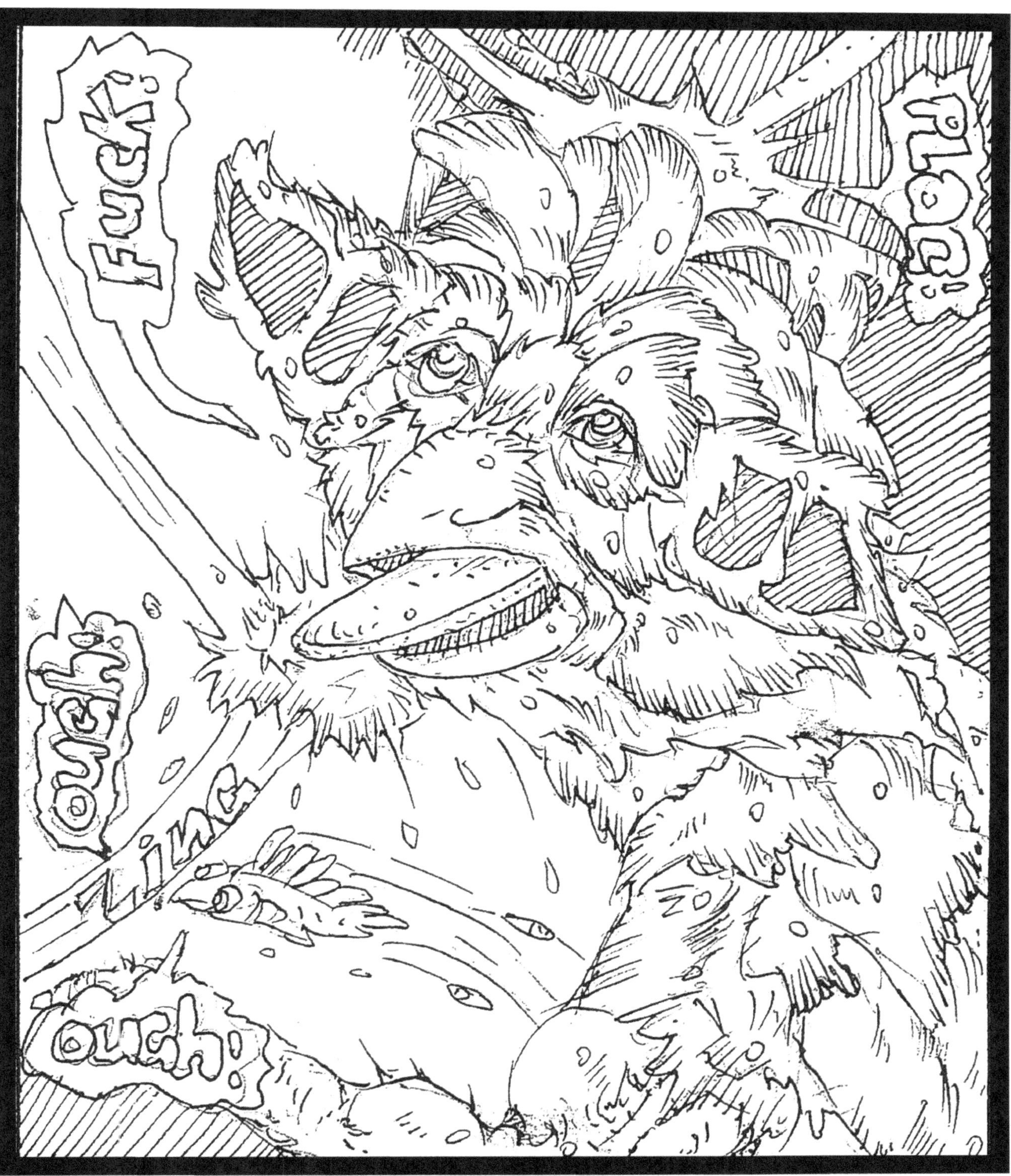

FUCK!
PLORB
OUCH!
ZING
OUCH!

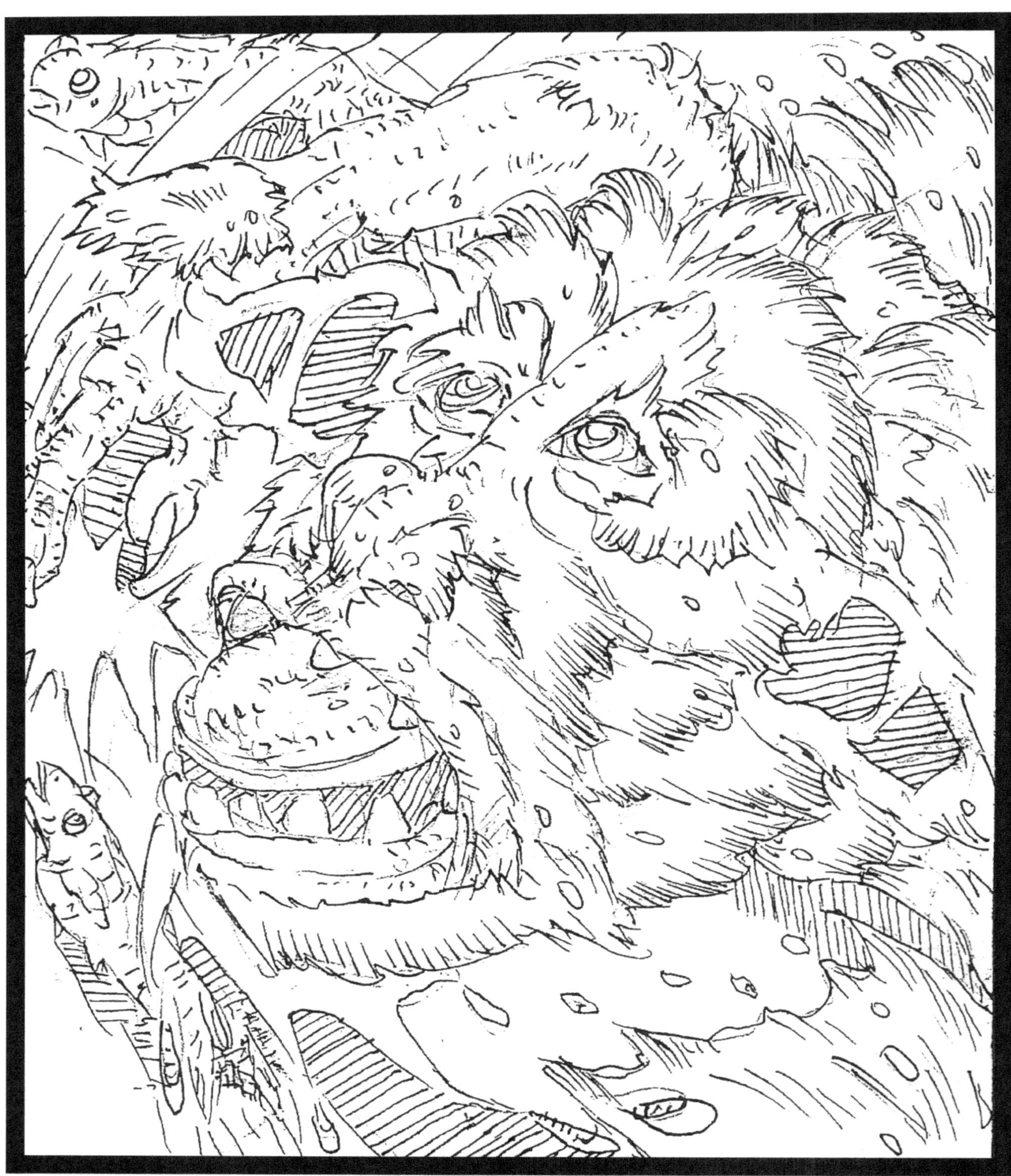

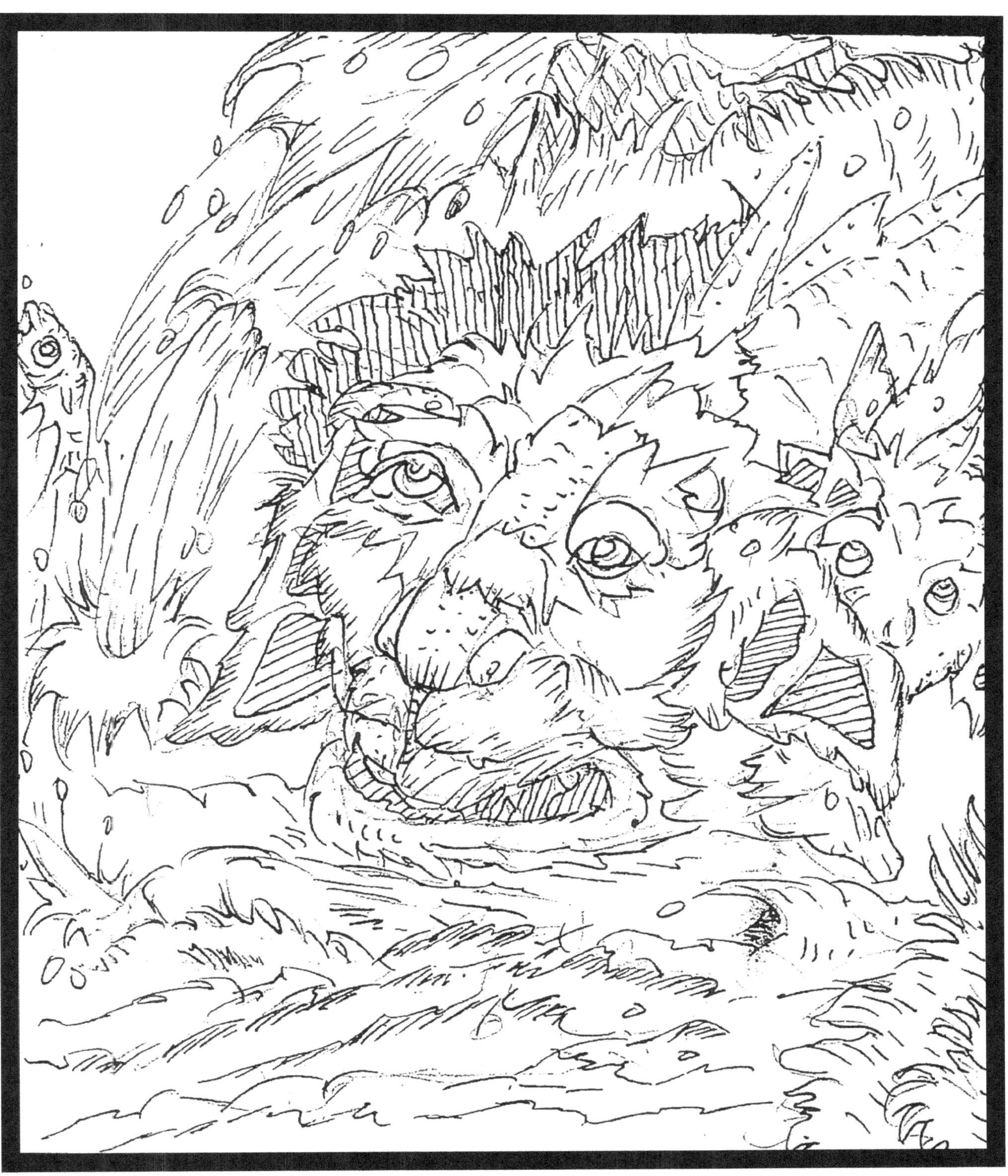

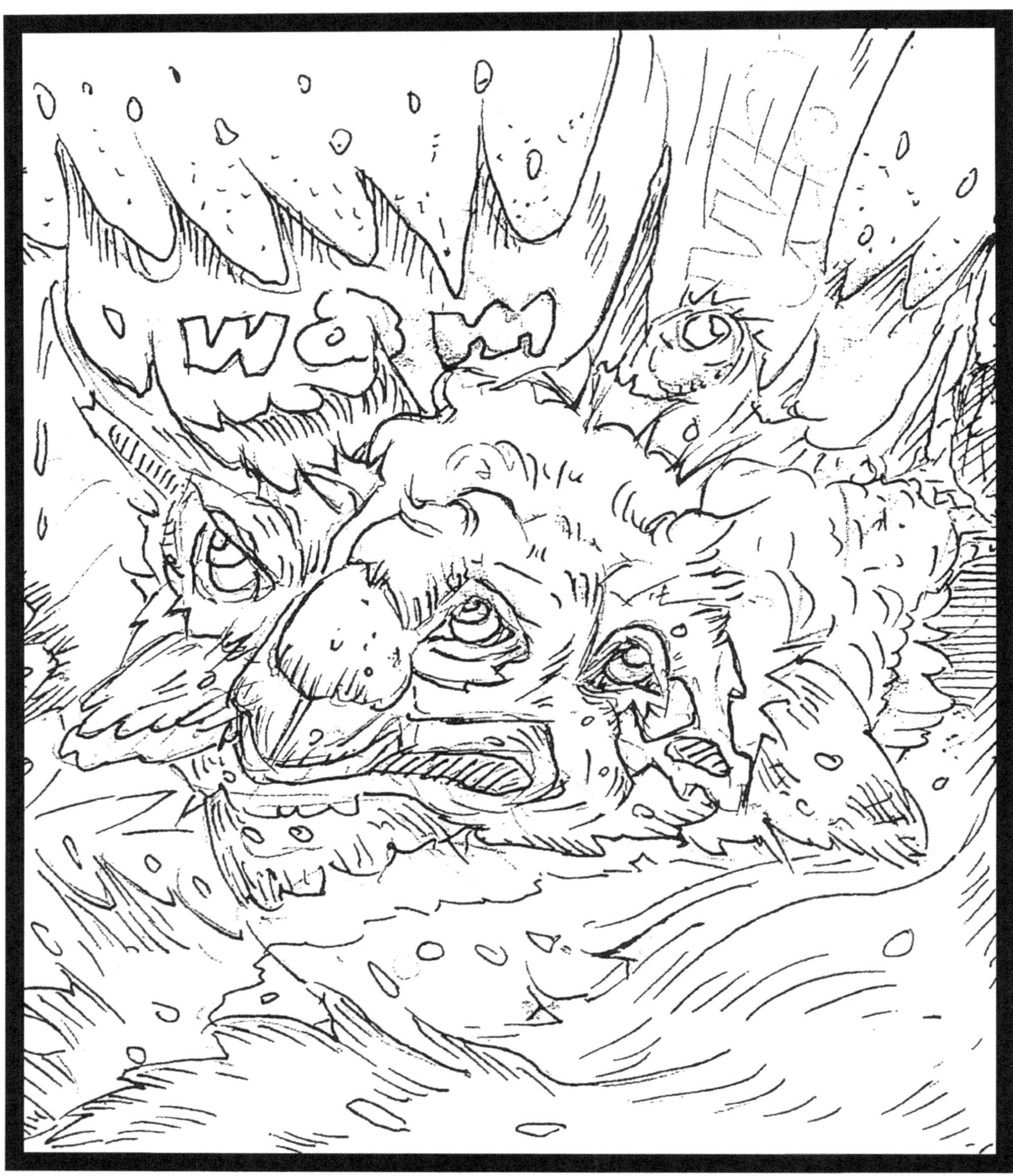

wam

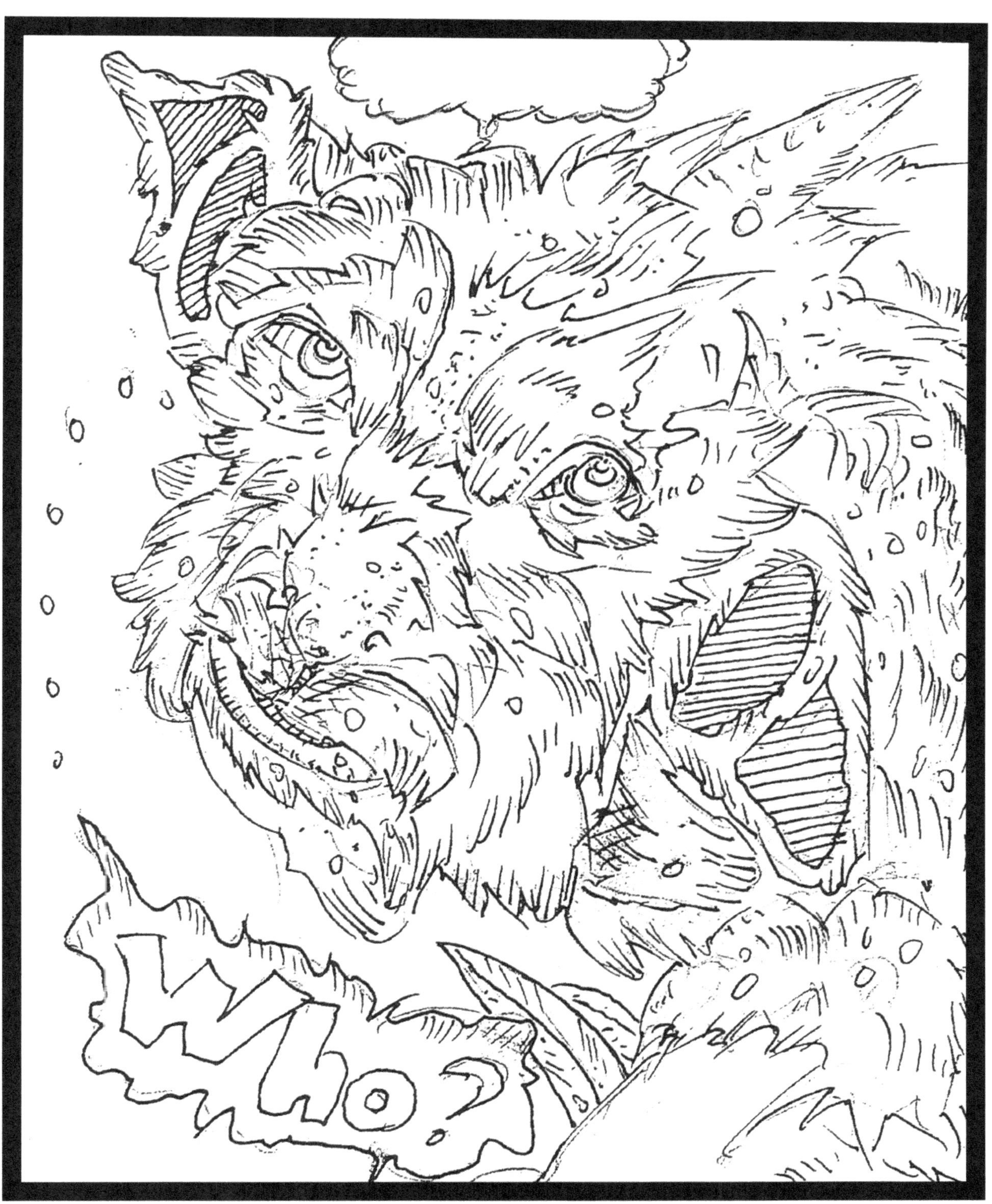

WHO?

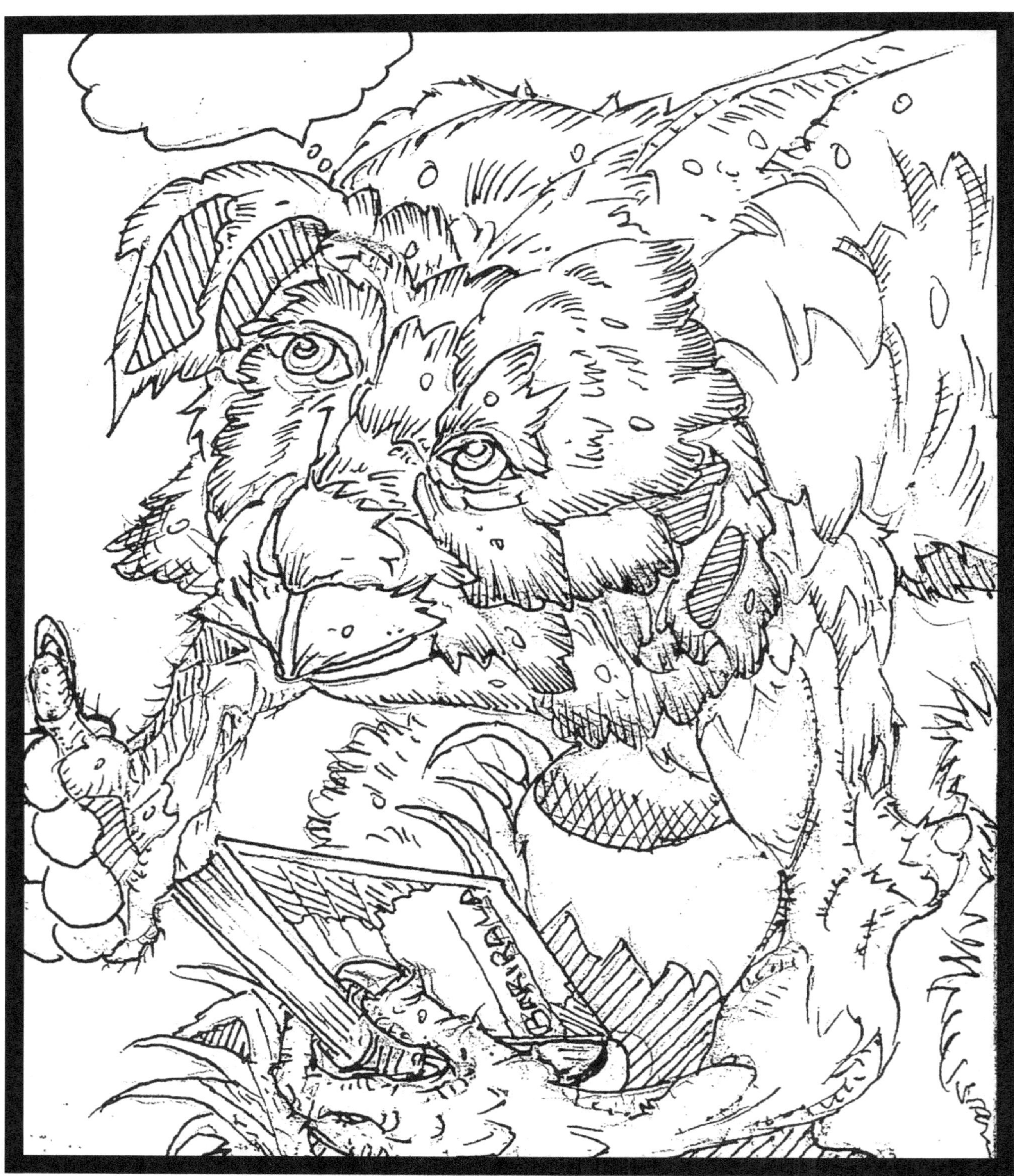

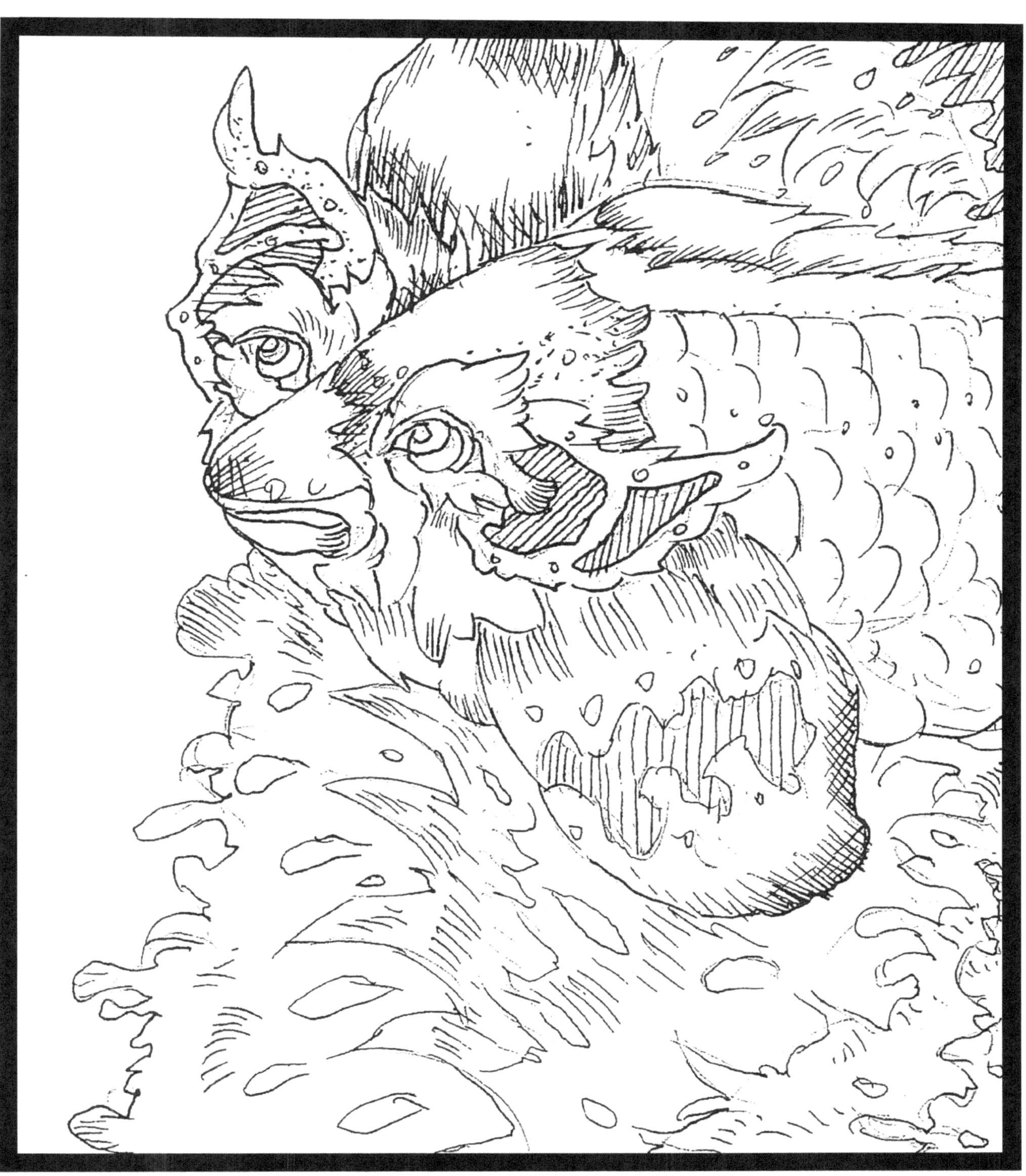

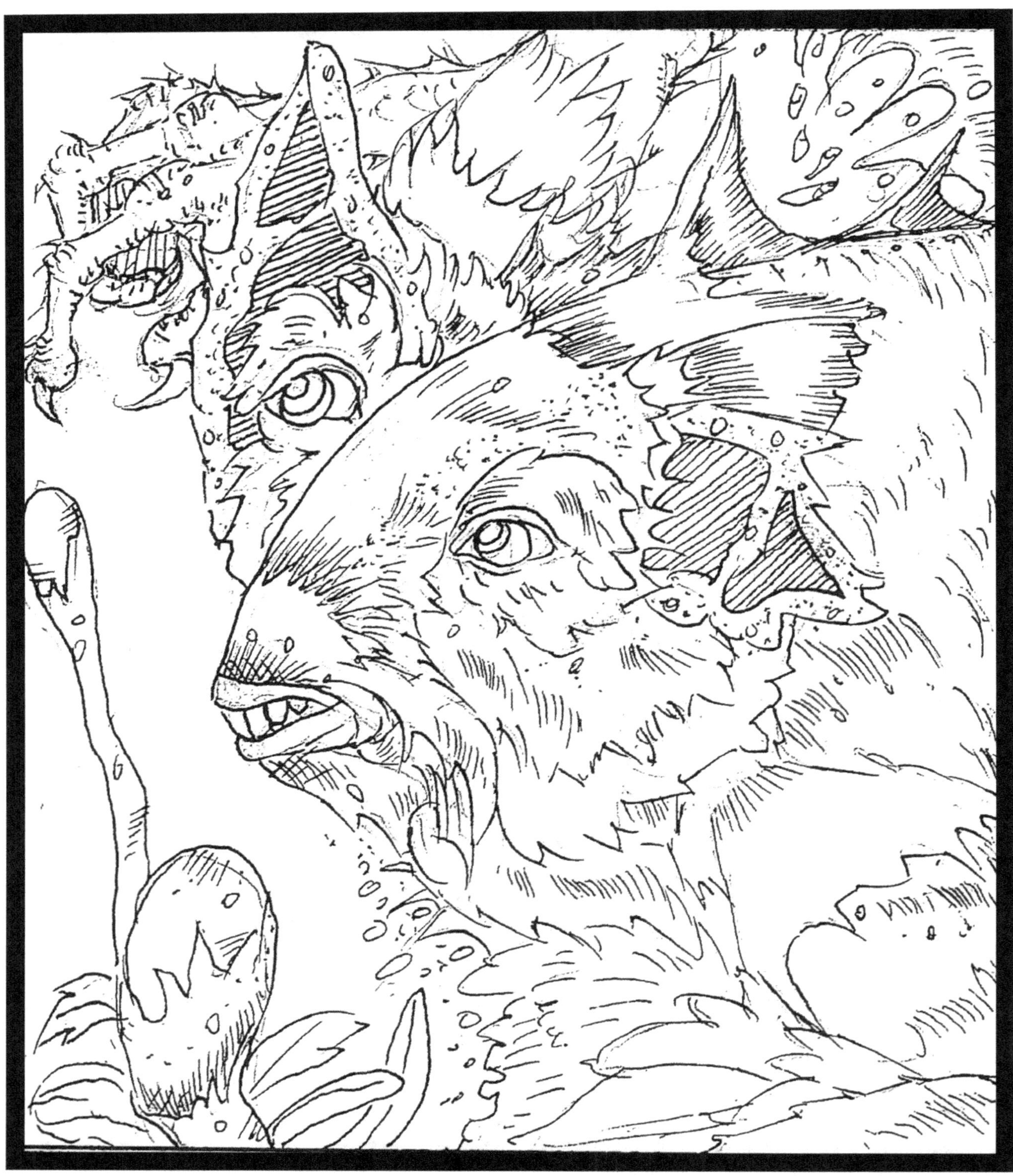

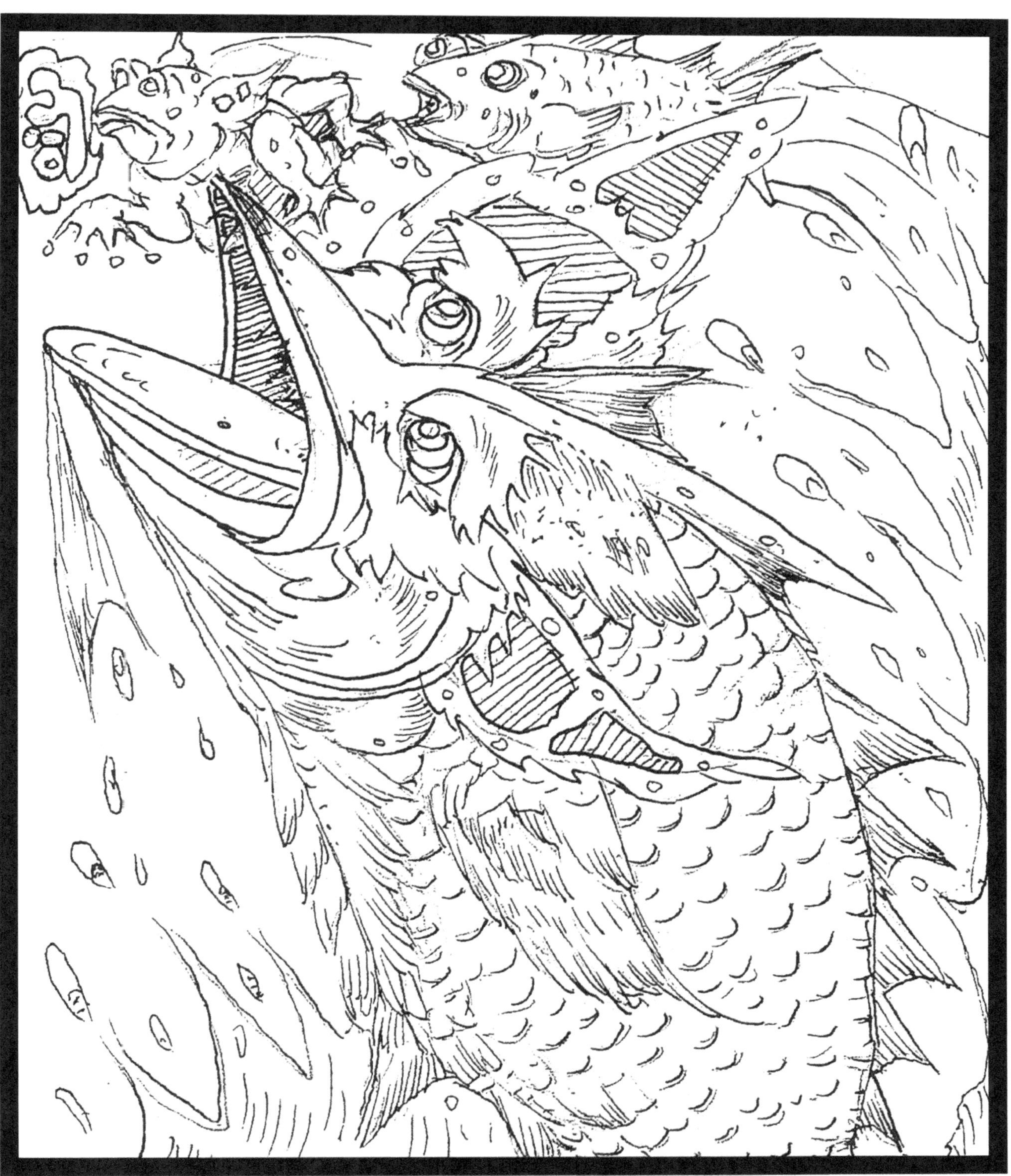

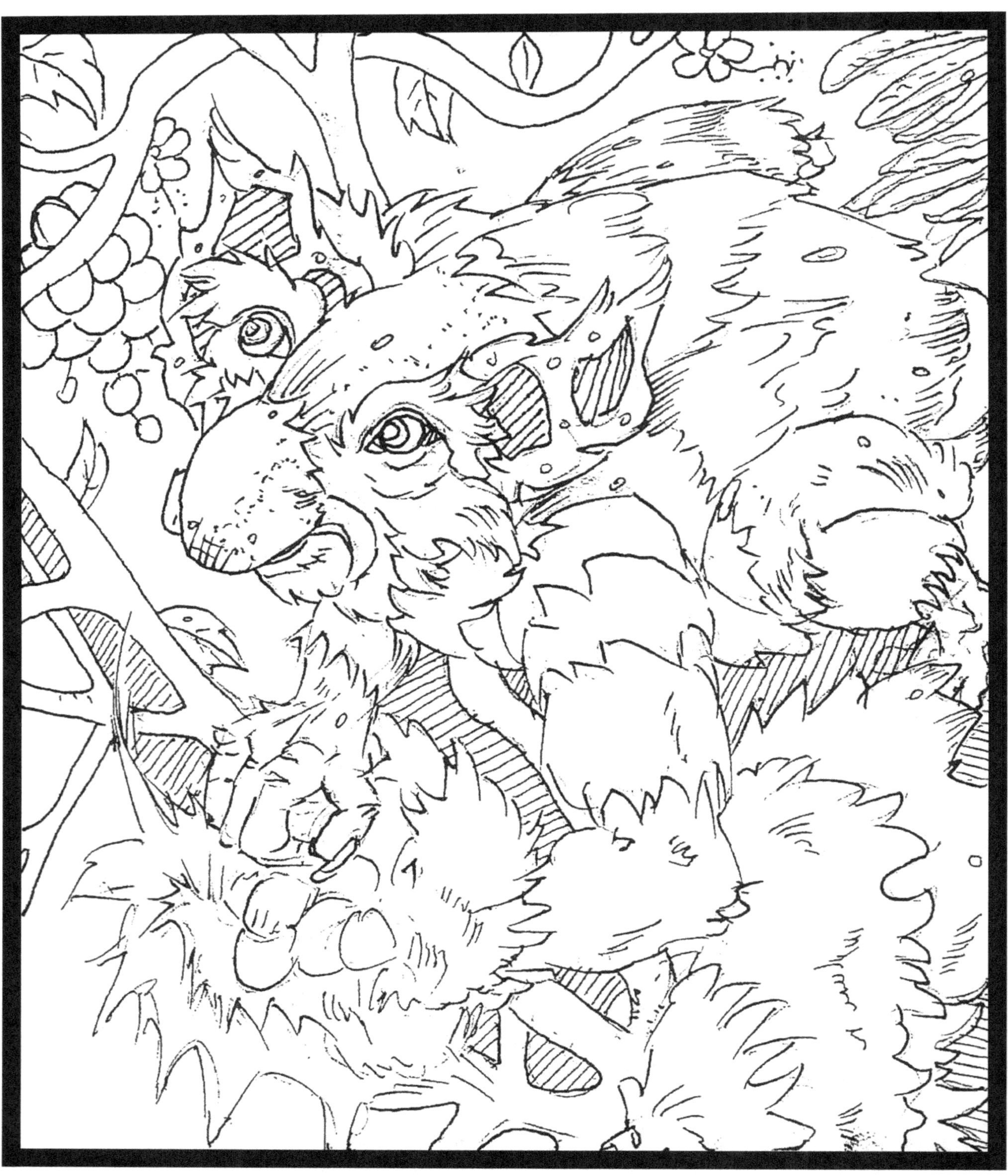

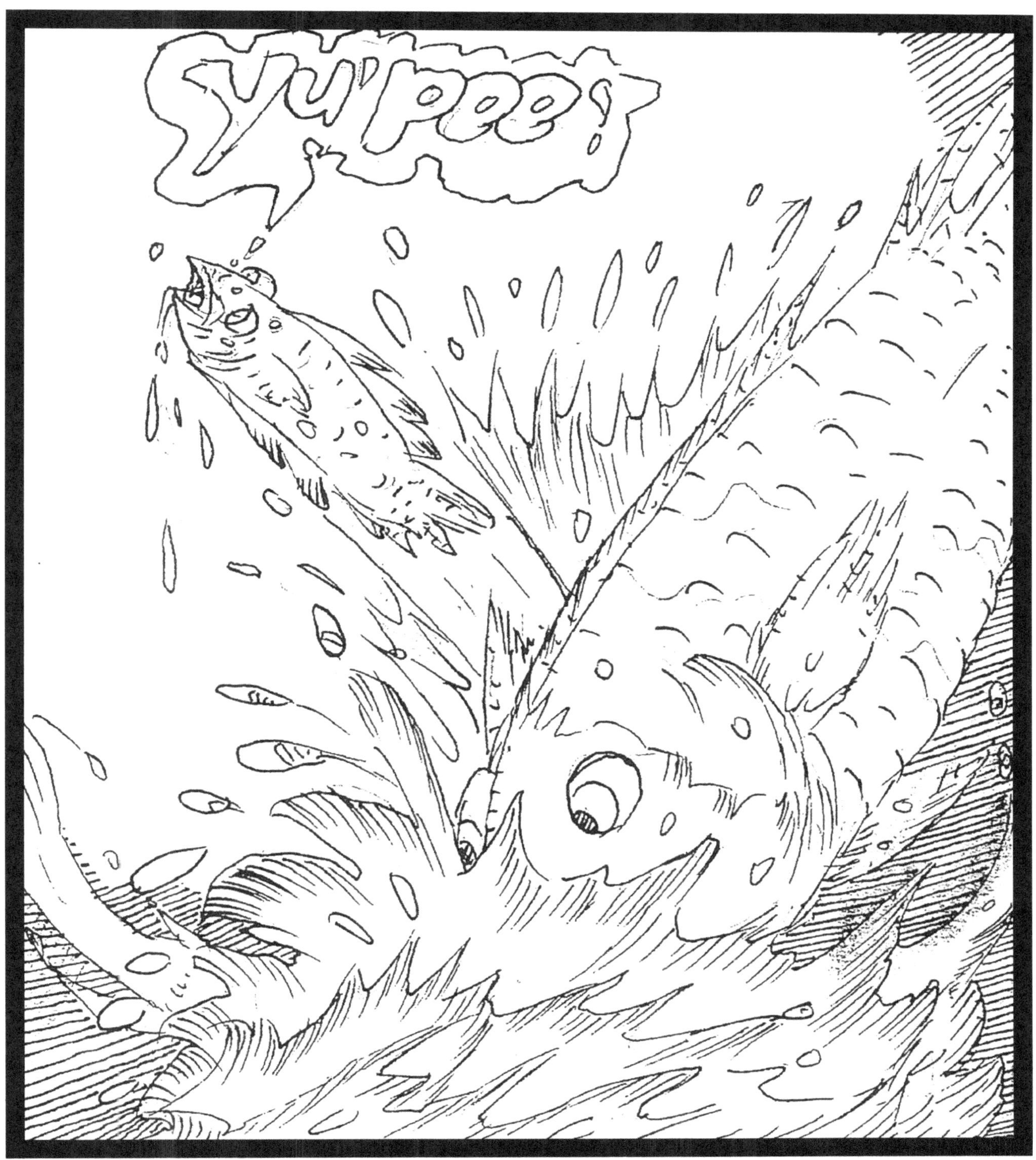

Yu'pee!

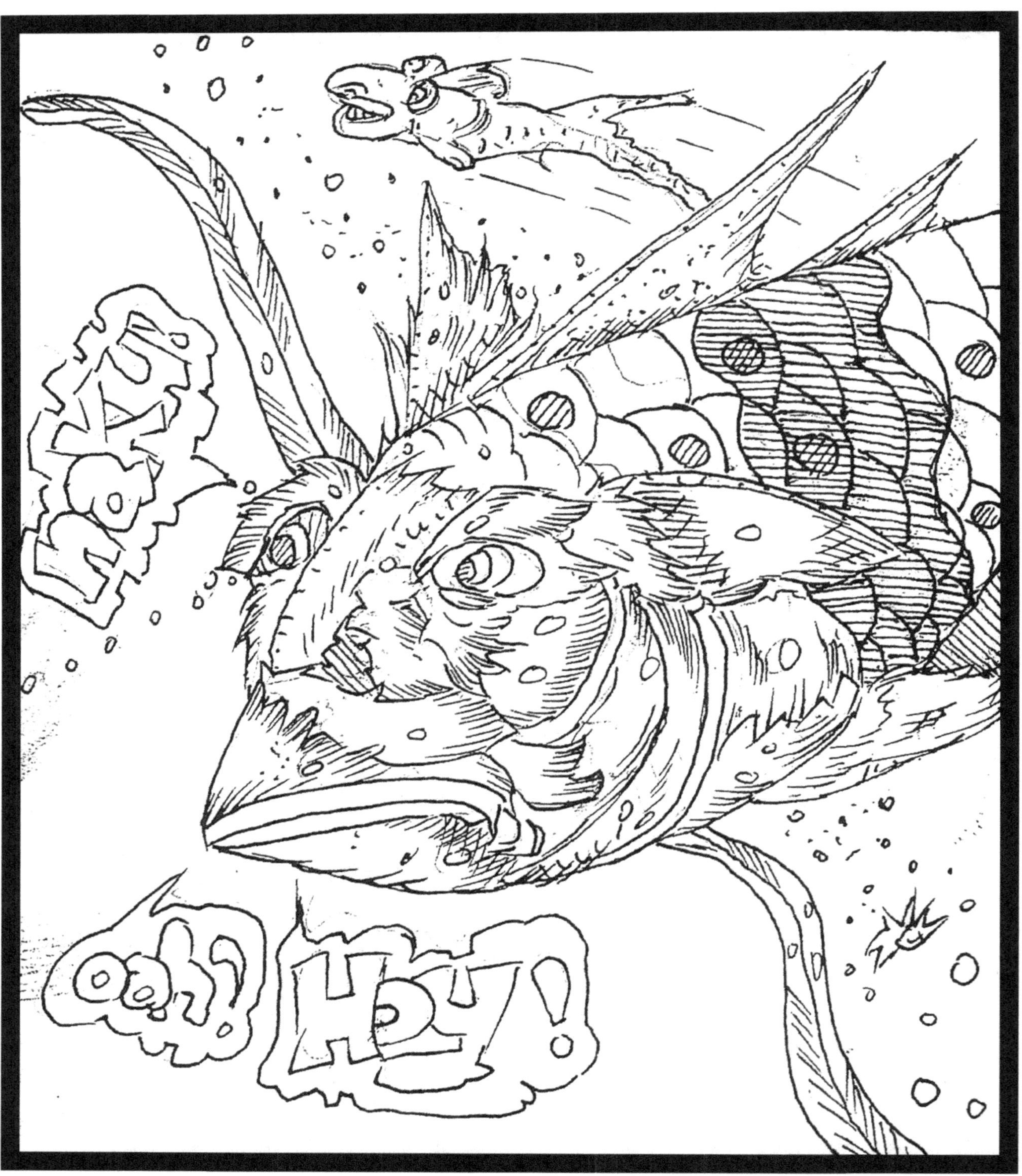
nak!
Ooh! Hey!

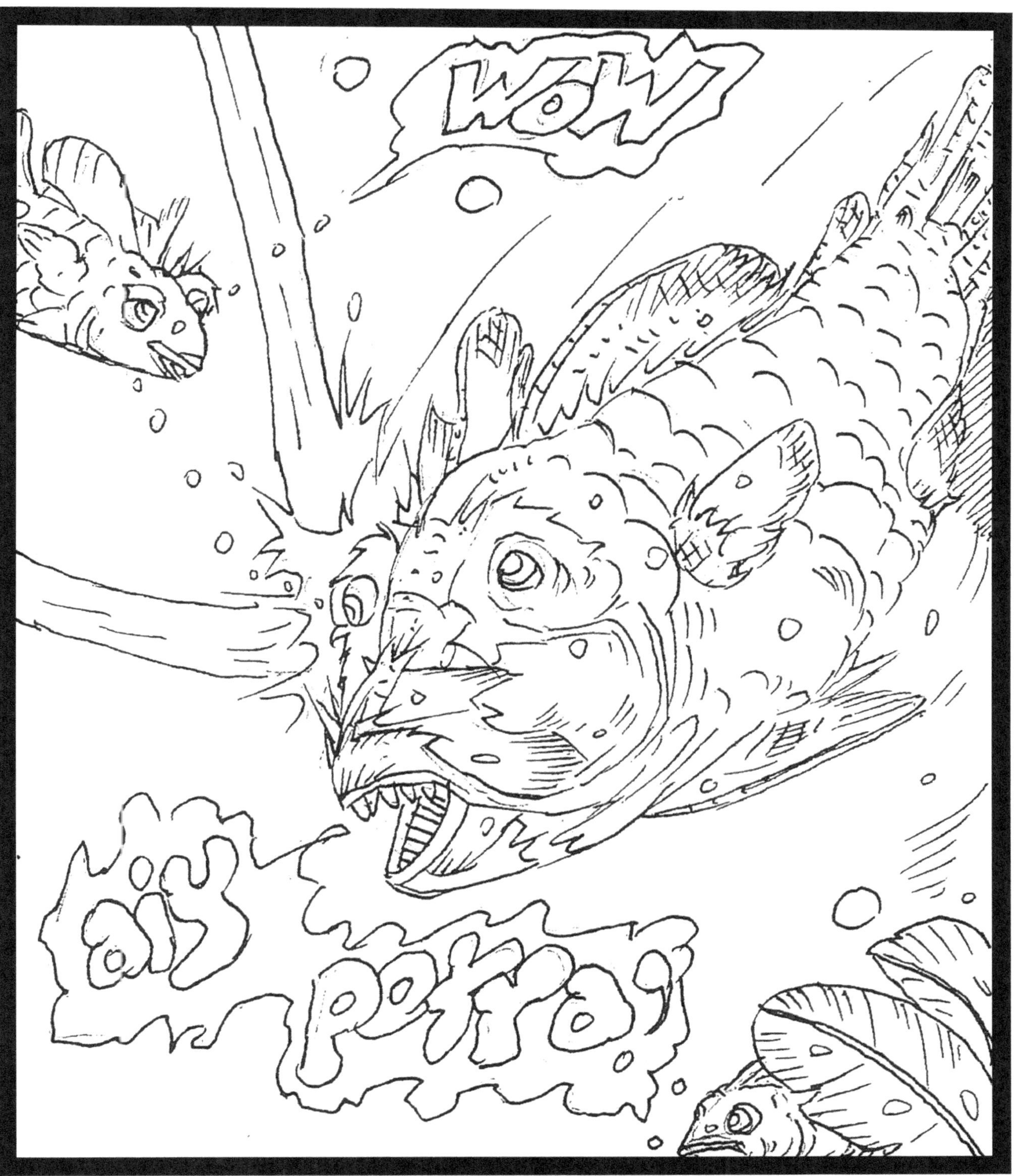

WOW
ai!
petra!

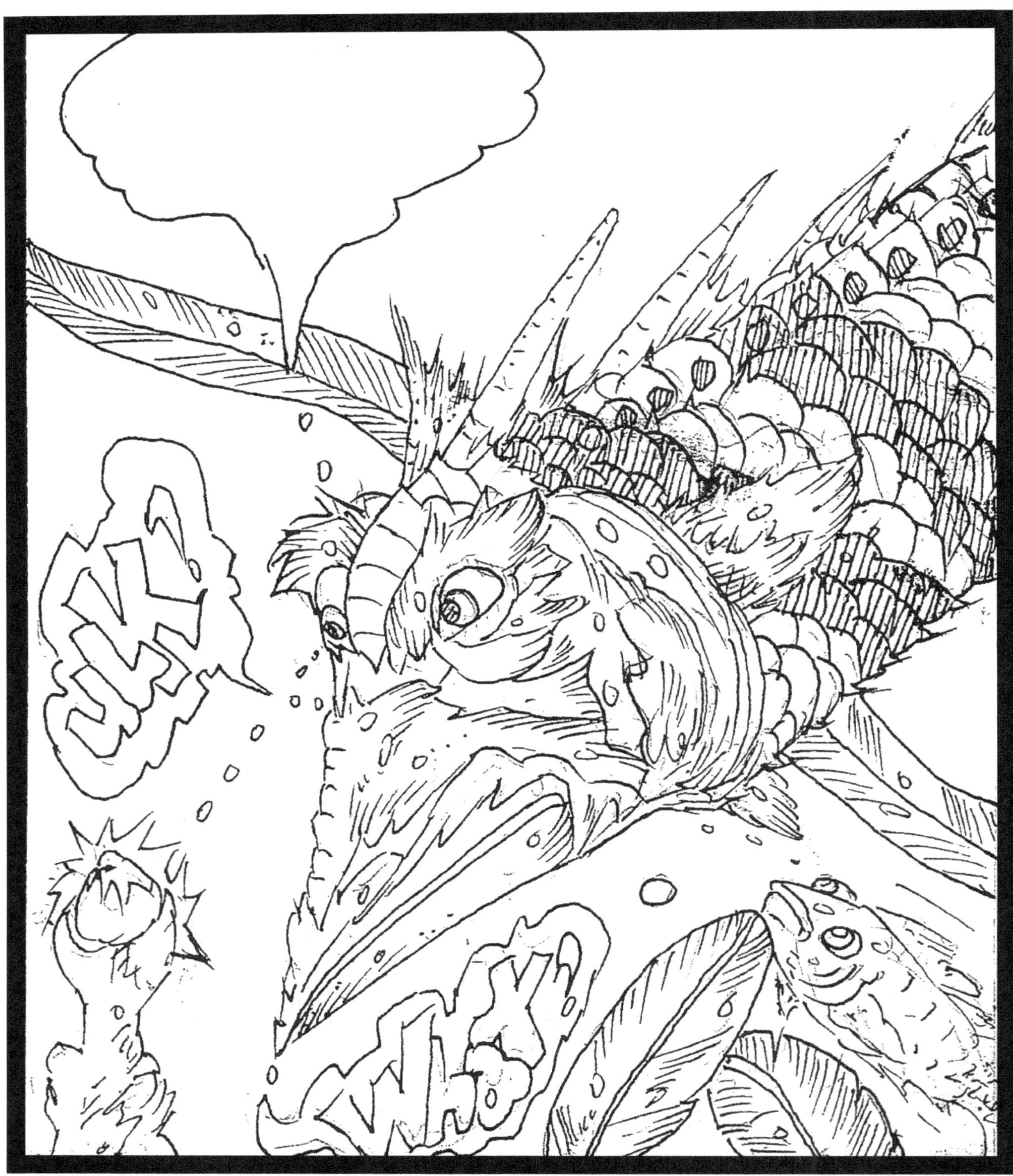
ULK?
SKWHO?

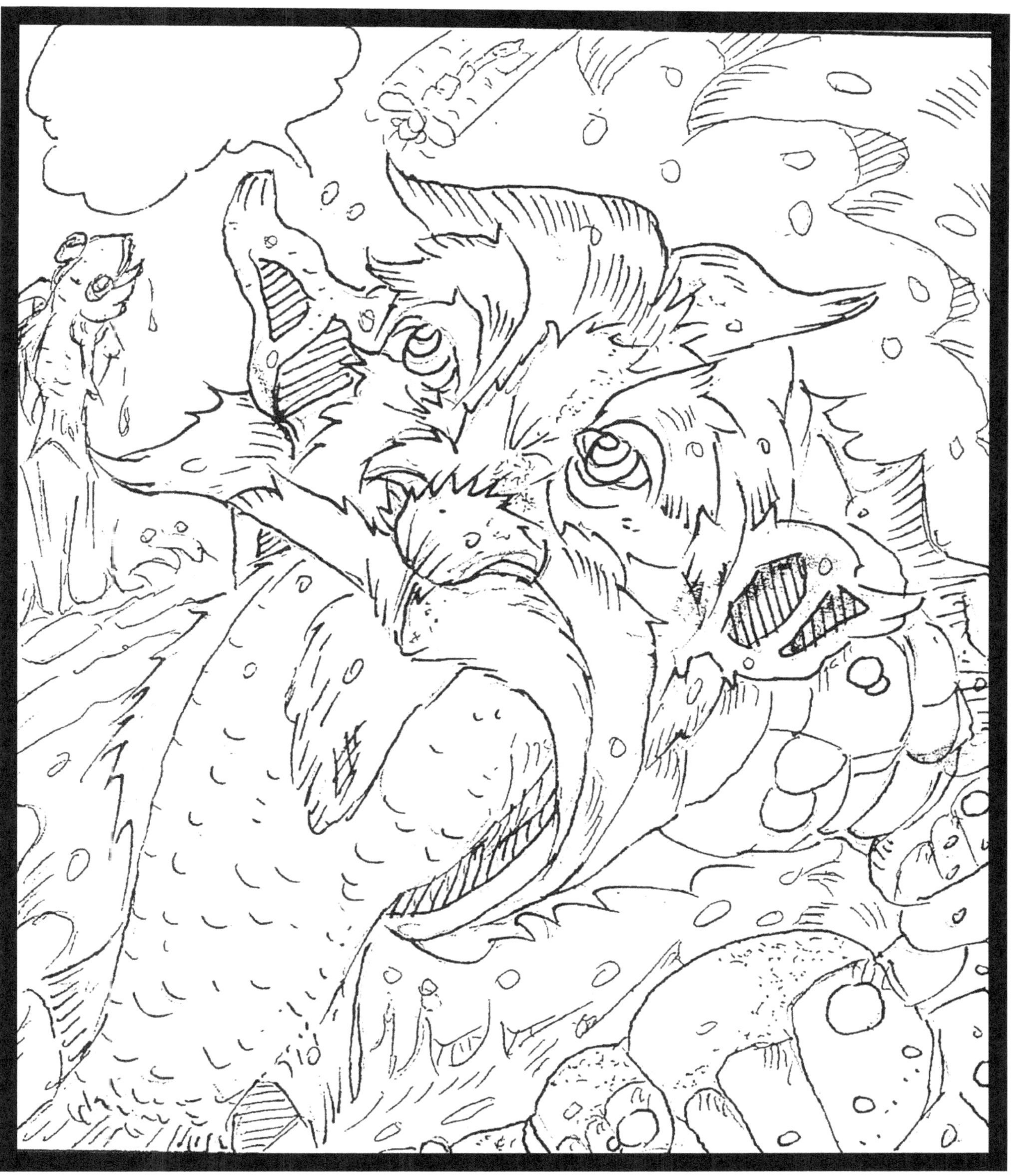

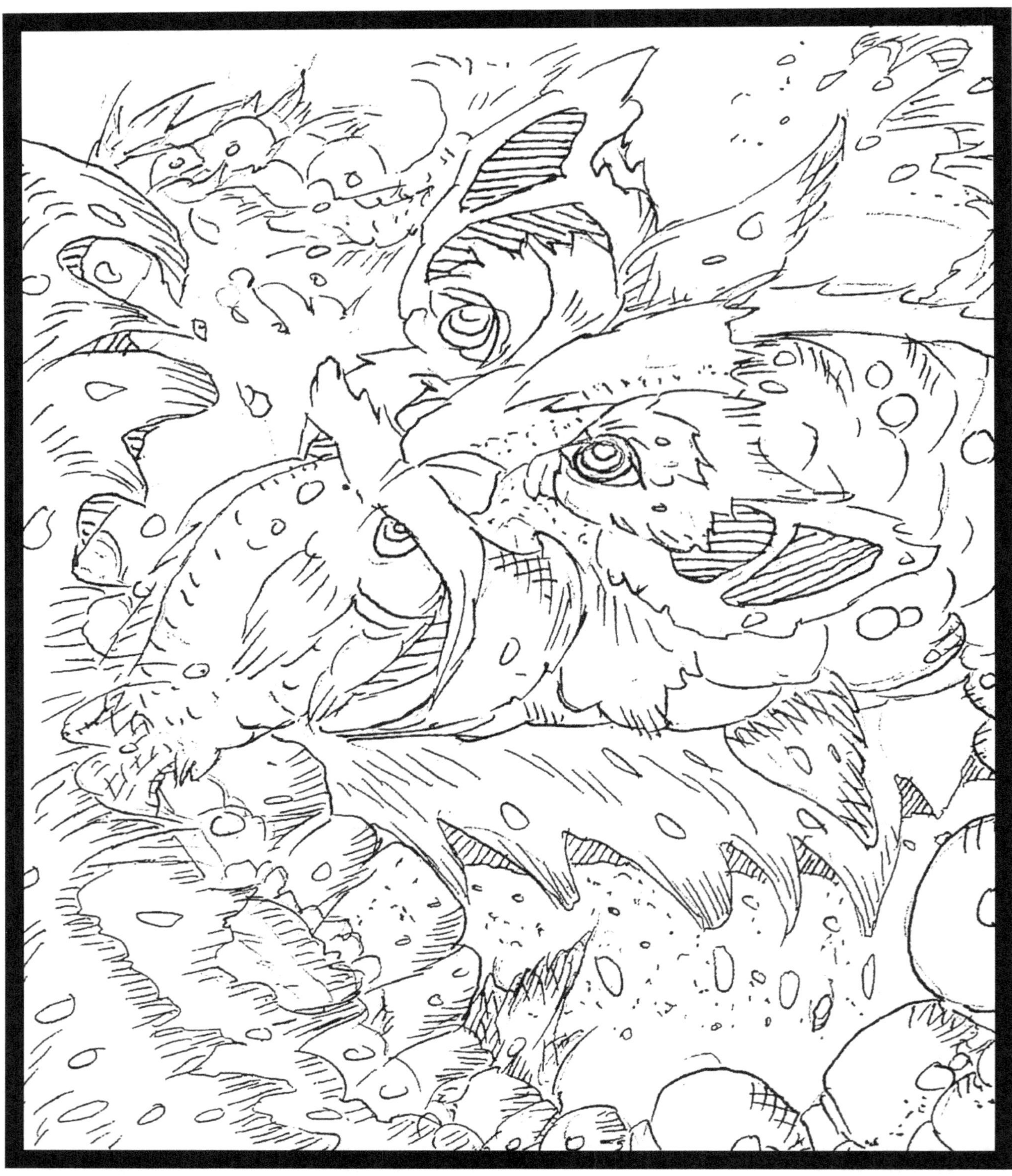

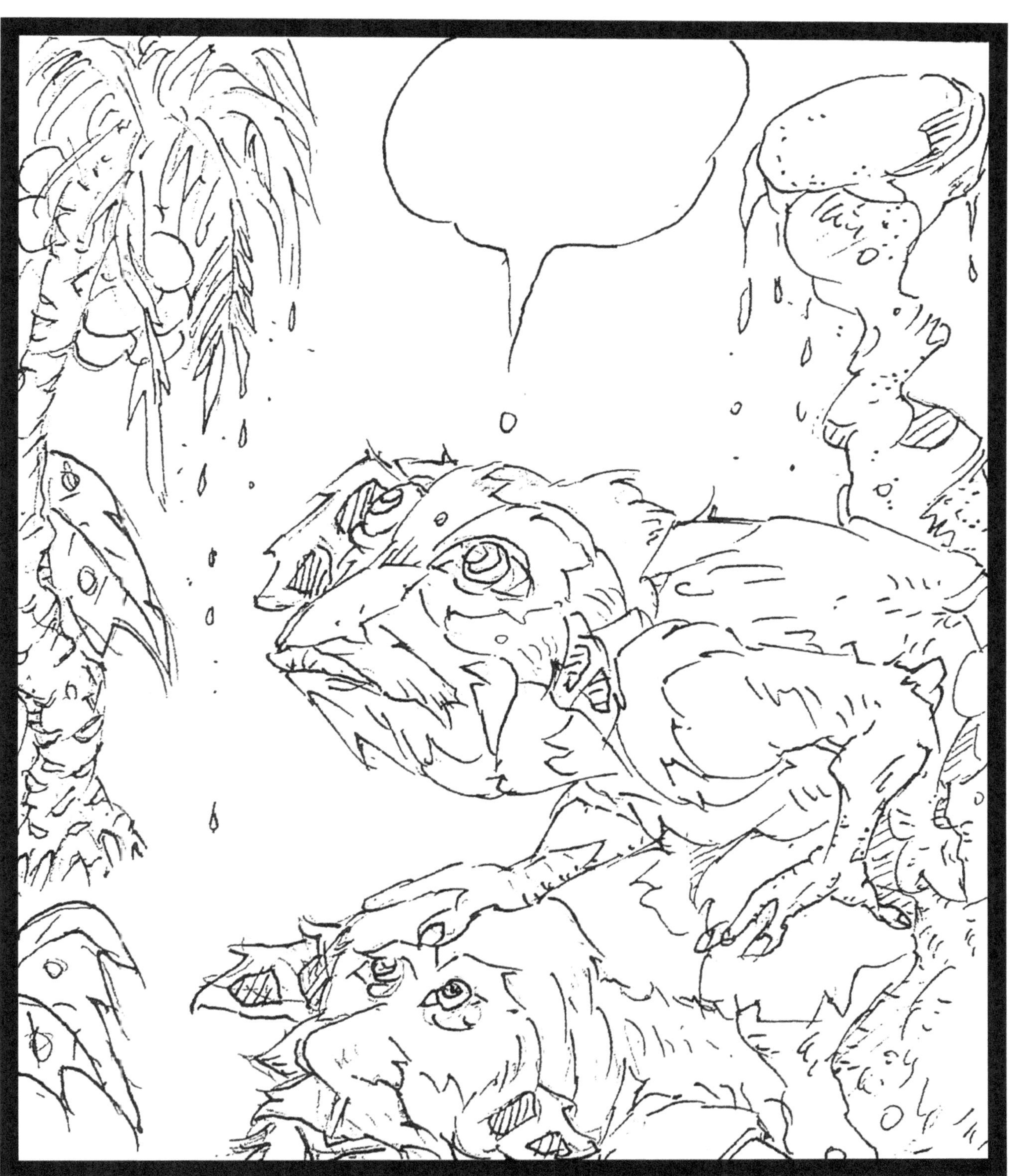

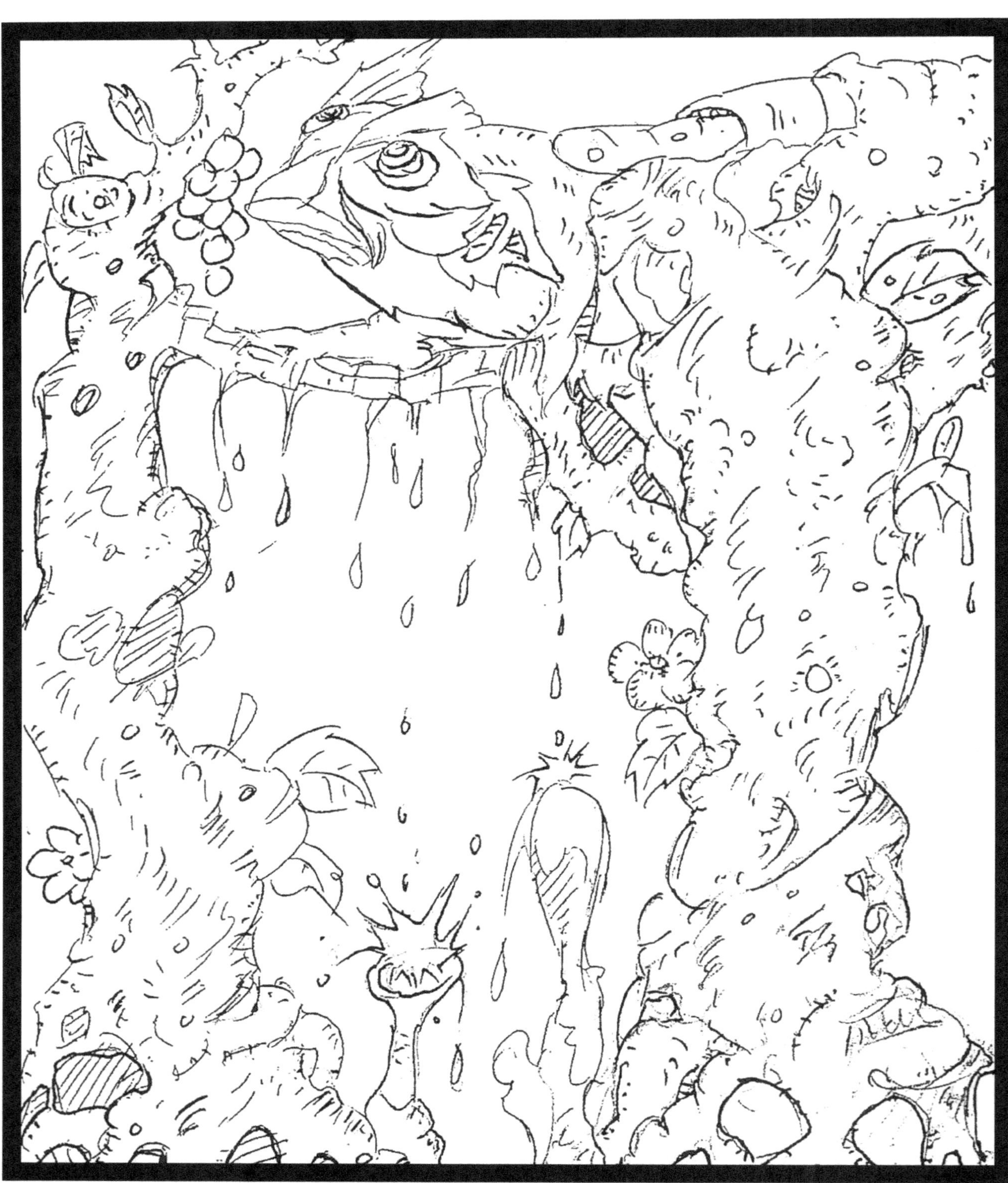

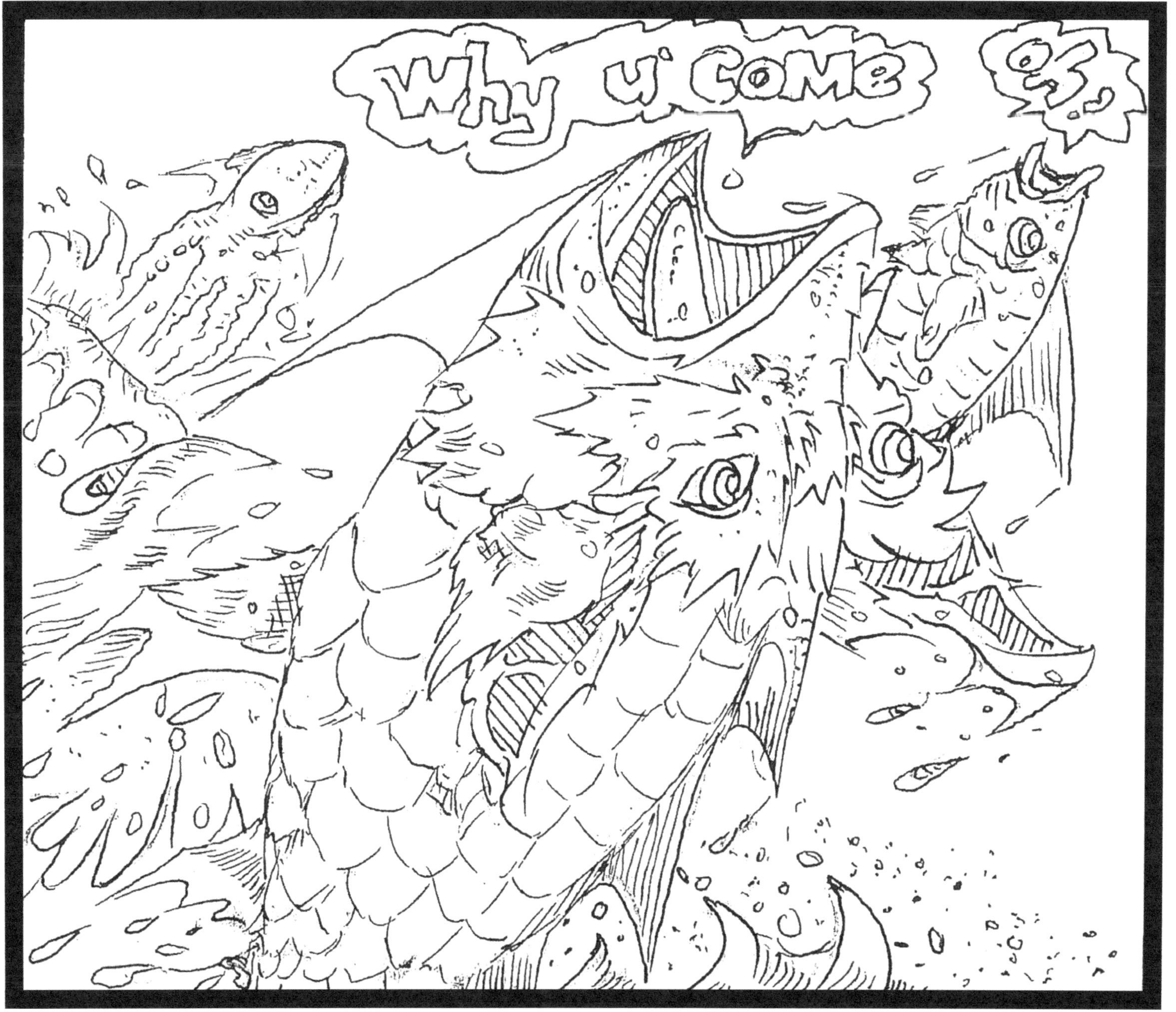

why u come
eh?

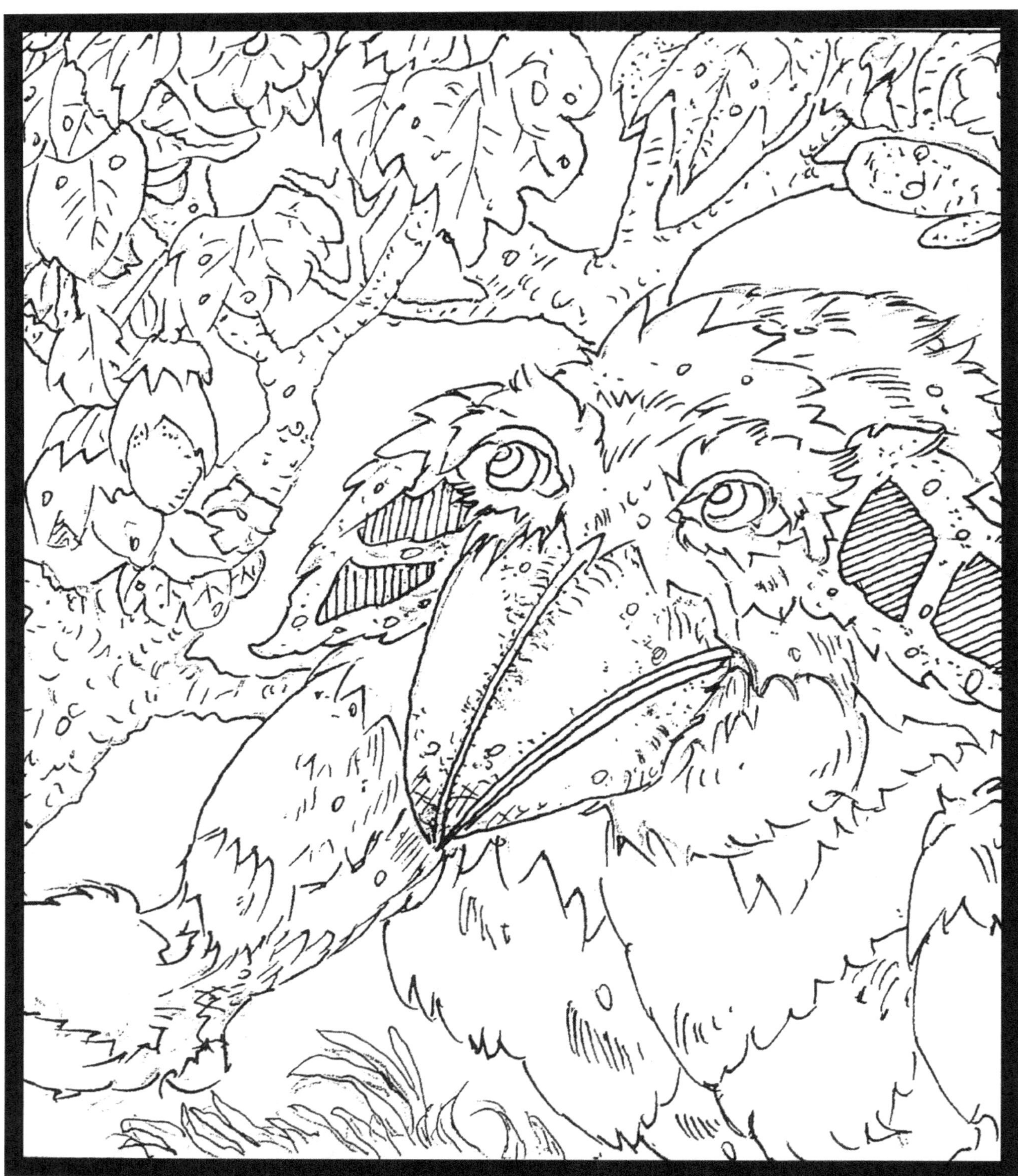

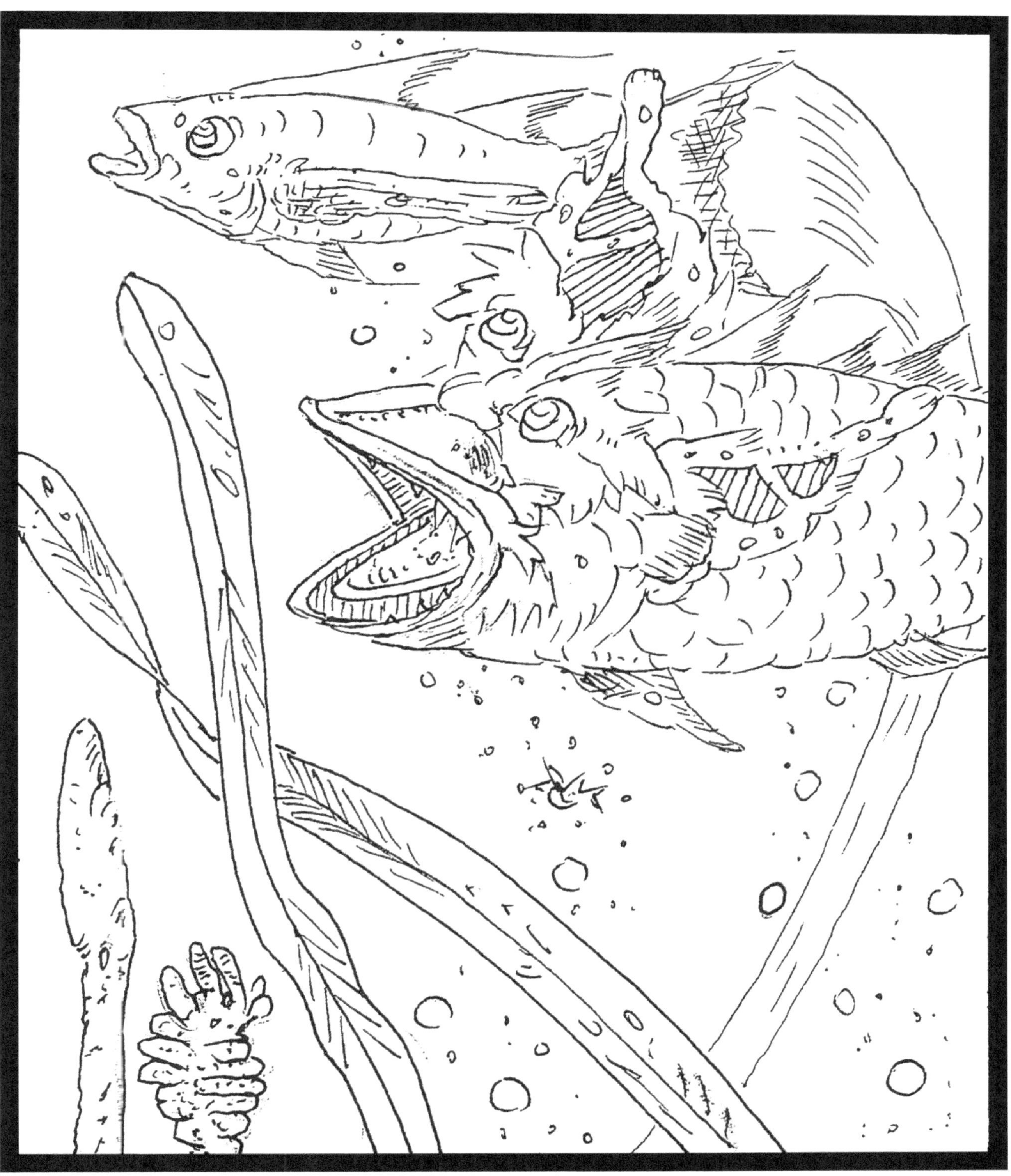

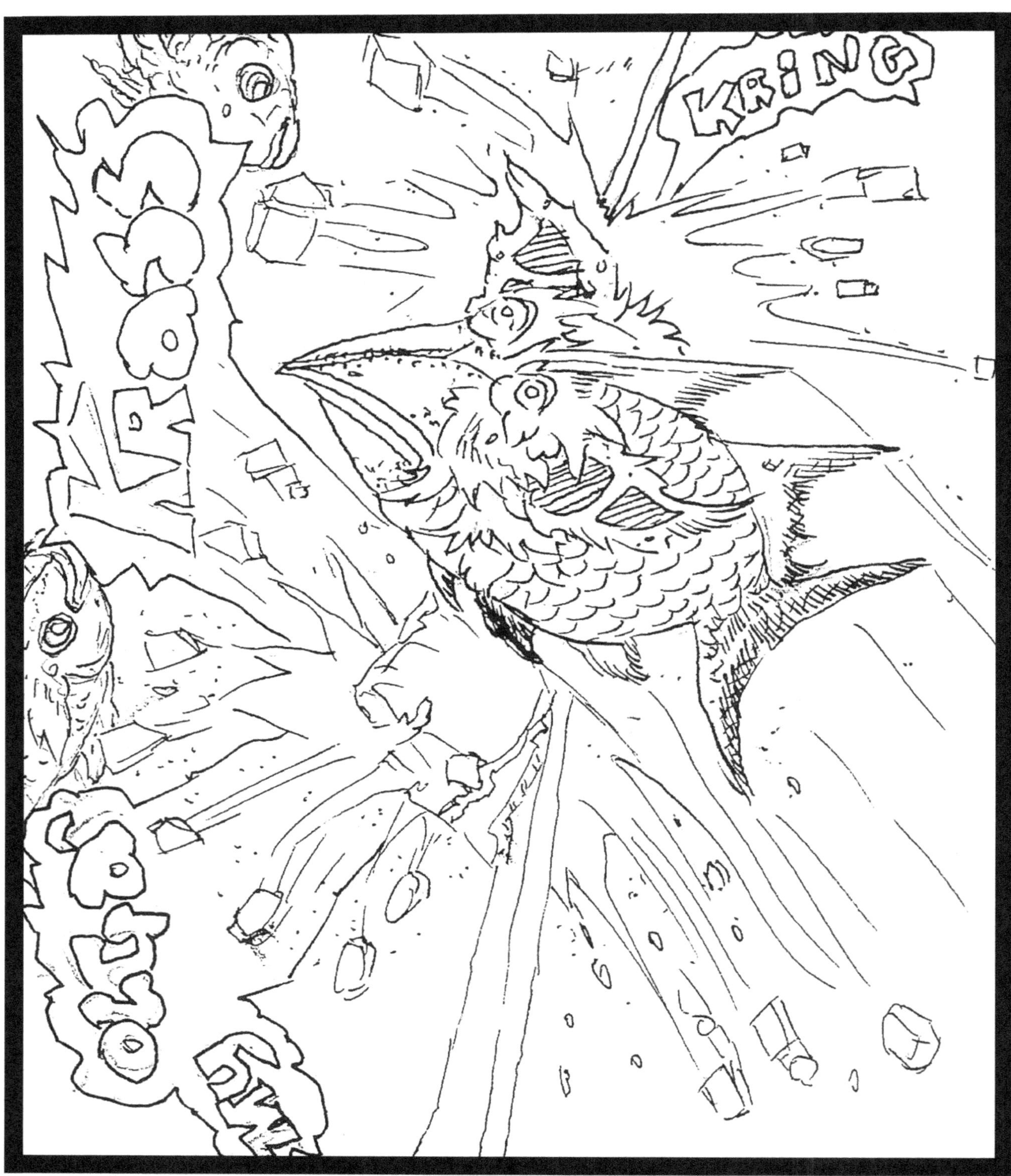

KRING
KRASSSH

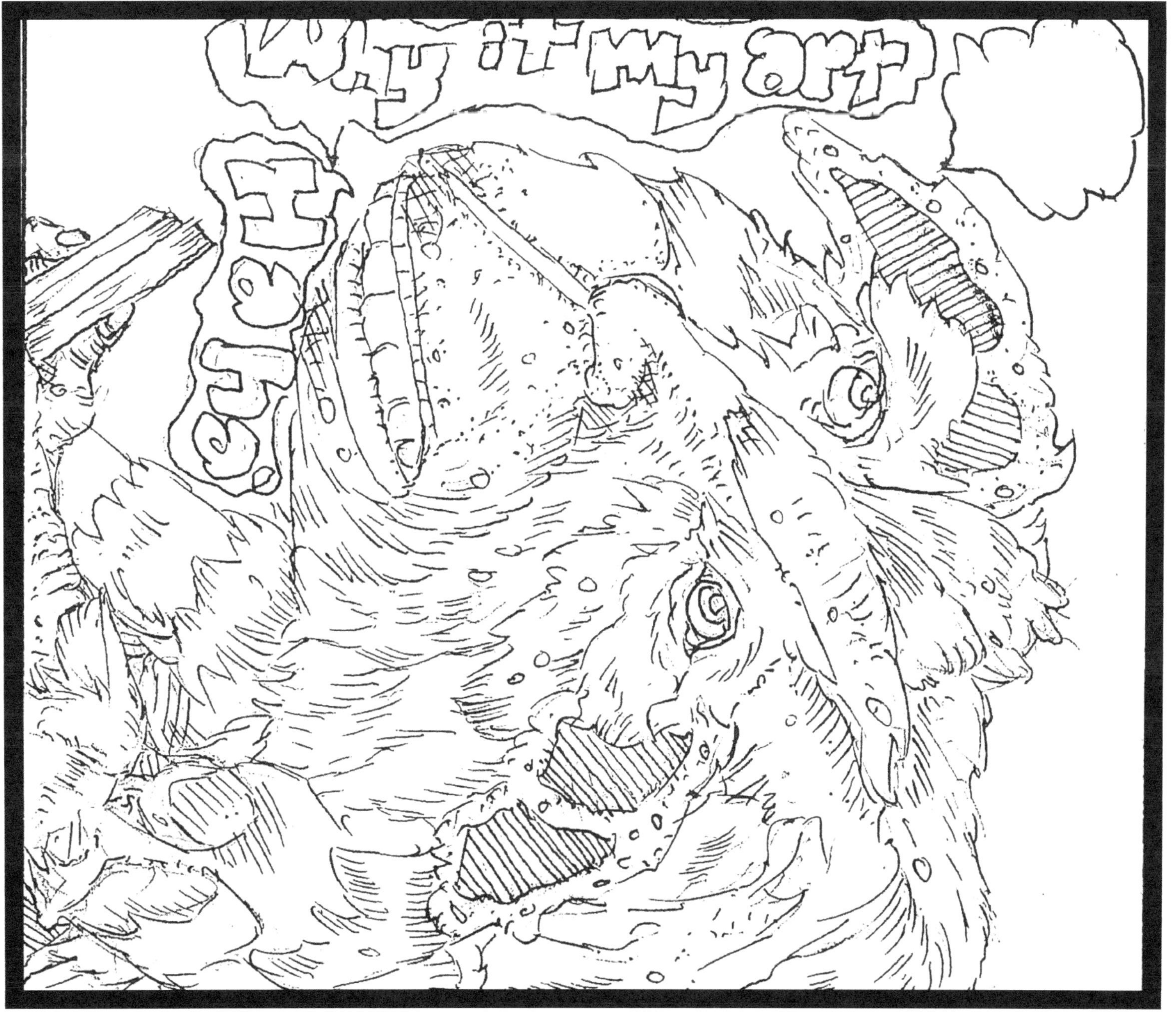

Why it my art
Haha

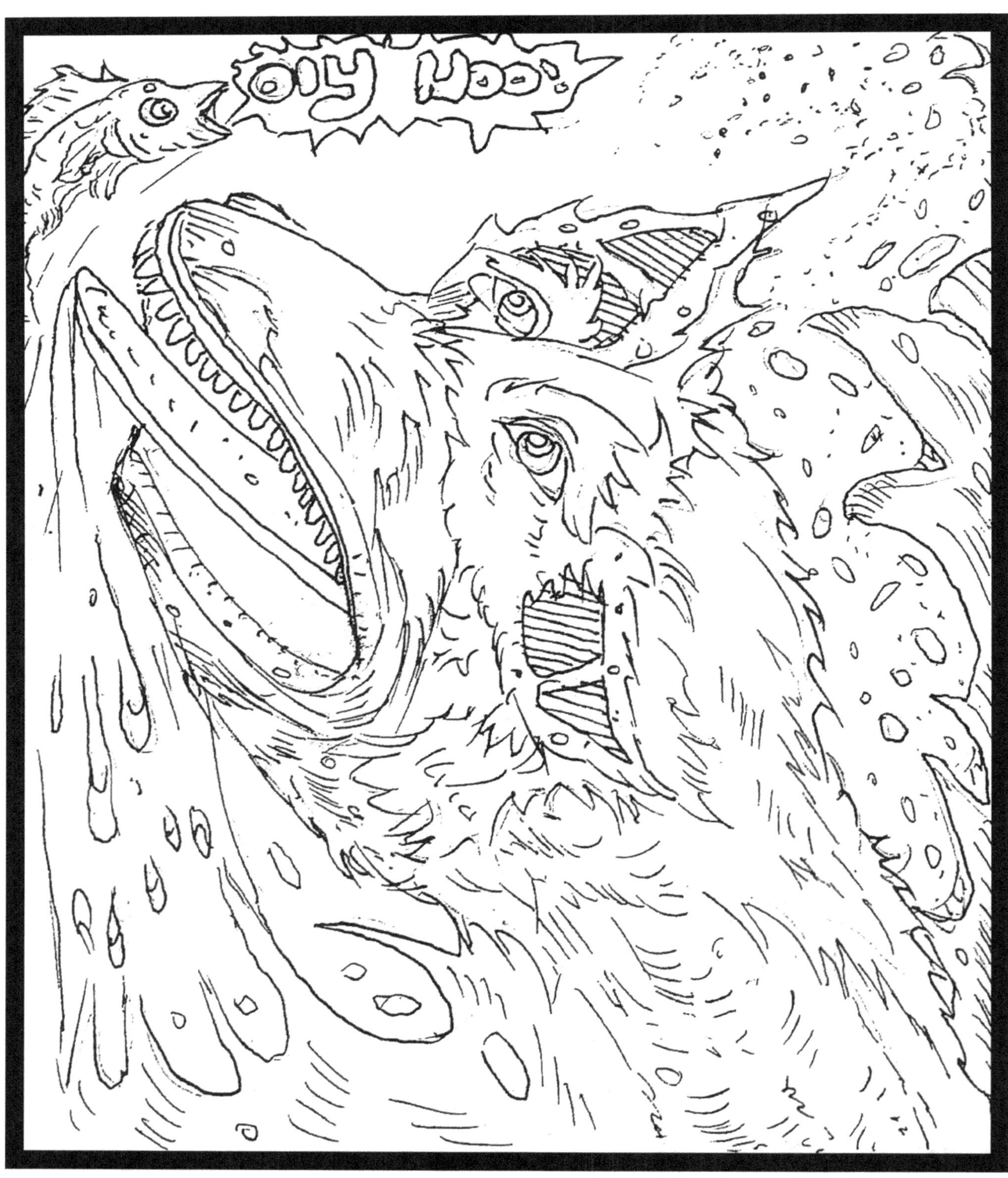
OILY MOO!

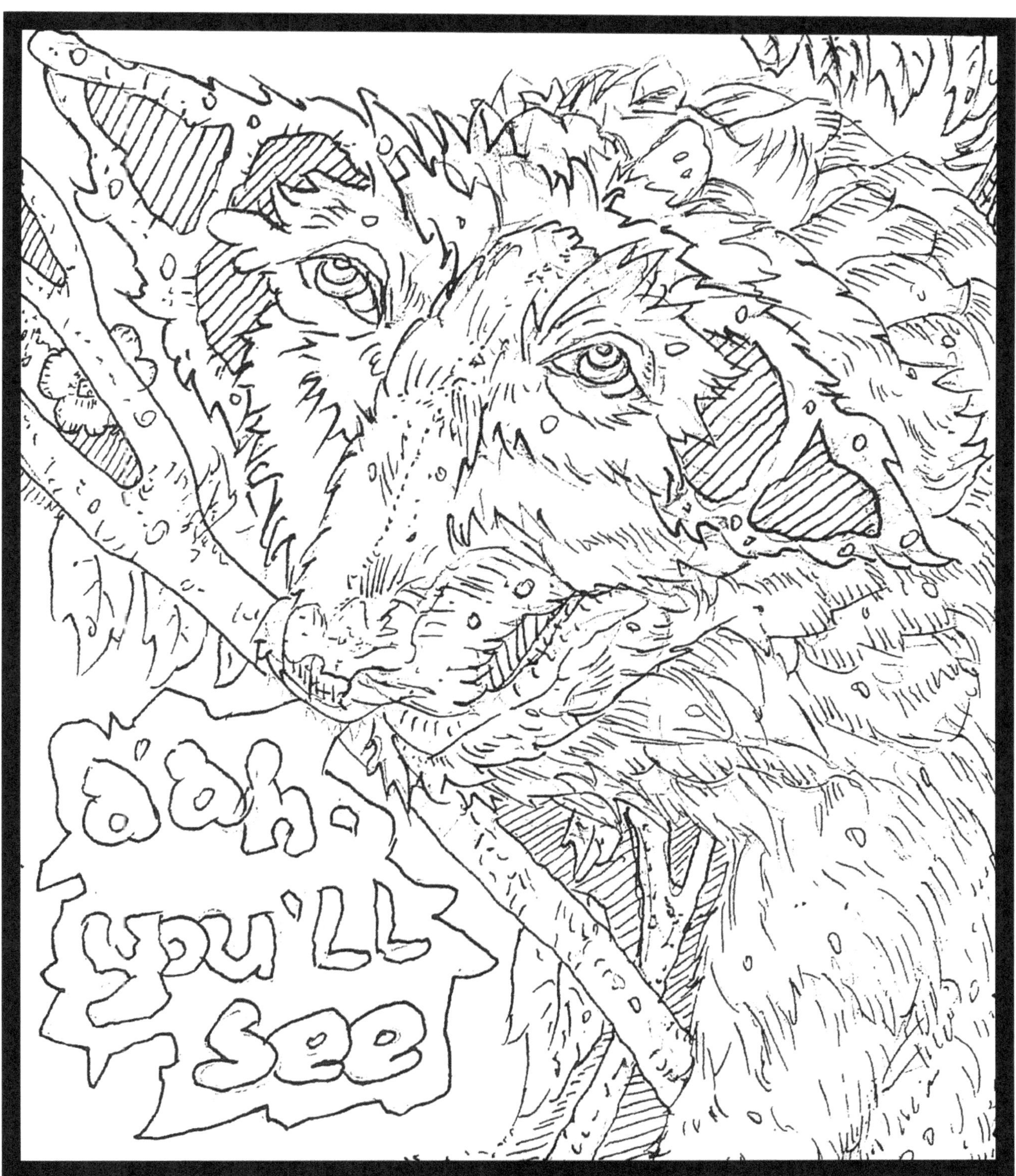
d'ah.
you'll
see

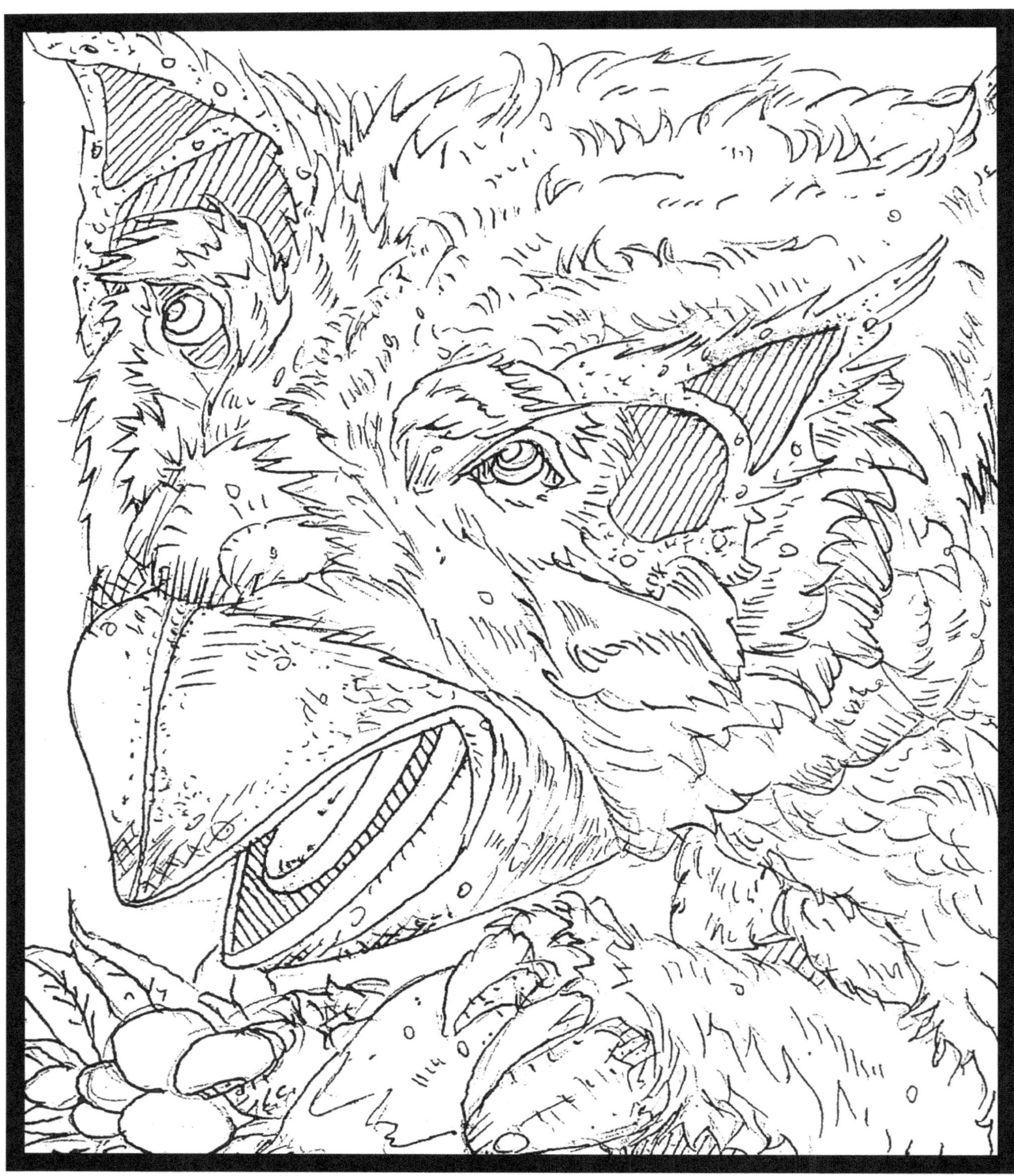

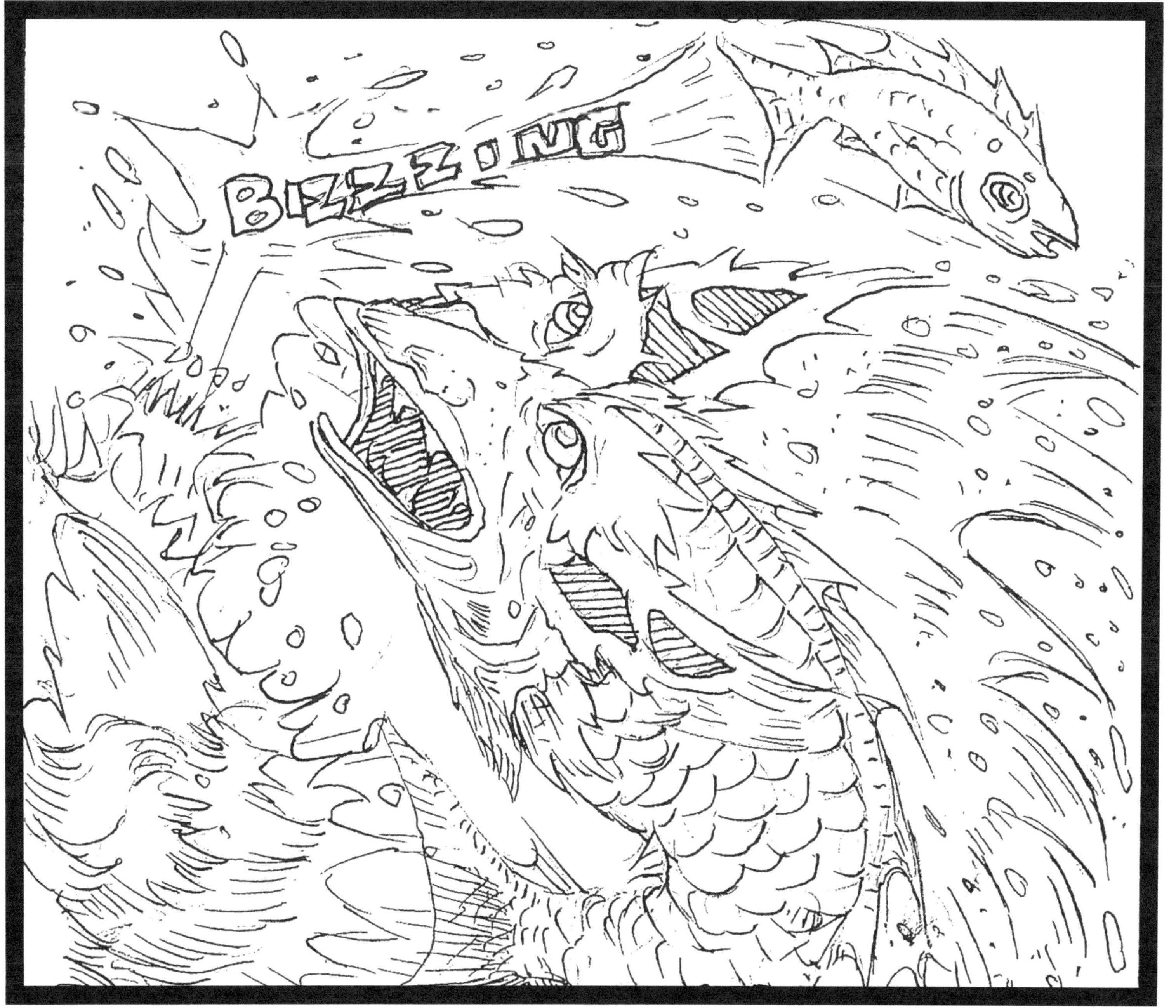

BIZZZING

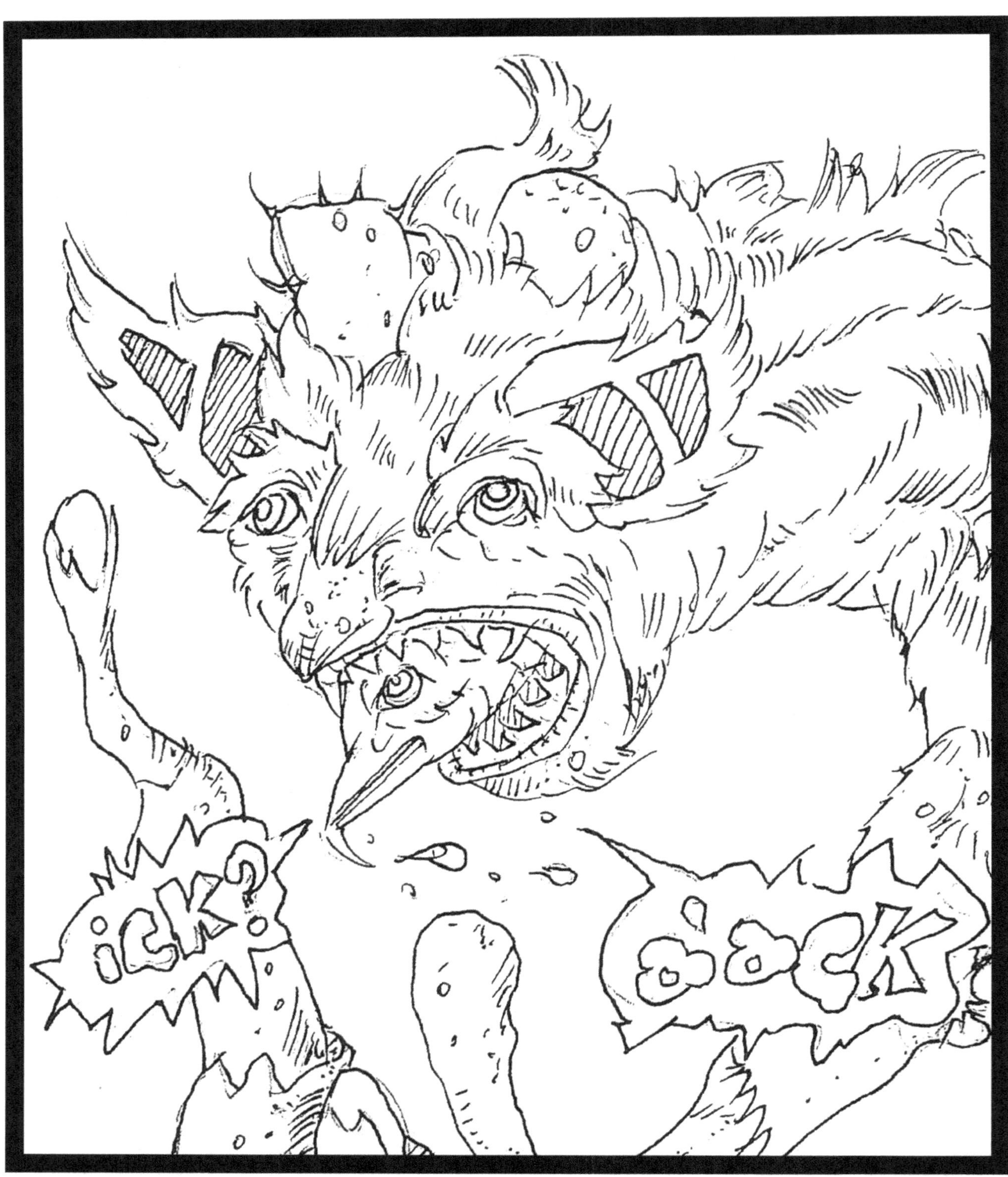

iCK?
bACK

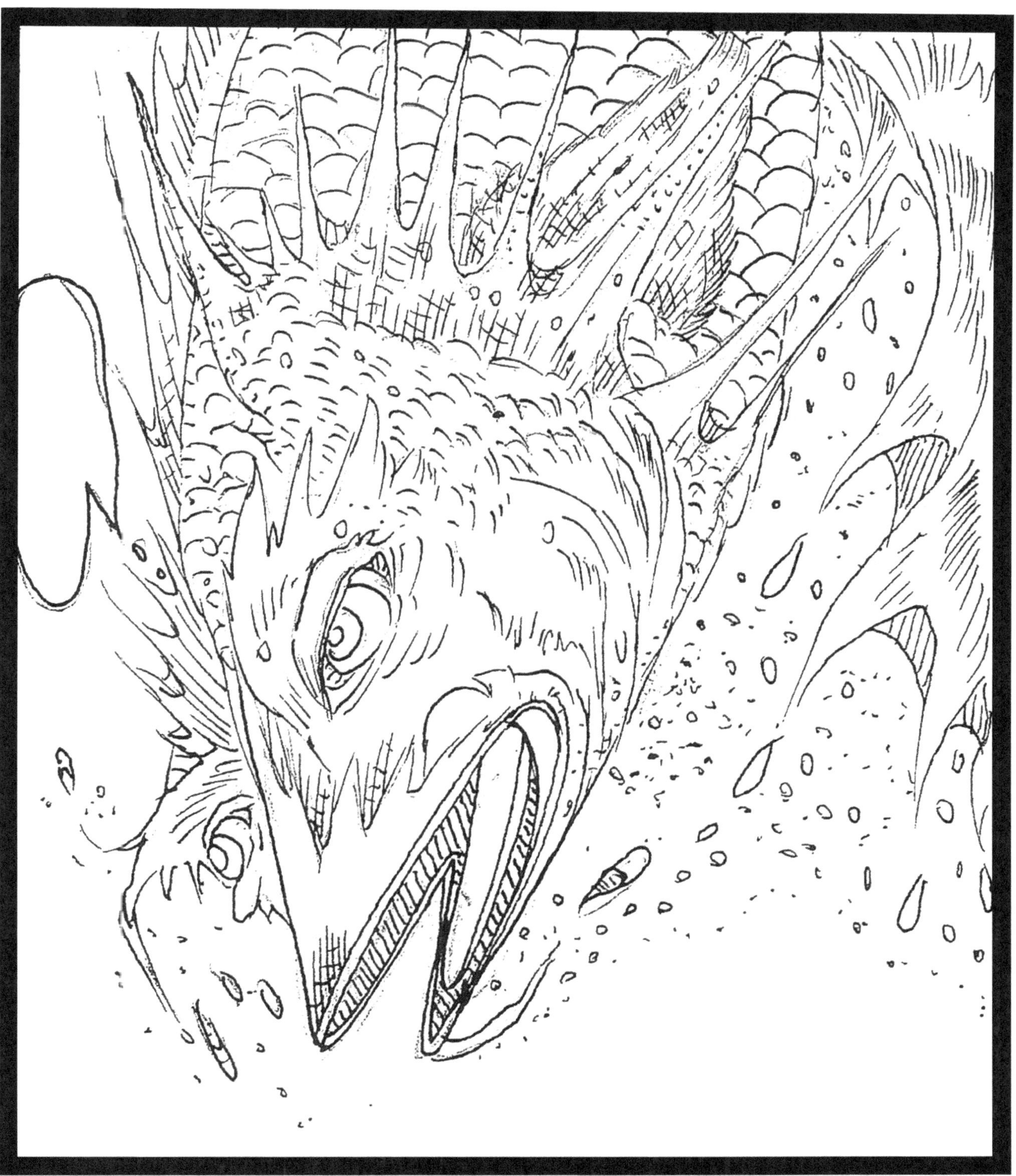

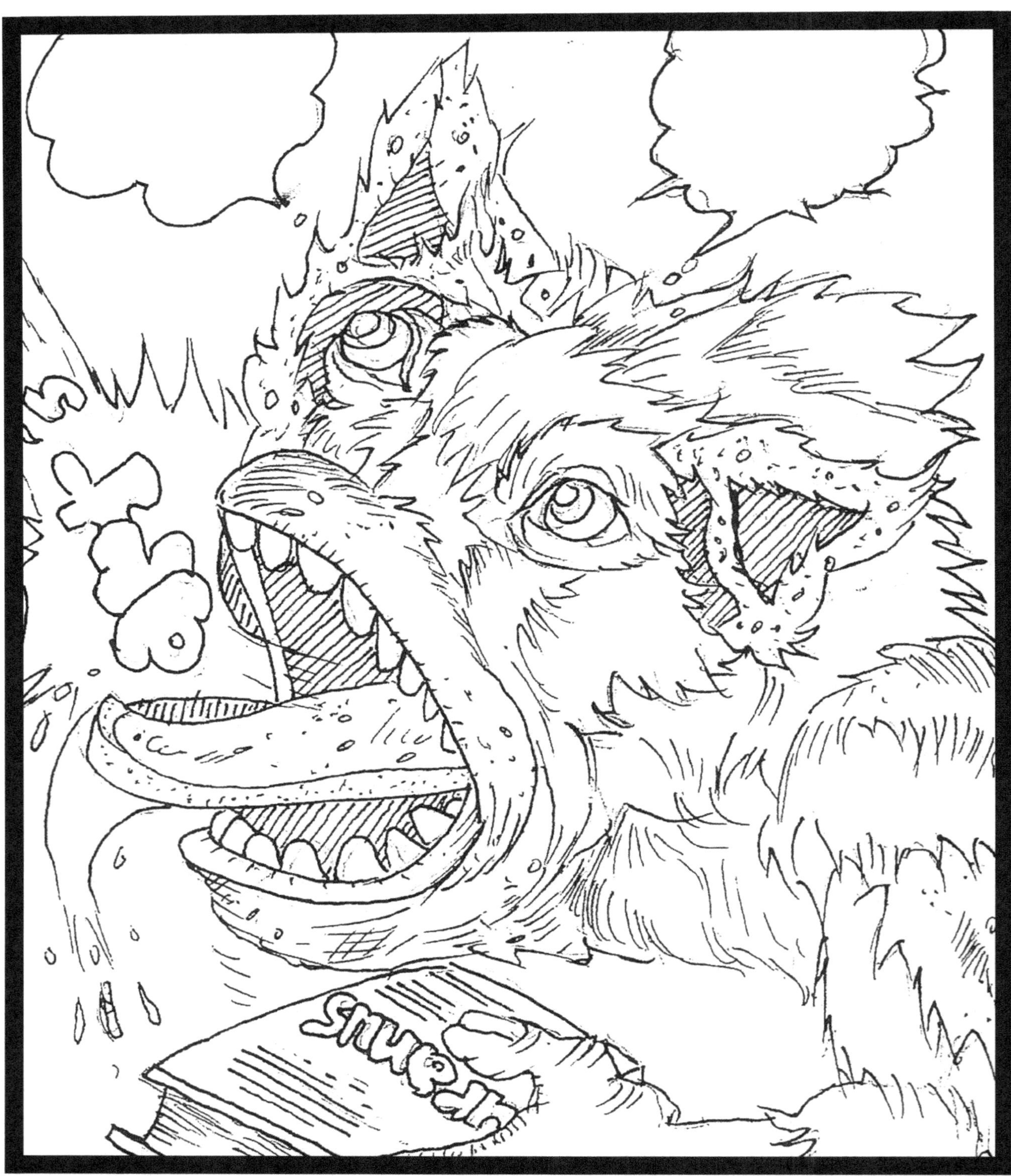

SMUBS

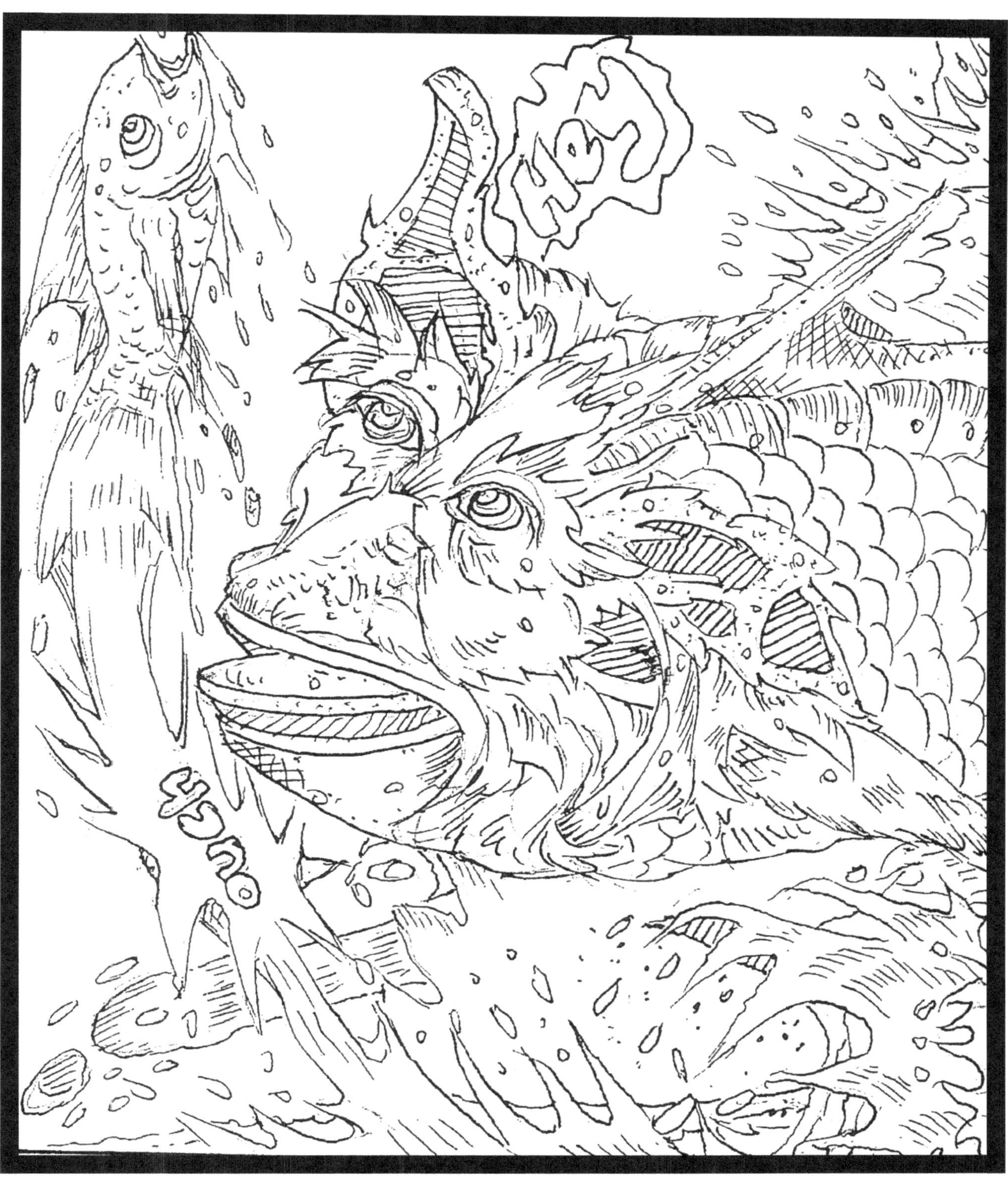
HEY
OUCH

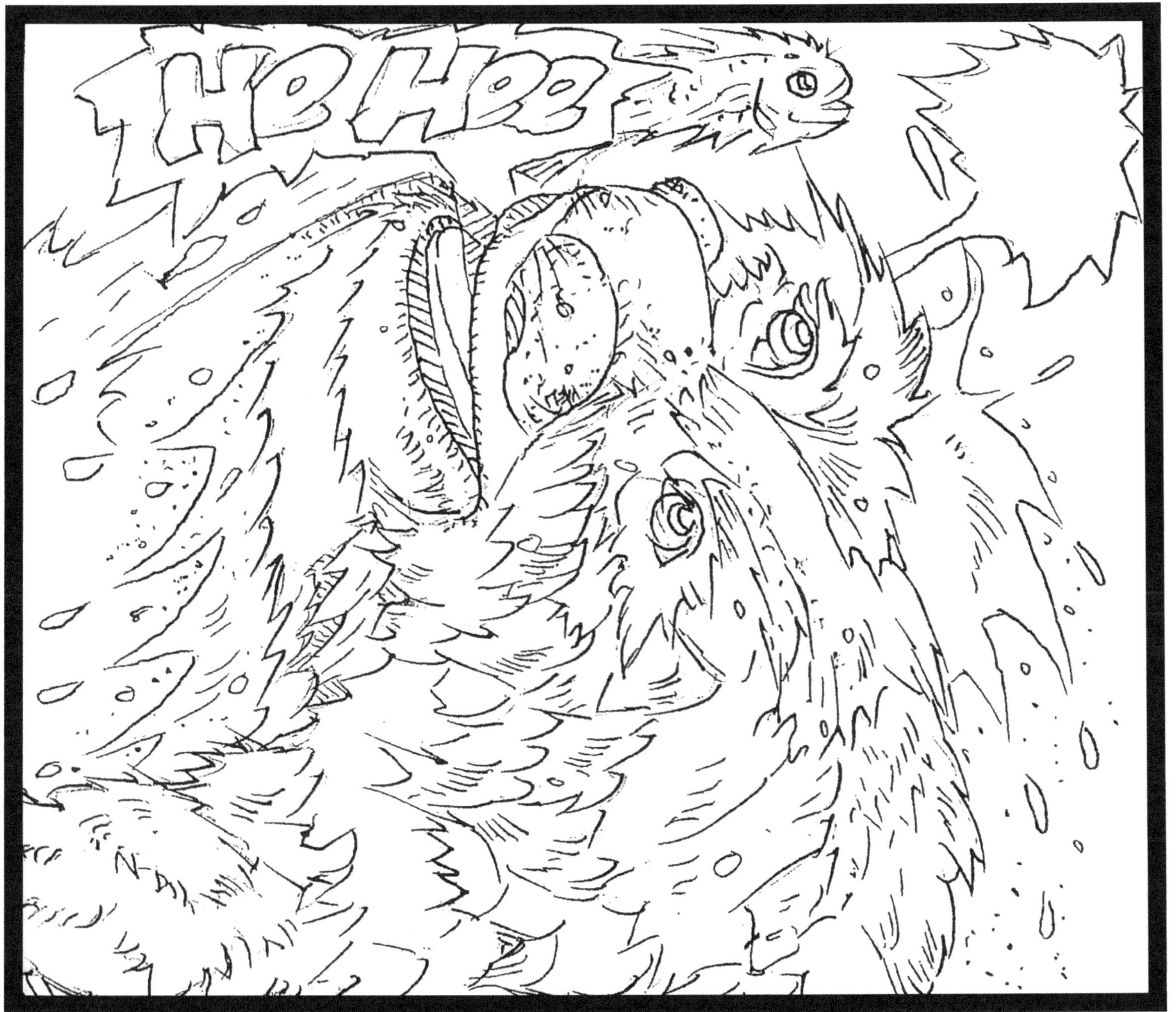

THe HeE

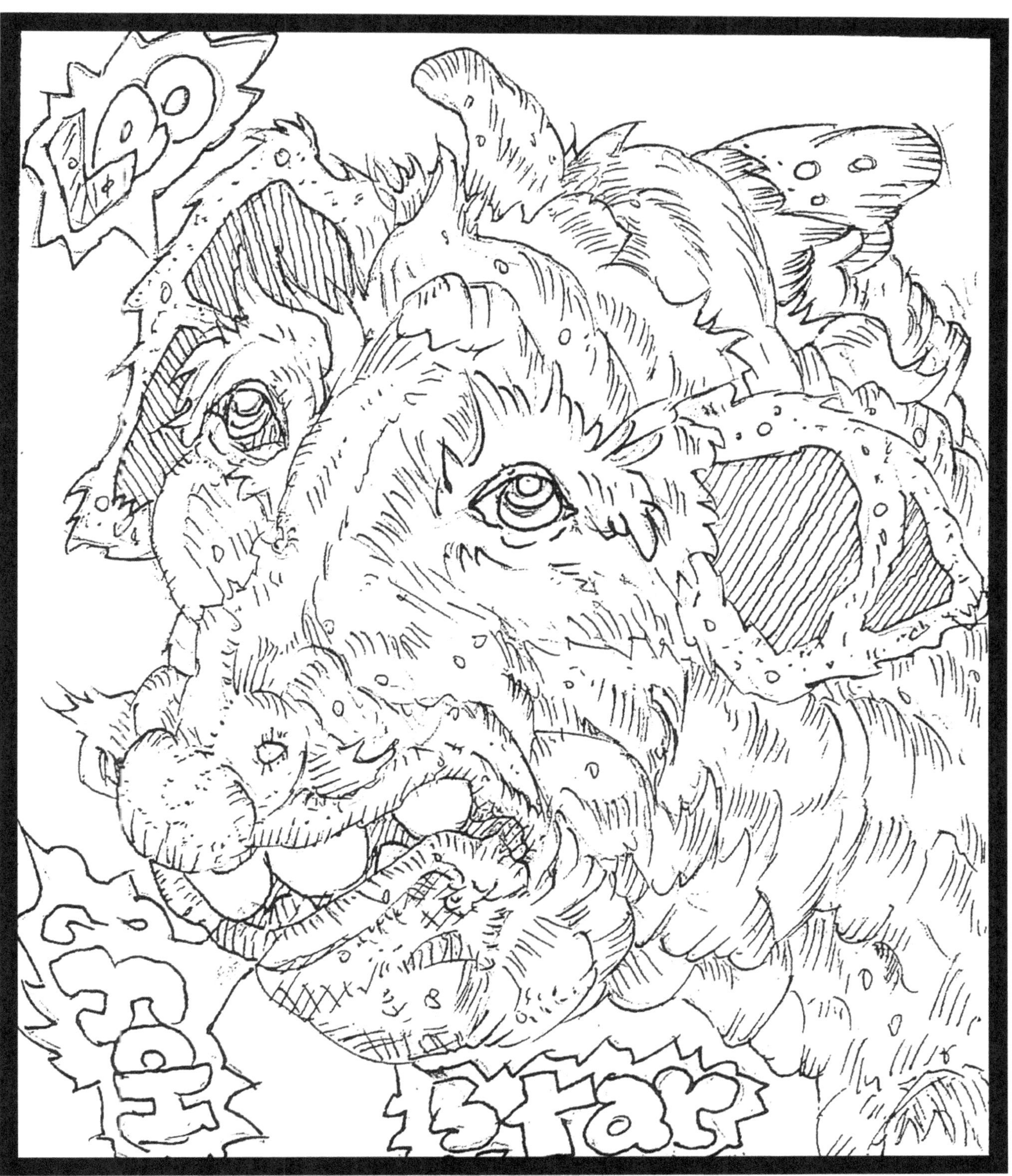
Leo
Greg
star

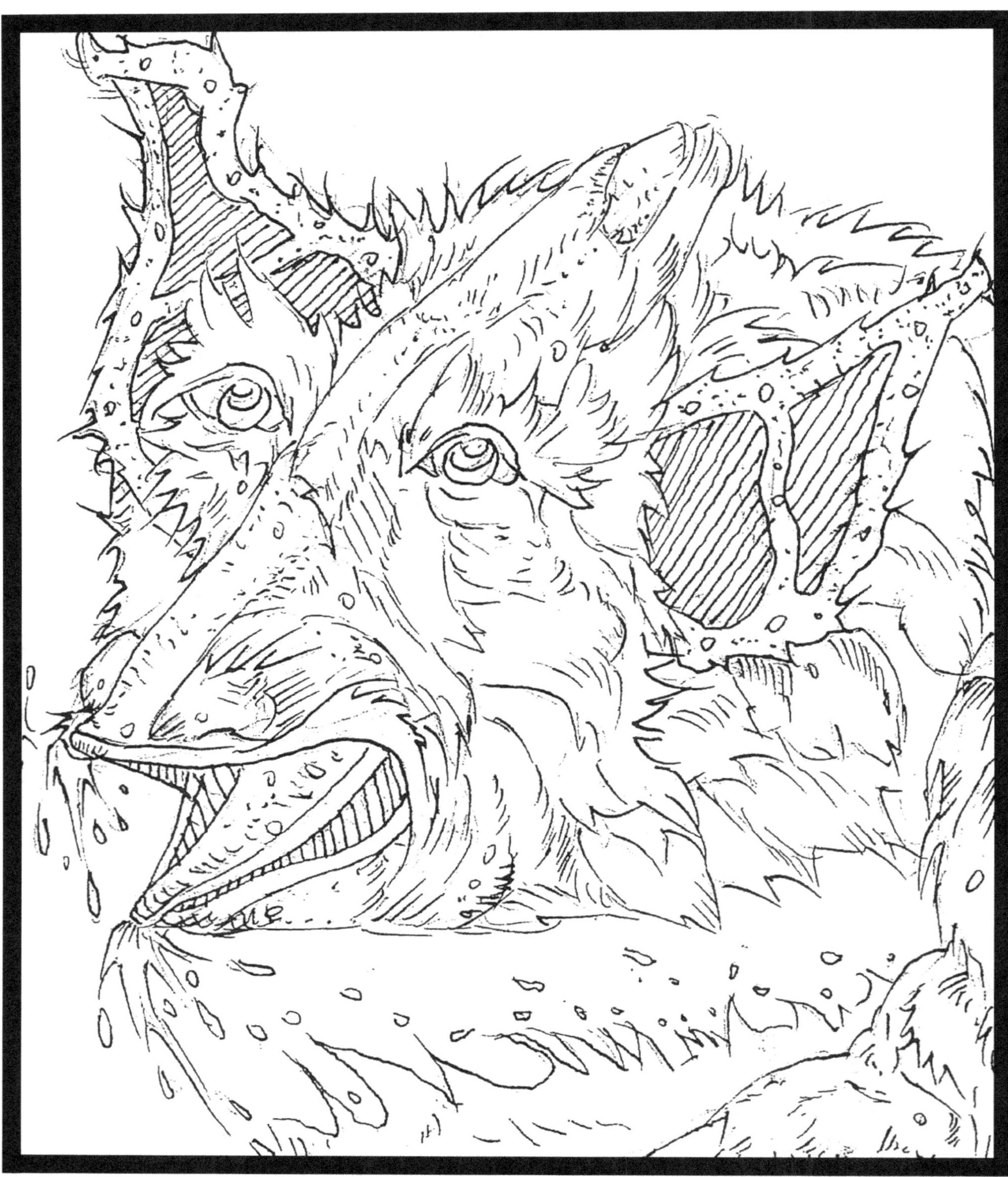

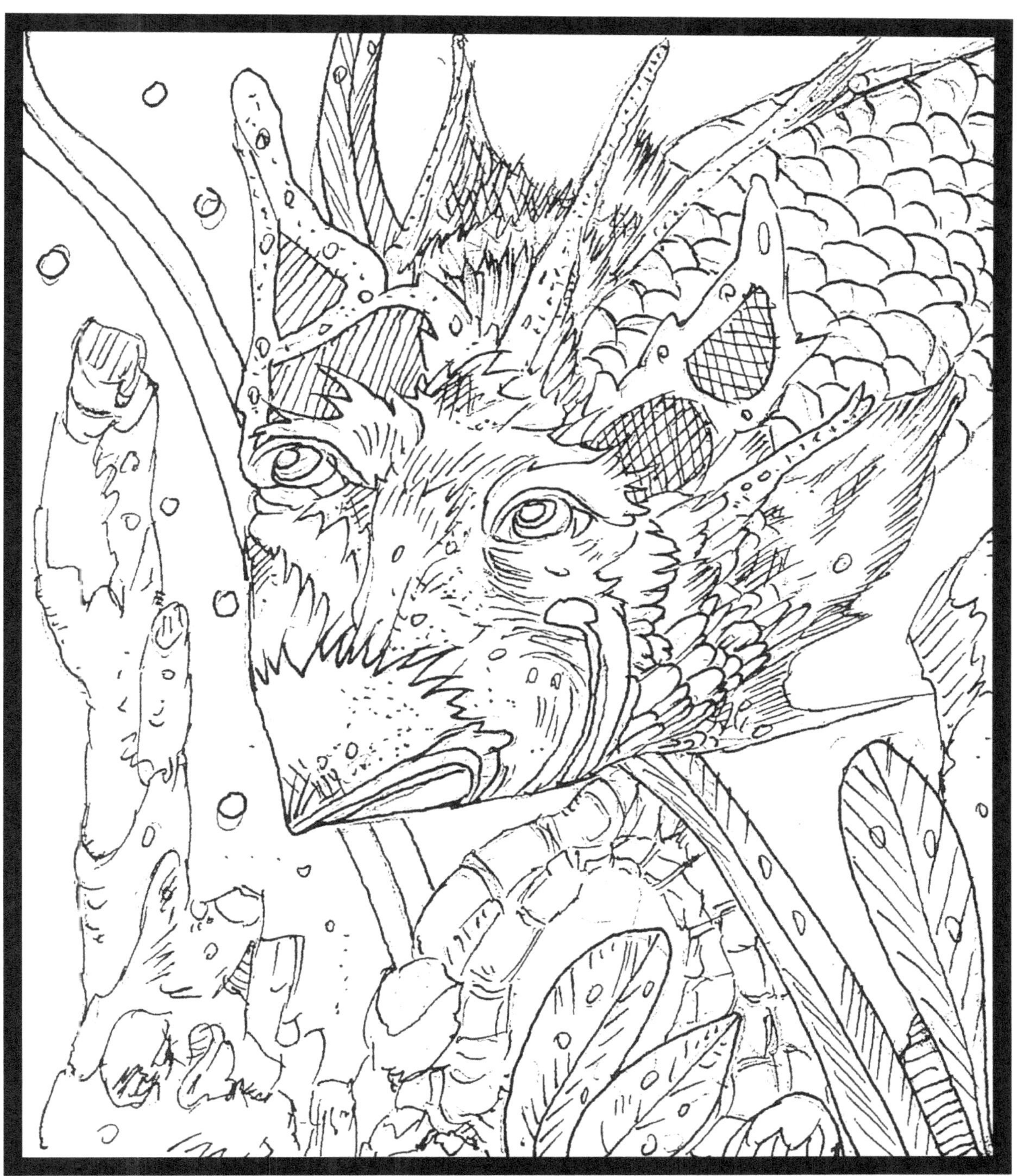

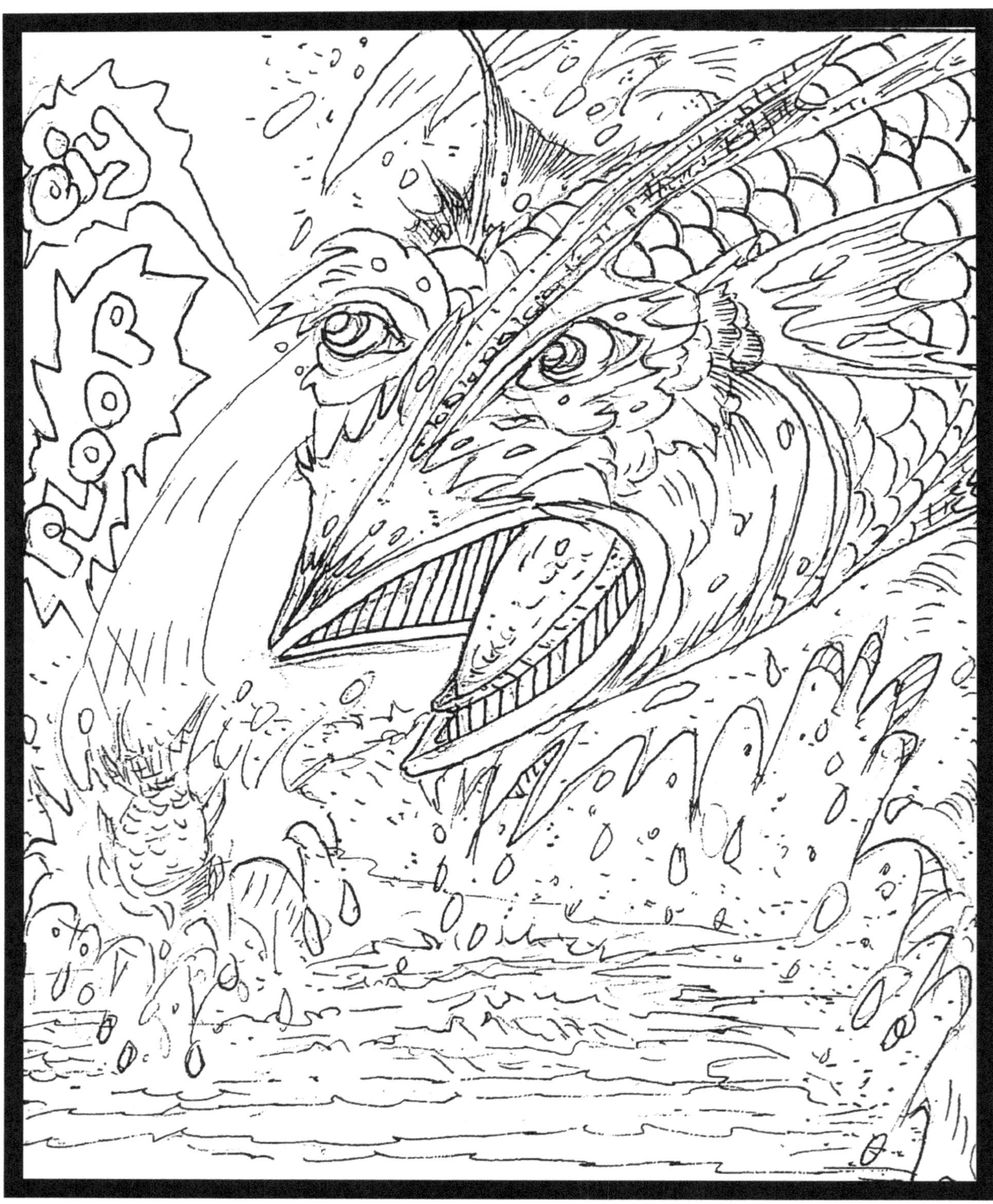

SPLOOP

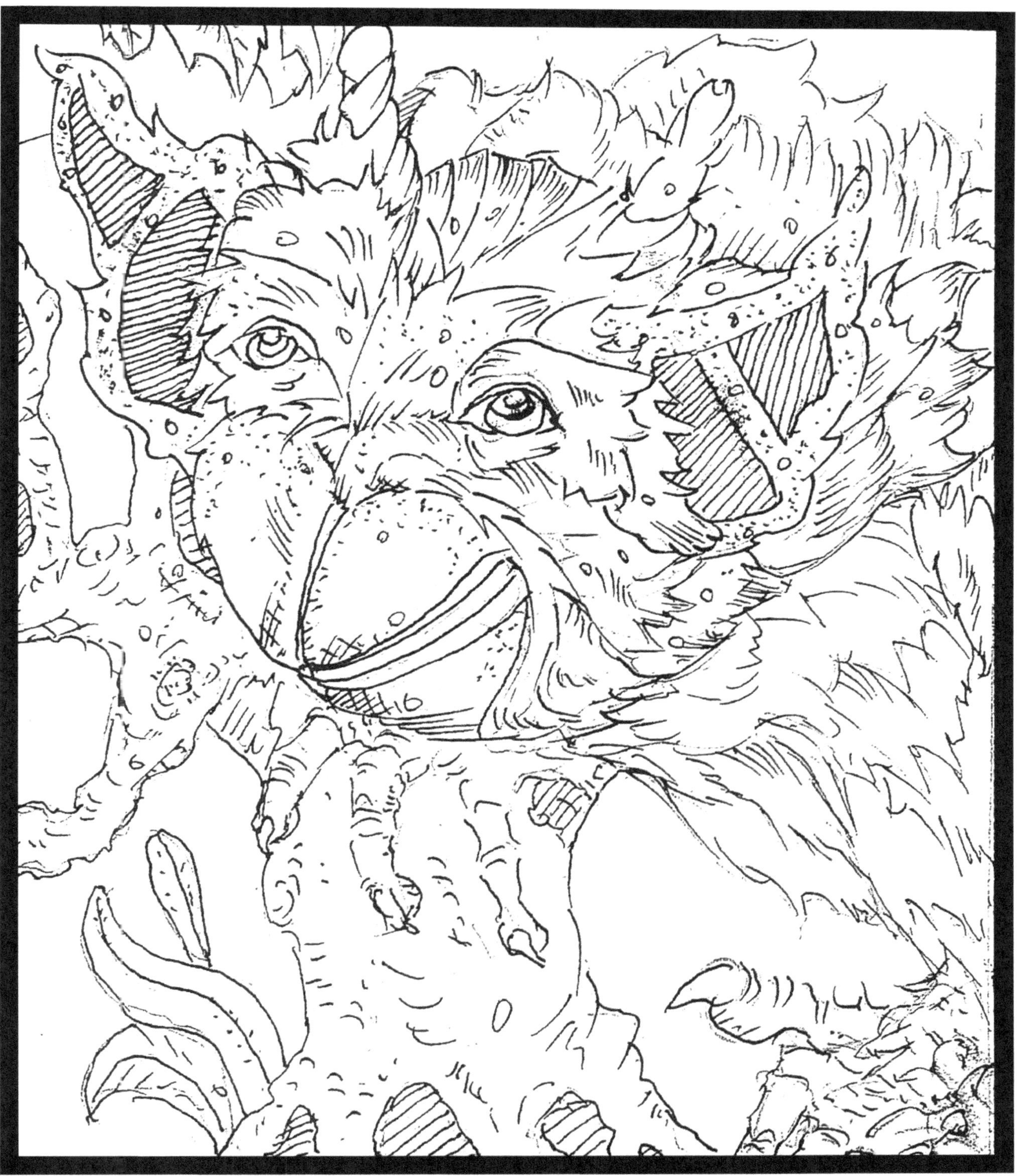

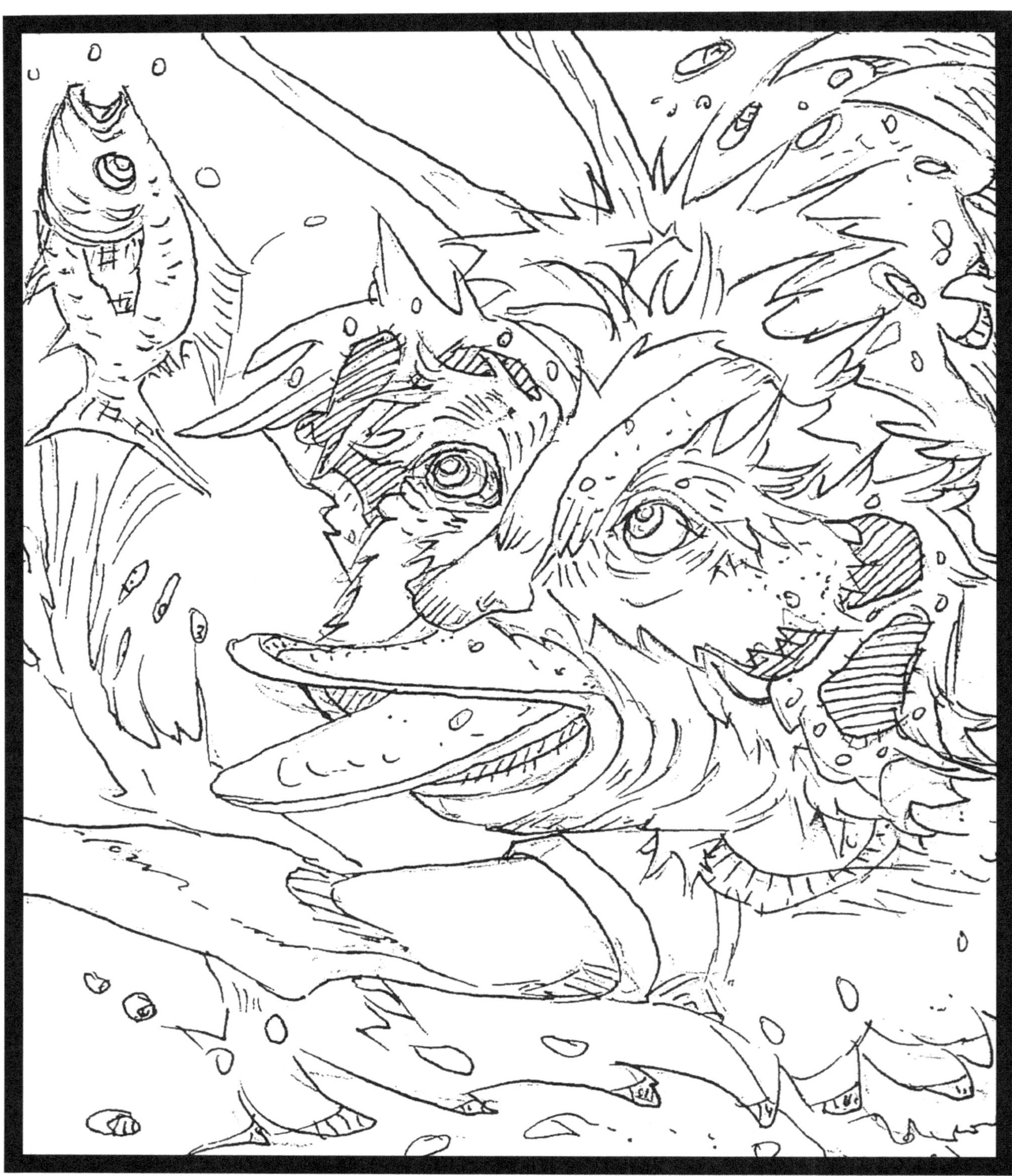

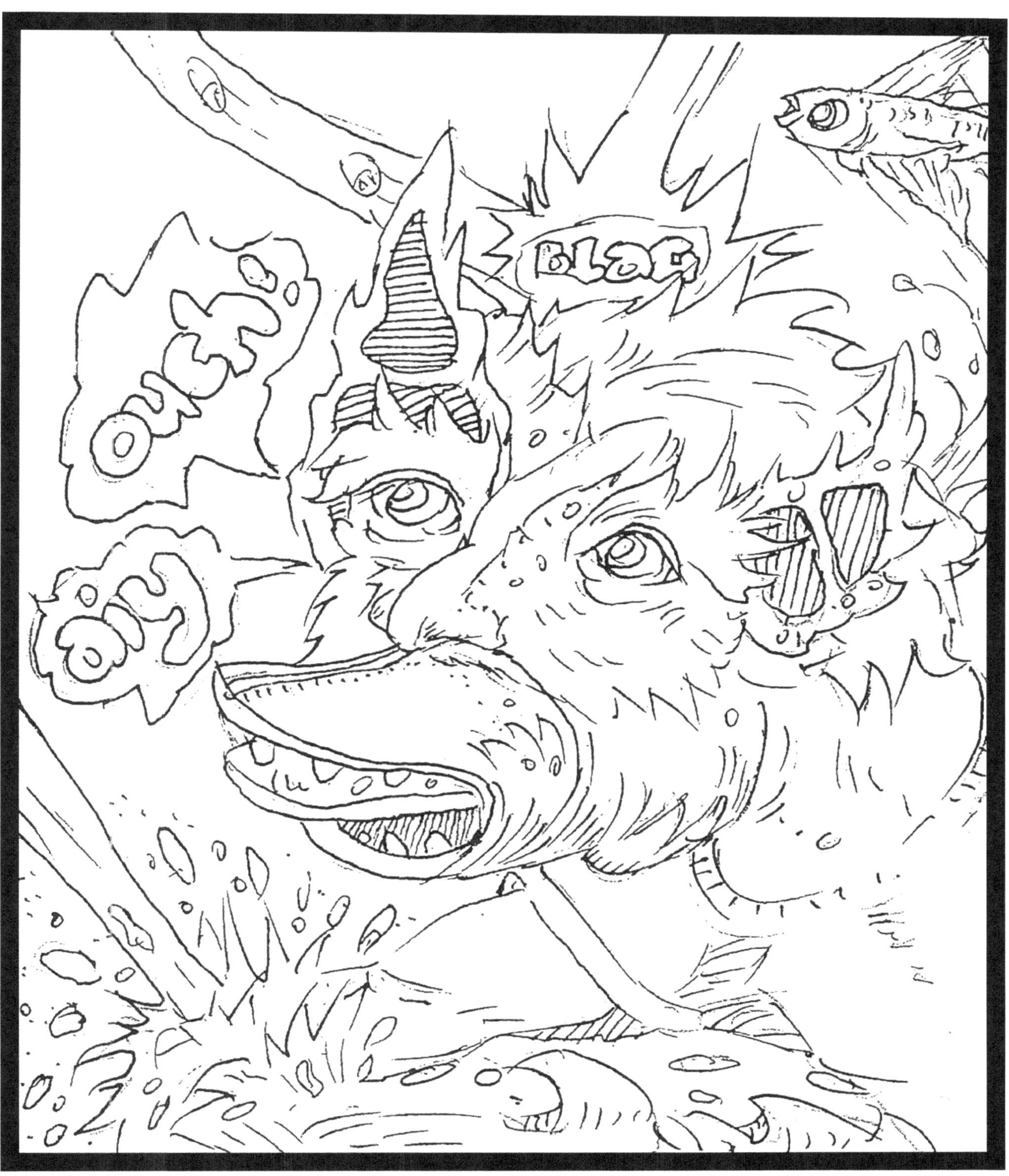

OUCH!
BLAP
AY

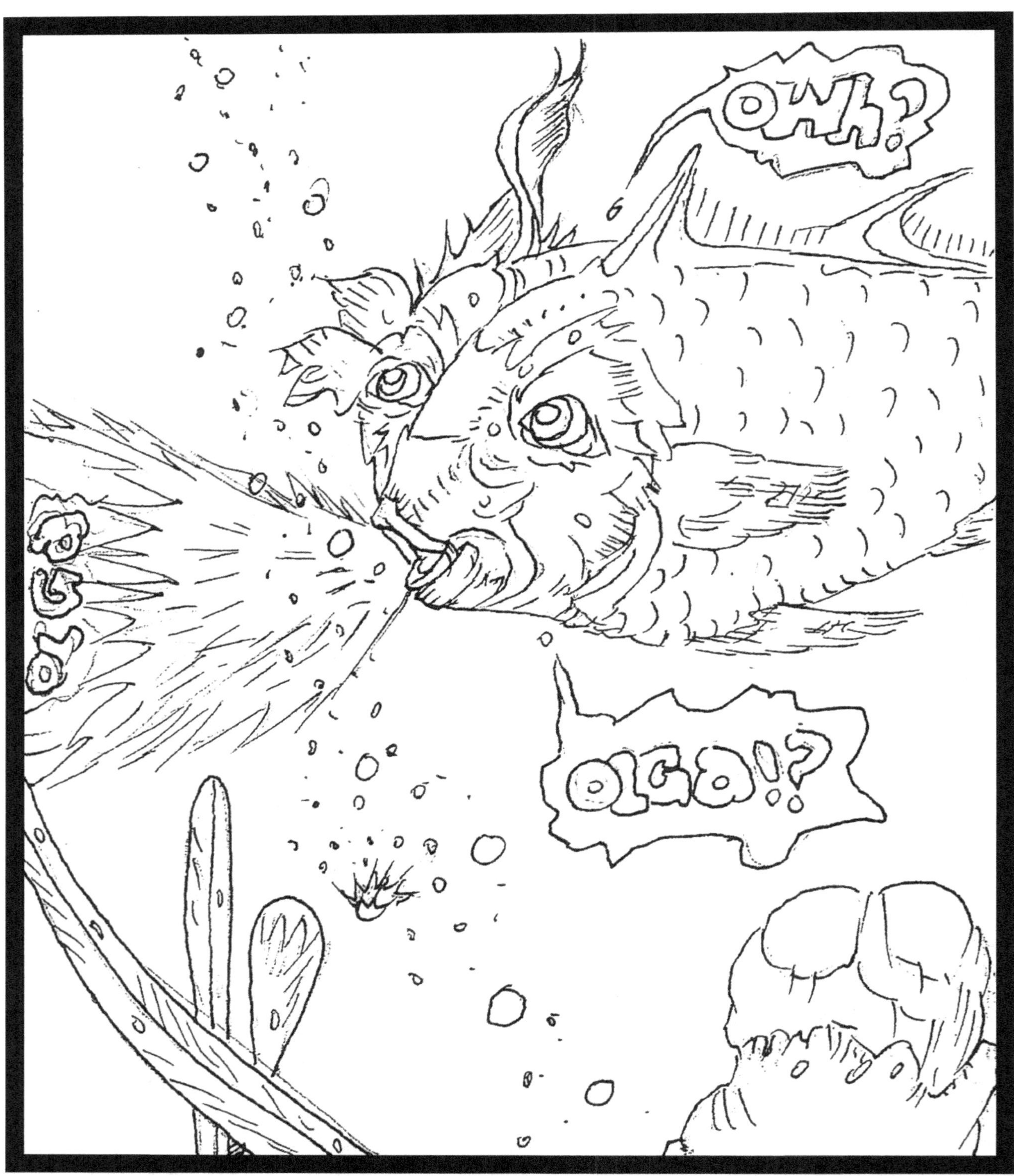

OW?
Olga
OLGA!?

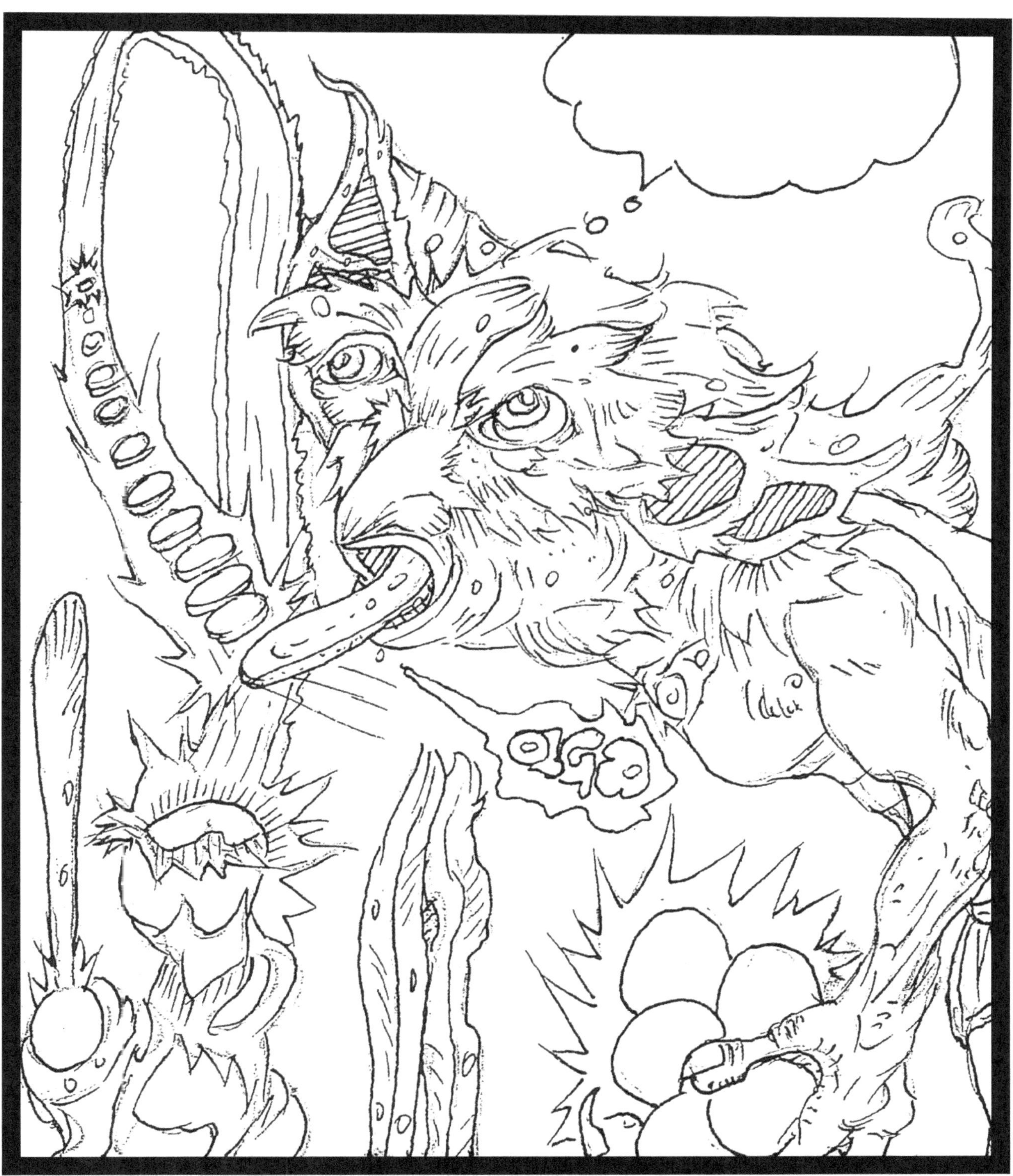

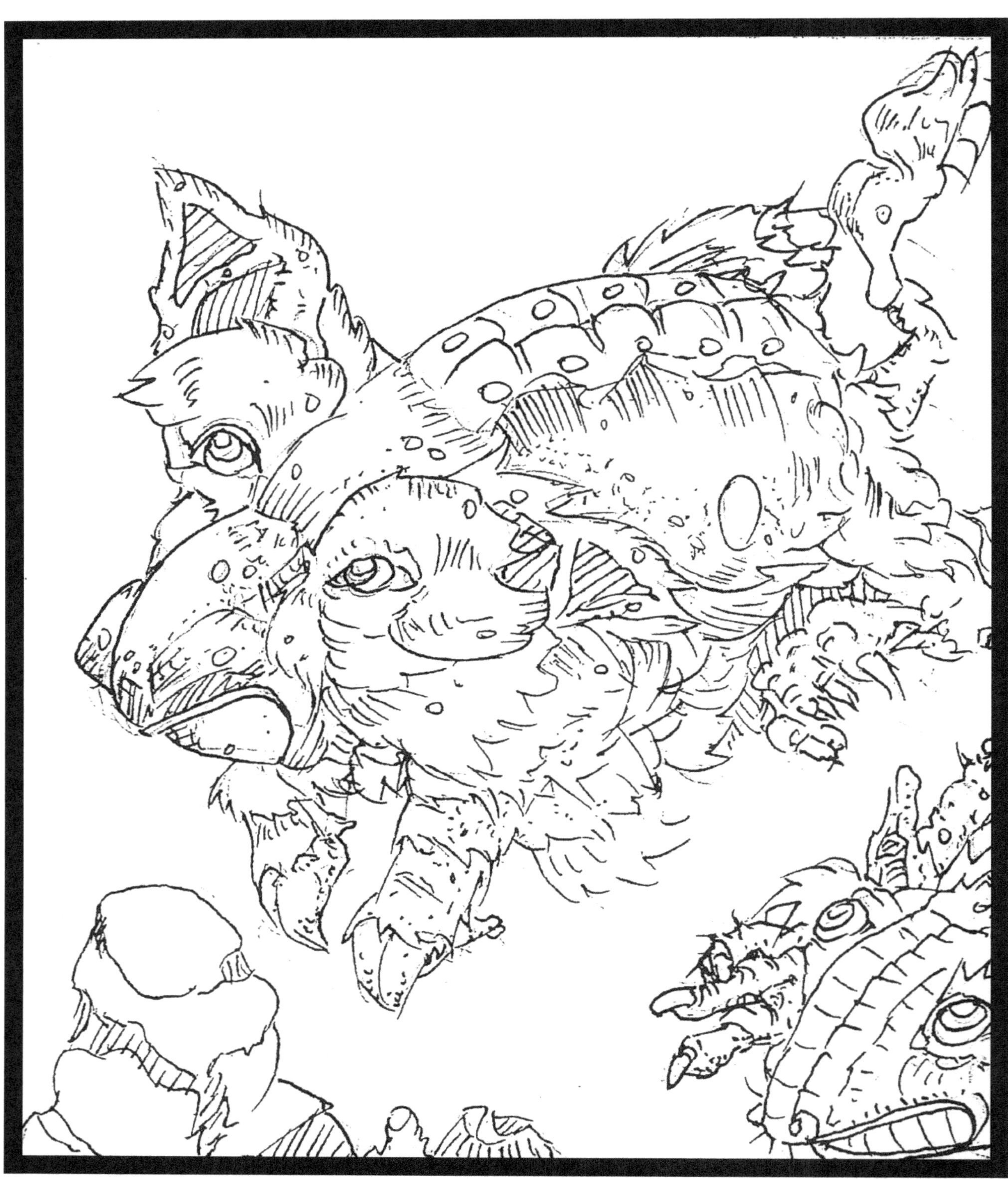

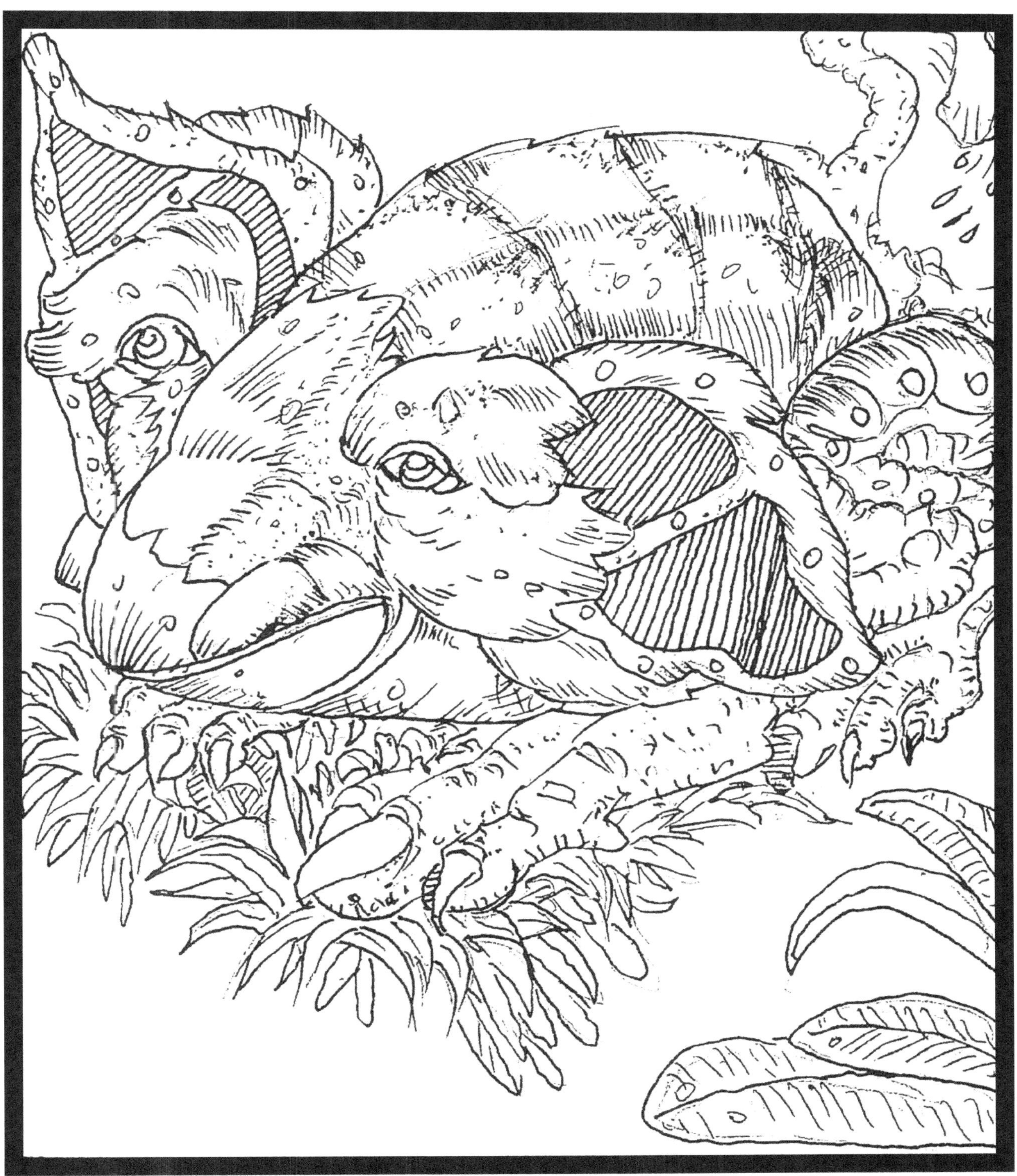

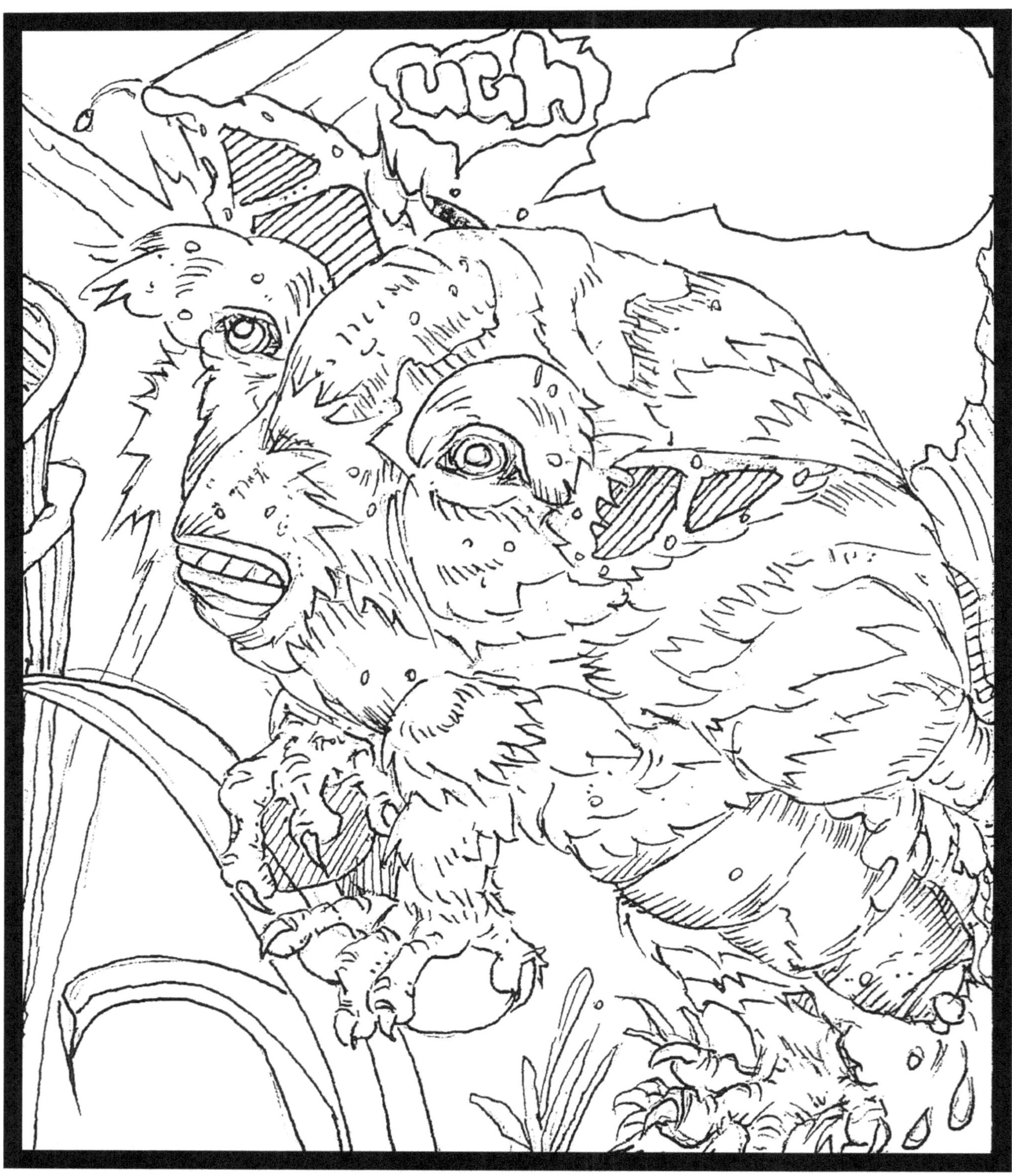
UGH

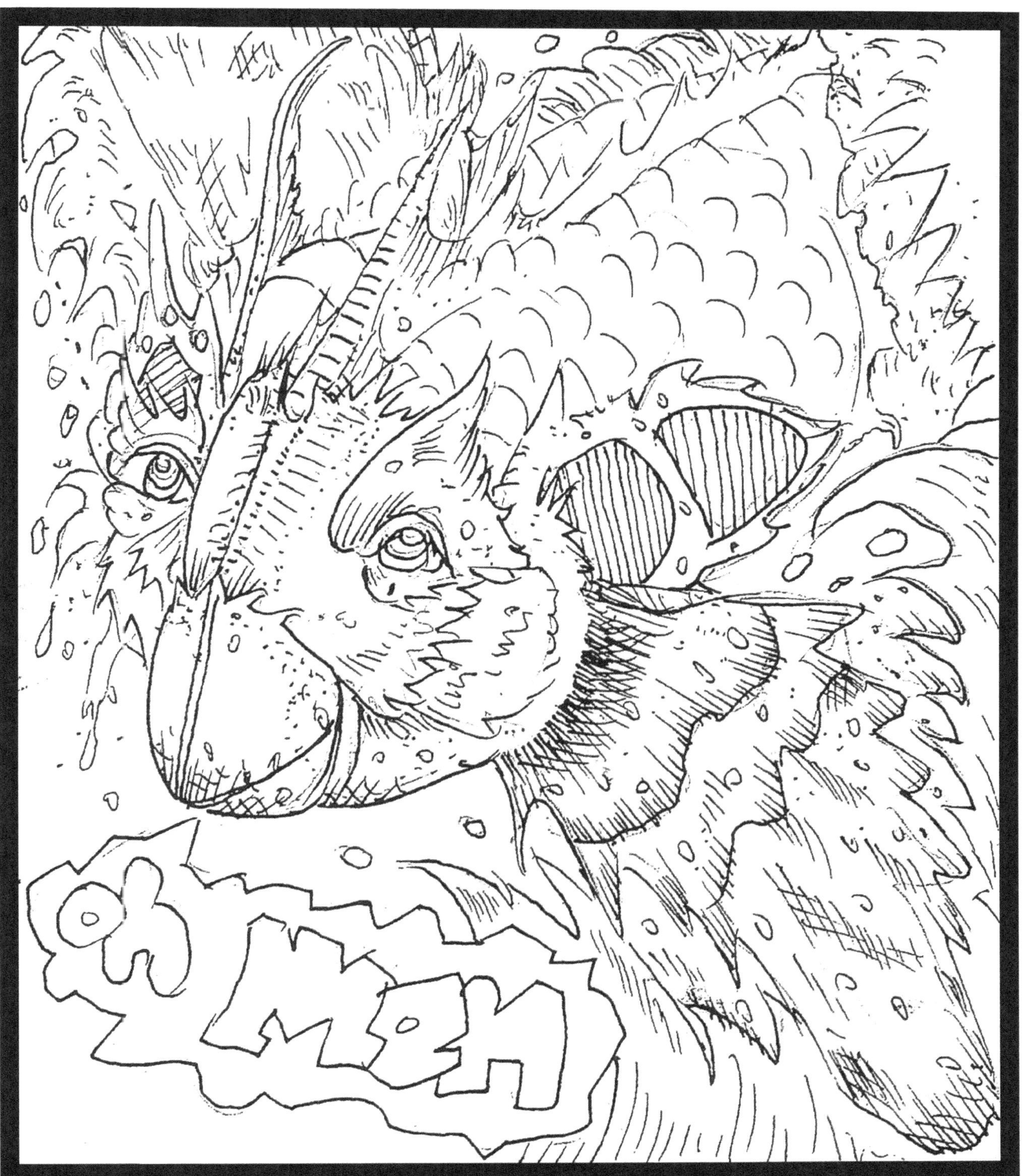
OH MAN

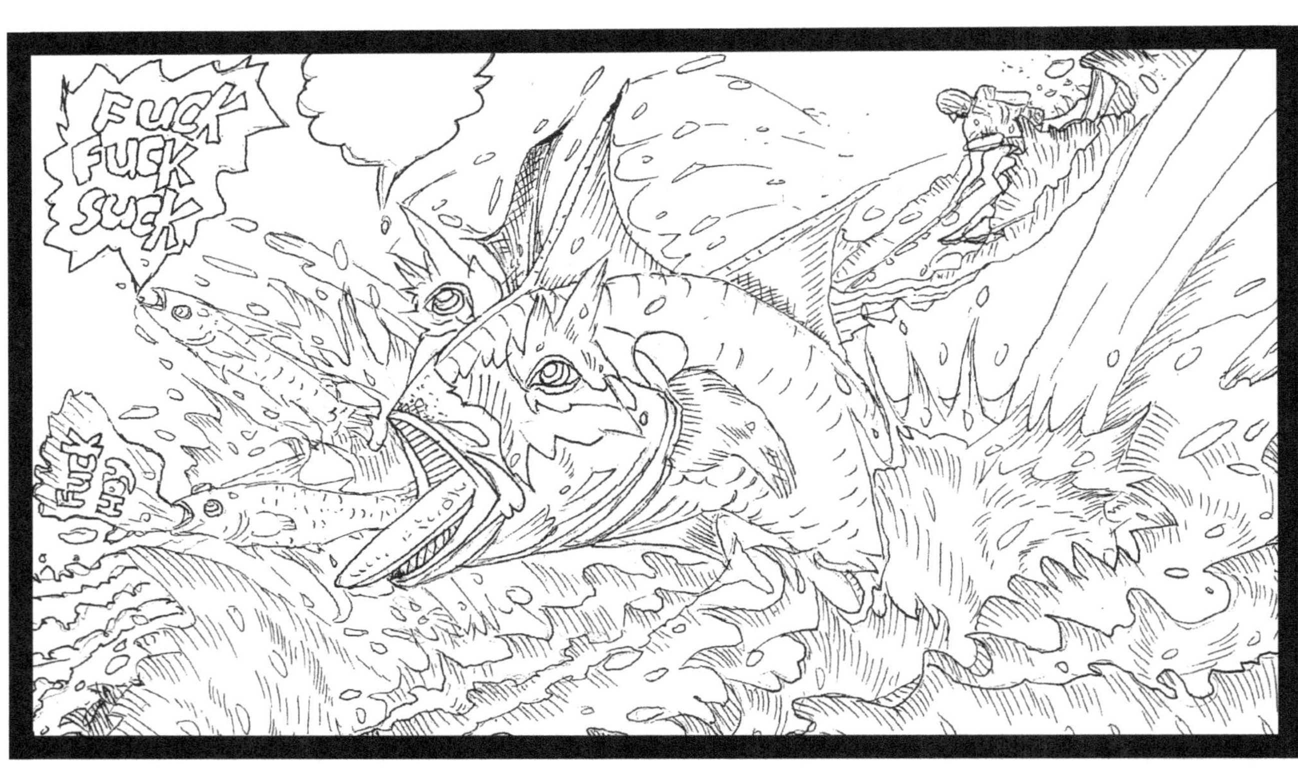

FUCK
FUCK
SUCK
FUCK HIM

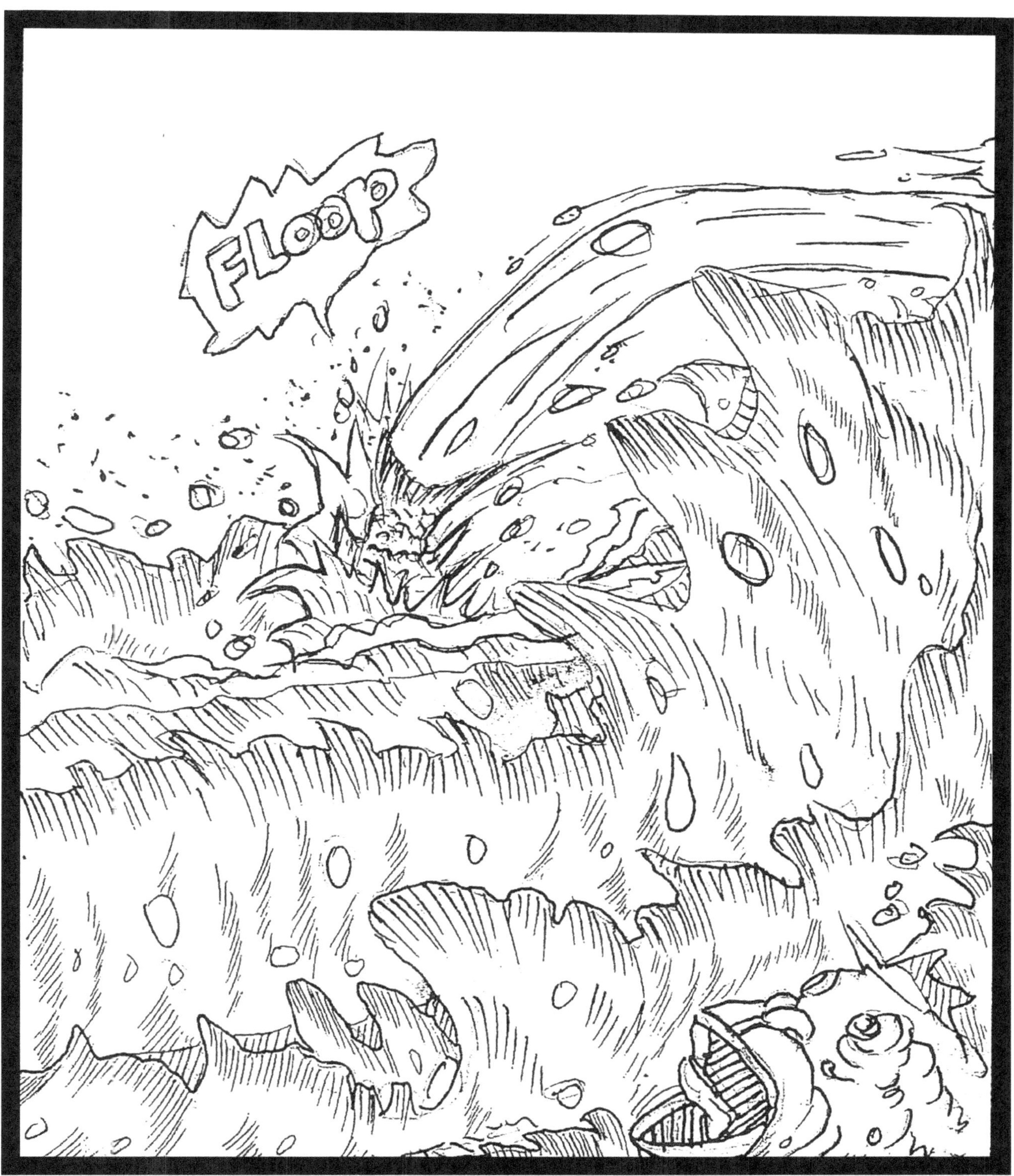

FLOOP

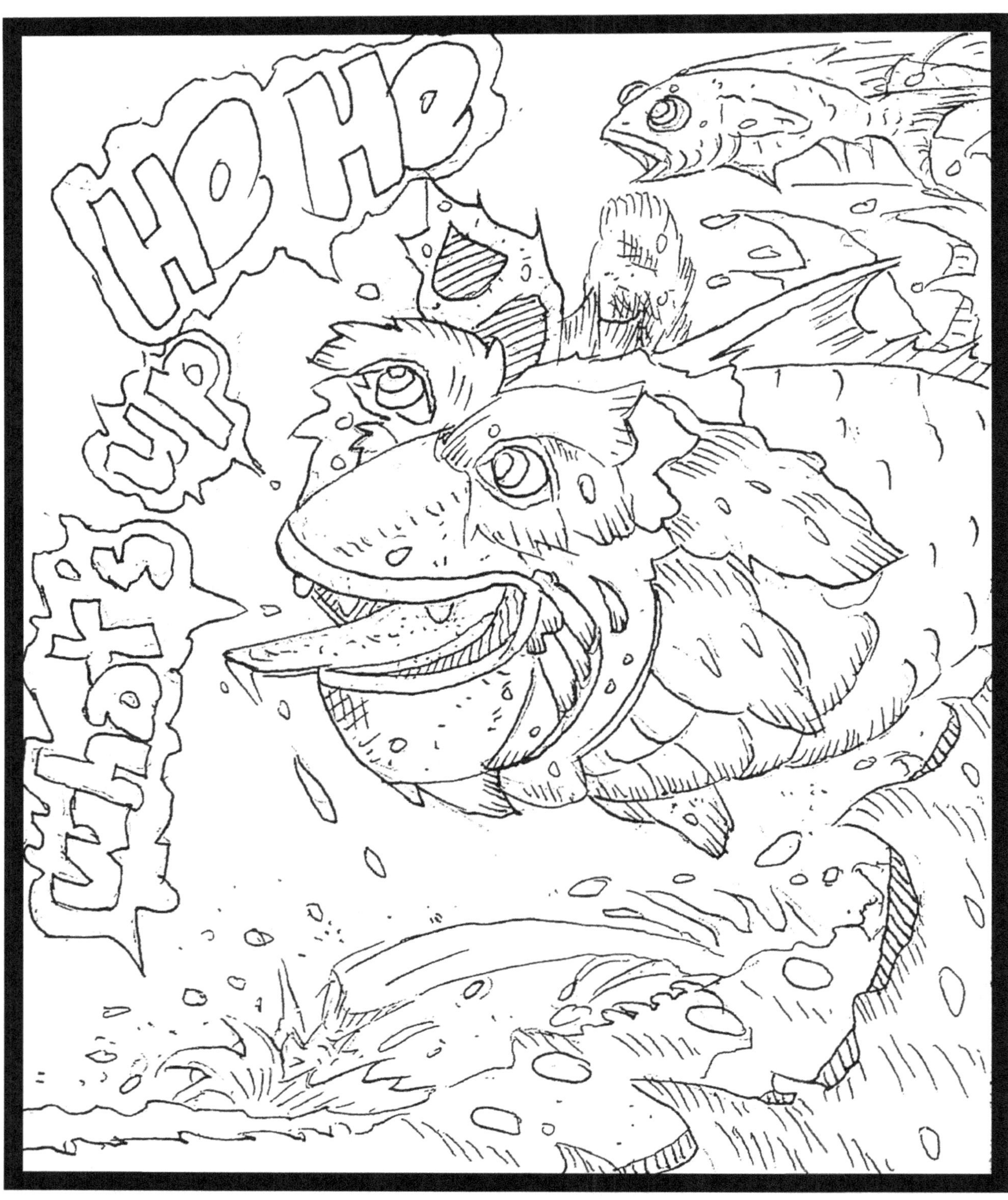

108

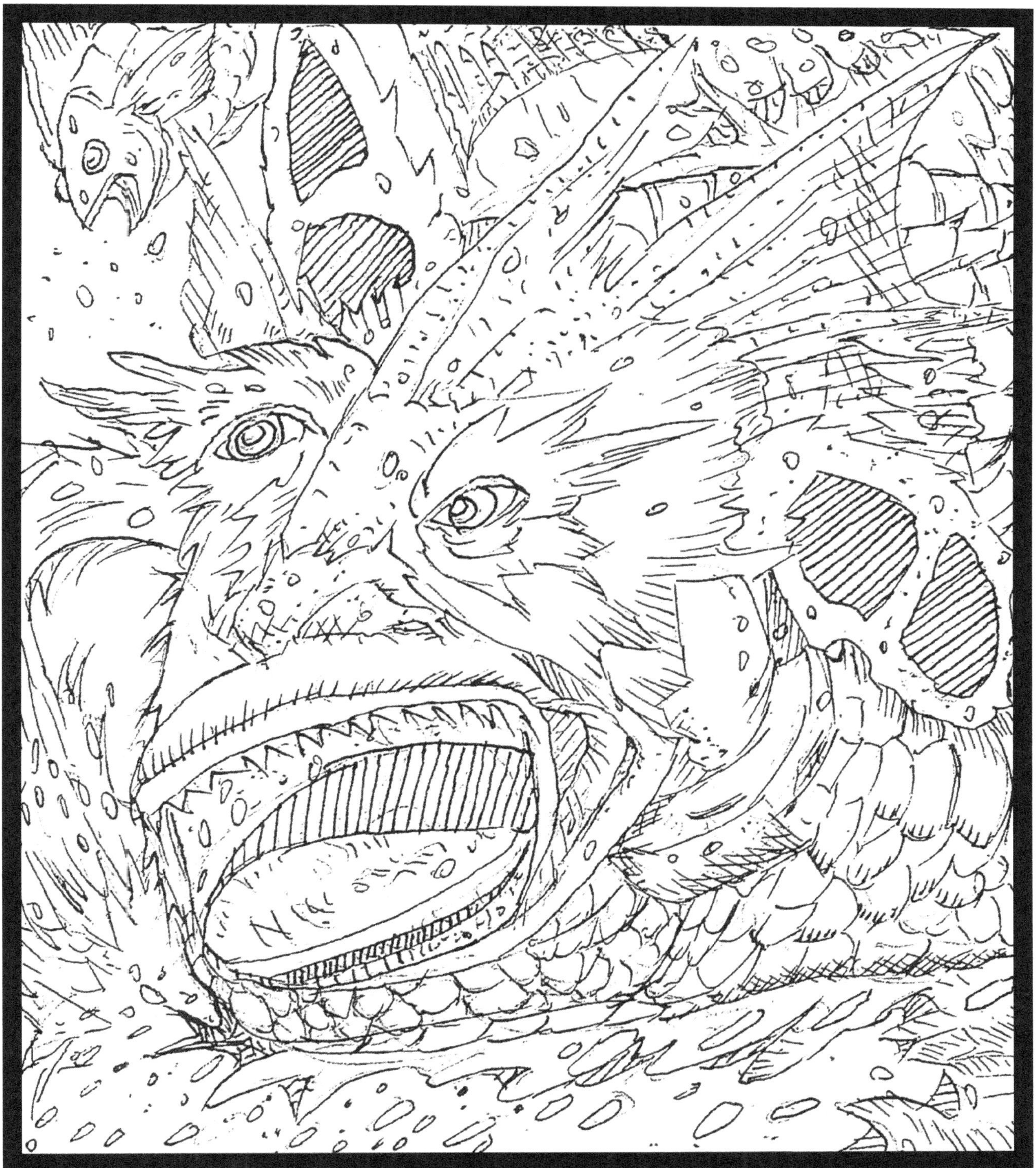

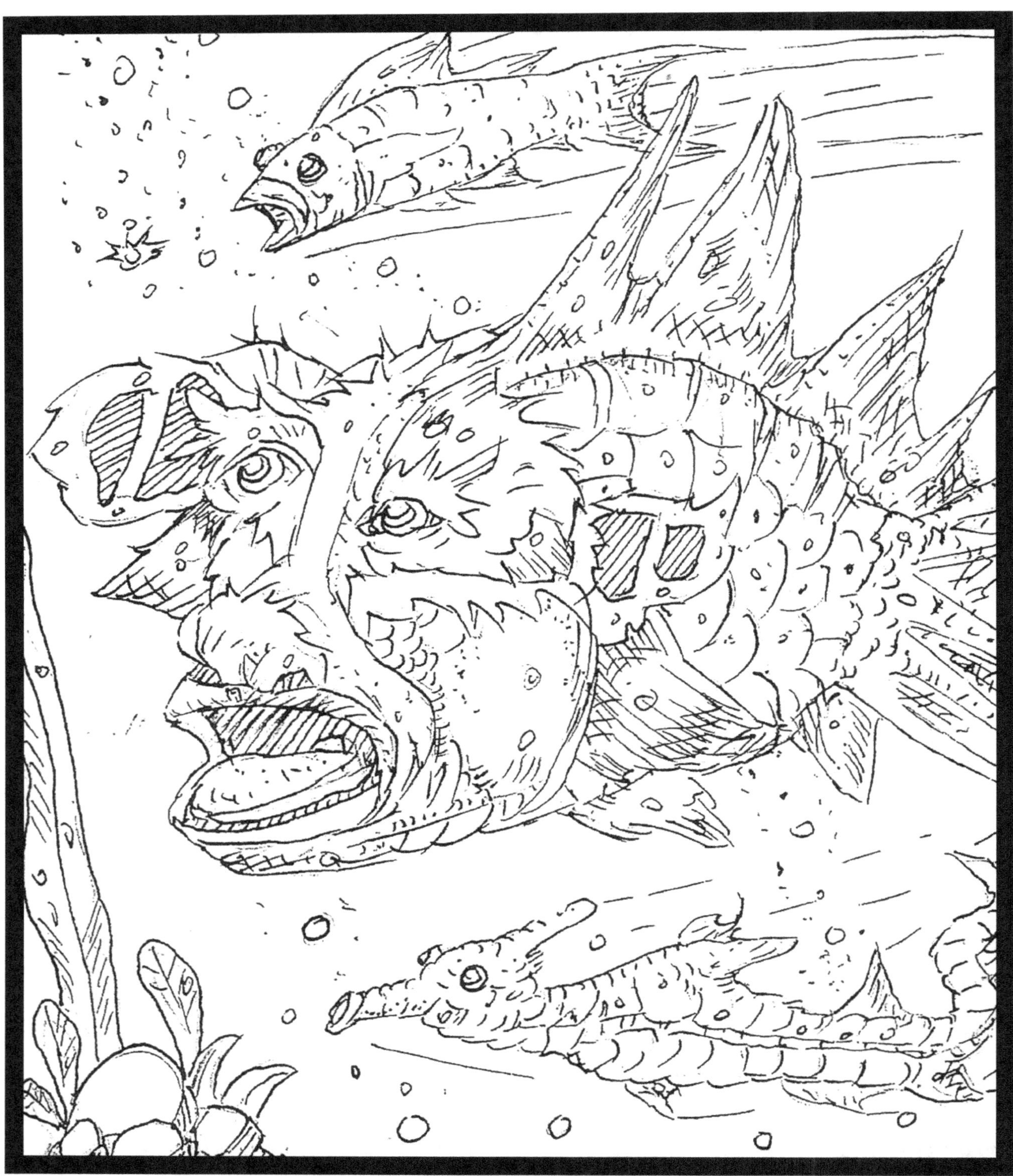

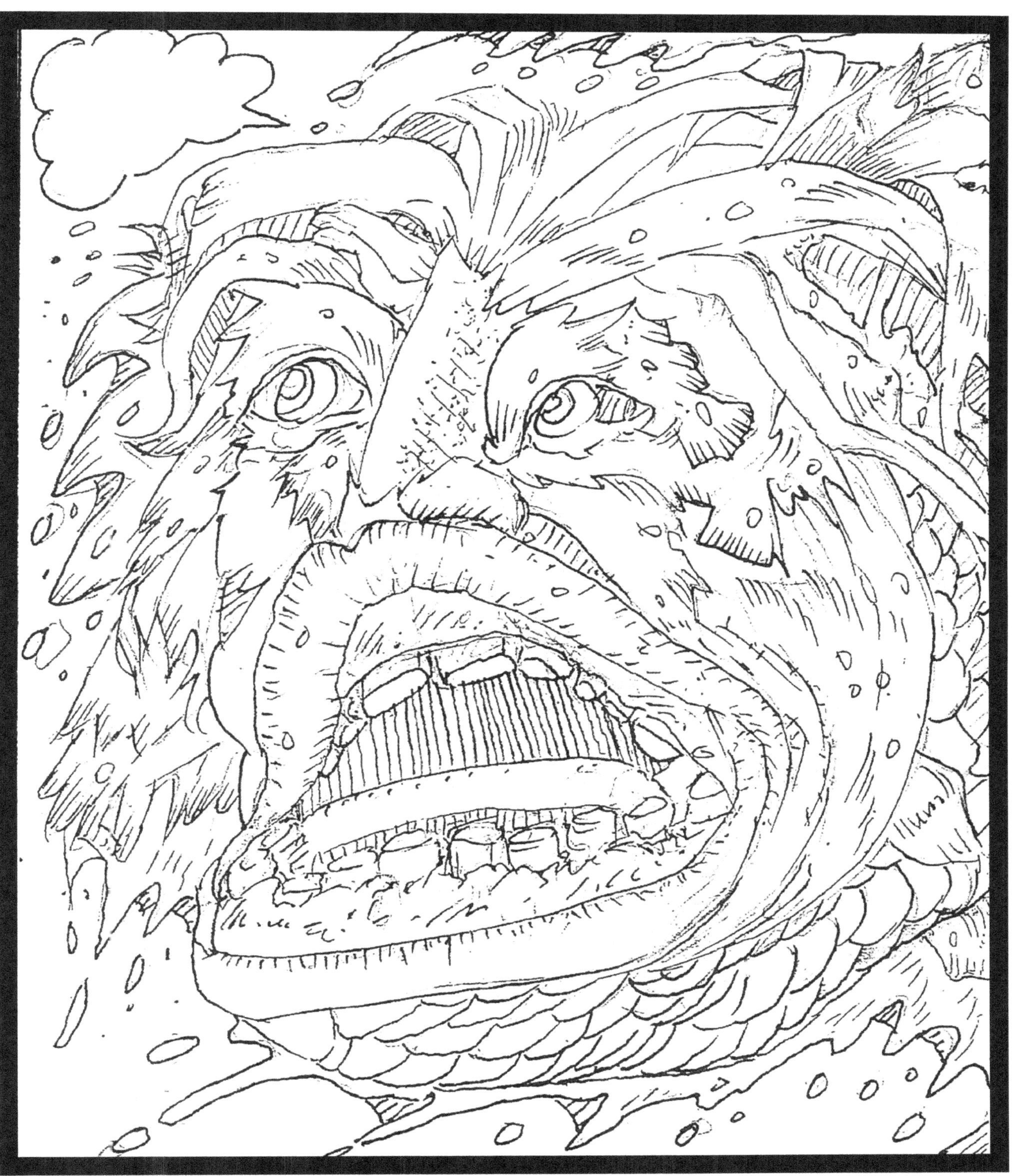

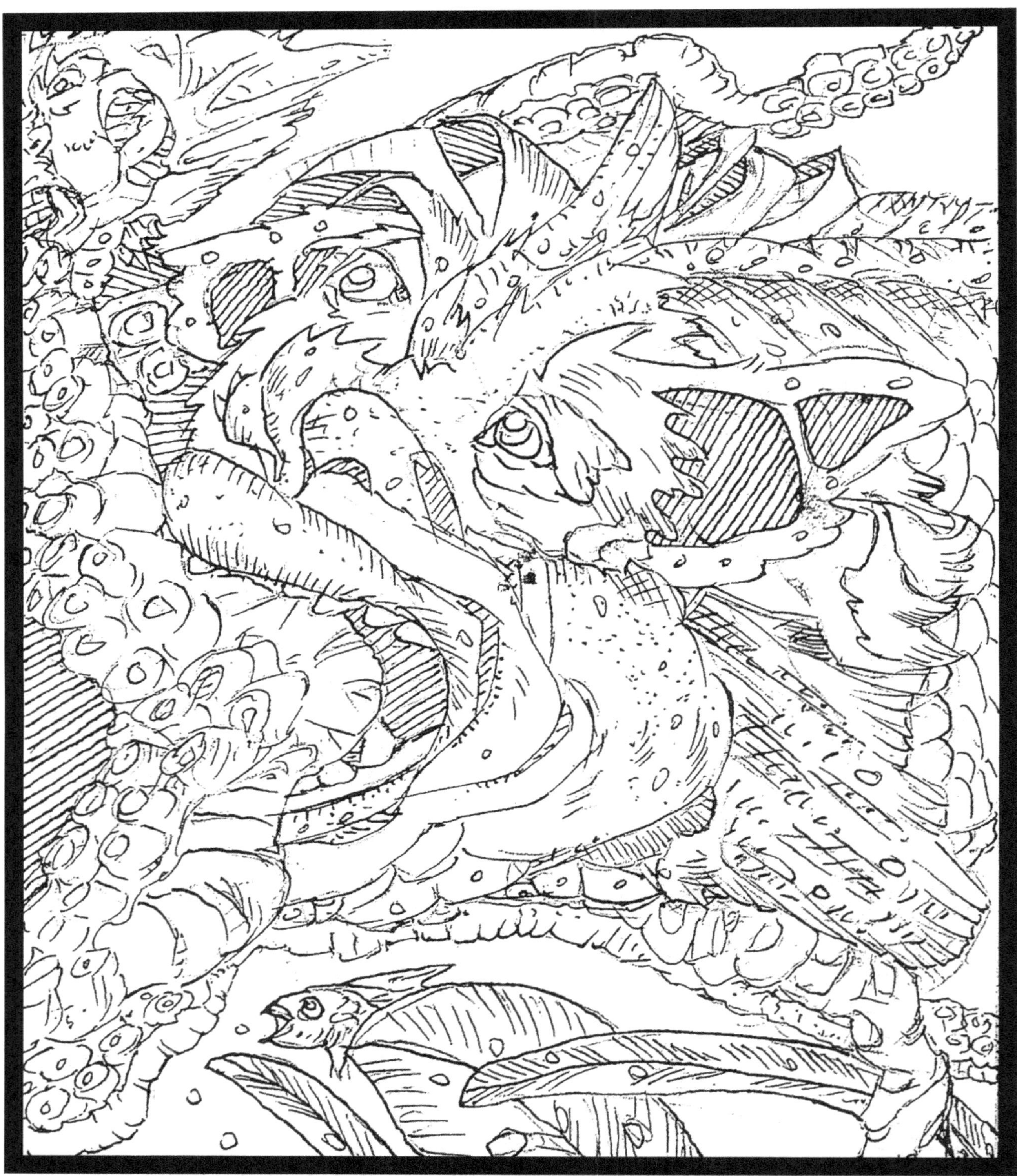

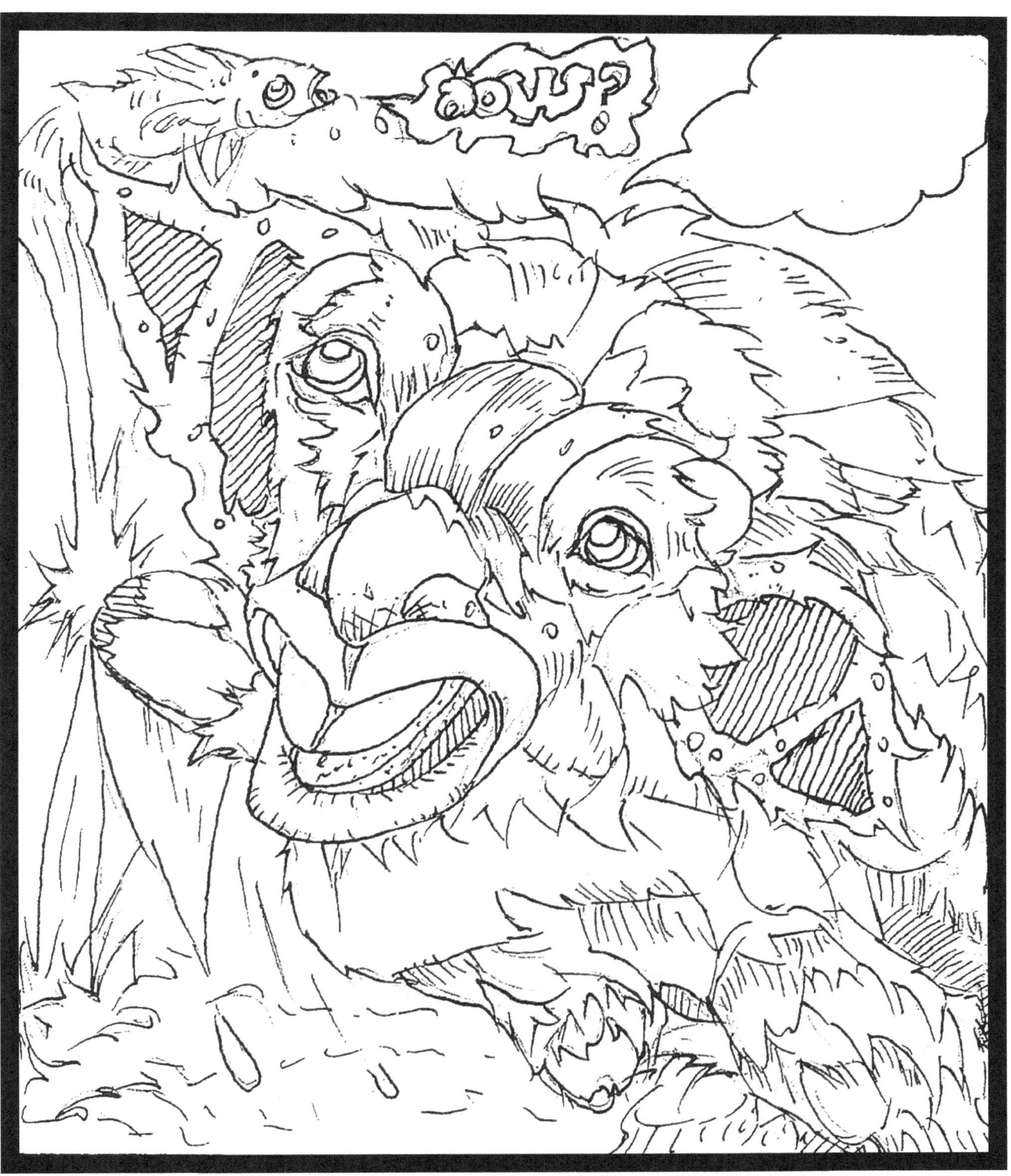
aovs?

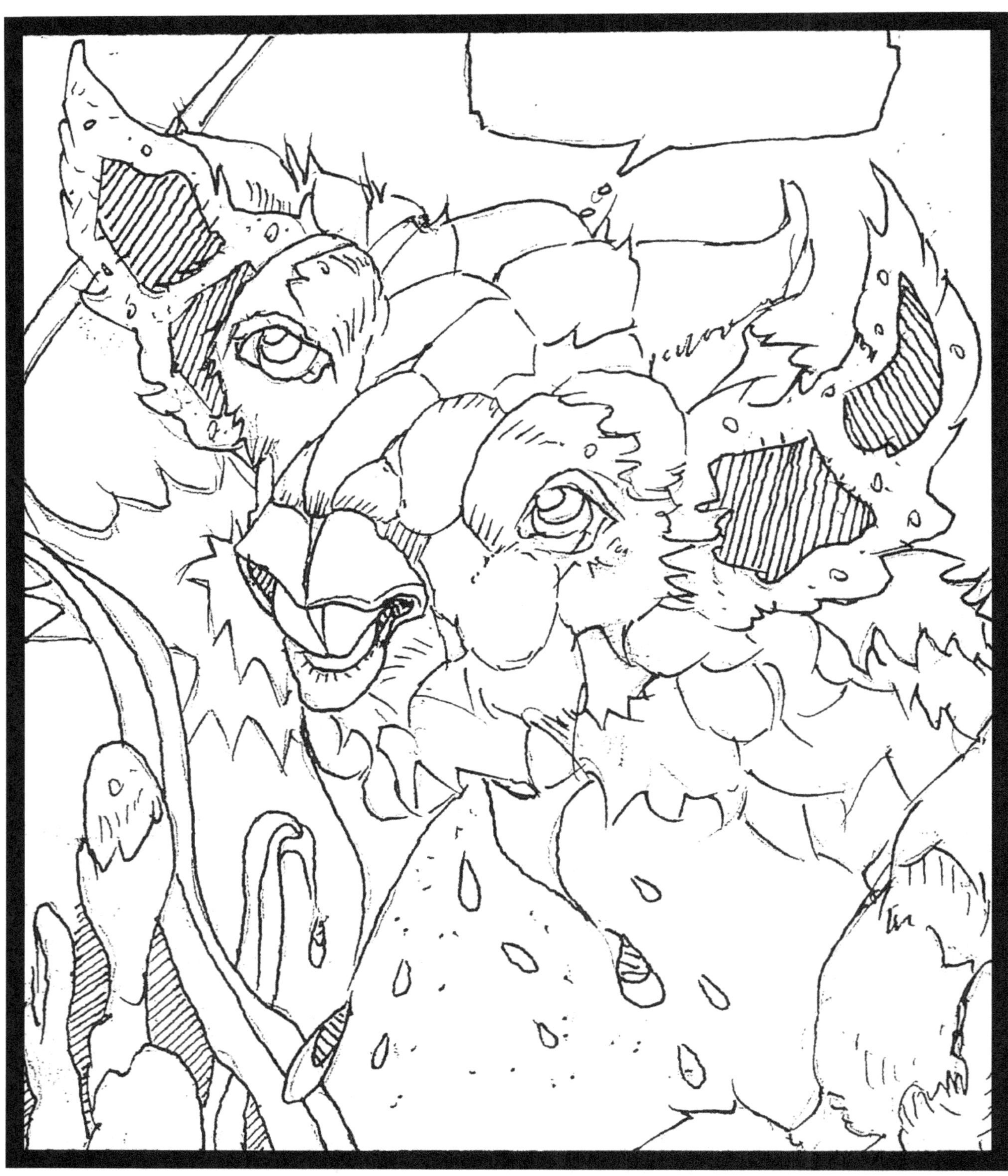

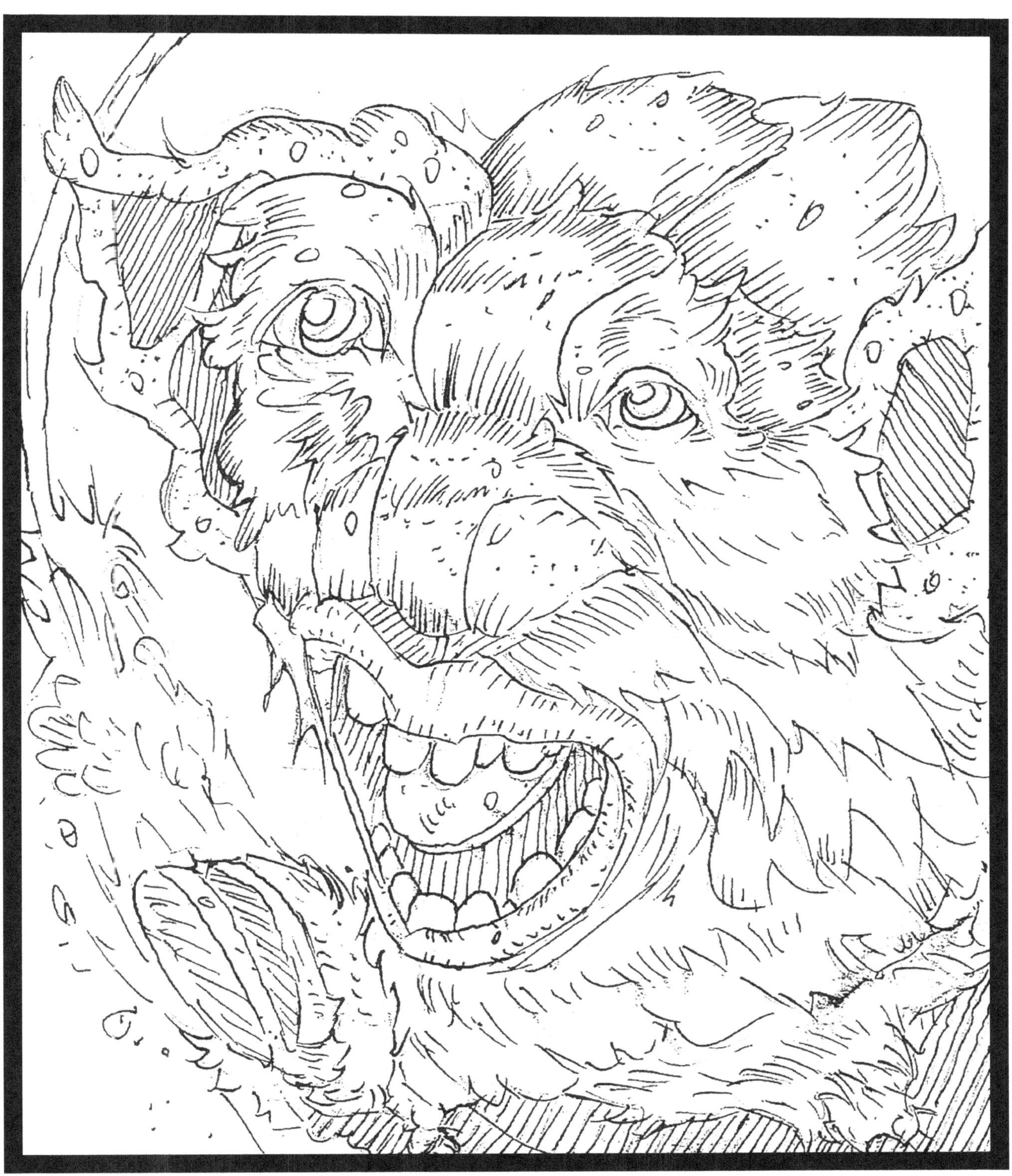

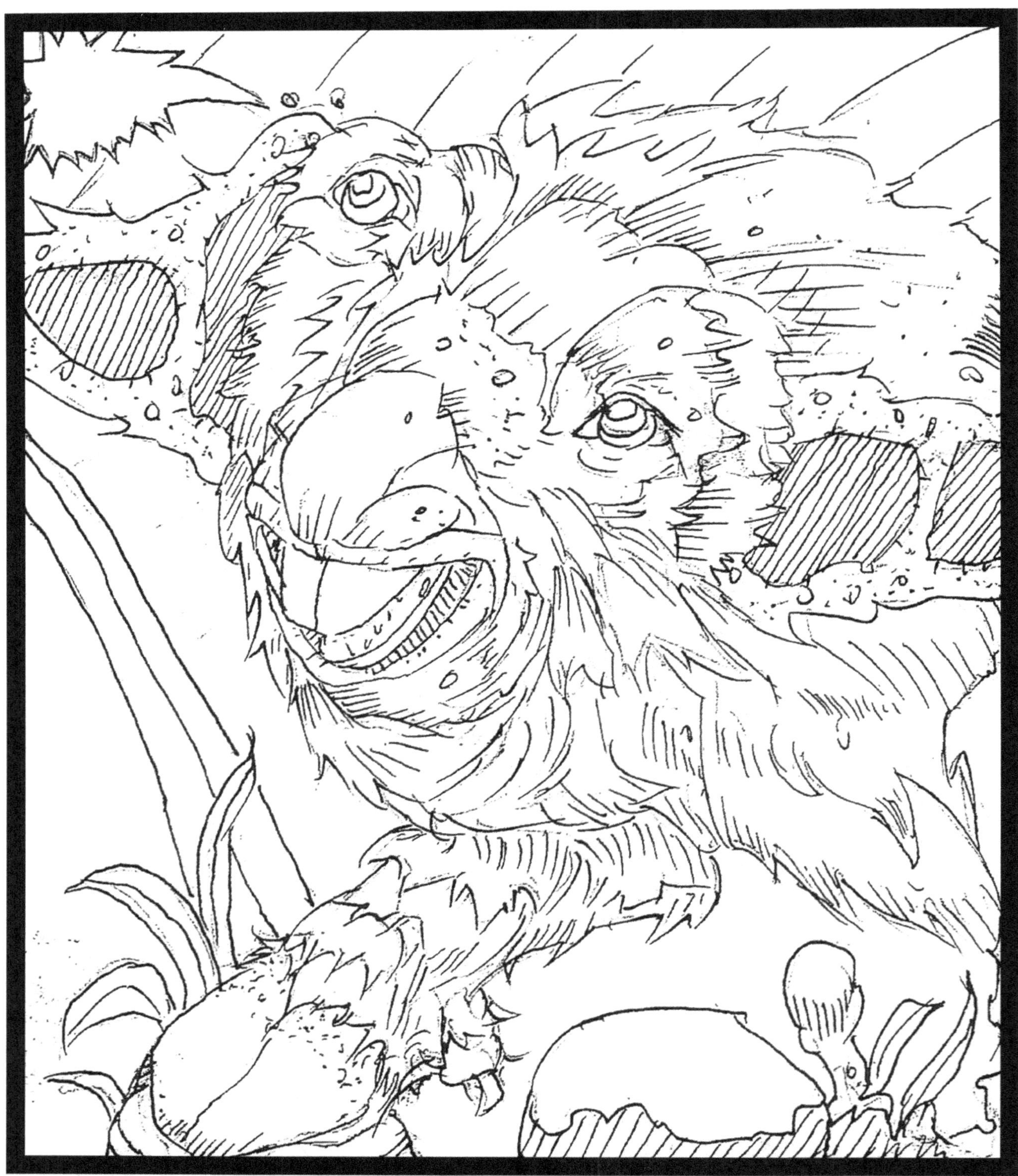

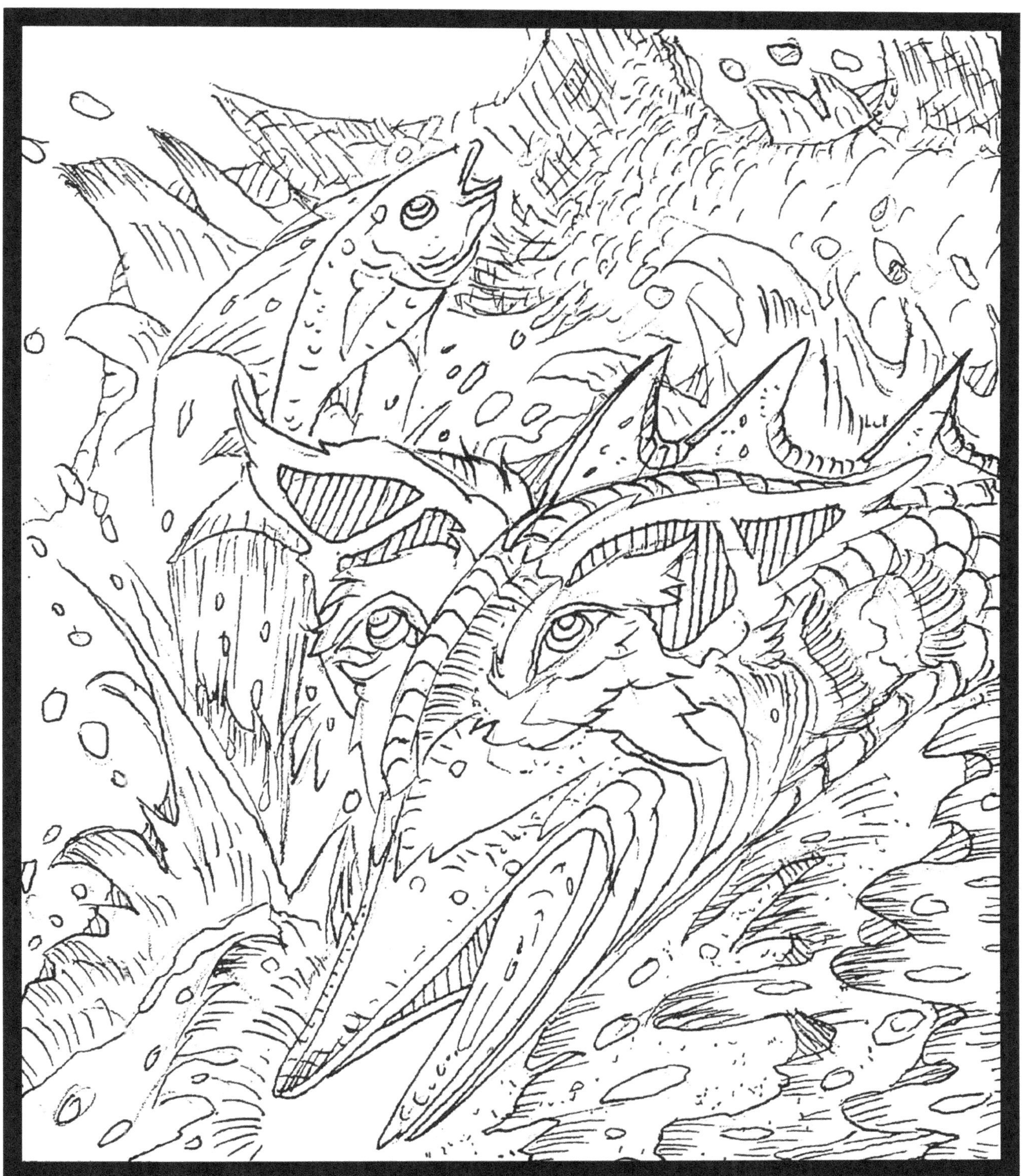

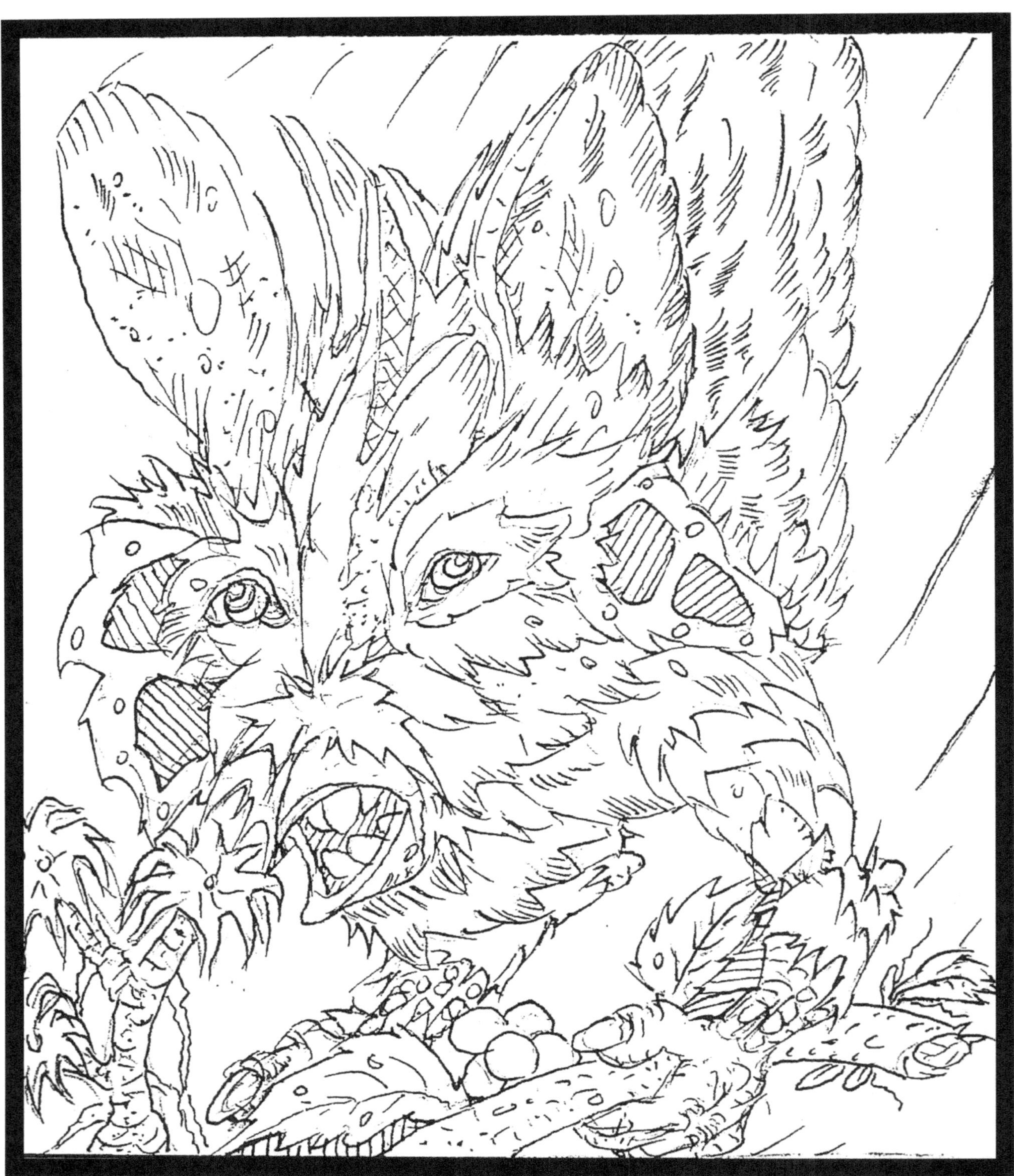

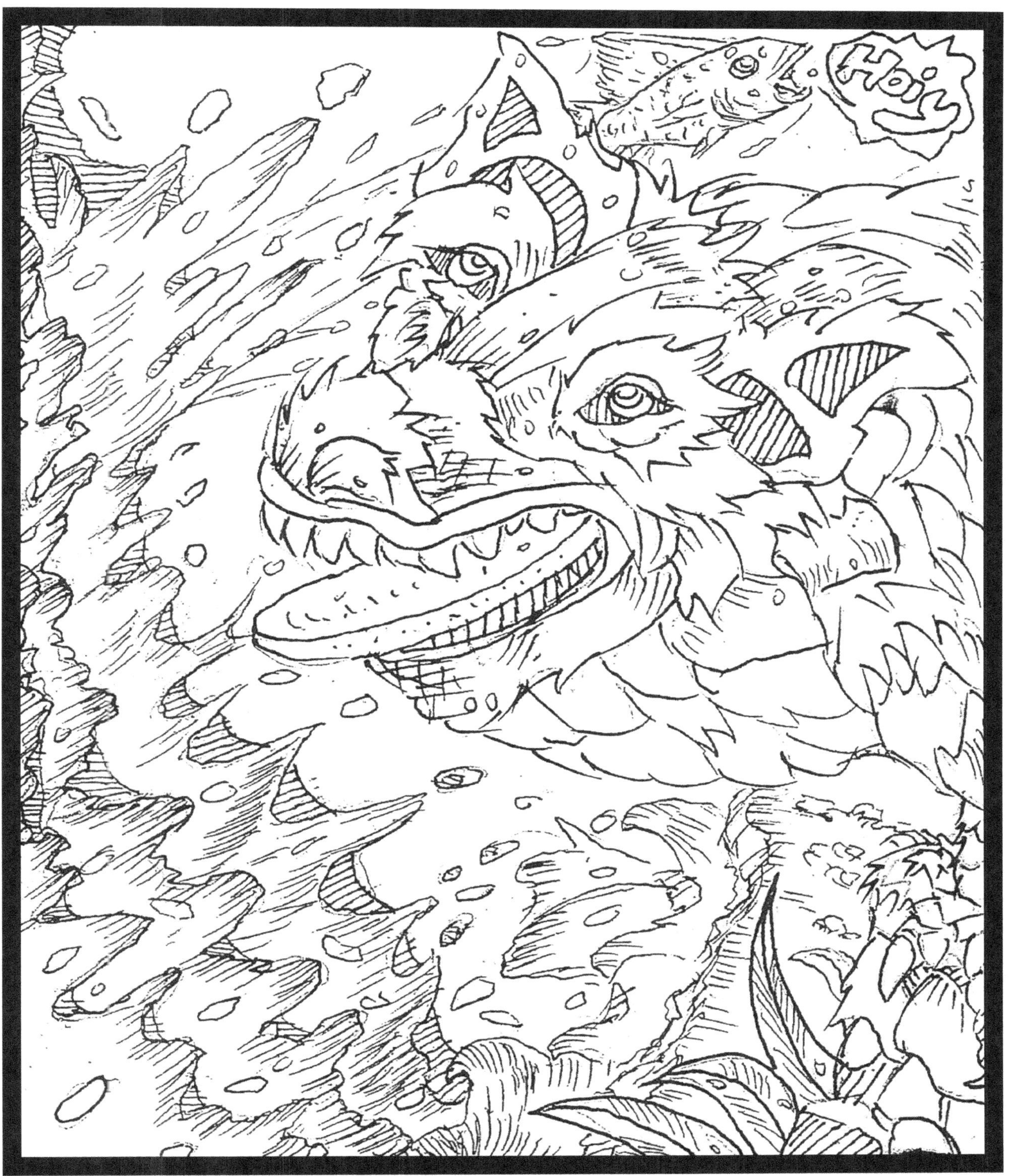

Holy

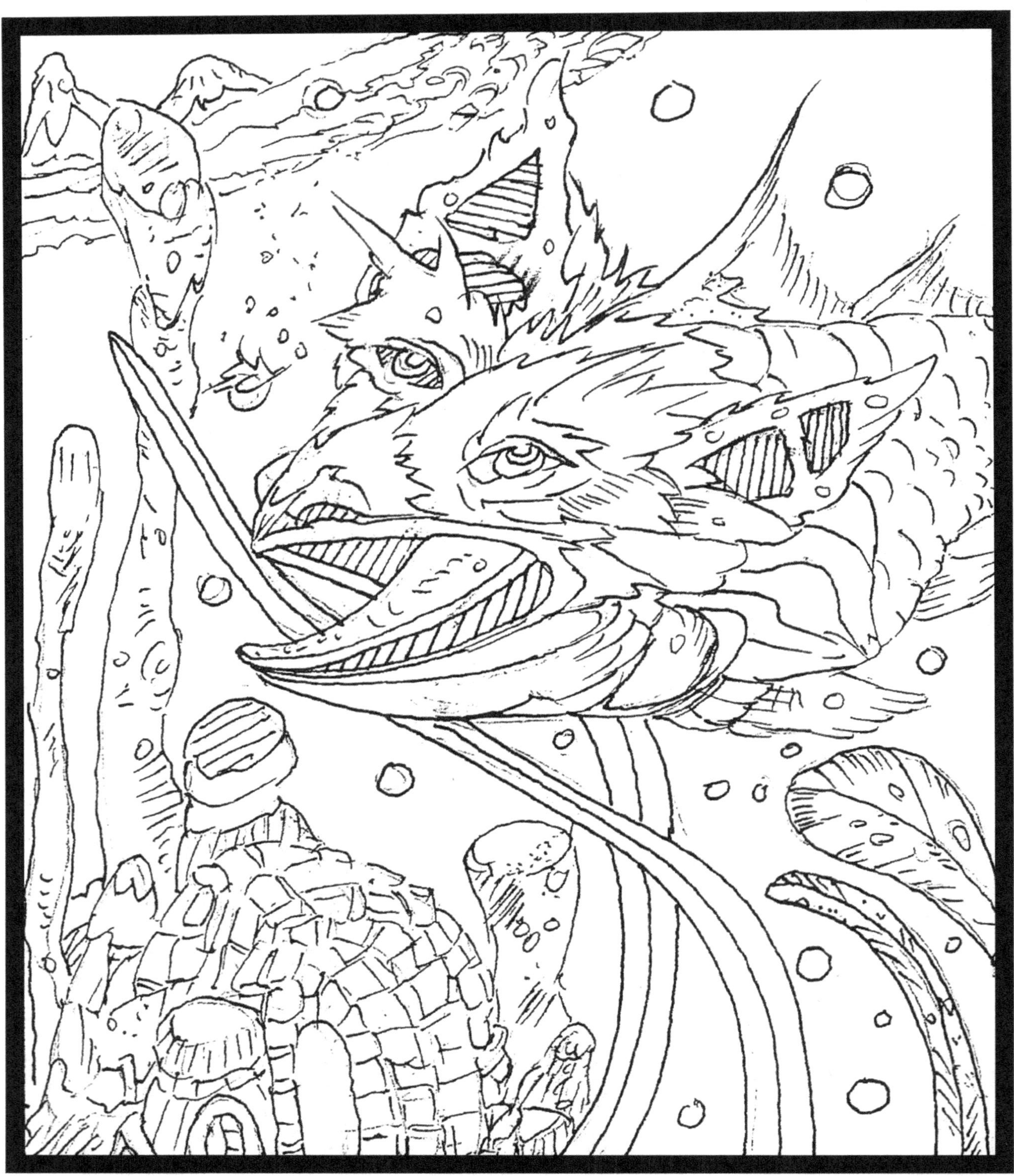

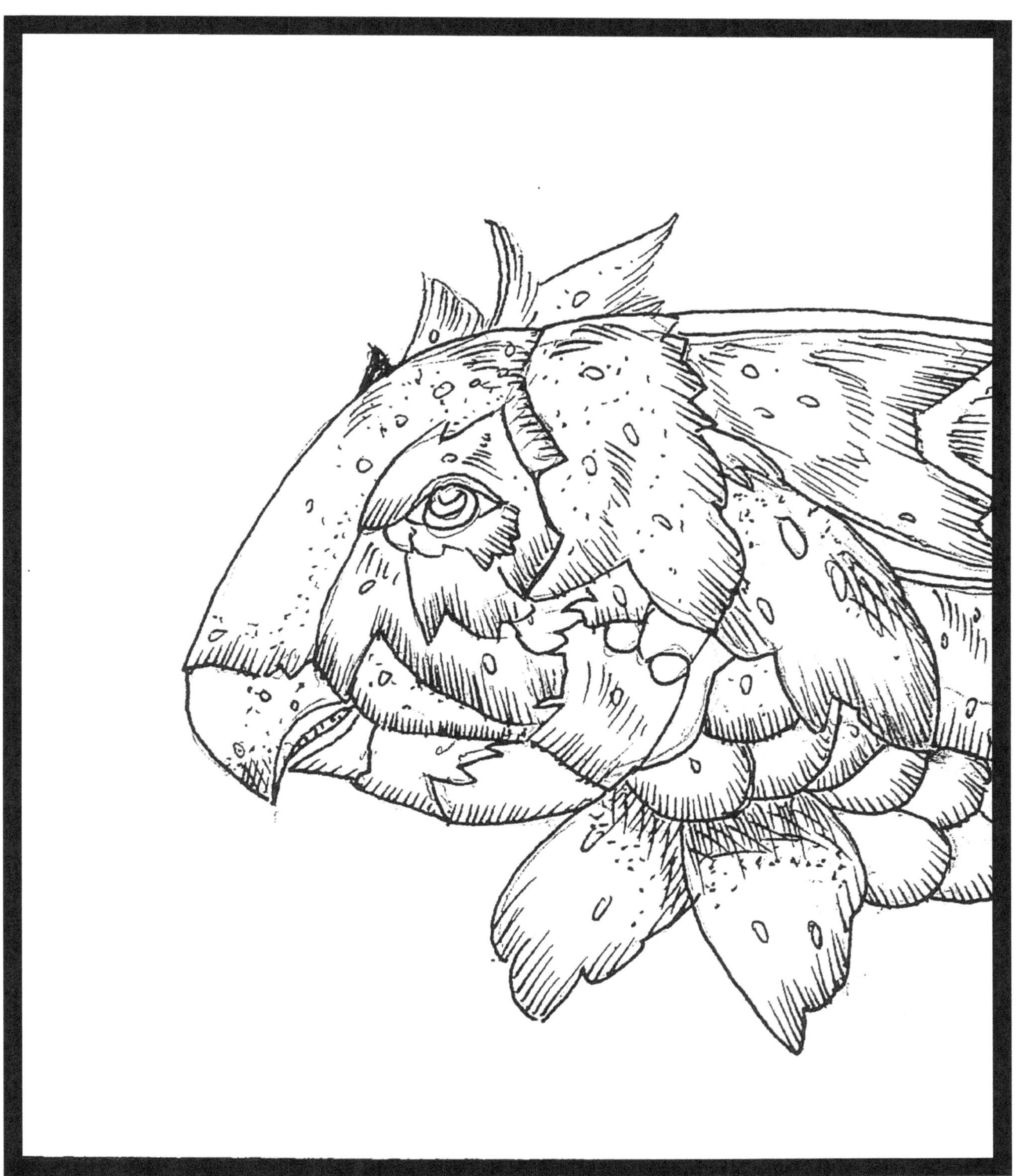

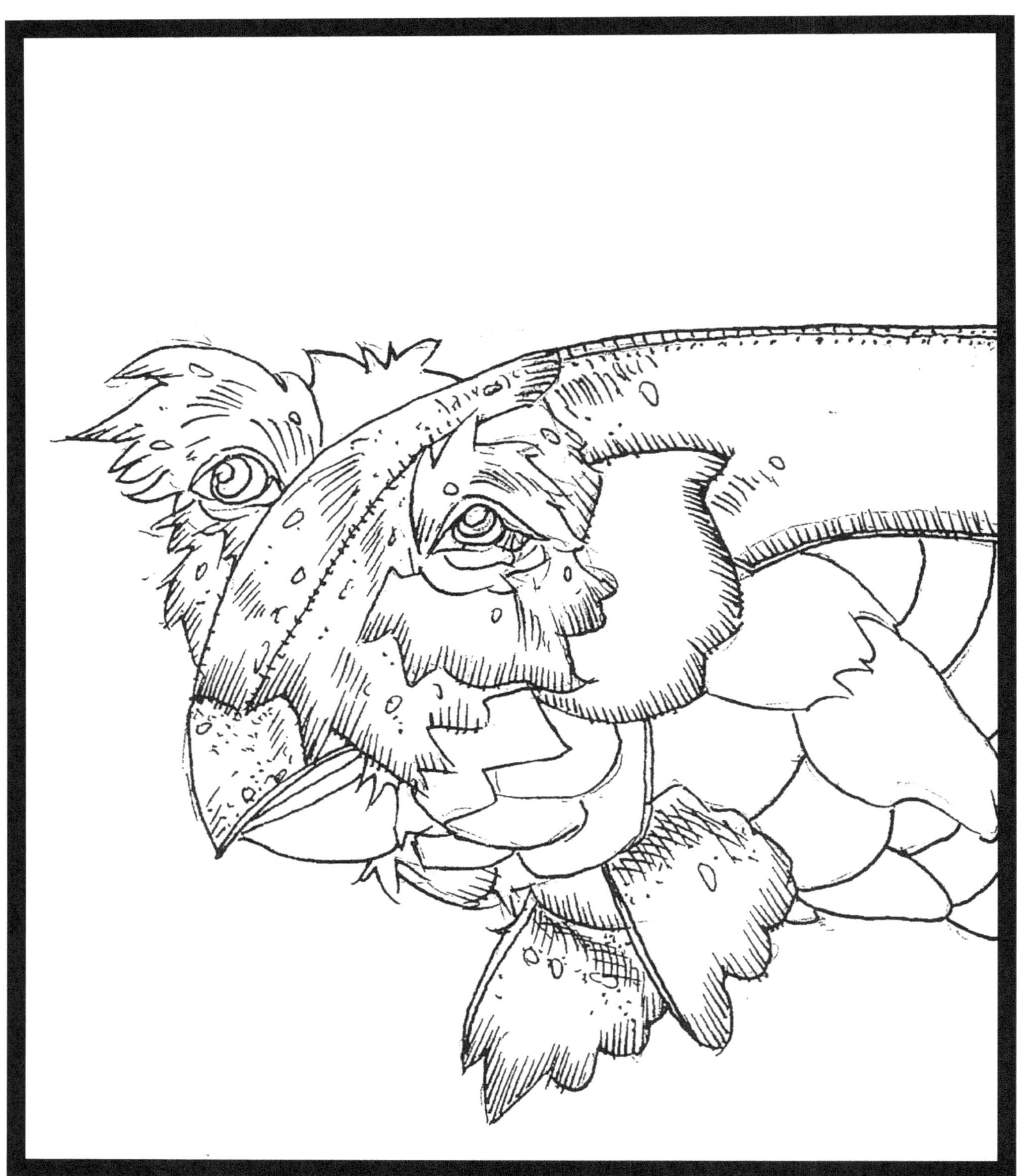

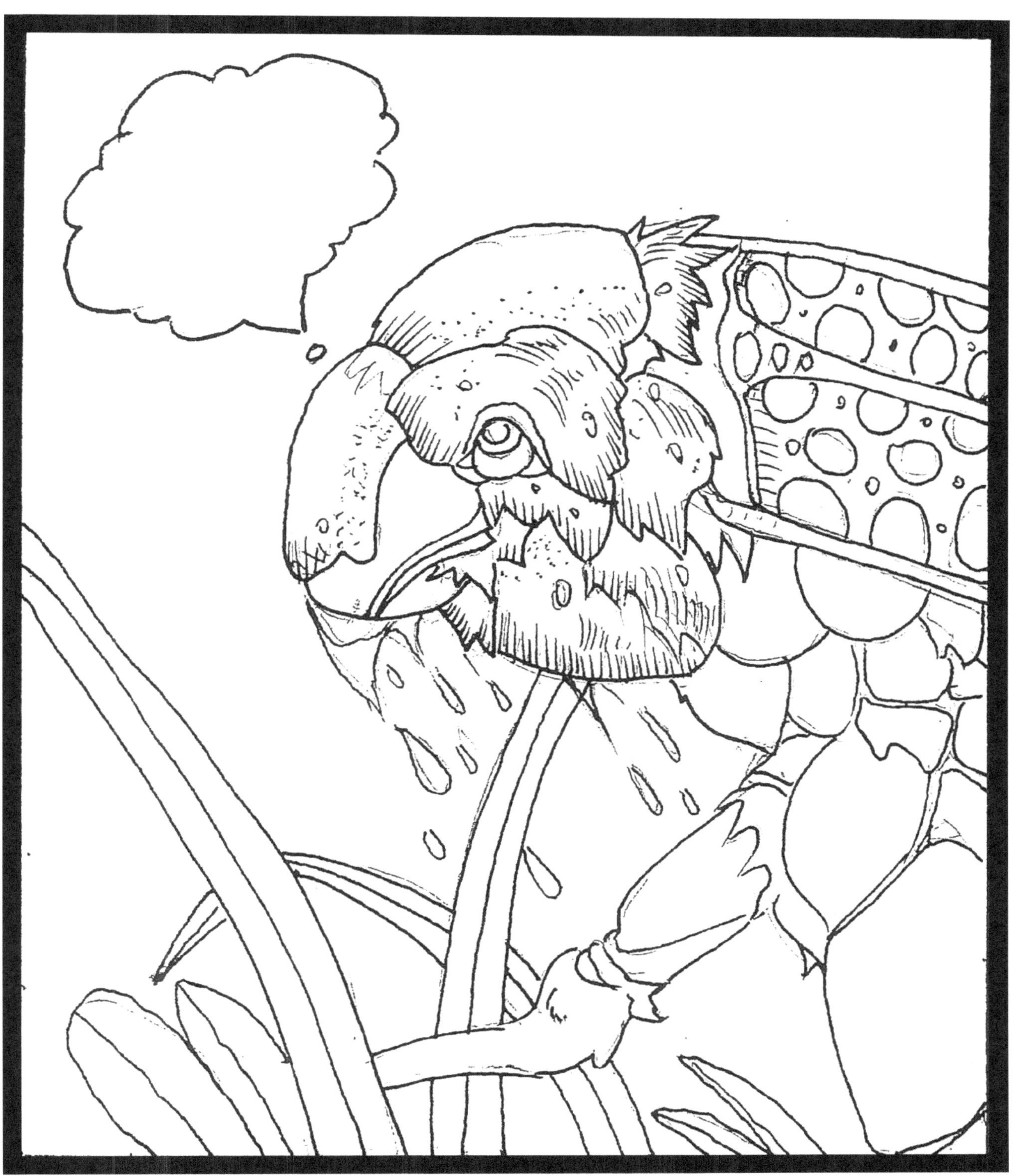

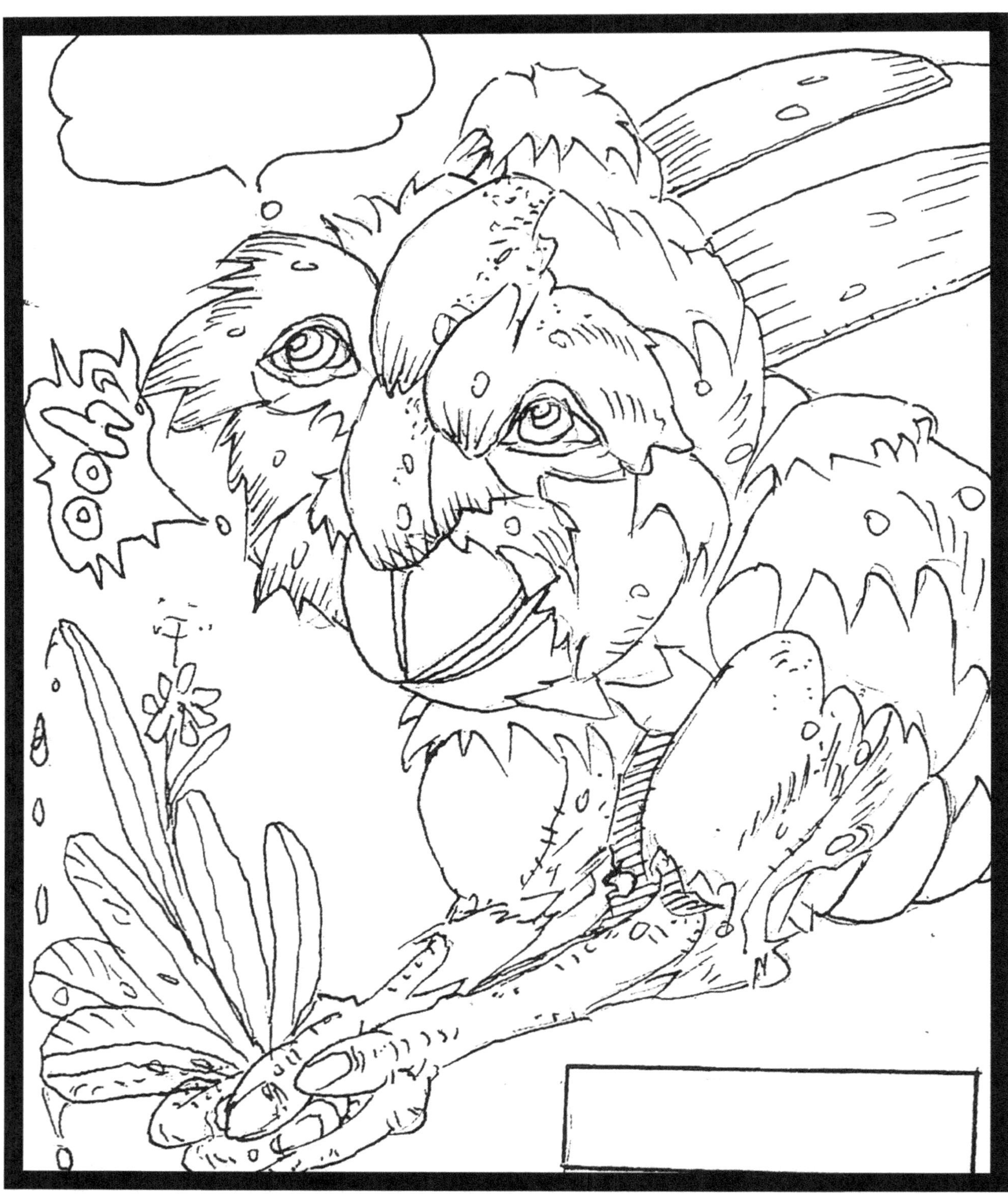

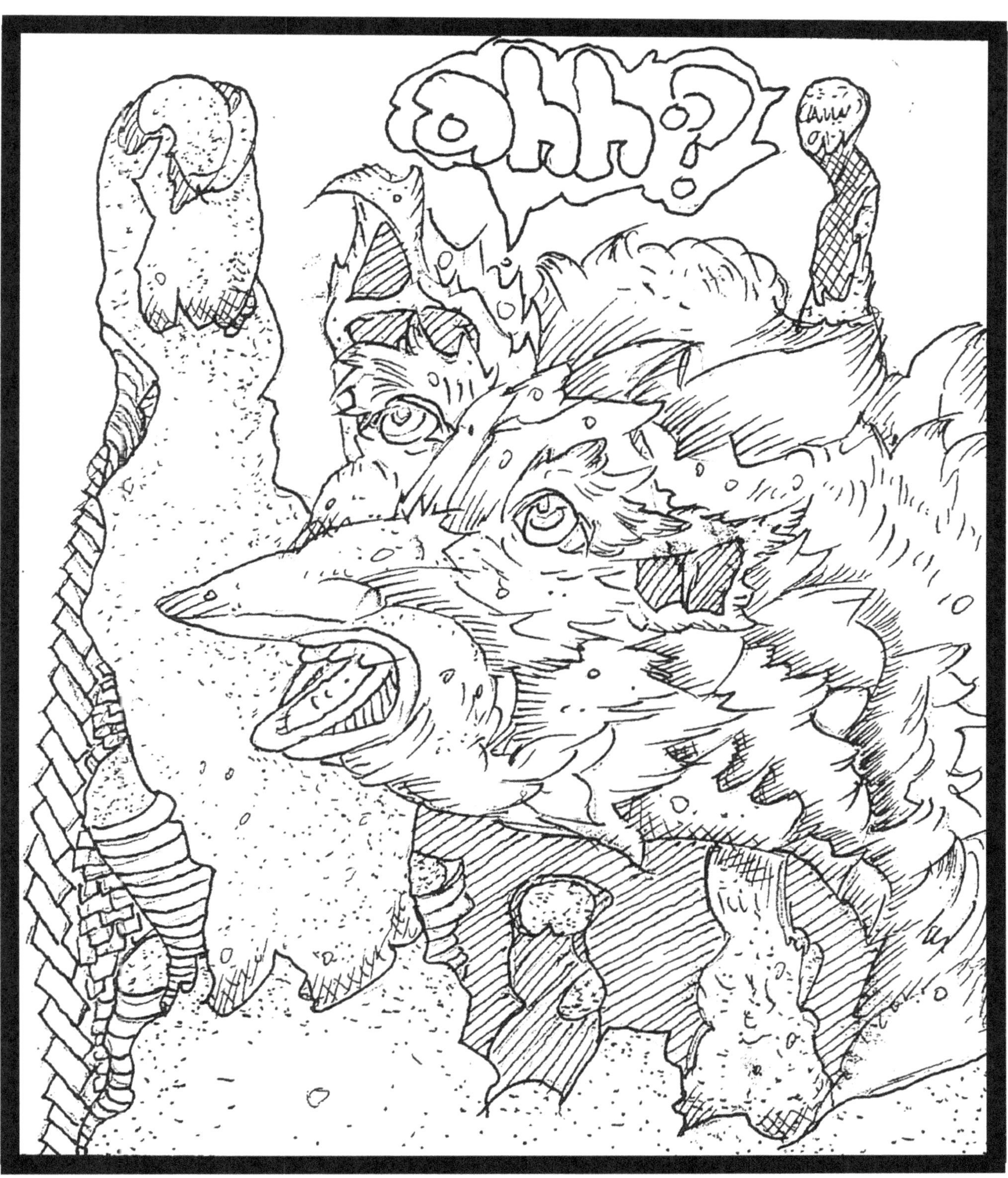

ohh?

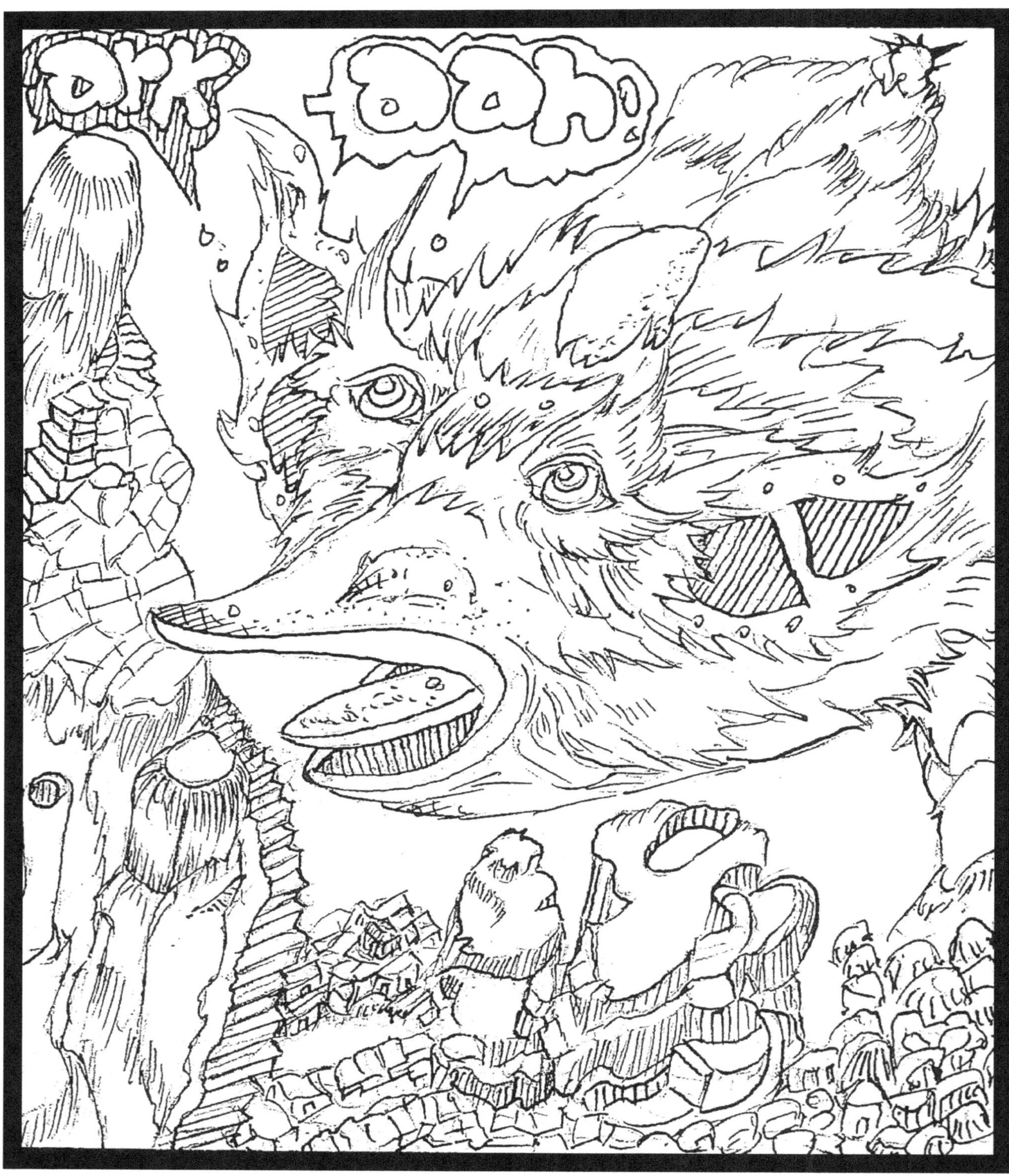
ork
aah

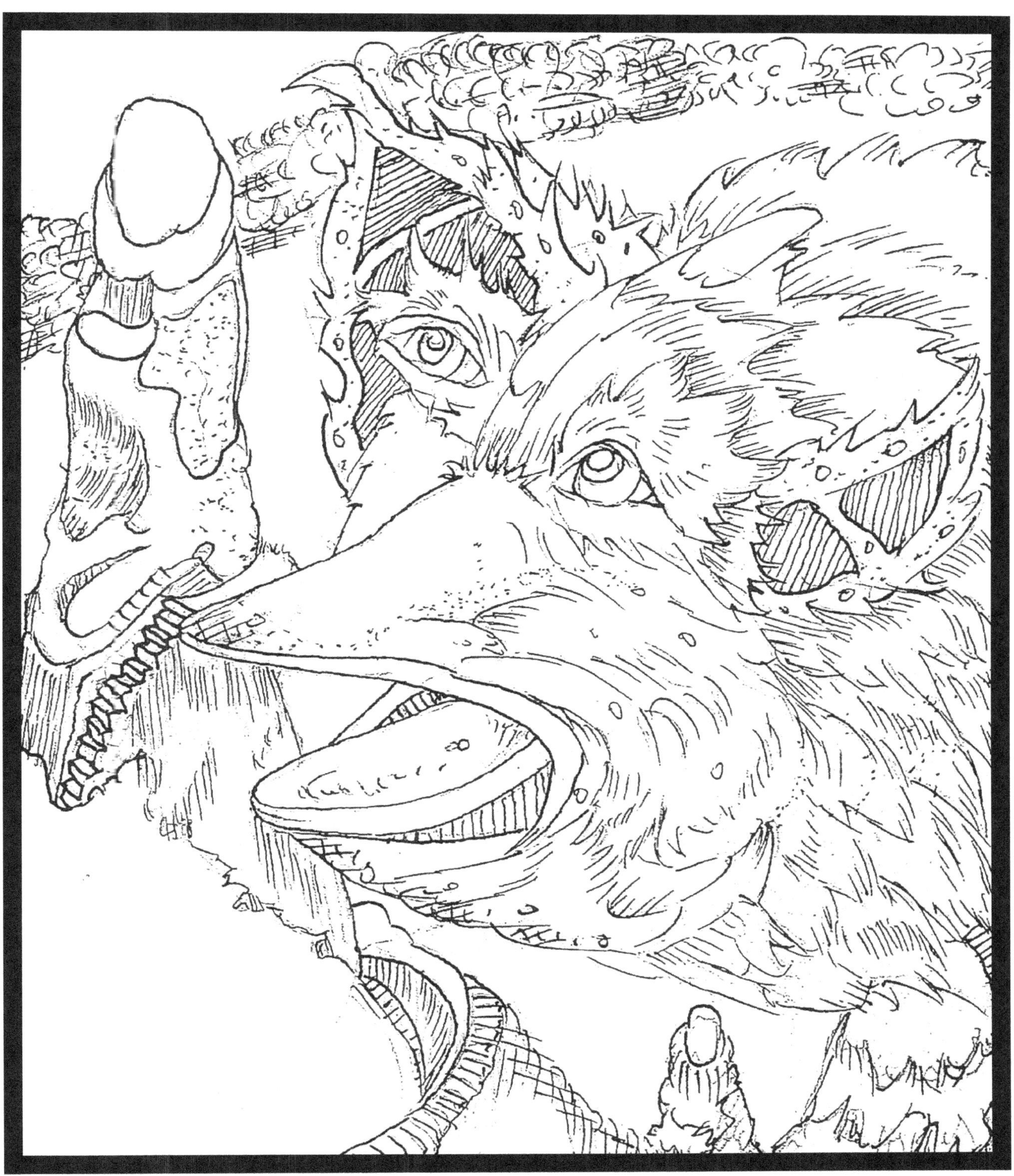

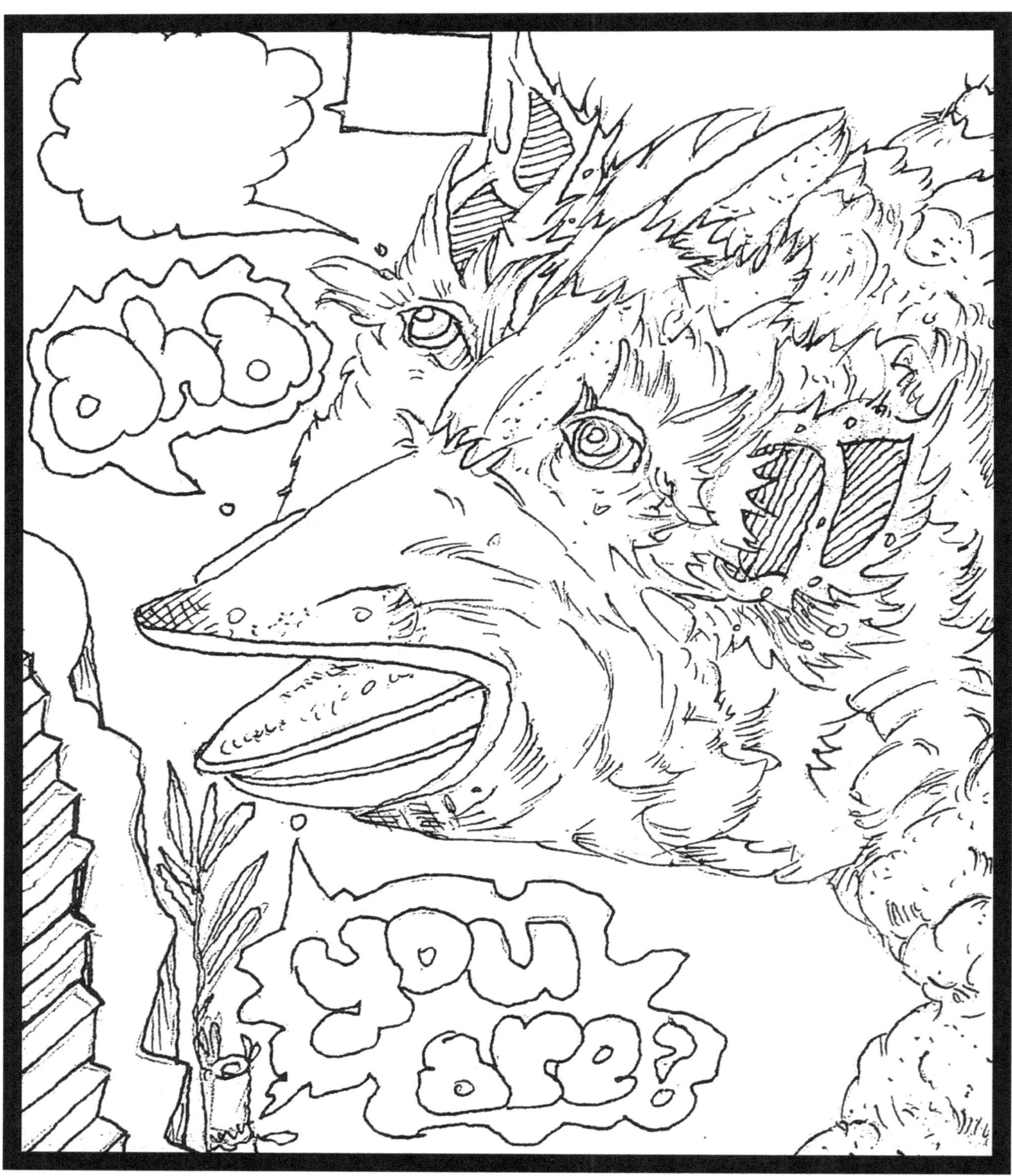
you are?

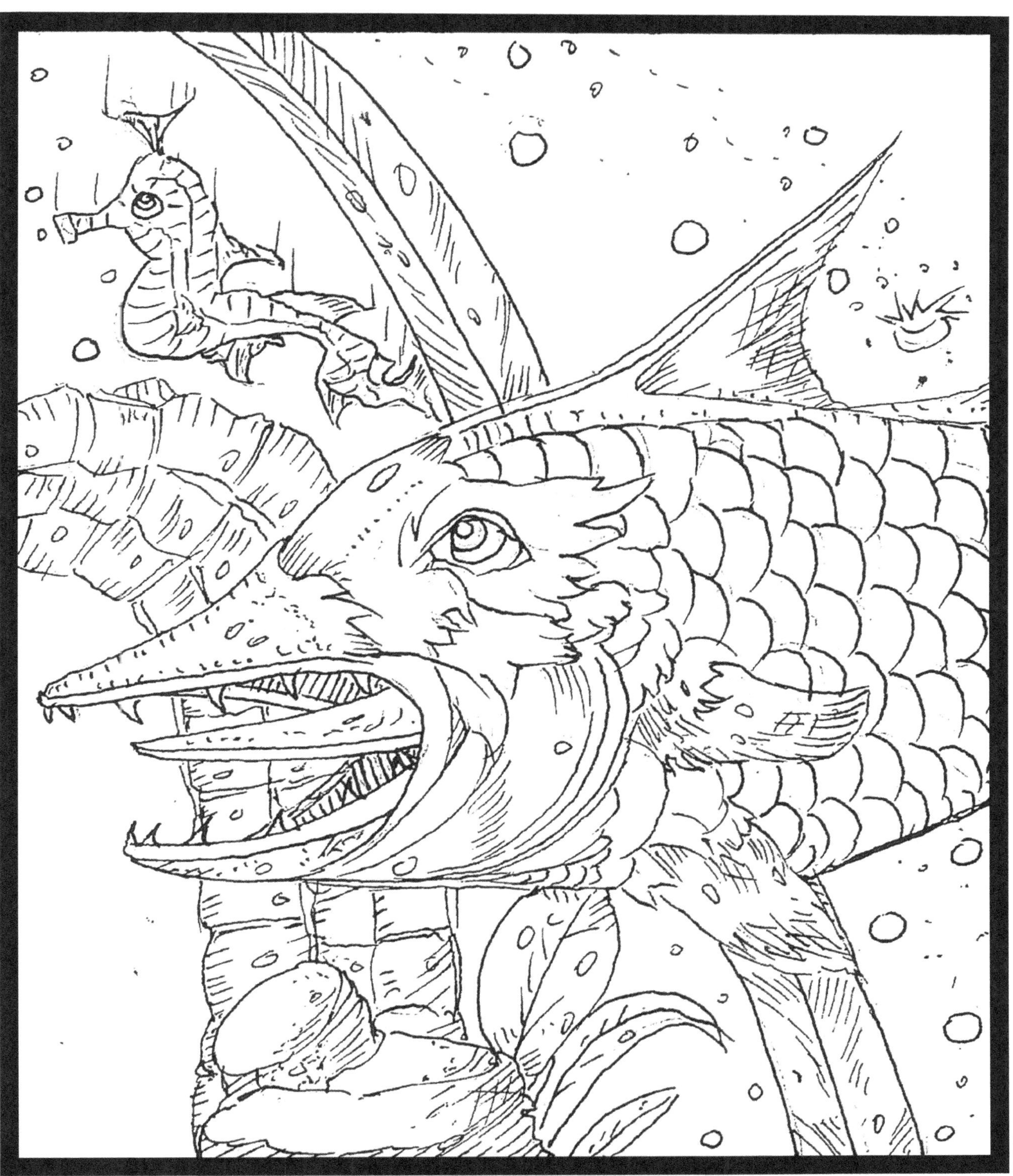

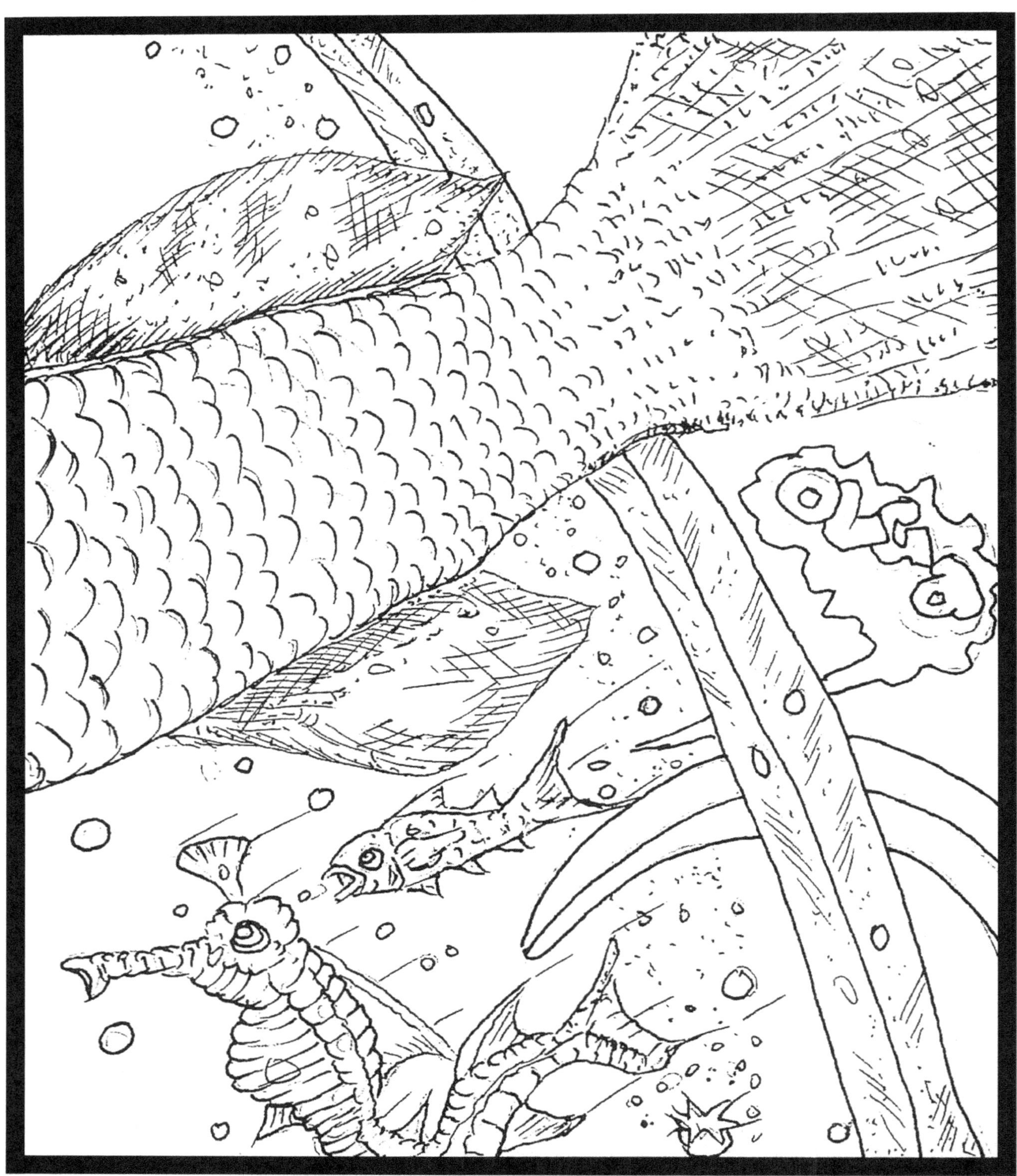

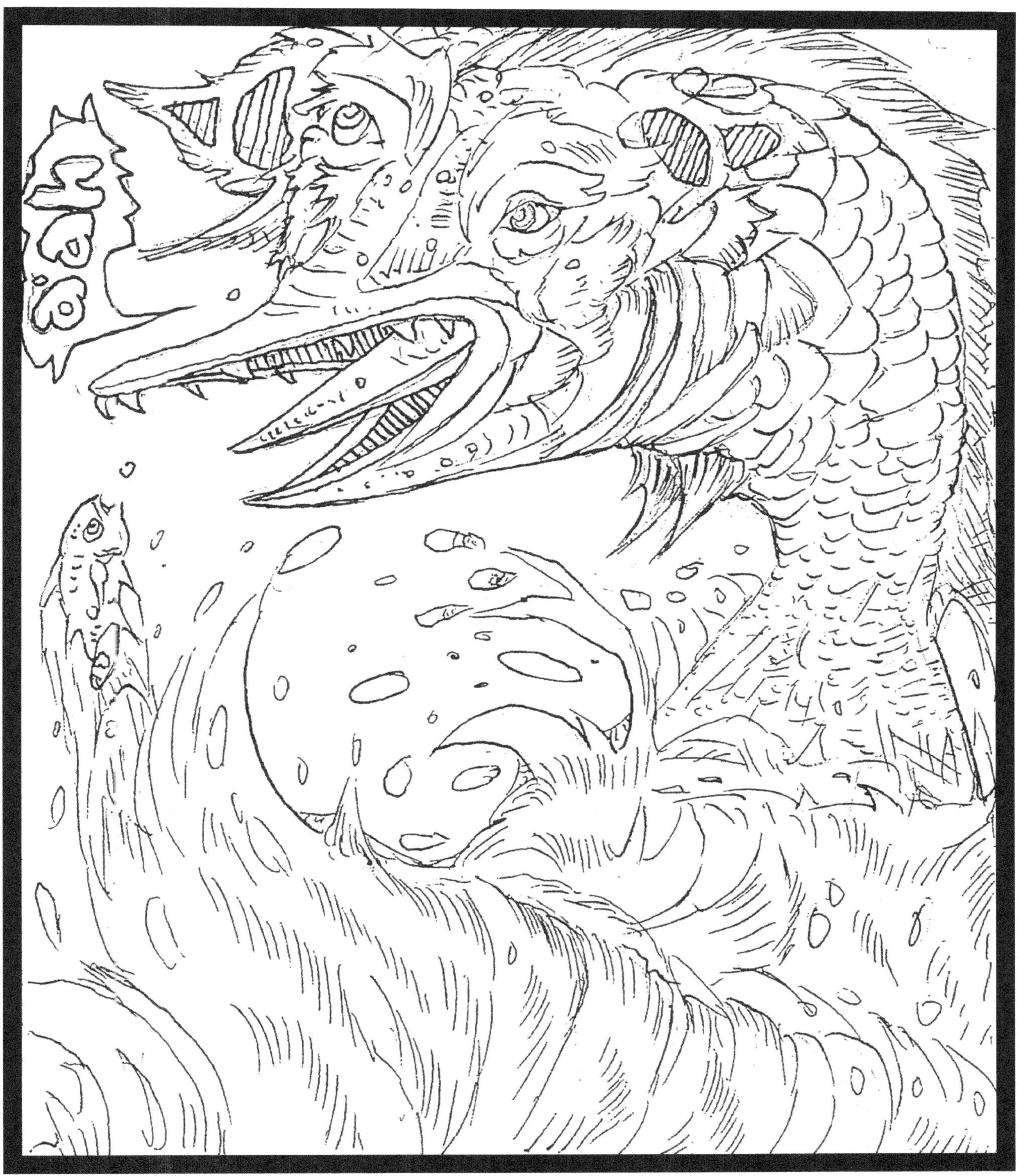

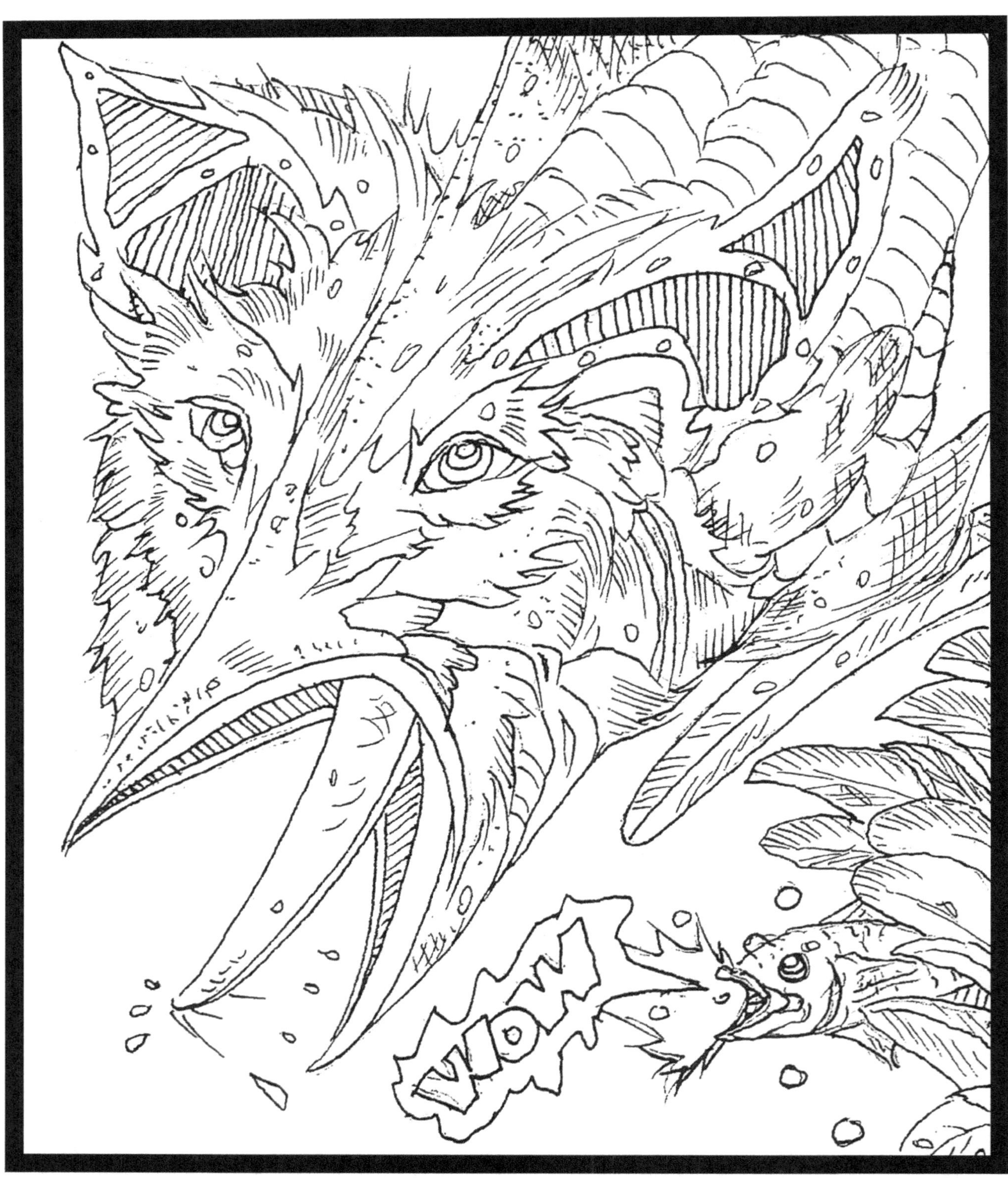
WOW

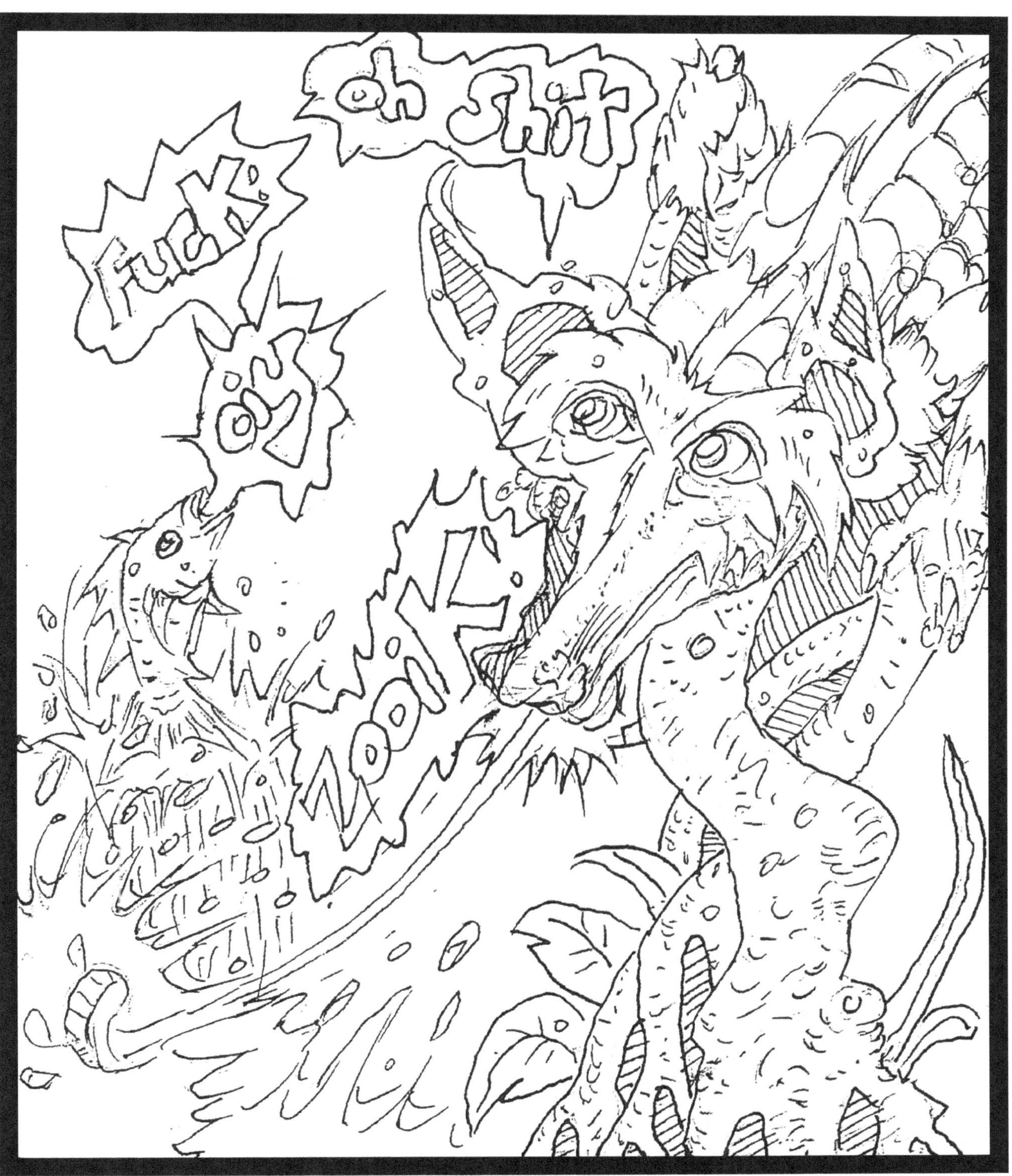

Fuck,
oh shit
oly
Zooik!

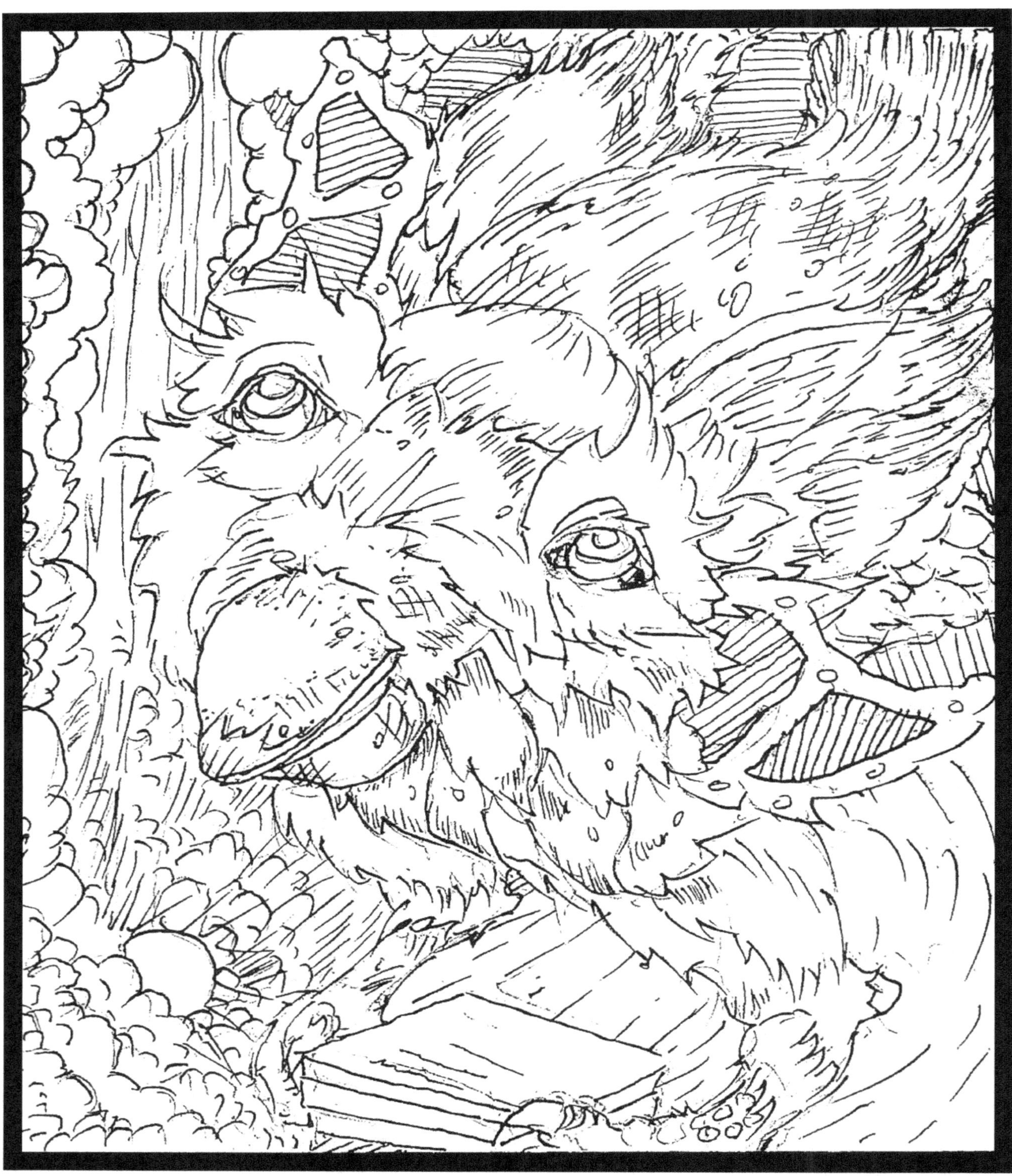

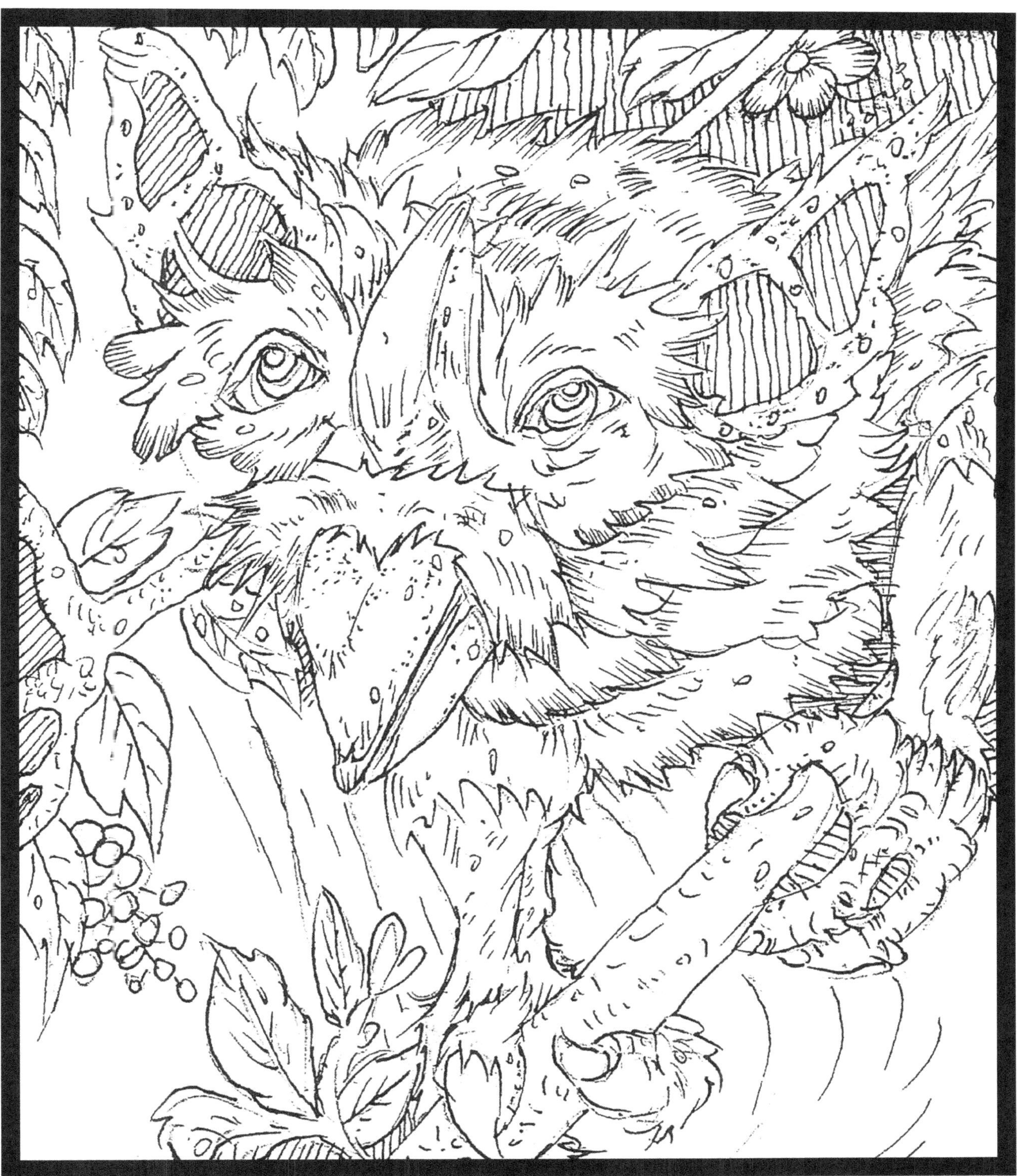

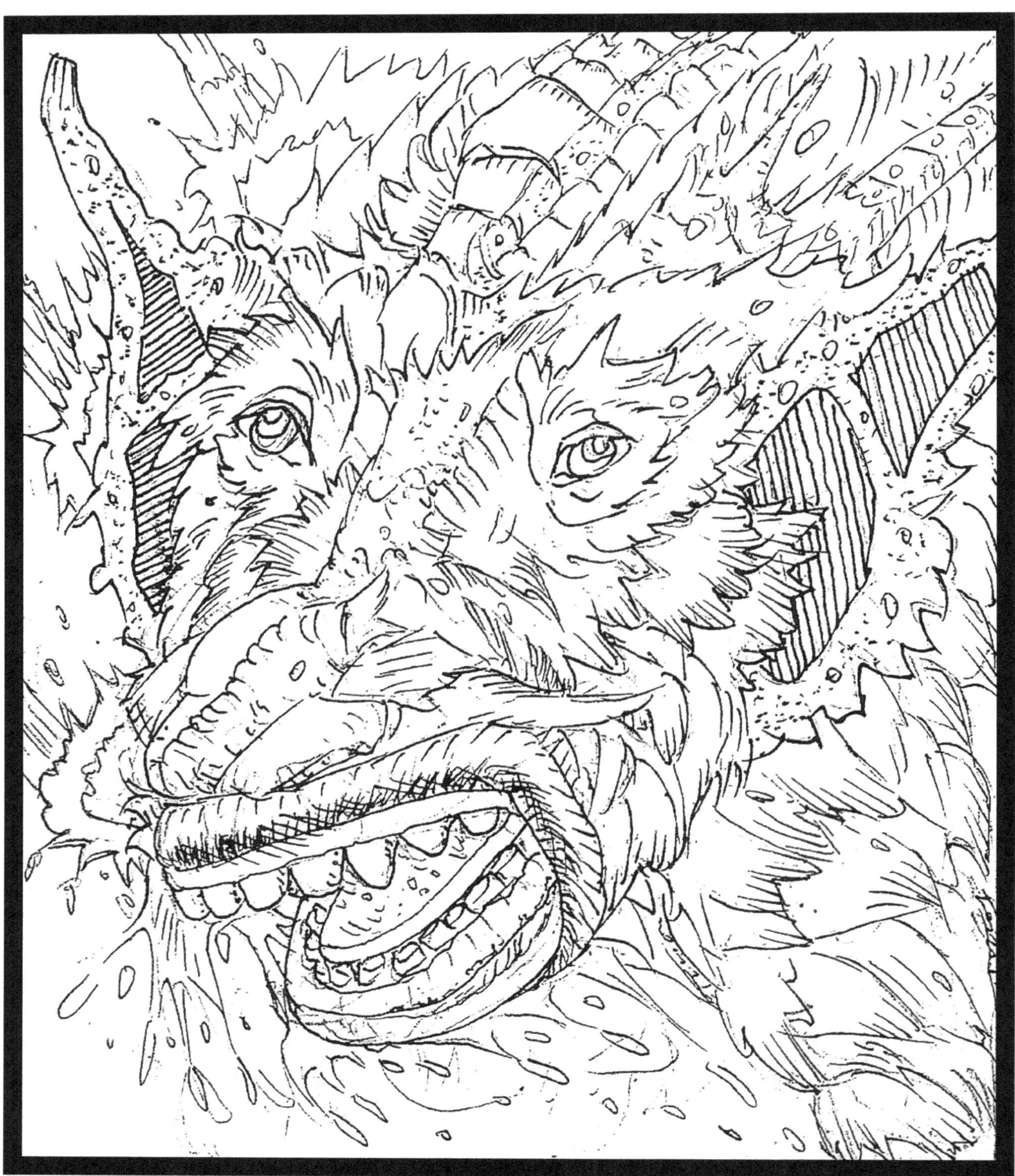

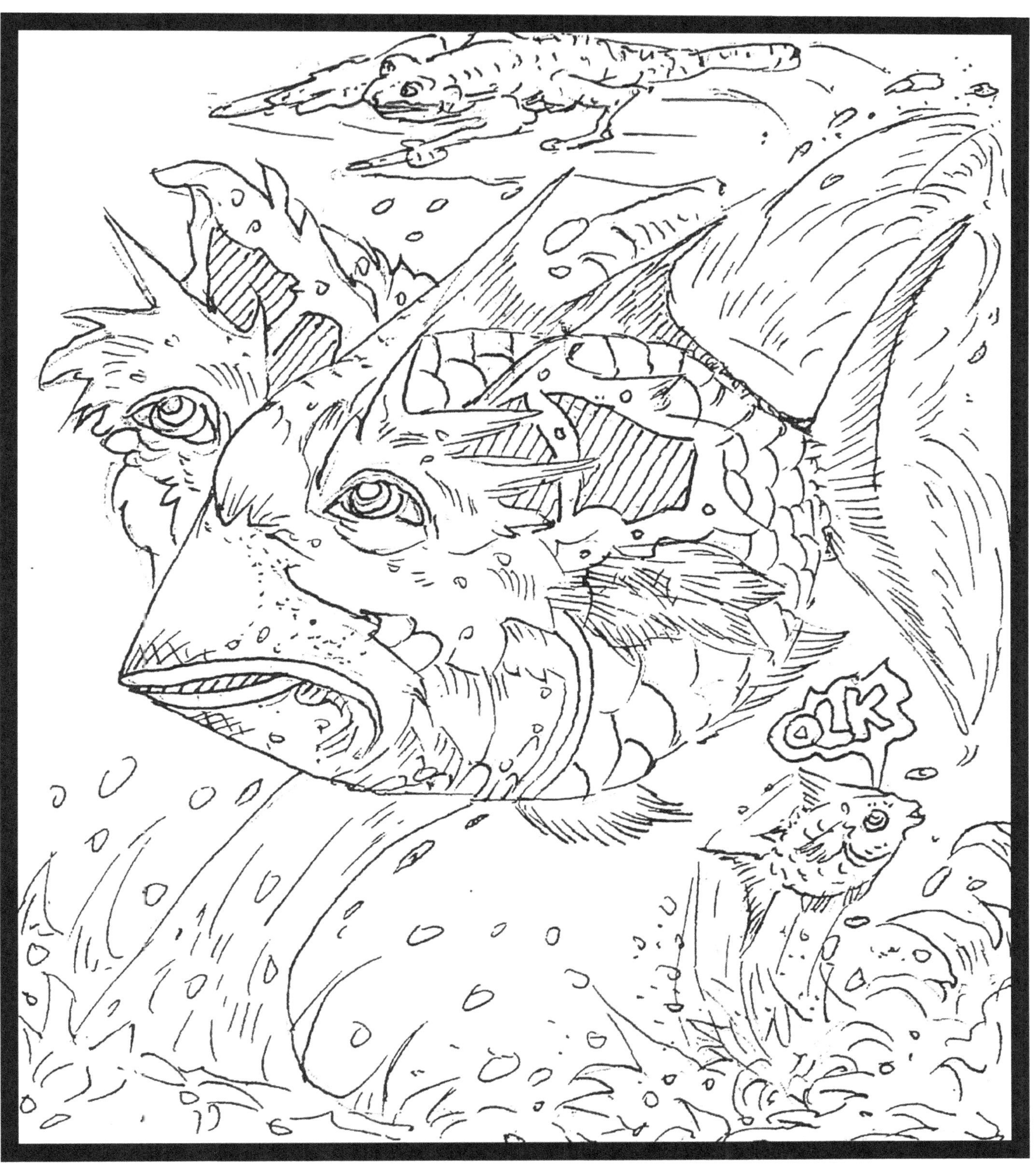
OLK

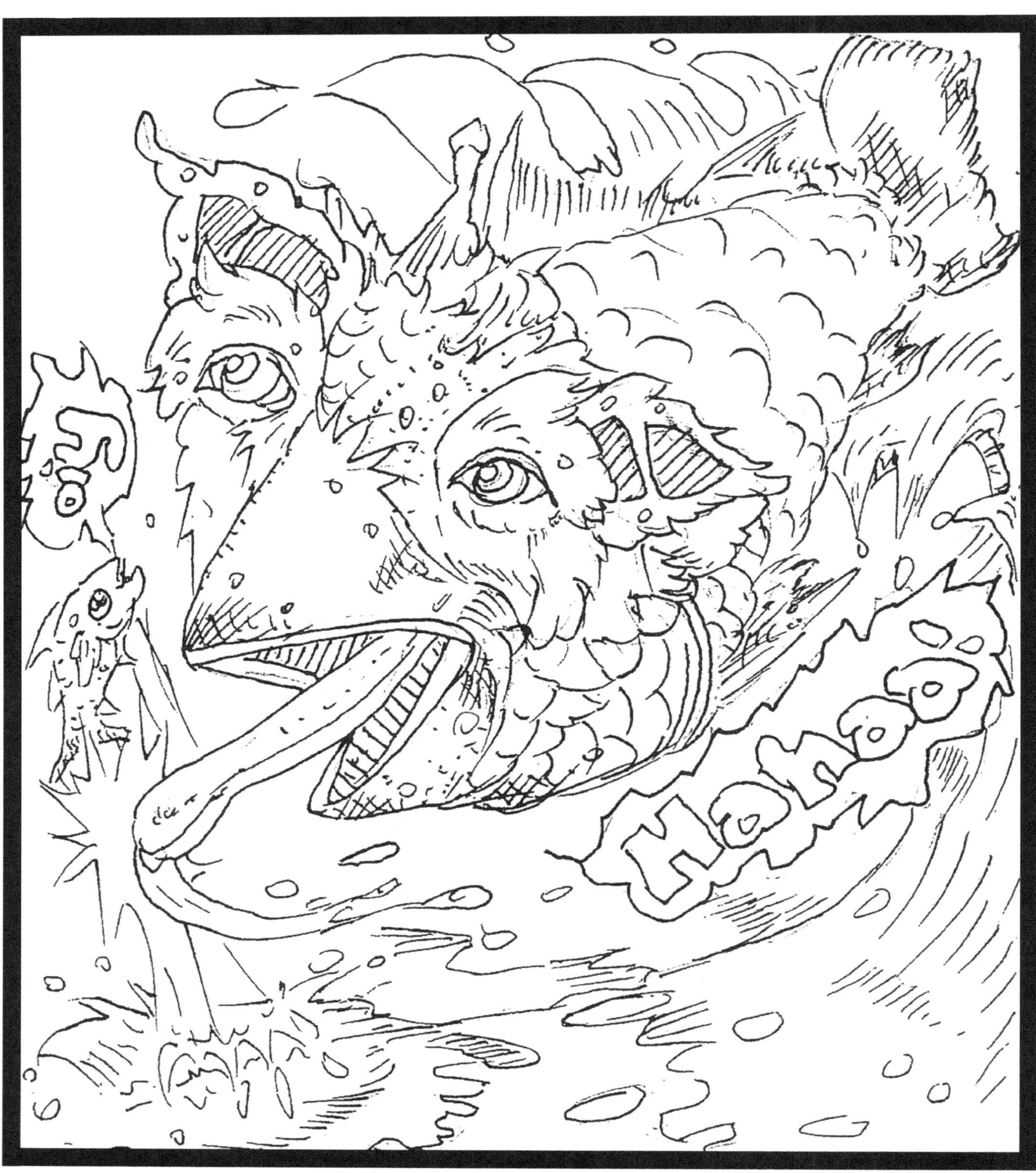

Ha ha ha

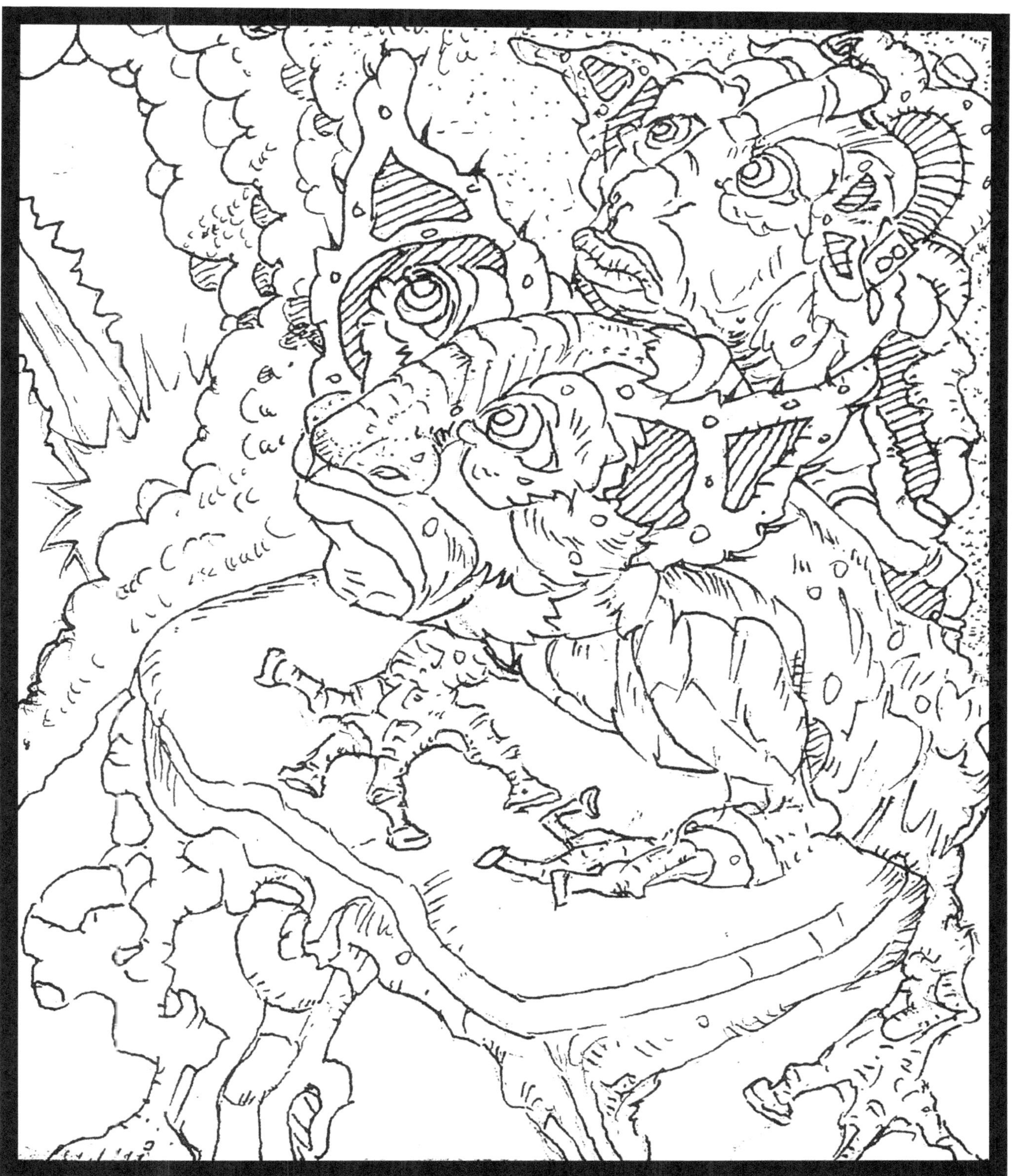

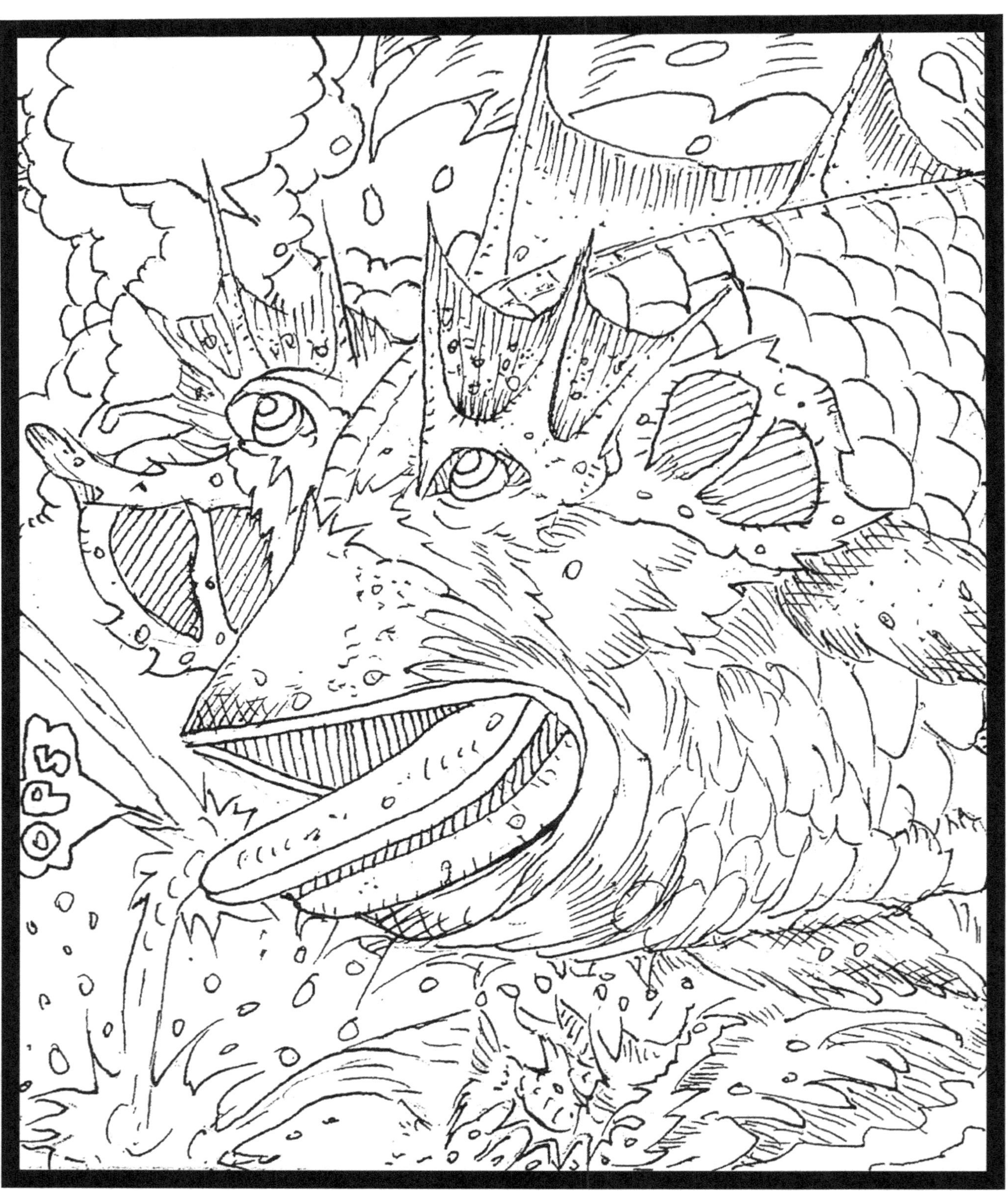
OPS

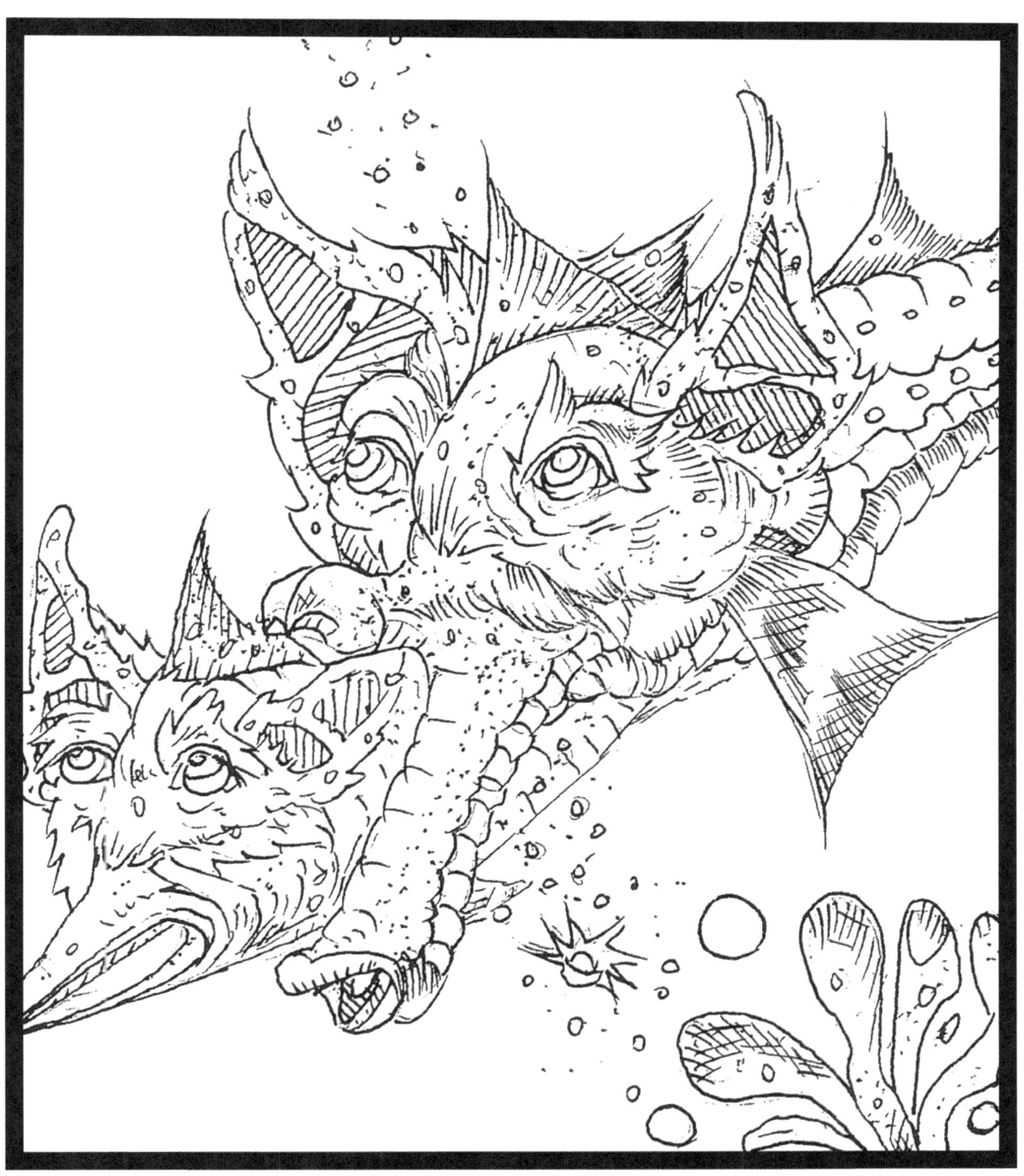

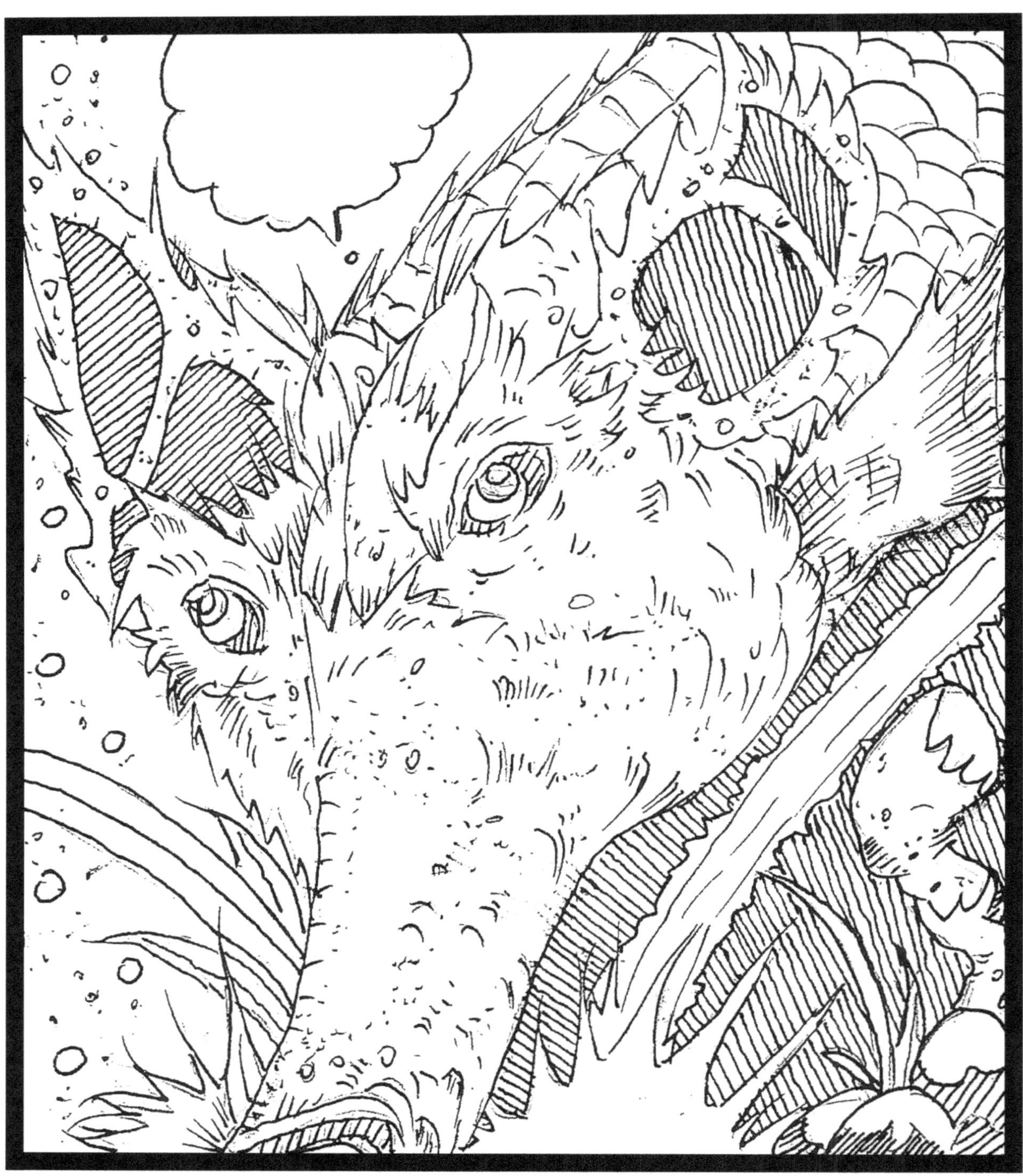

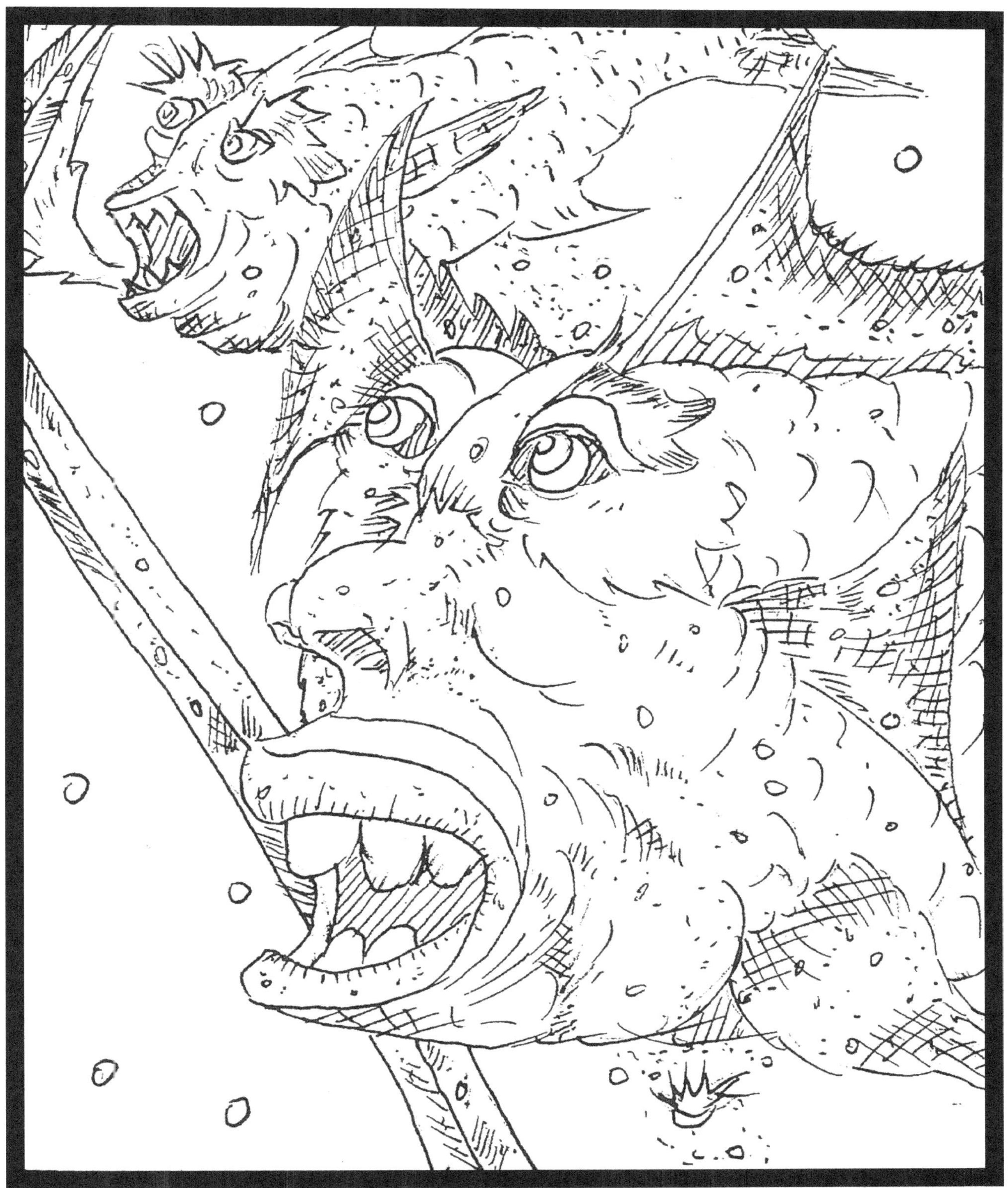

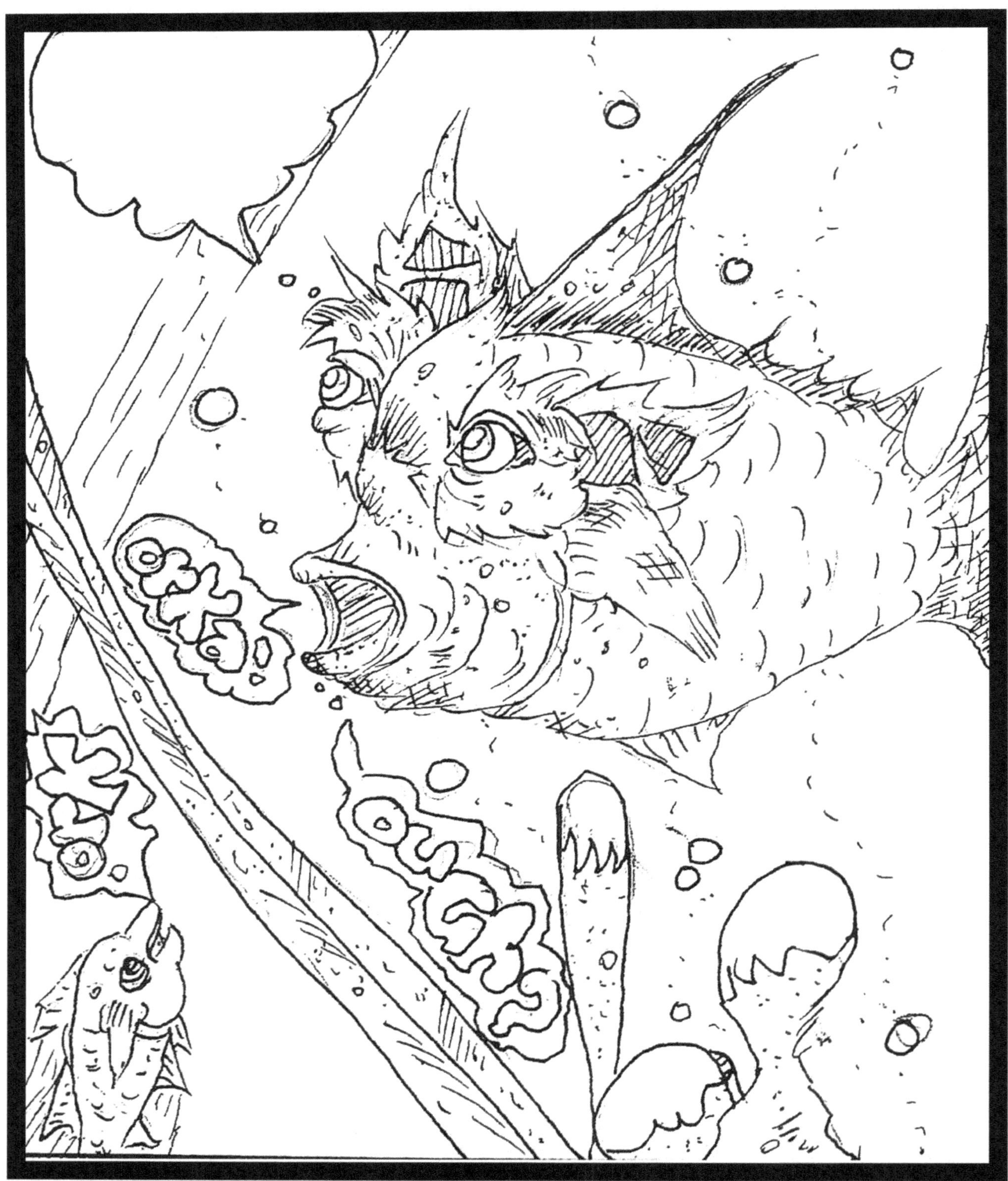
ORKa!
ougts

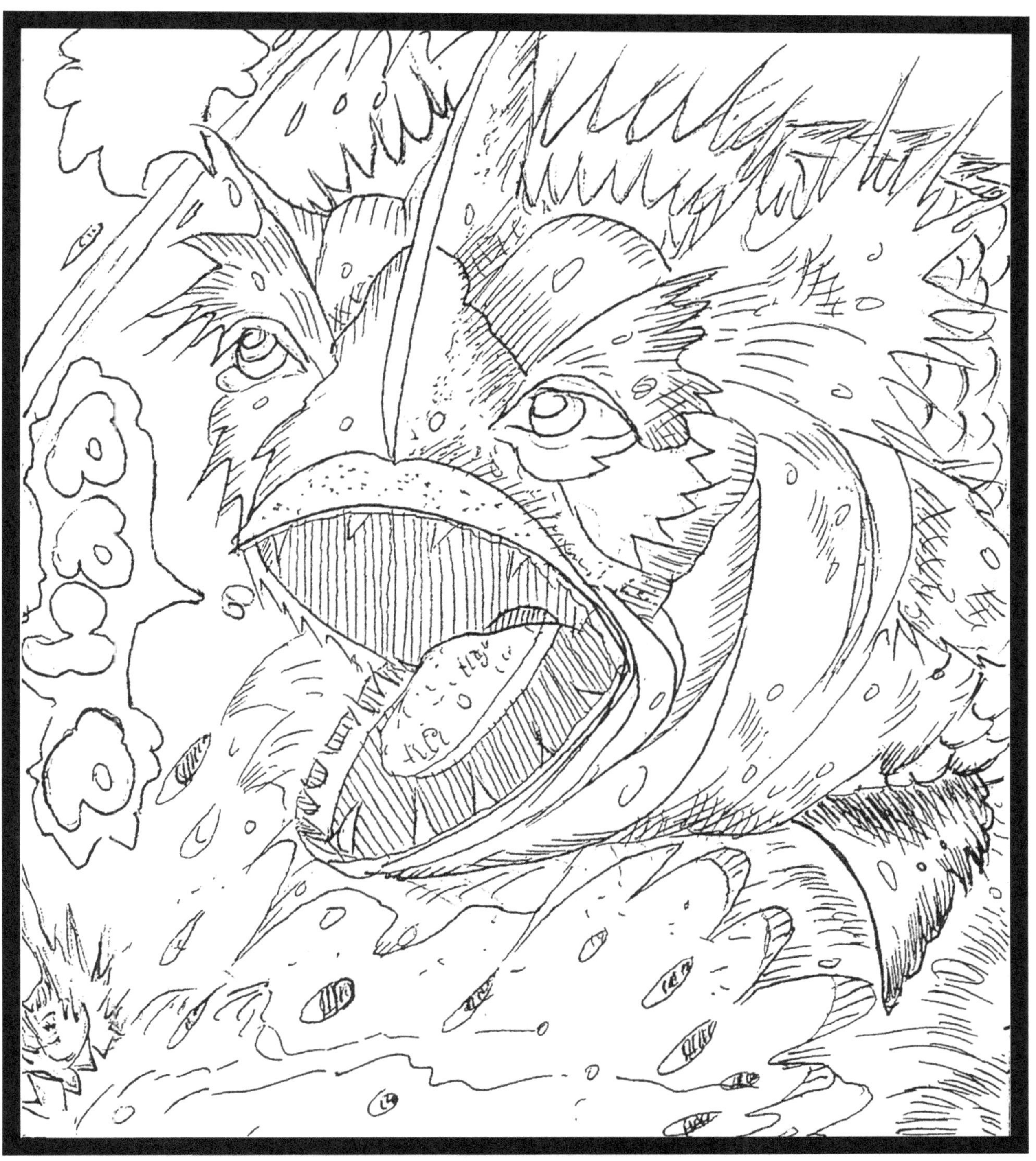

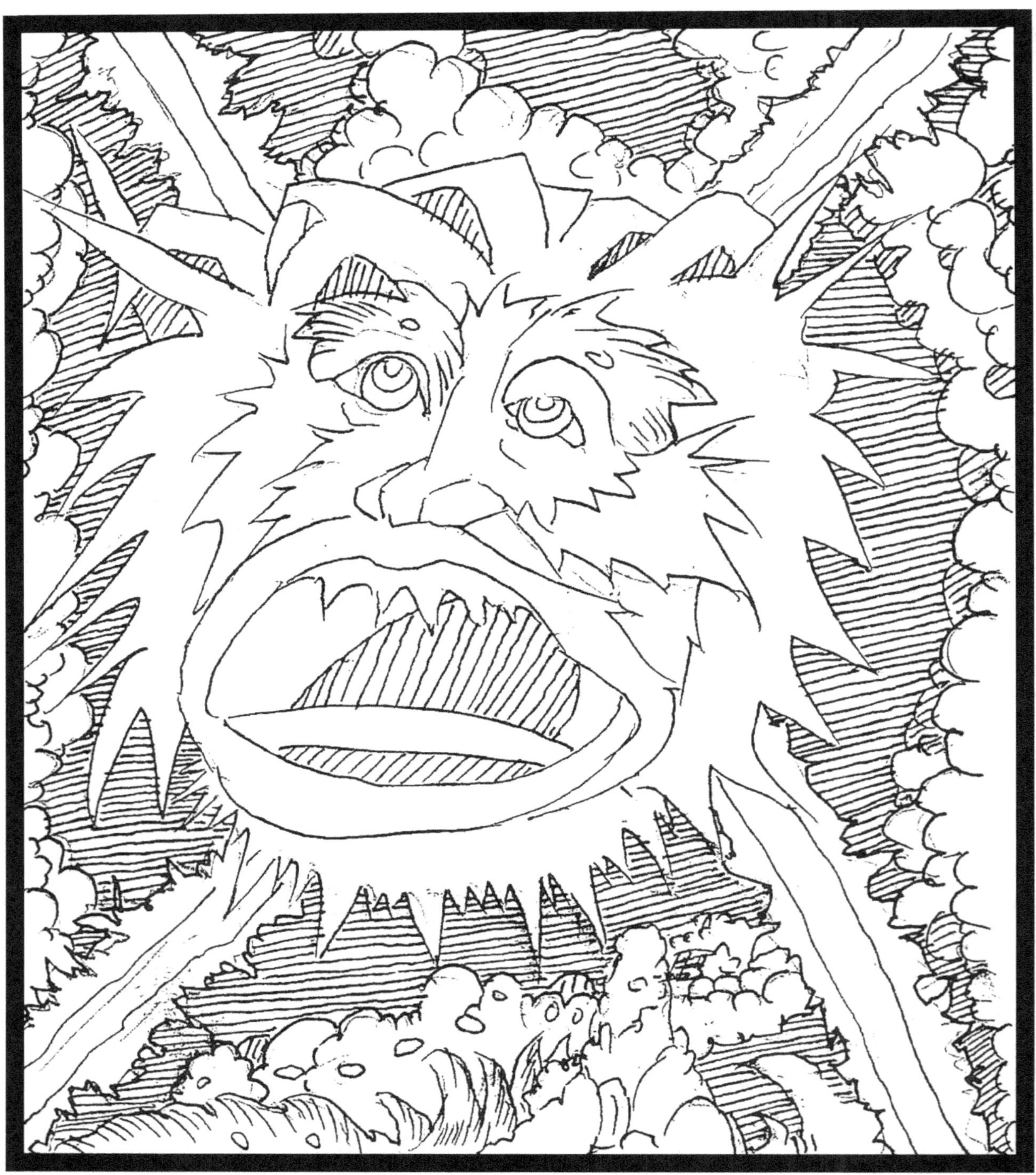

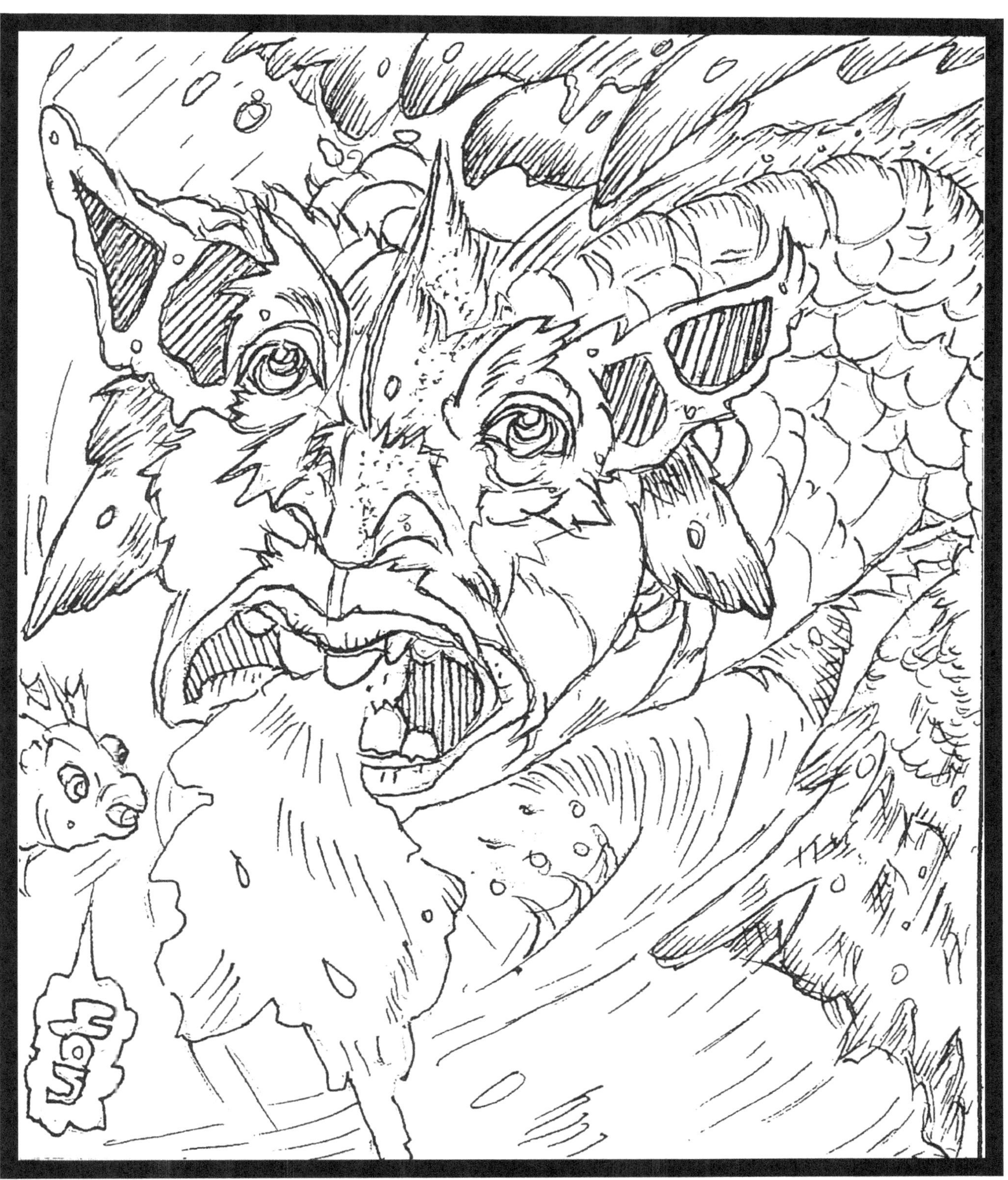

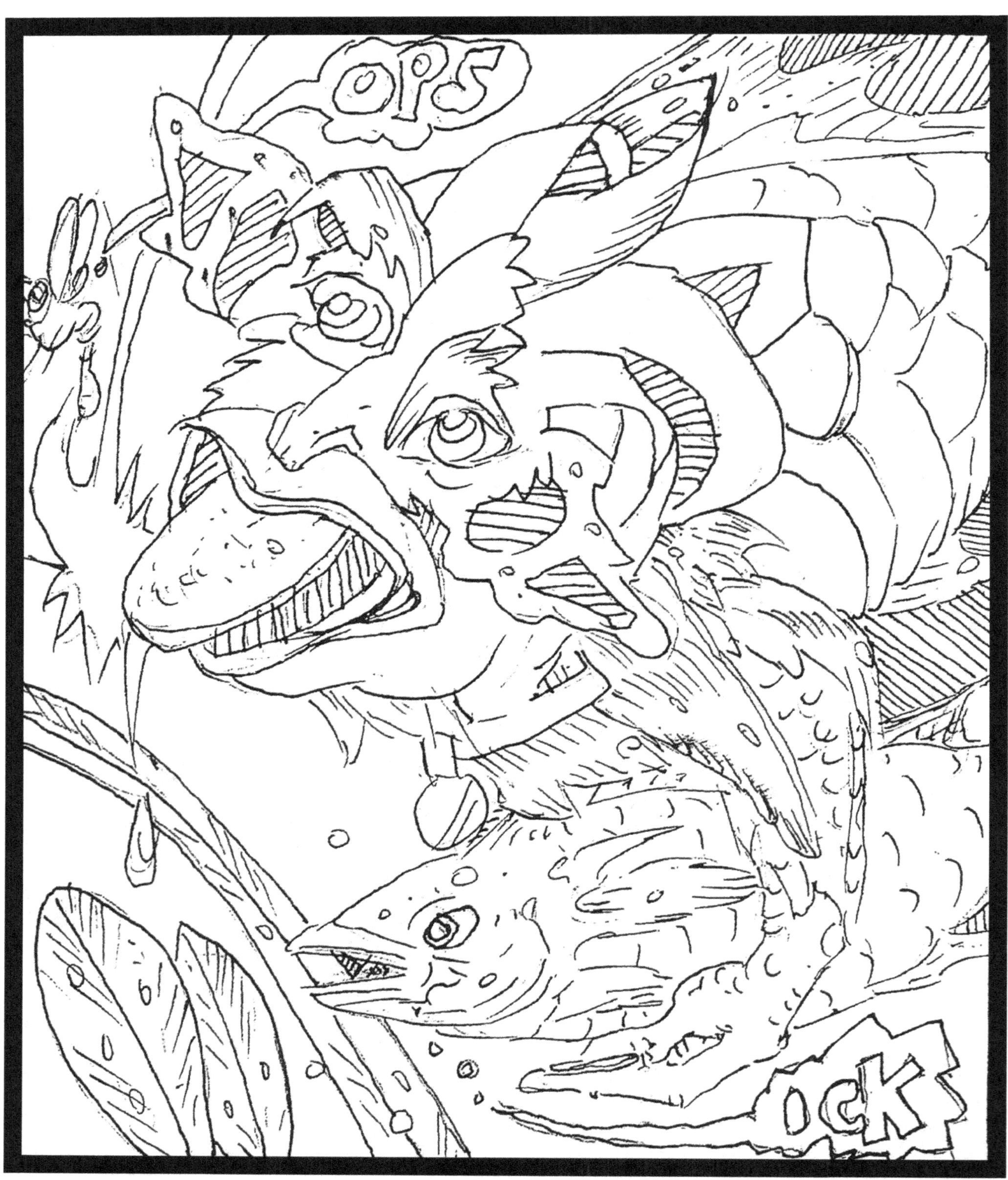
OPS
OCK

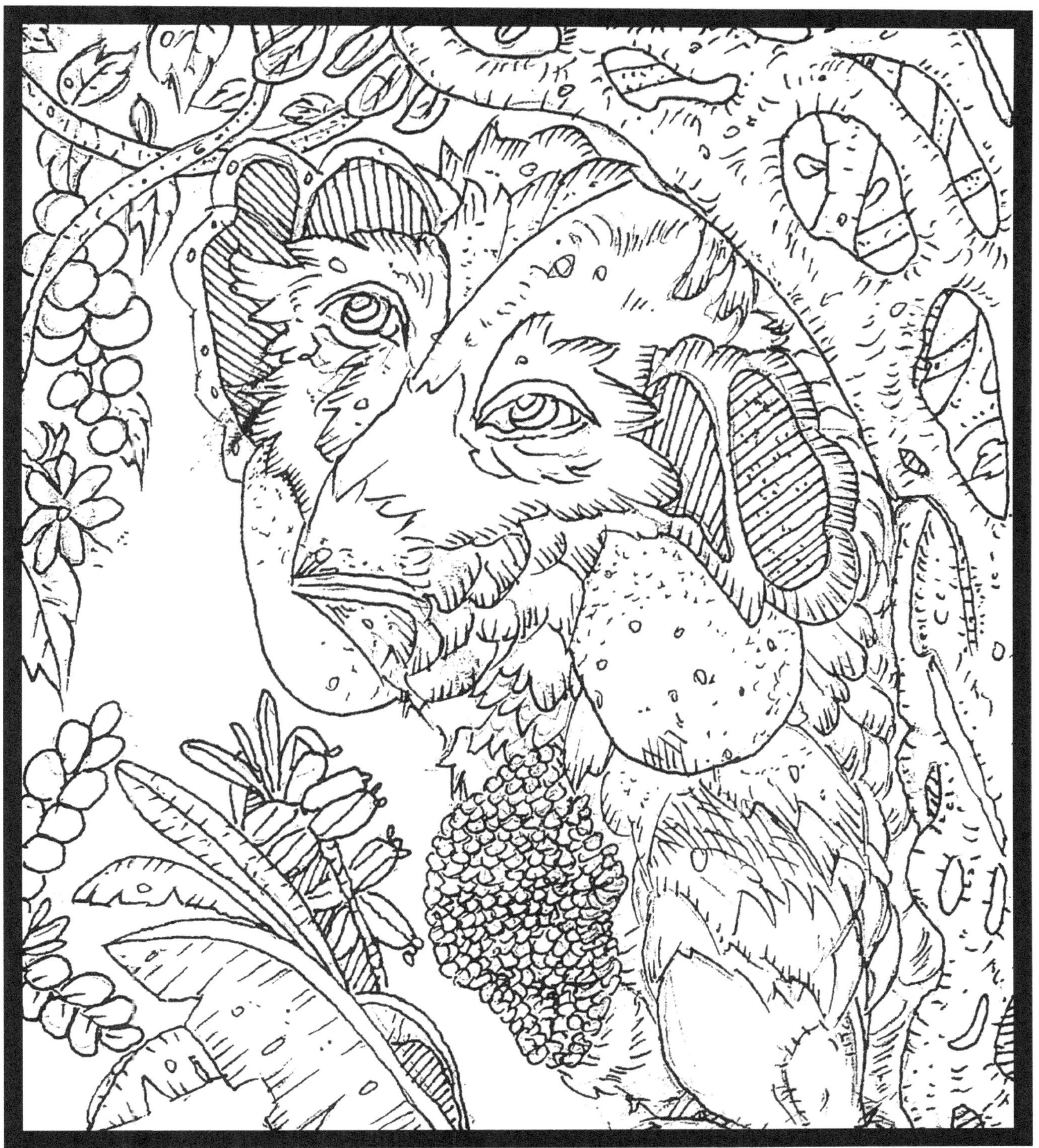

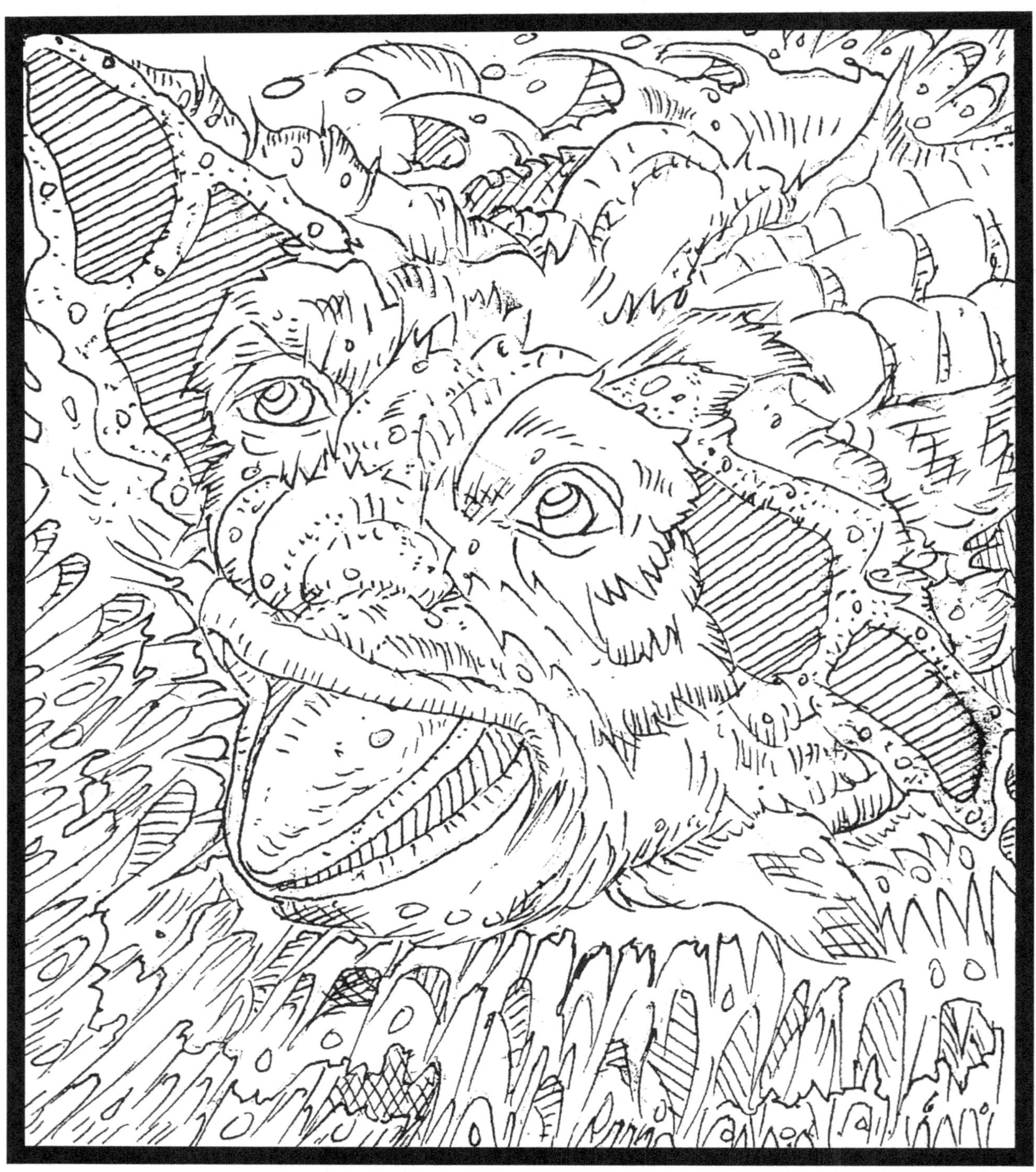

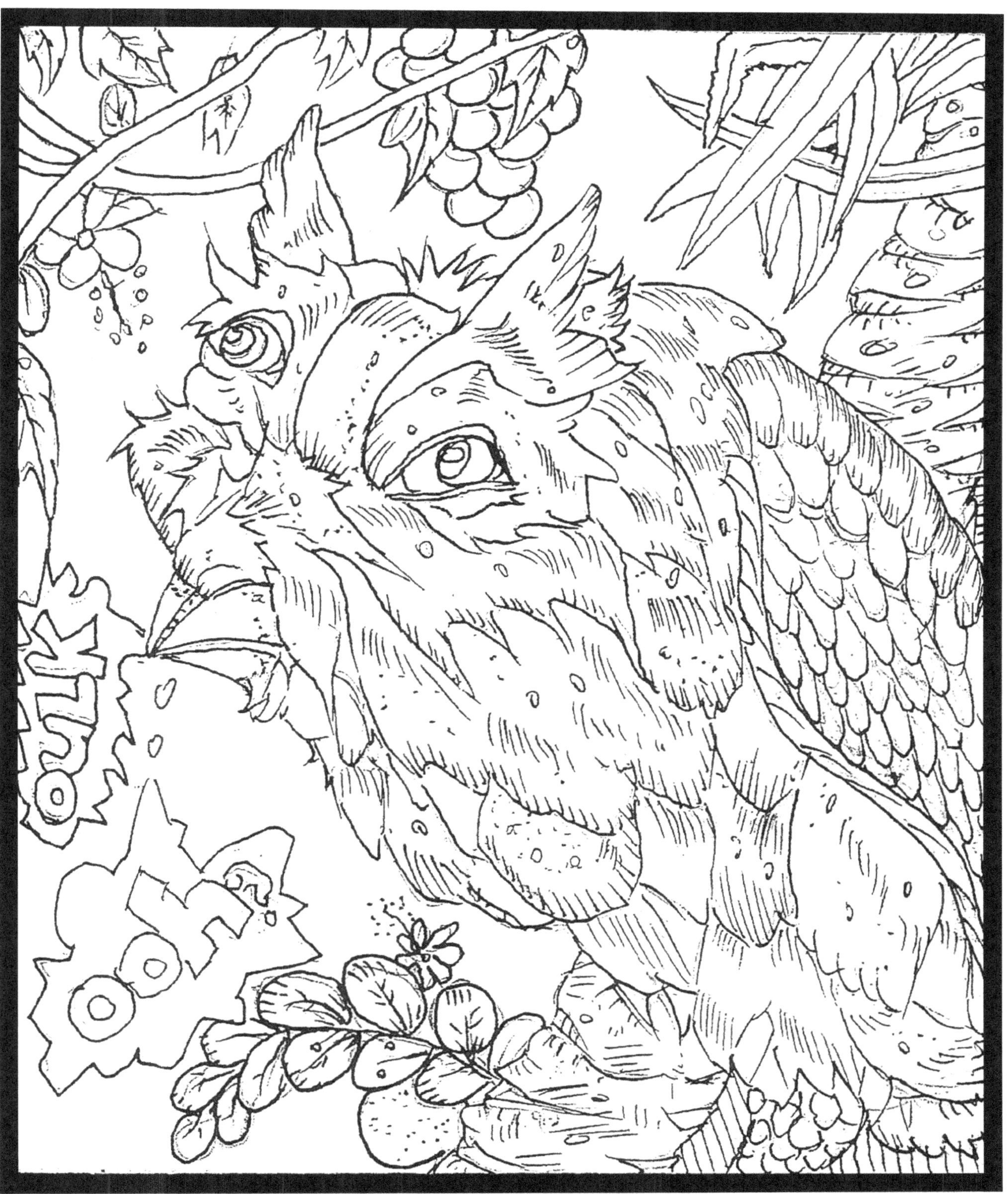

151

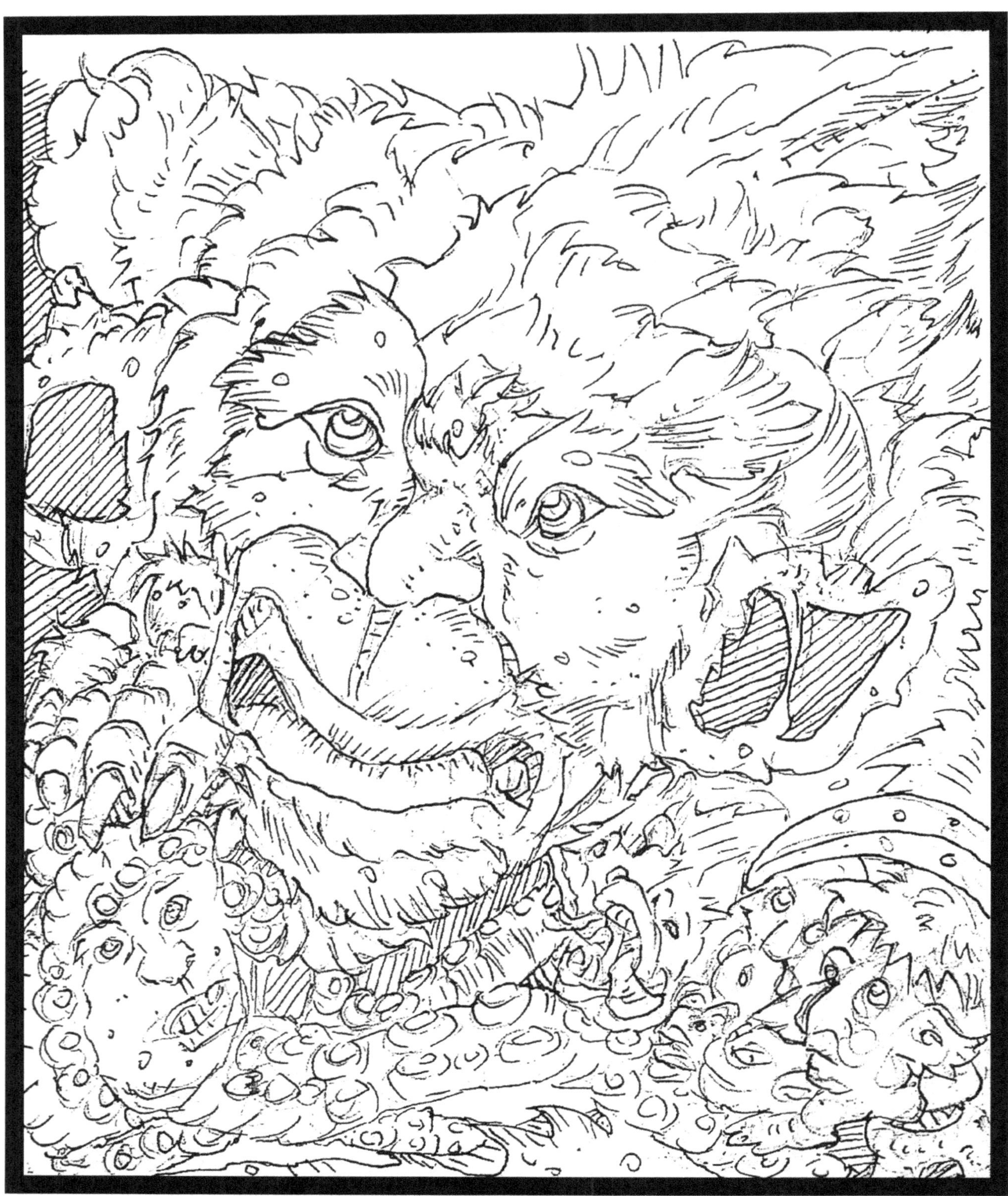

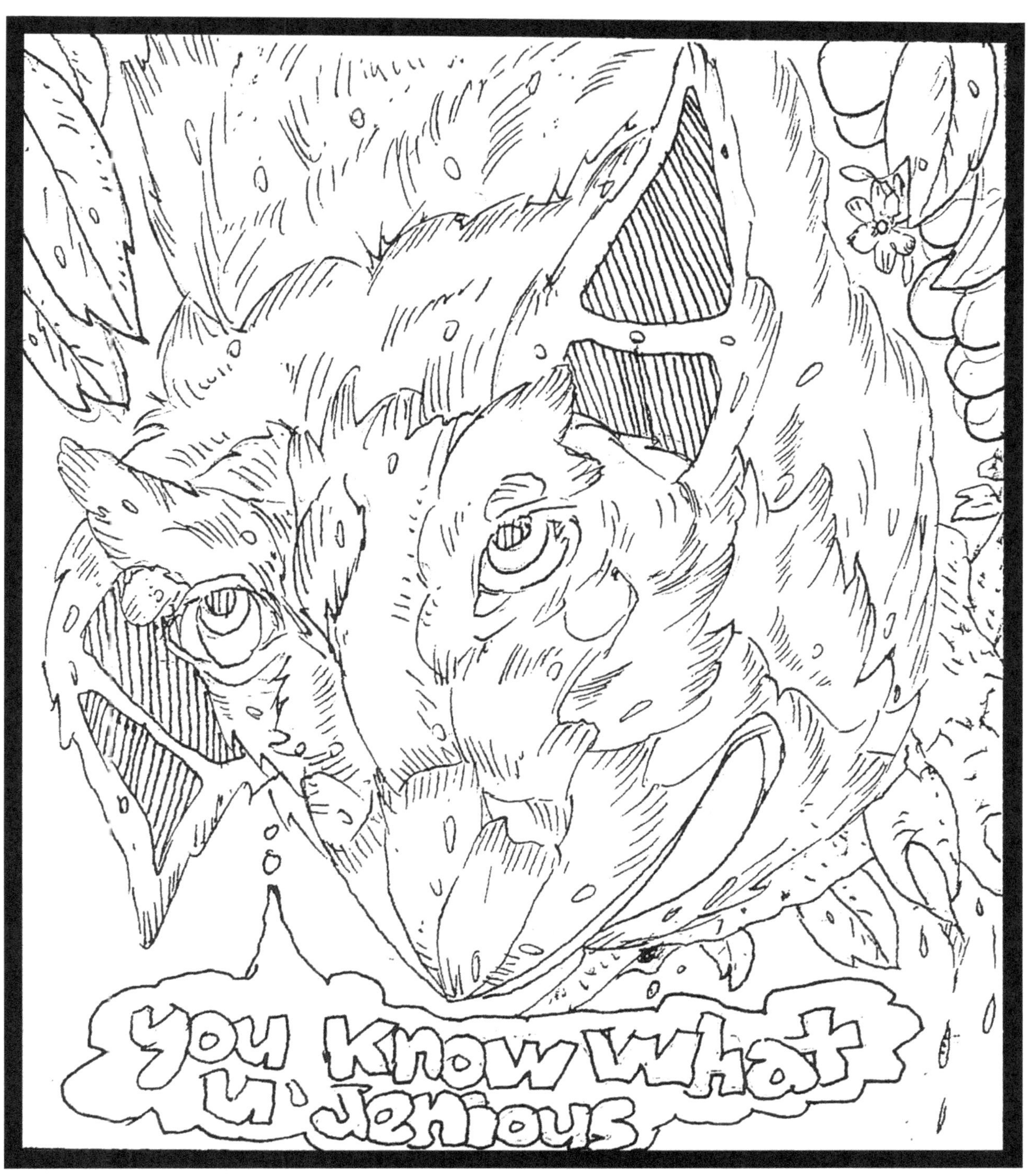

YOU KNOW WHAT
U JENIOUS

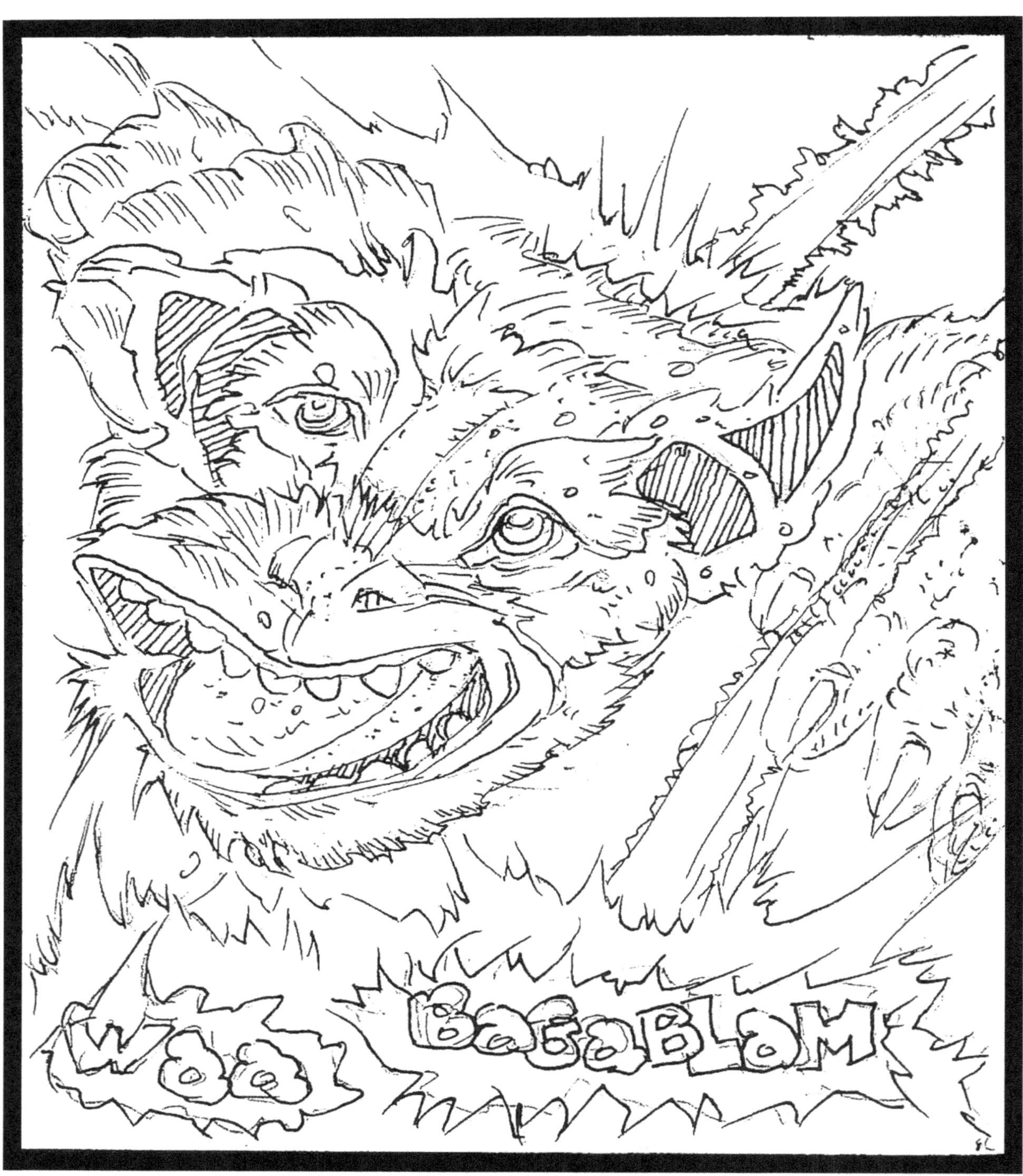

WOA
BASABLAM

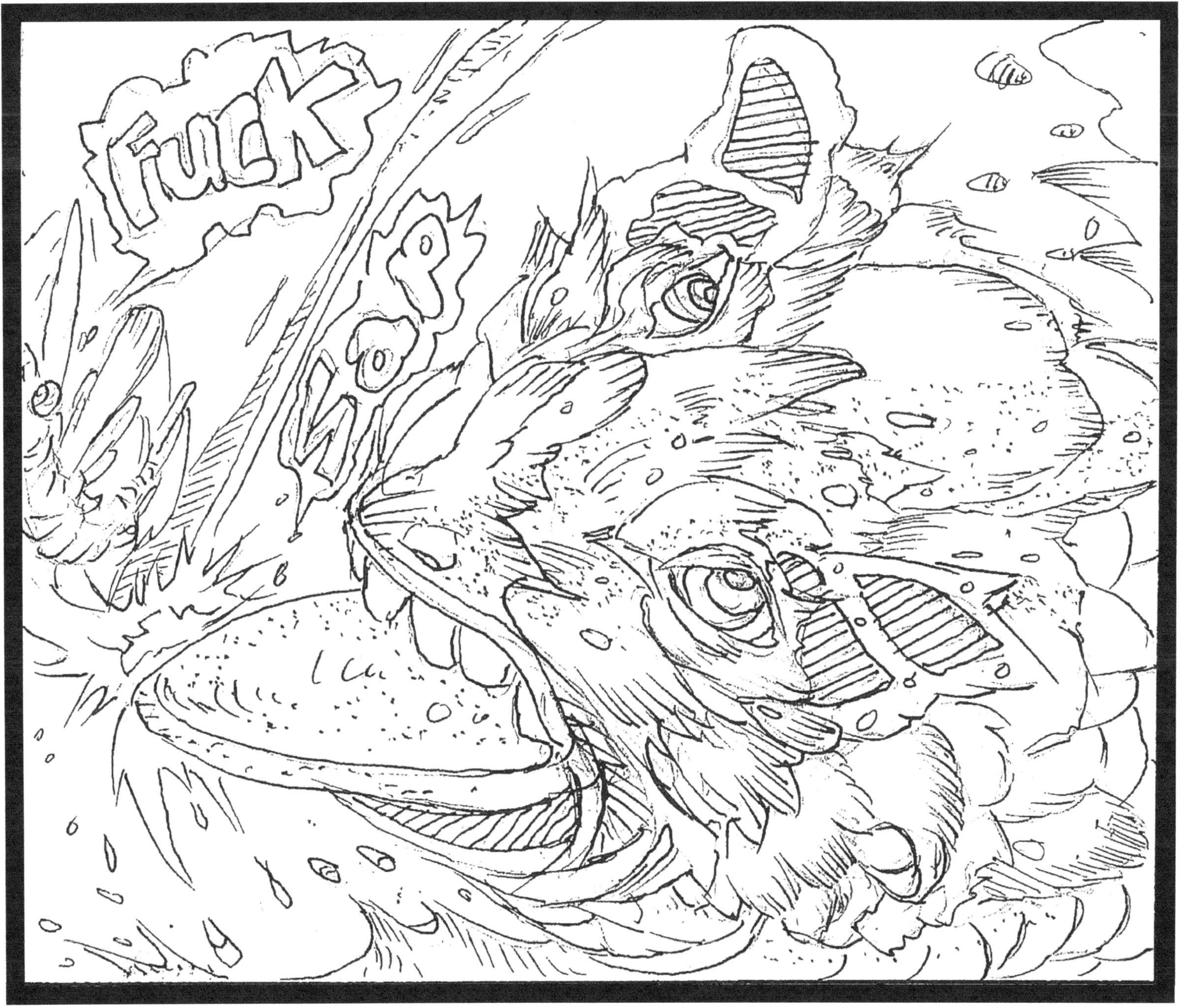
Fuck
Sap

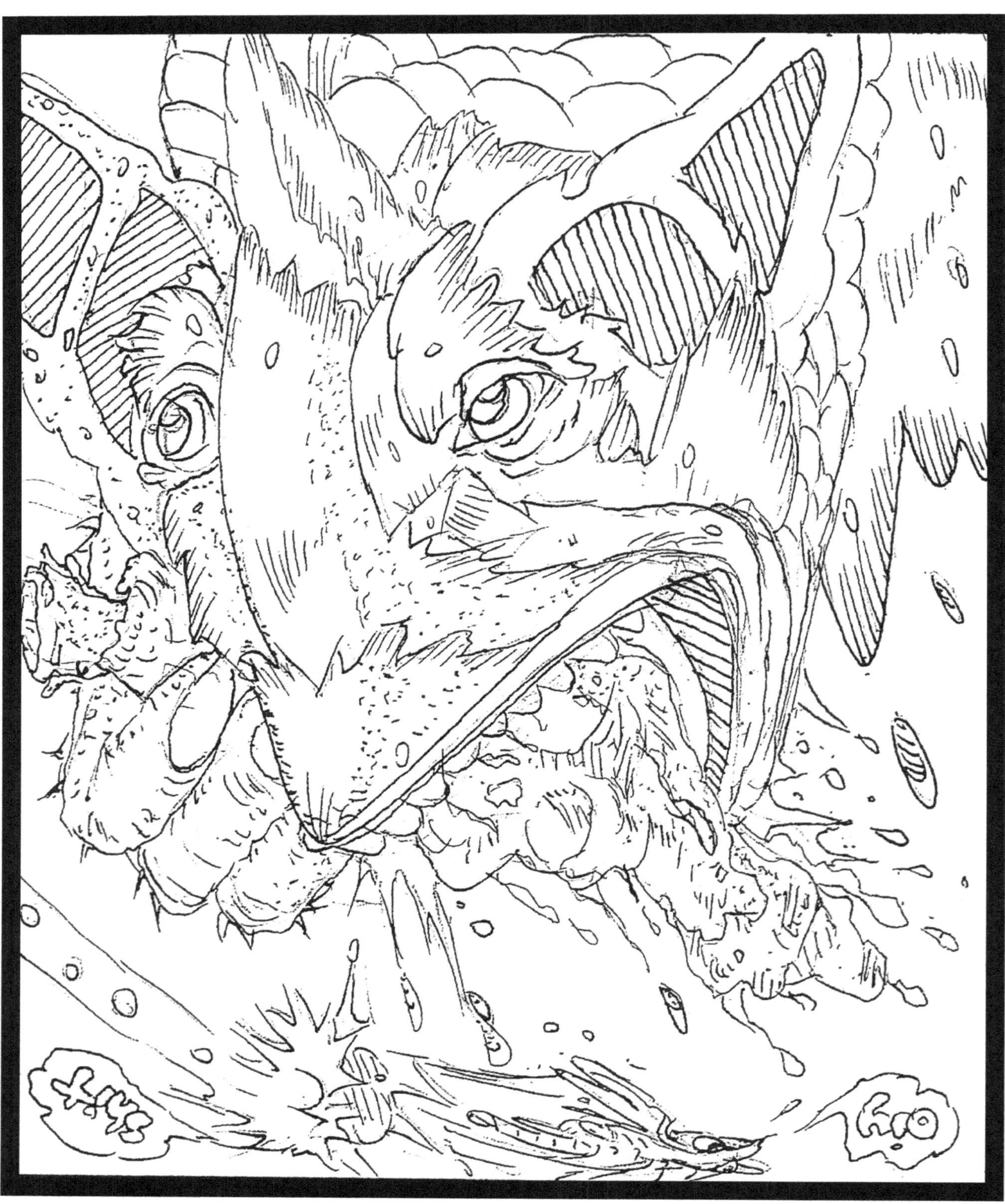

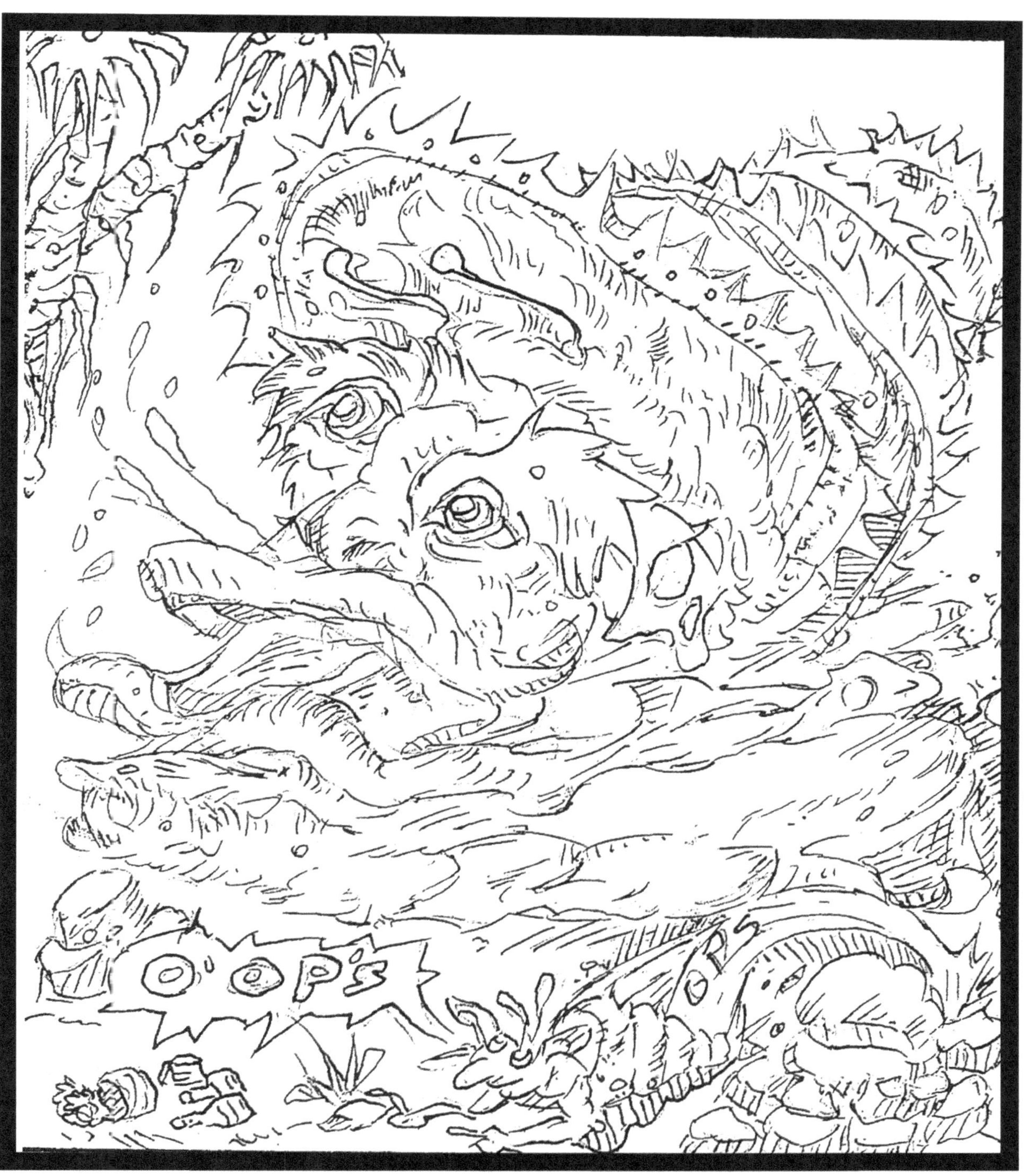
OOPS
OOPS

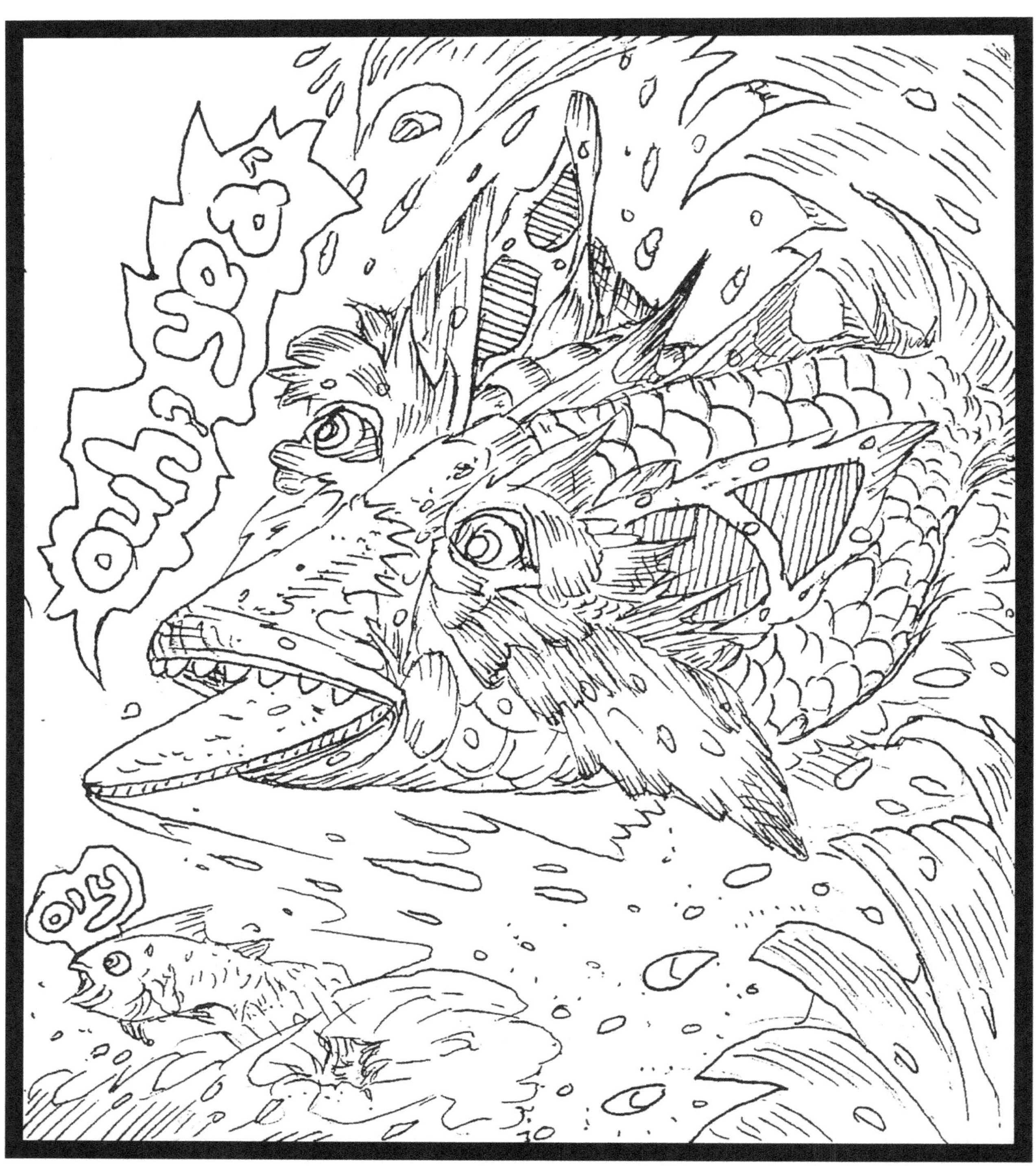
sea
ouh
glug

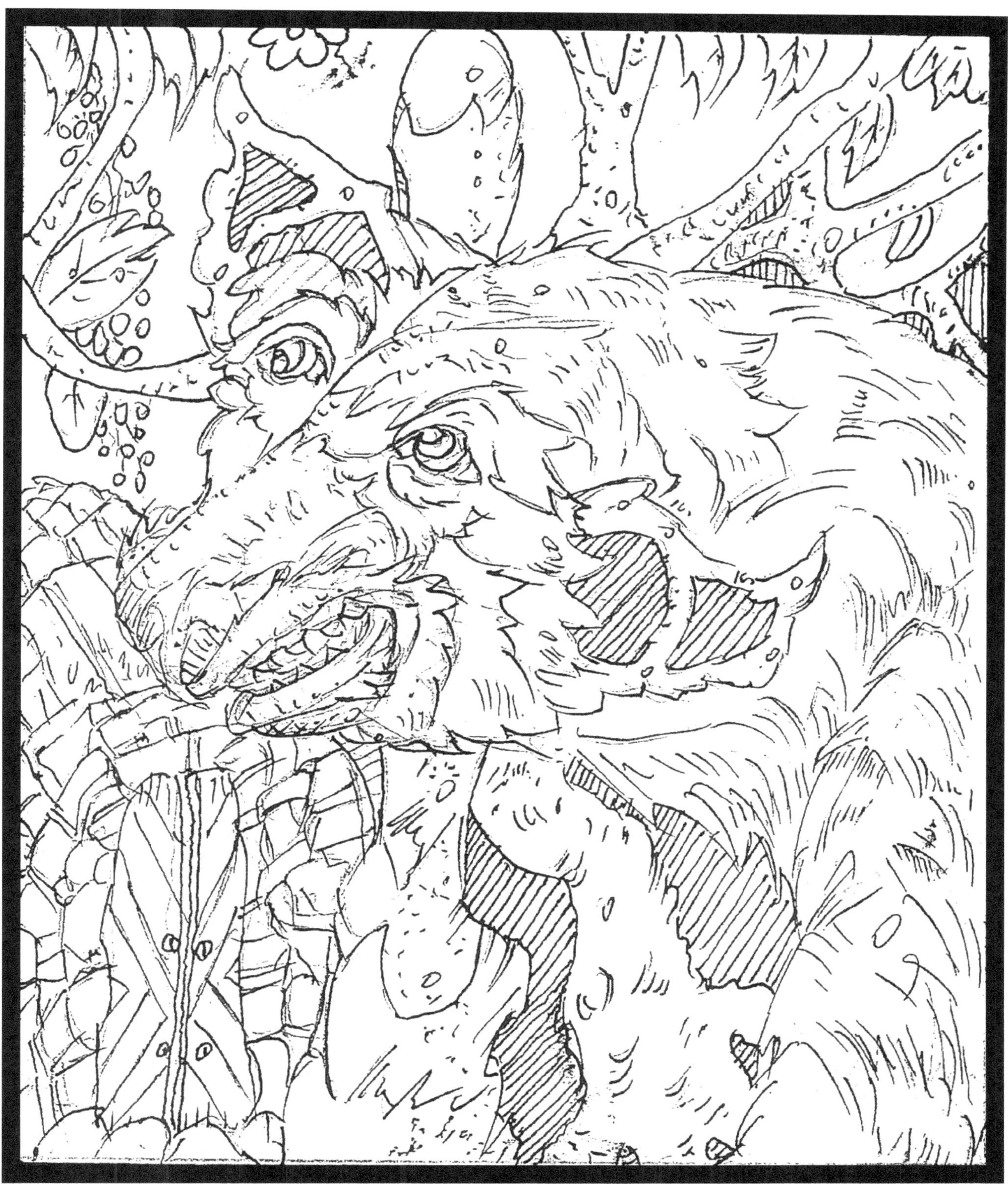

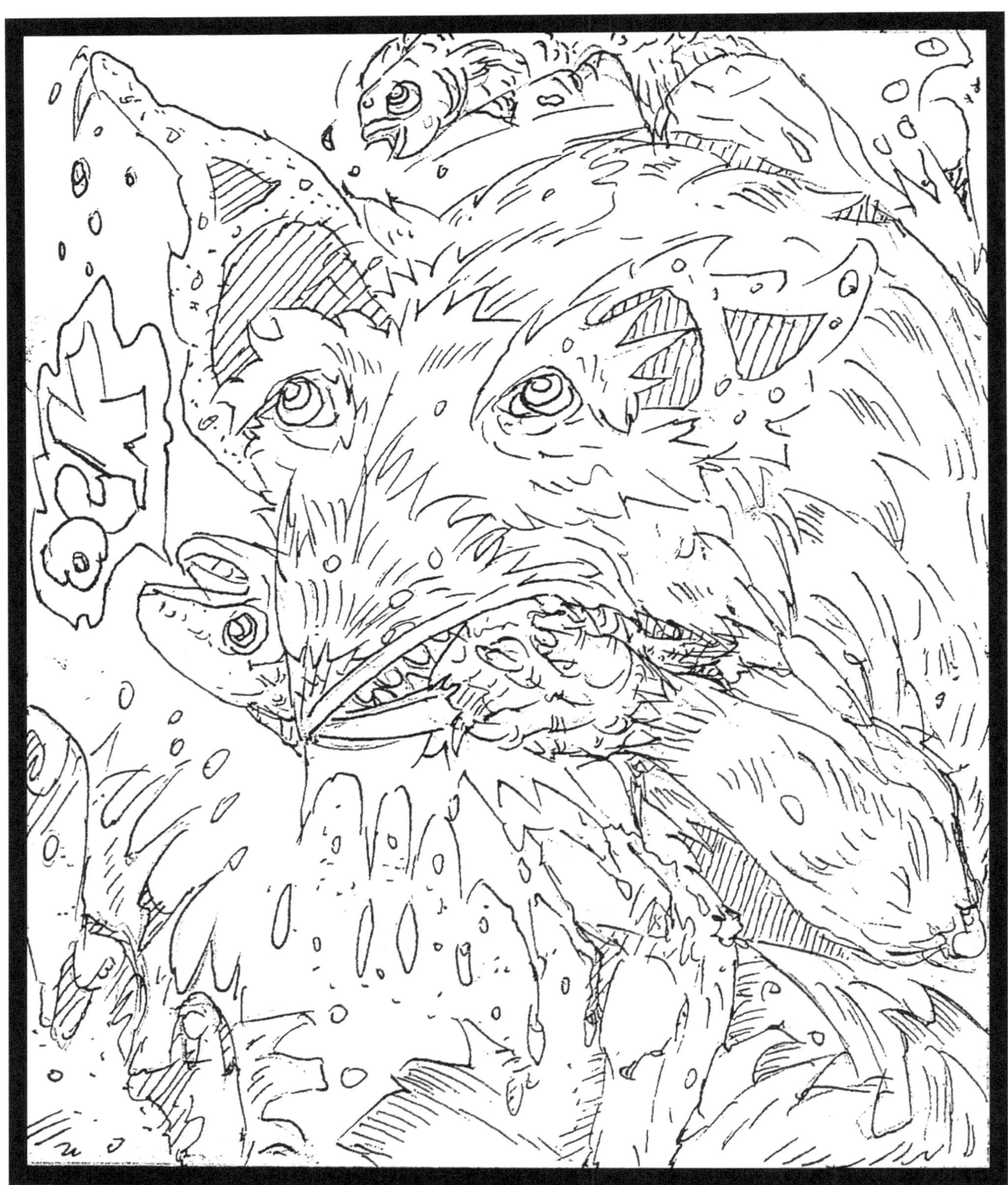

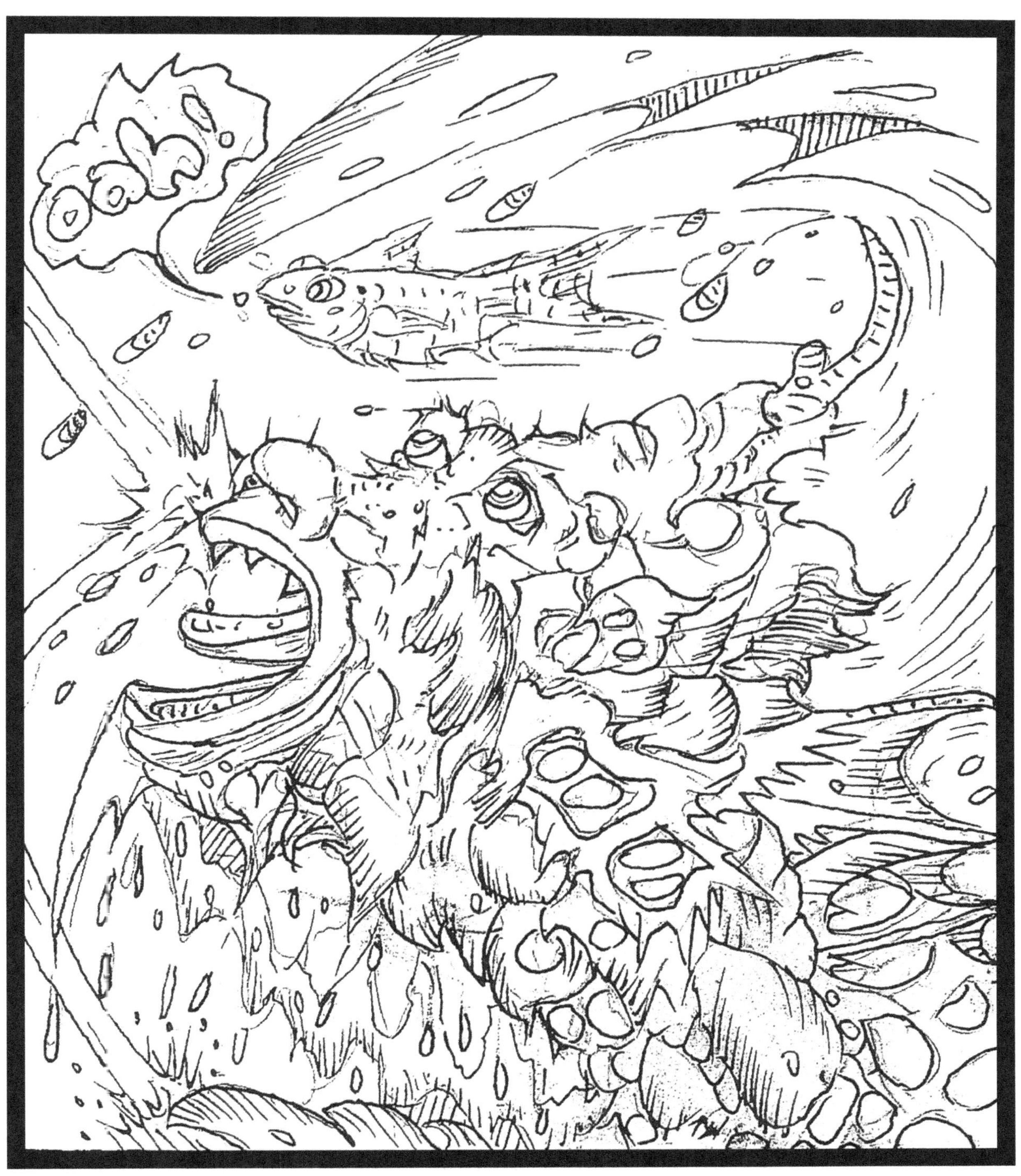

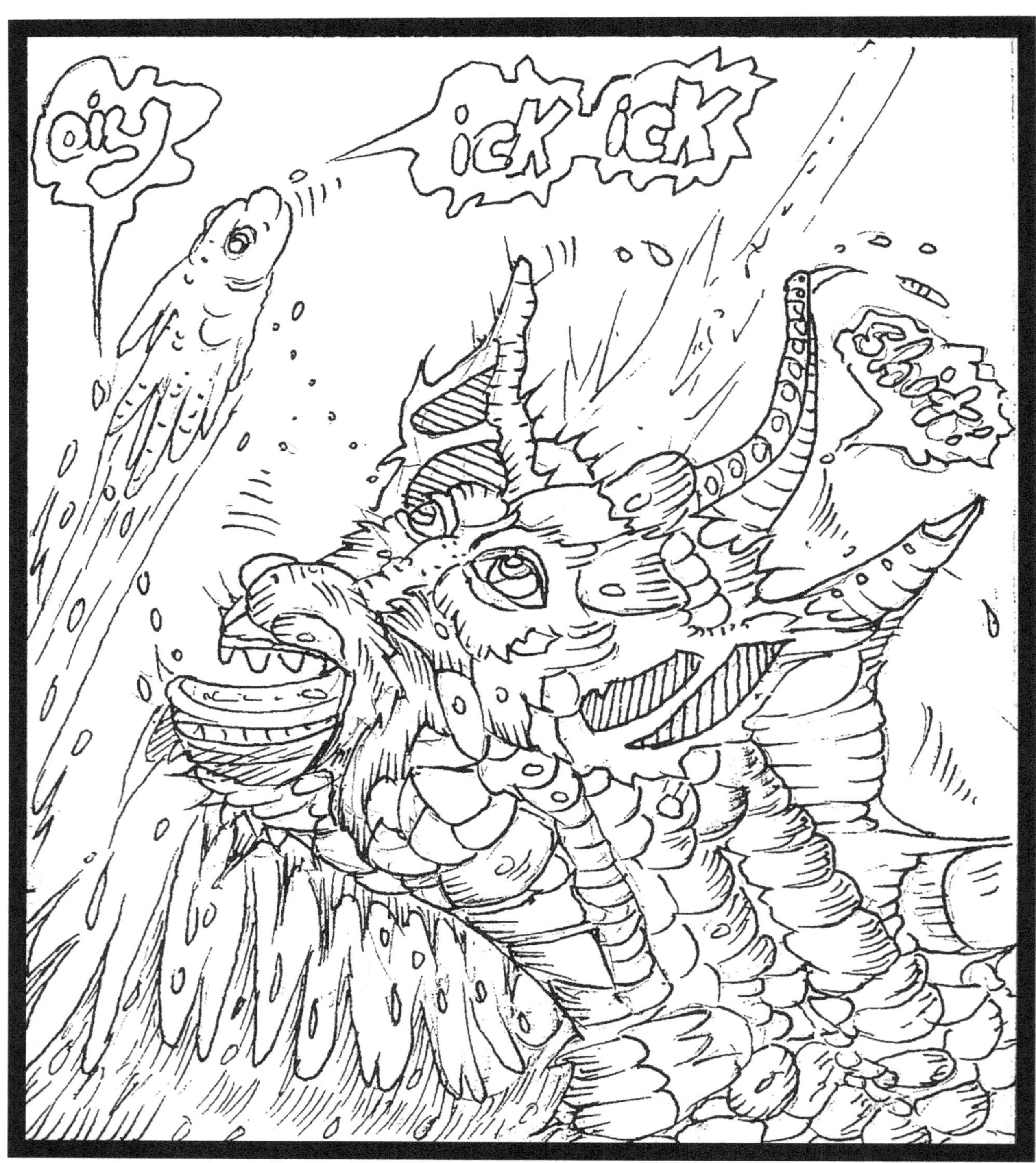

oily
ick ick
blatt

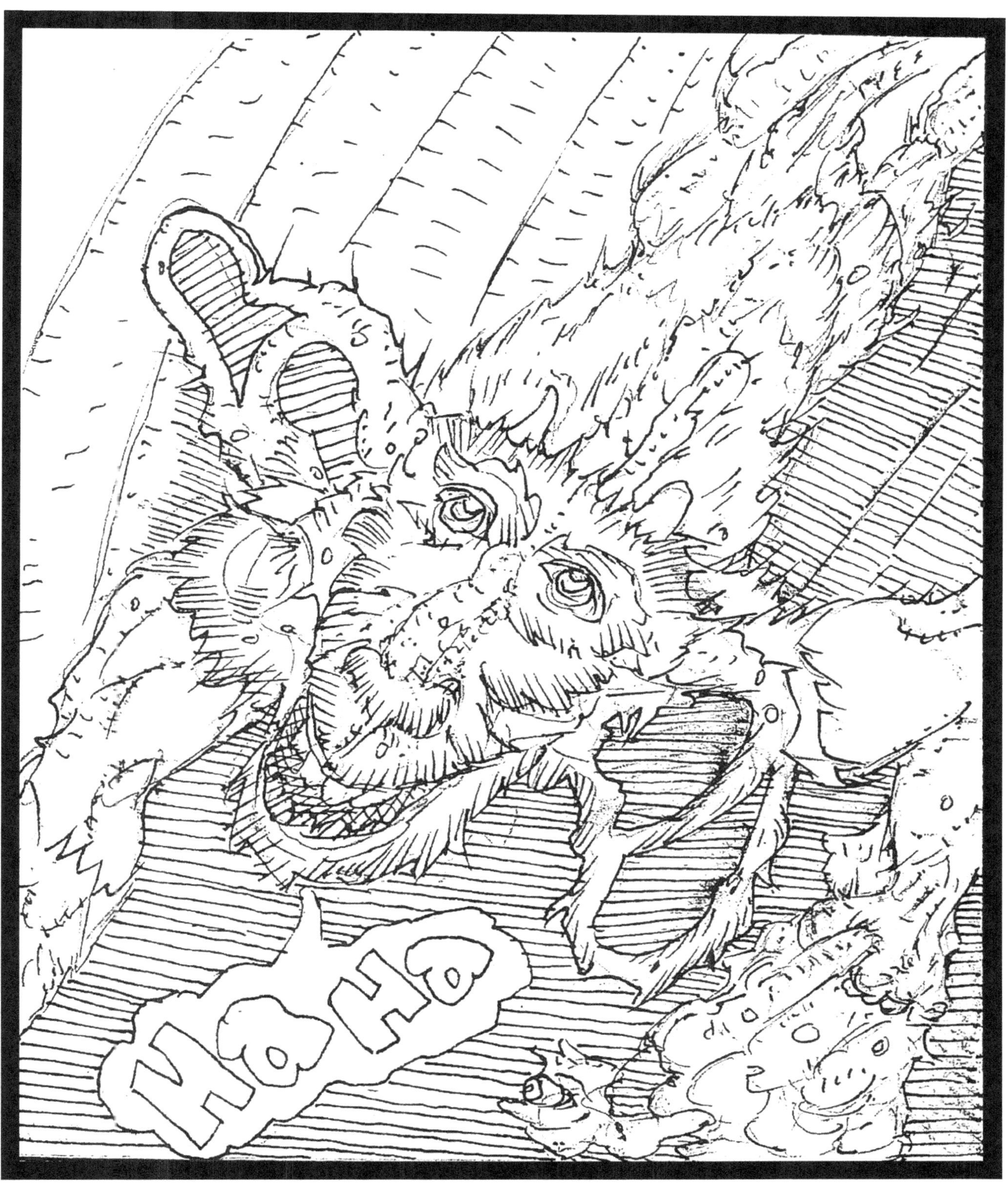
Ha Ha

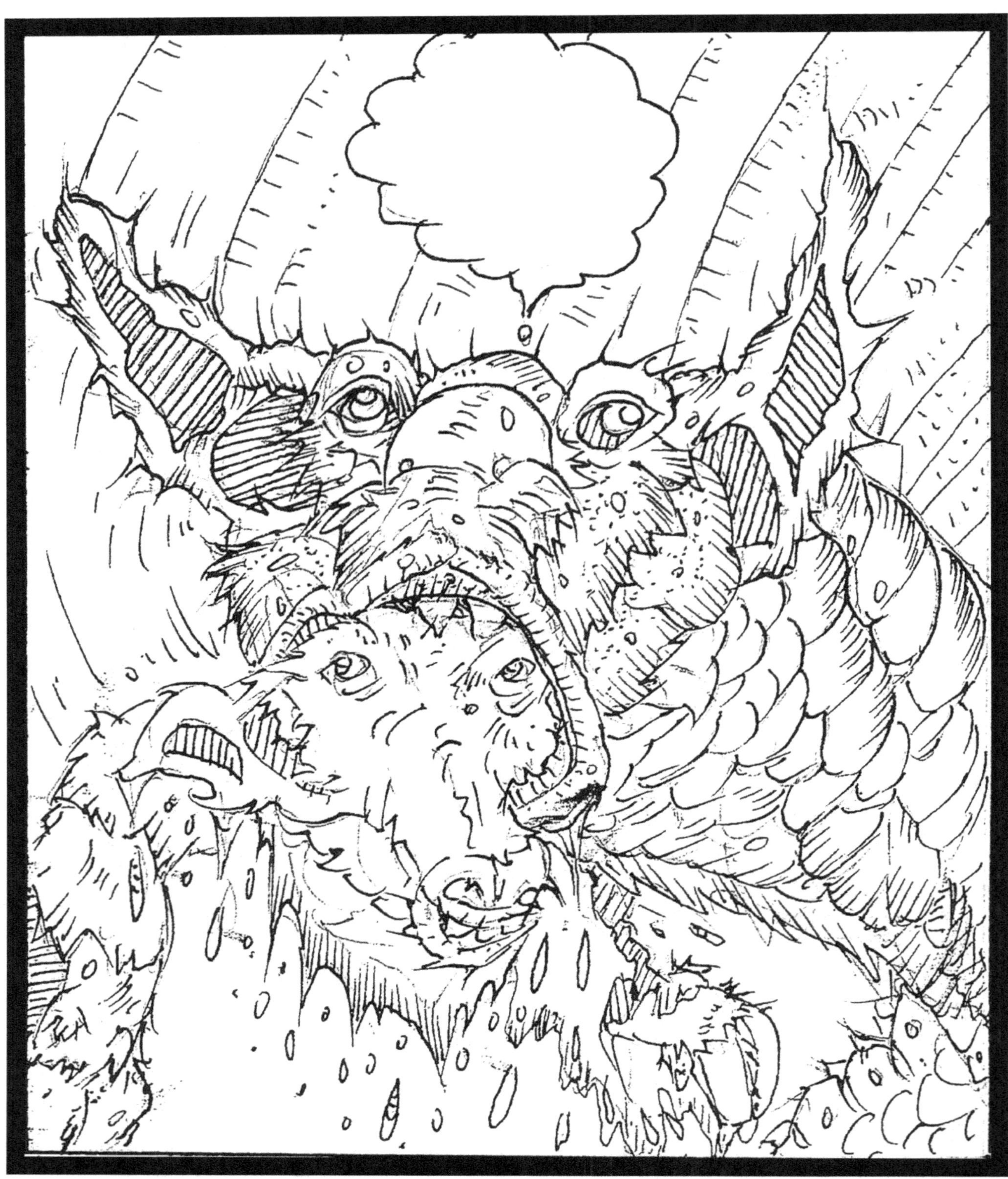

4000 YEARS AGO THERE WAS AN EPISODE WHICH SHOWED DIFFERENT LIVING THINGS THAT ROAMED ON EARTH. COULD THAT BE CALLED AN ALIEN…?

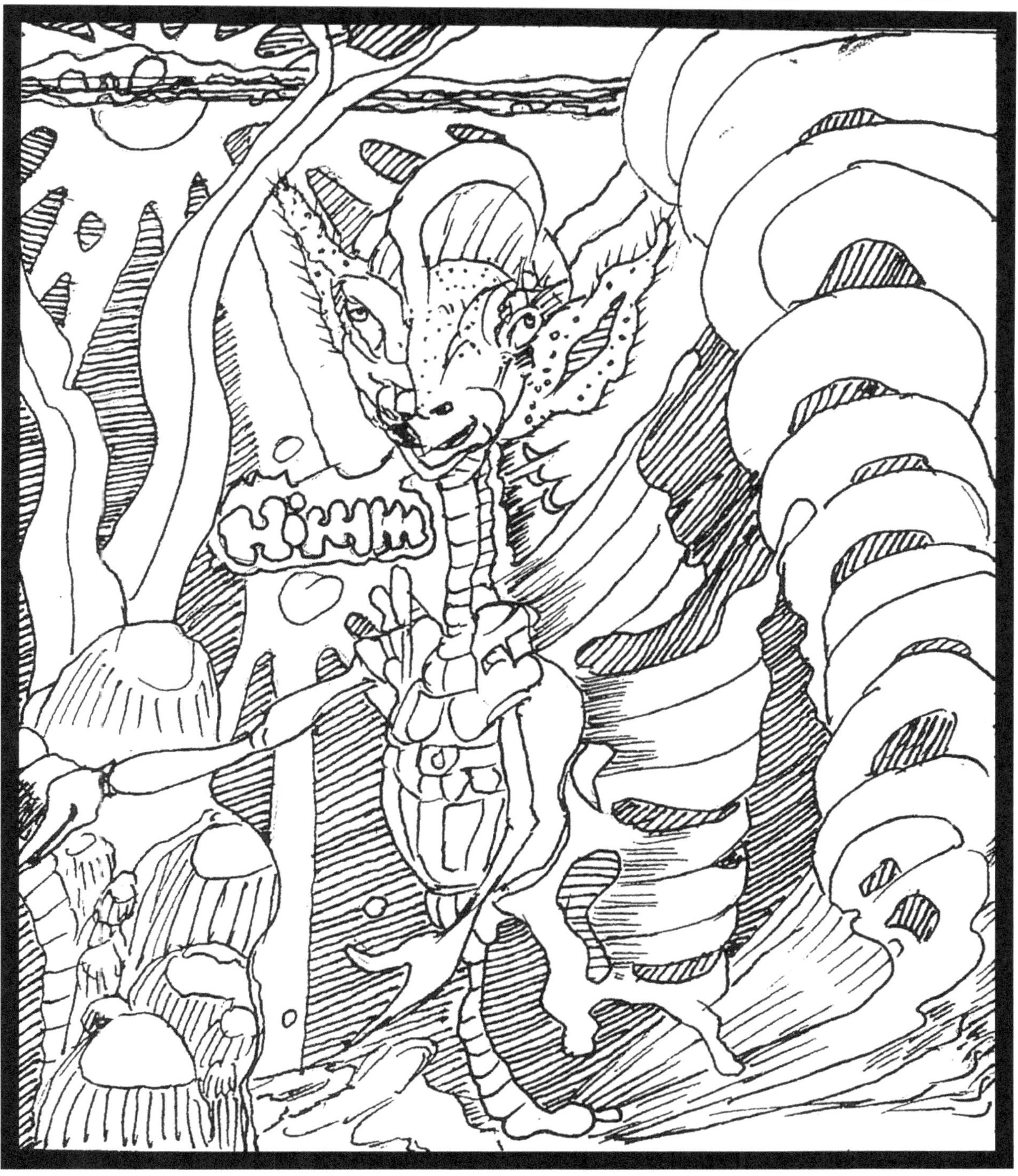

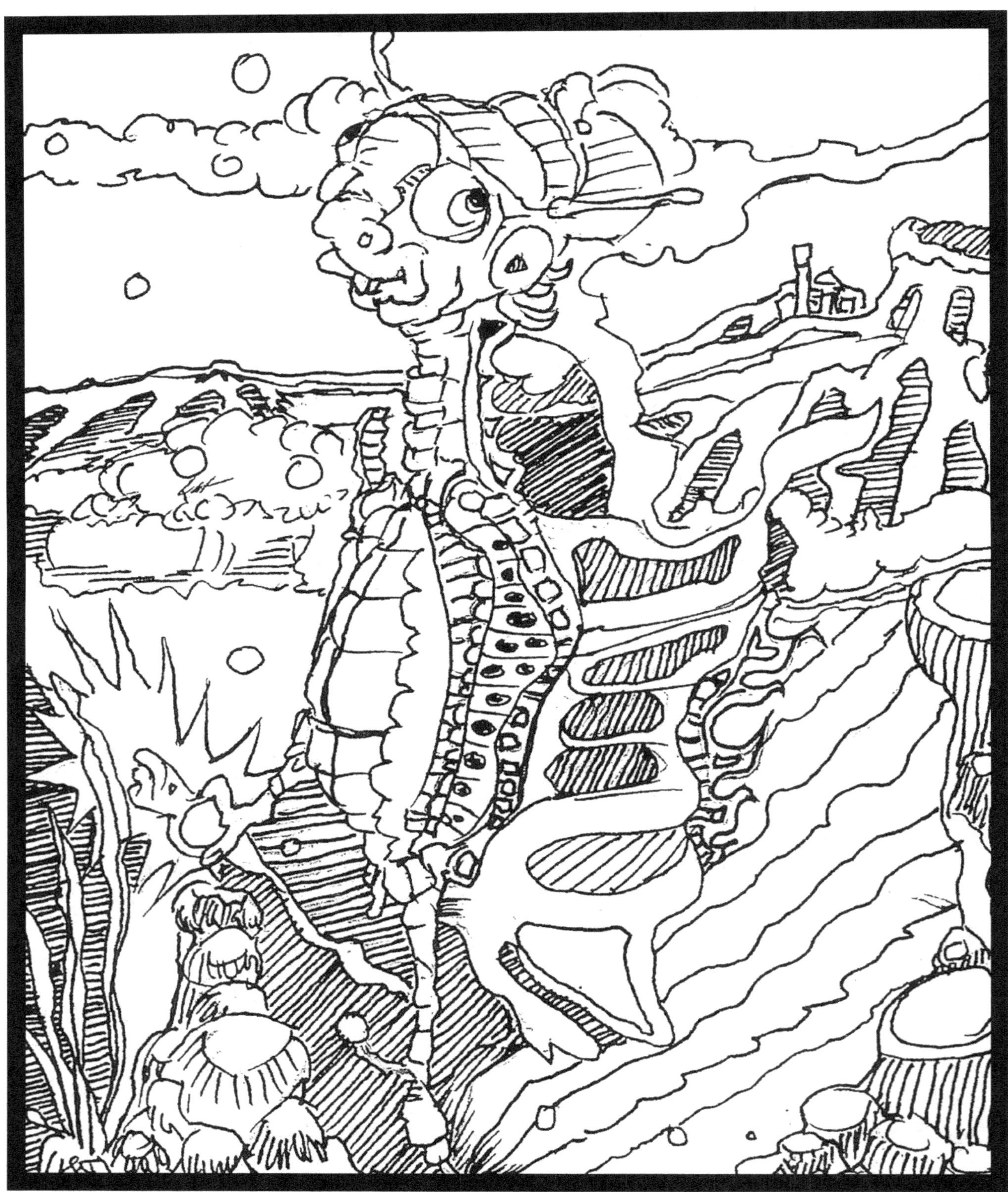

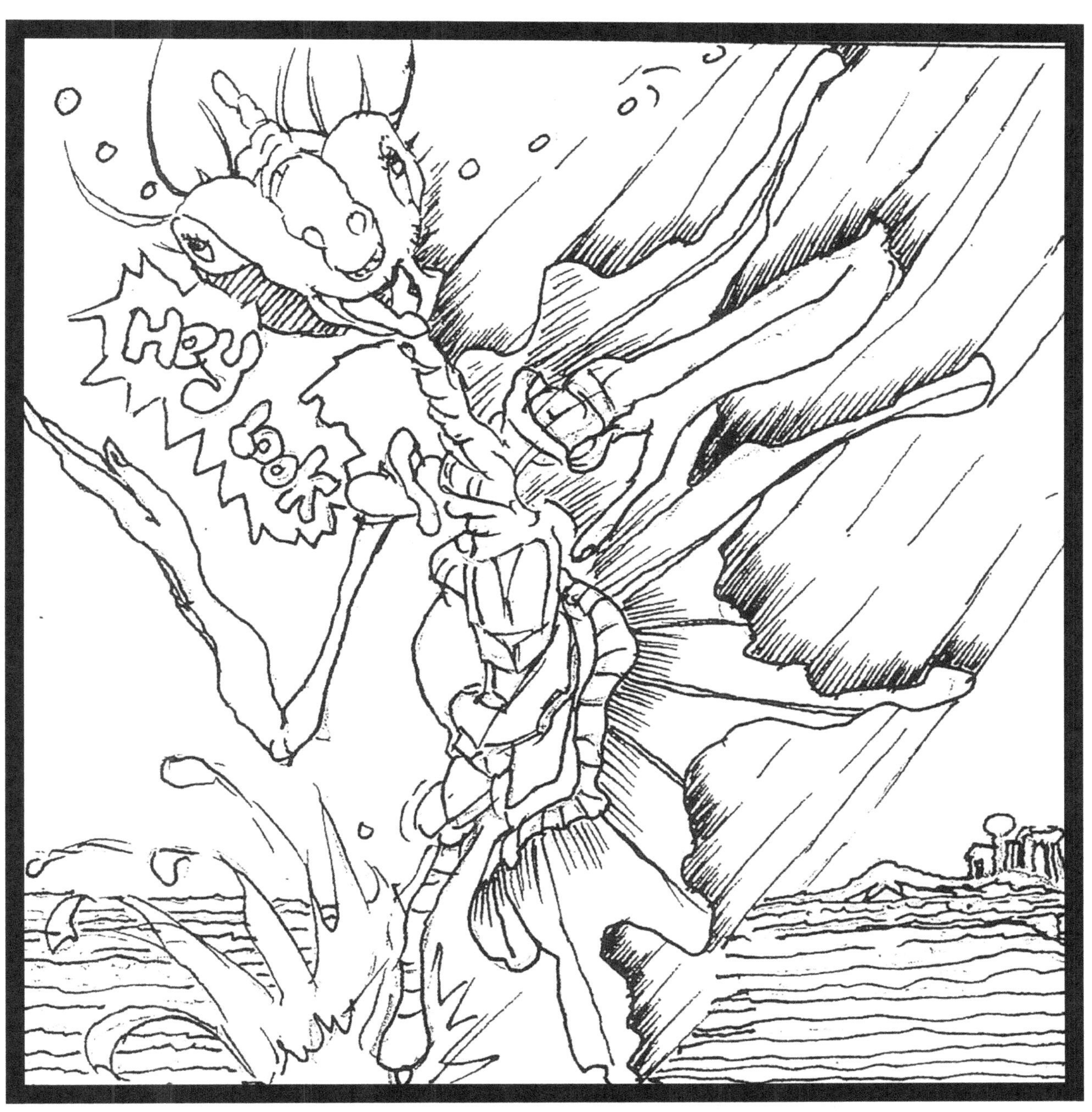

HEY
look

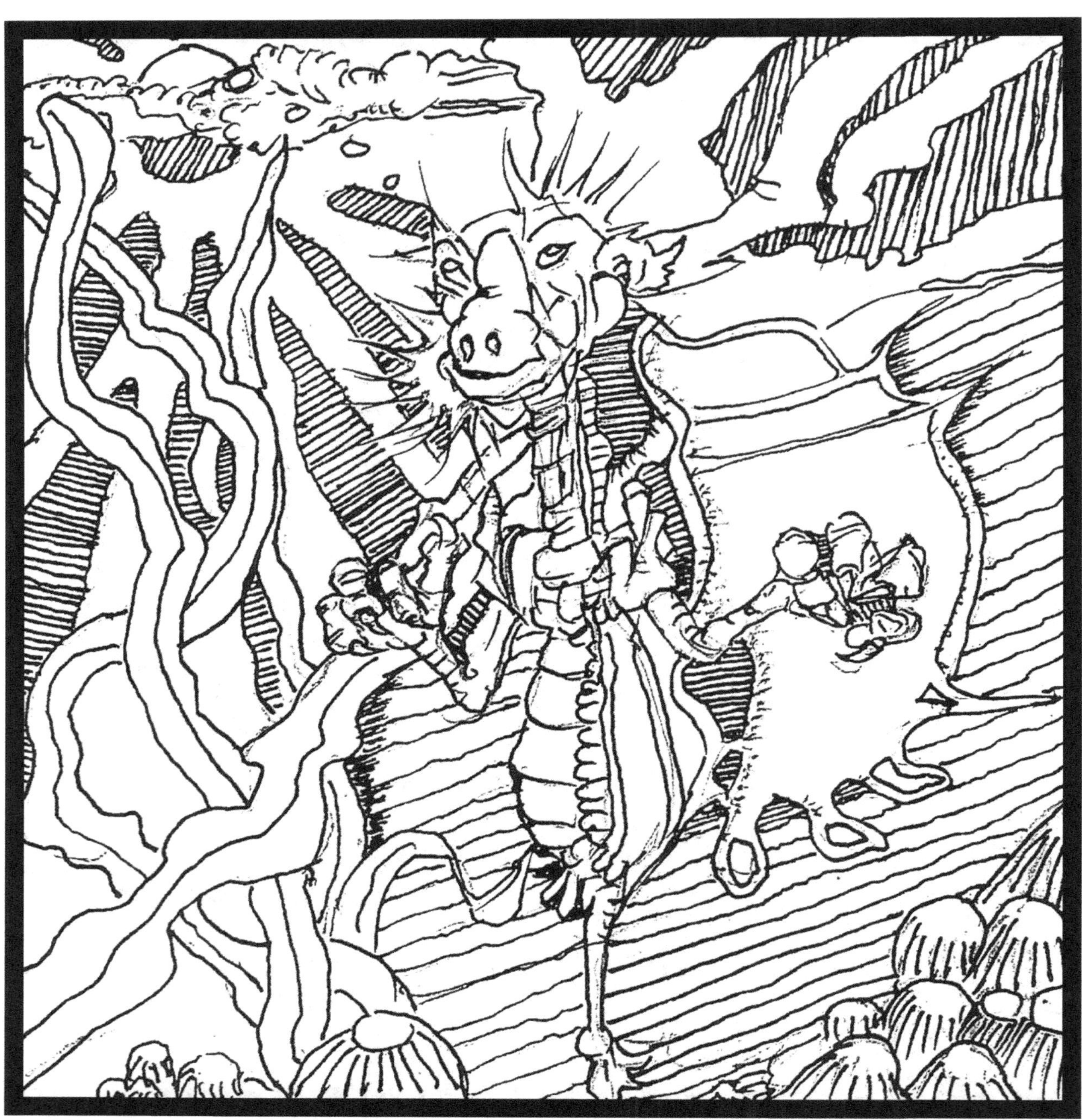

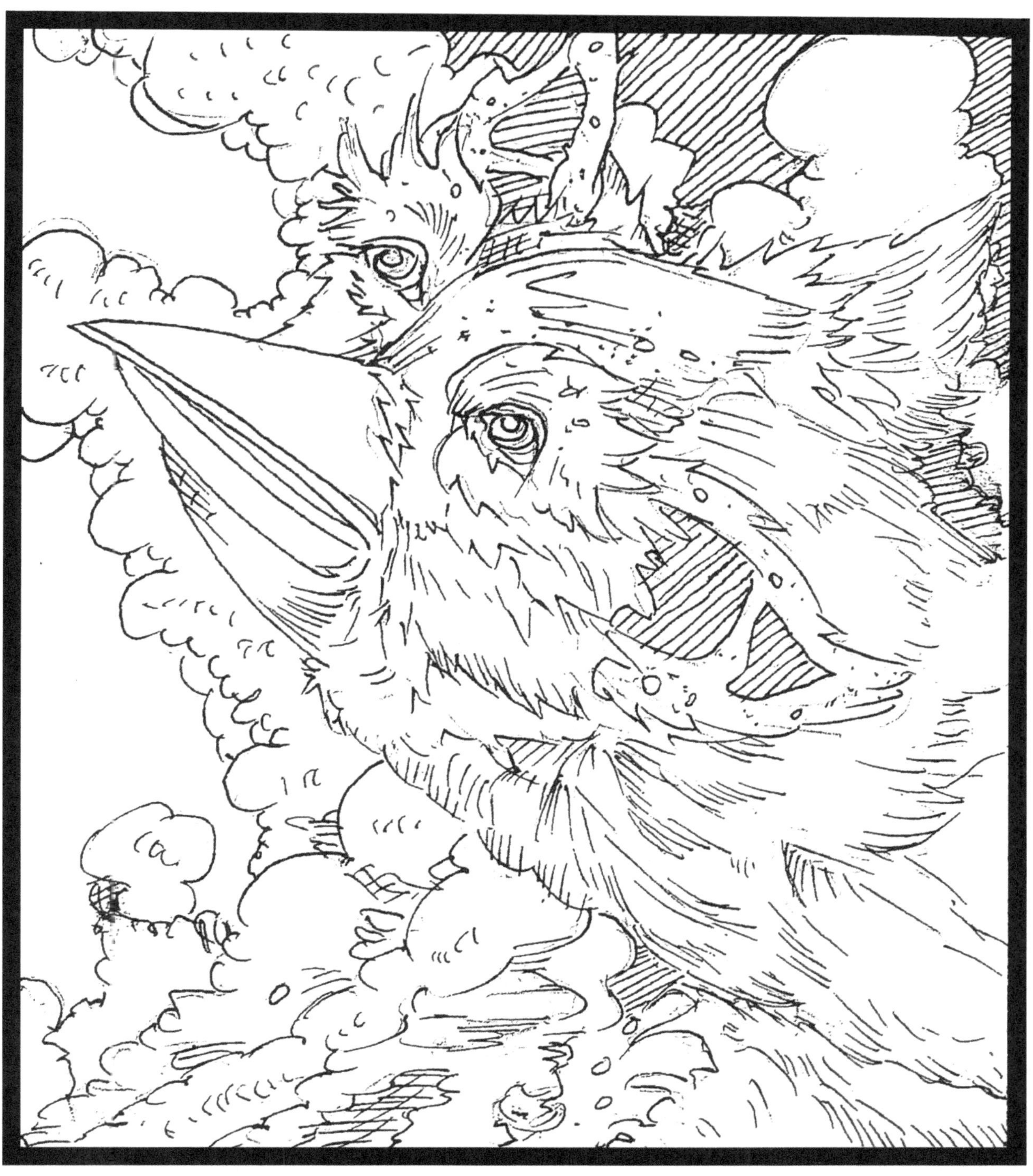

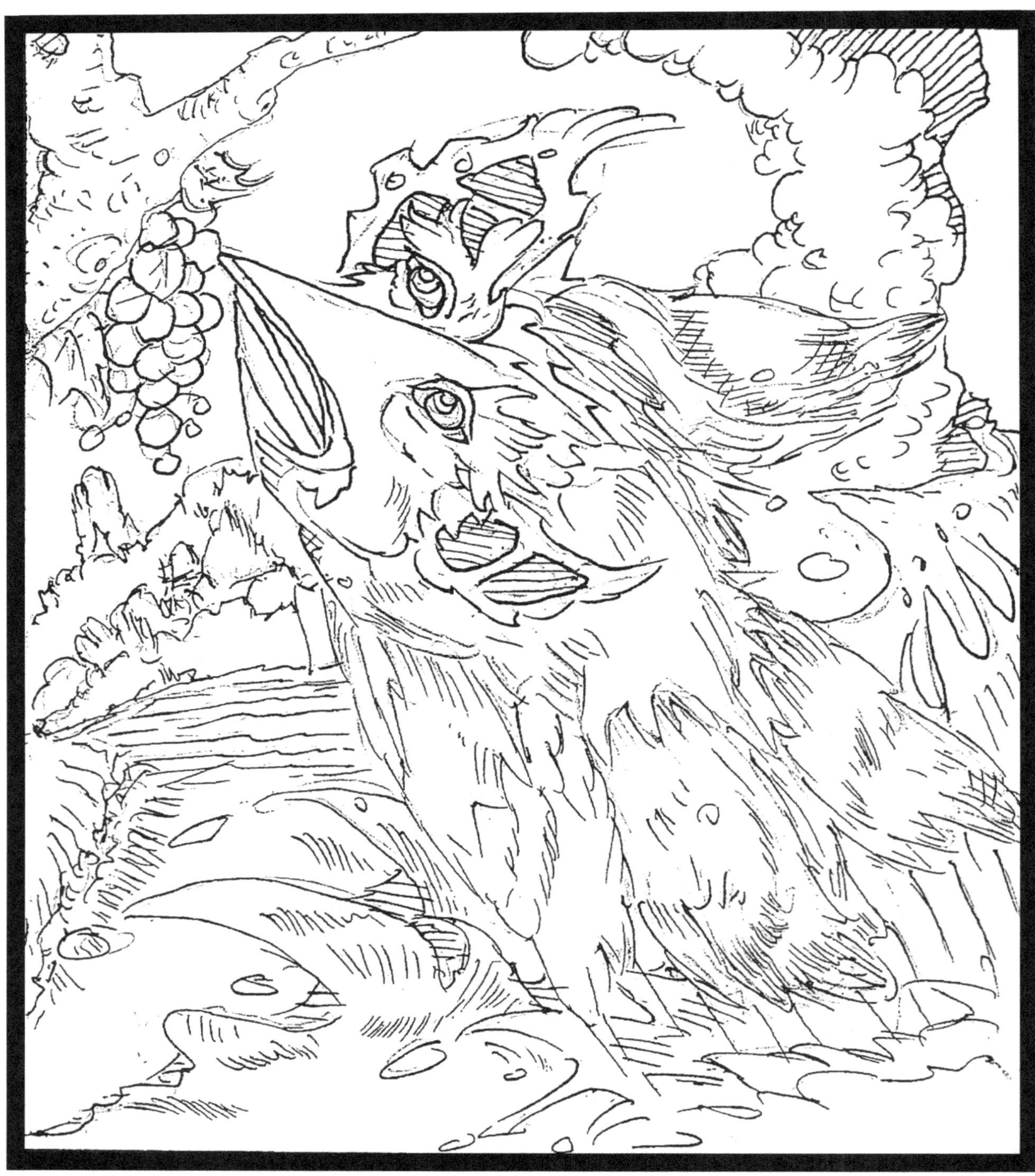

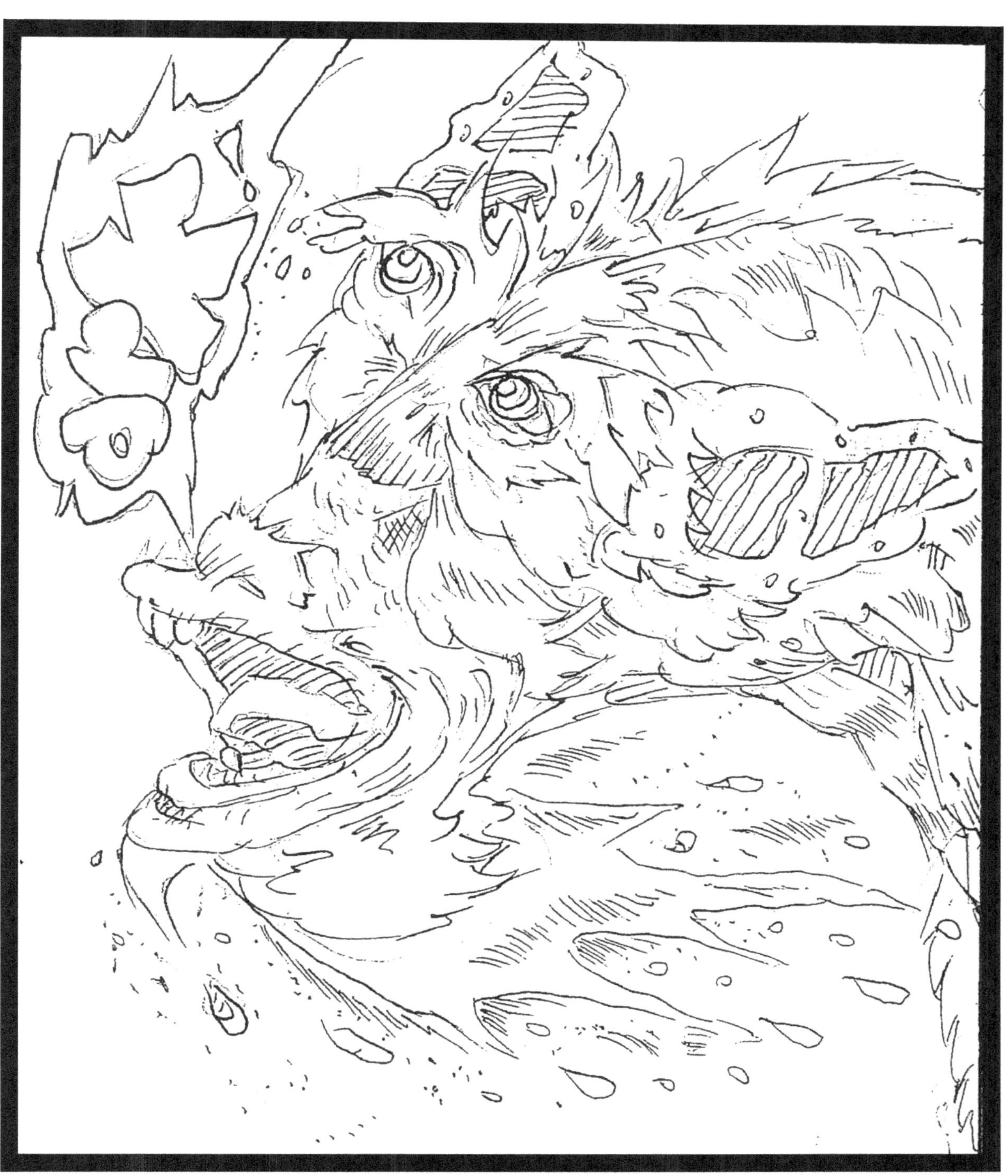

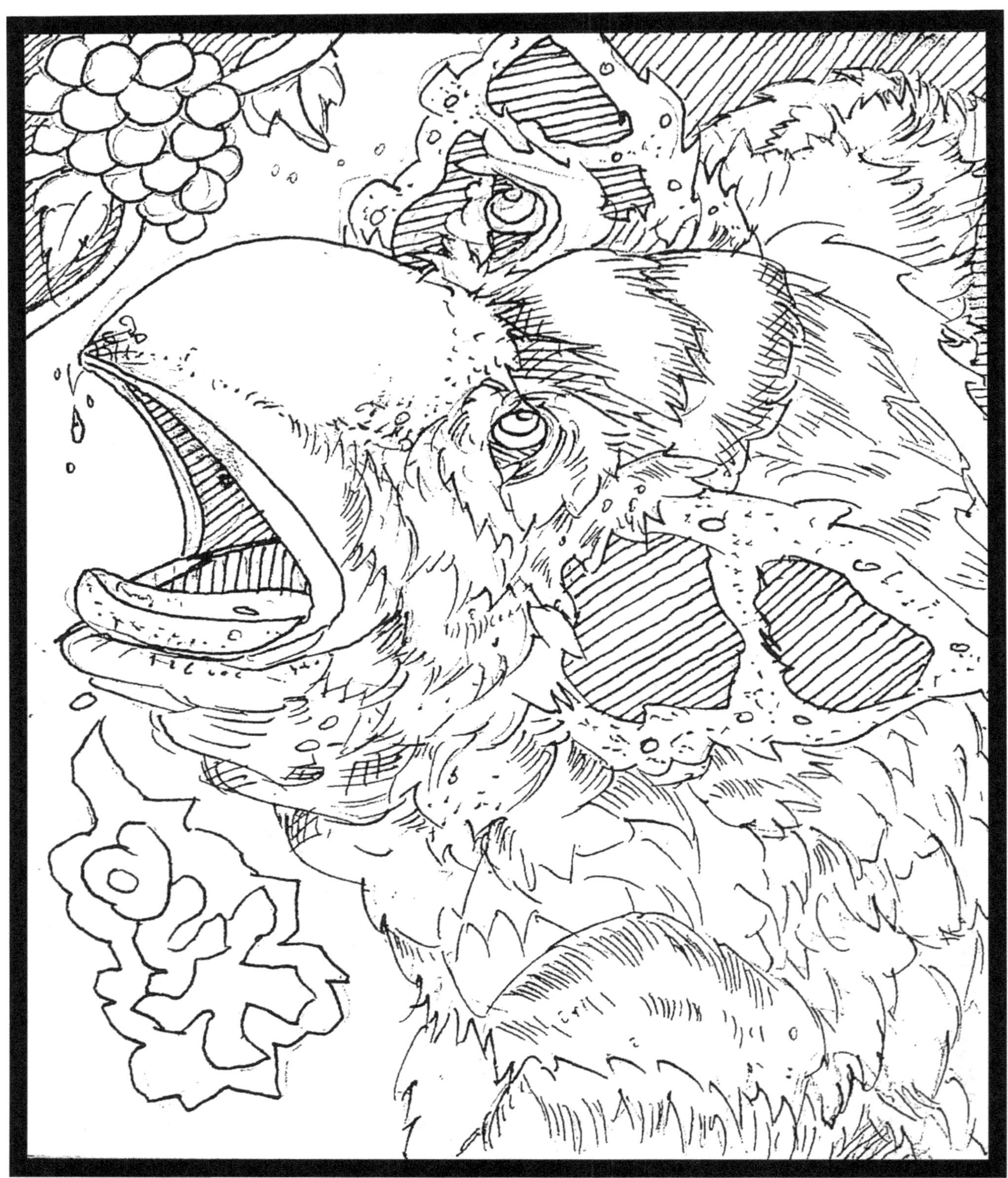

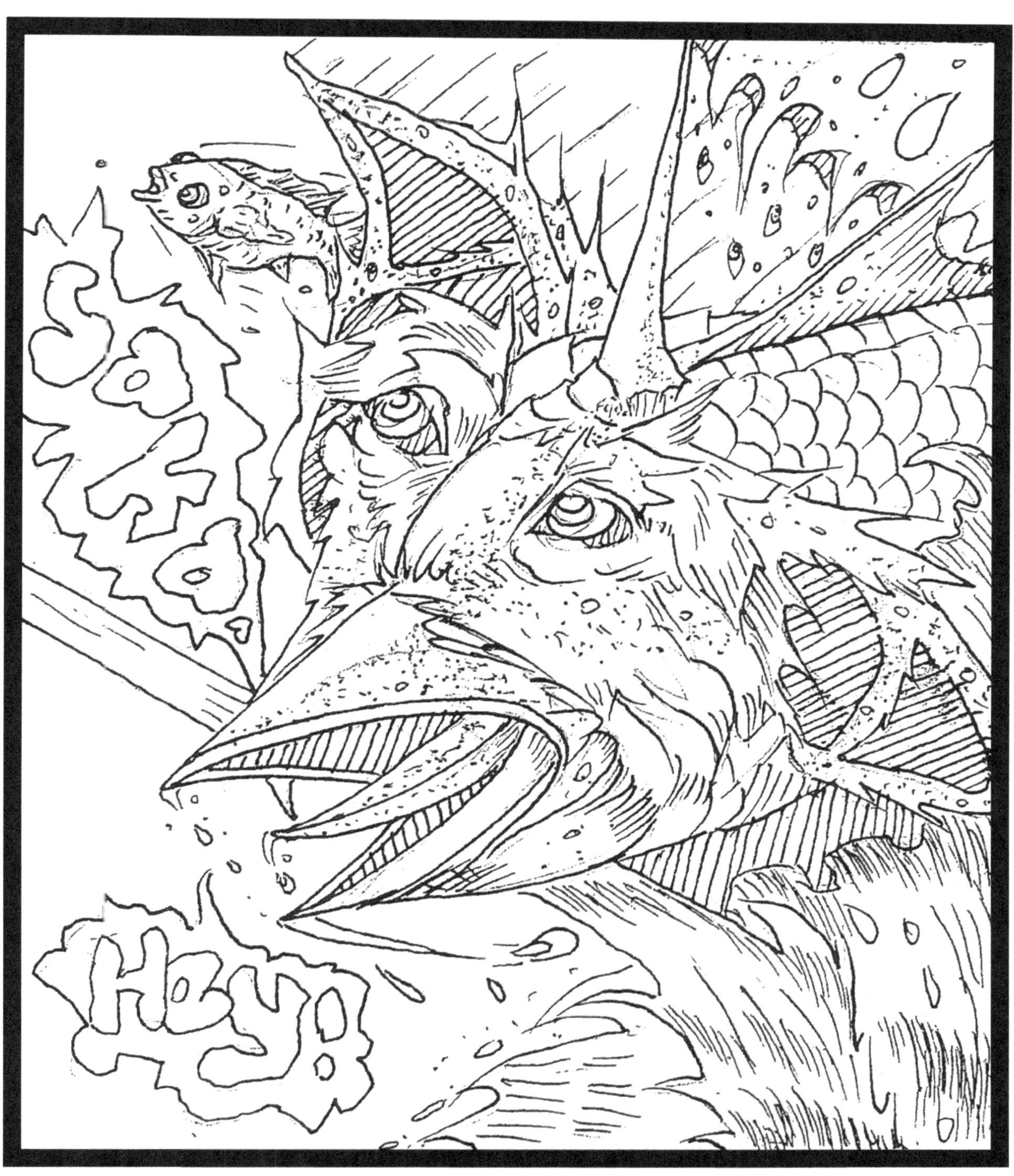

Sara
Hey!

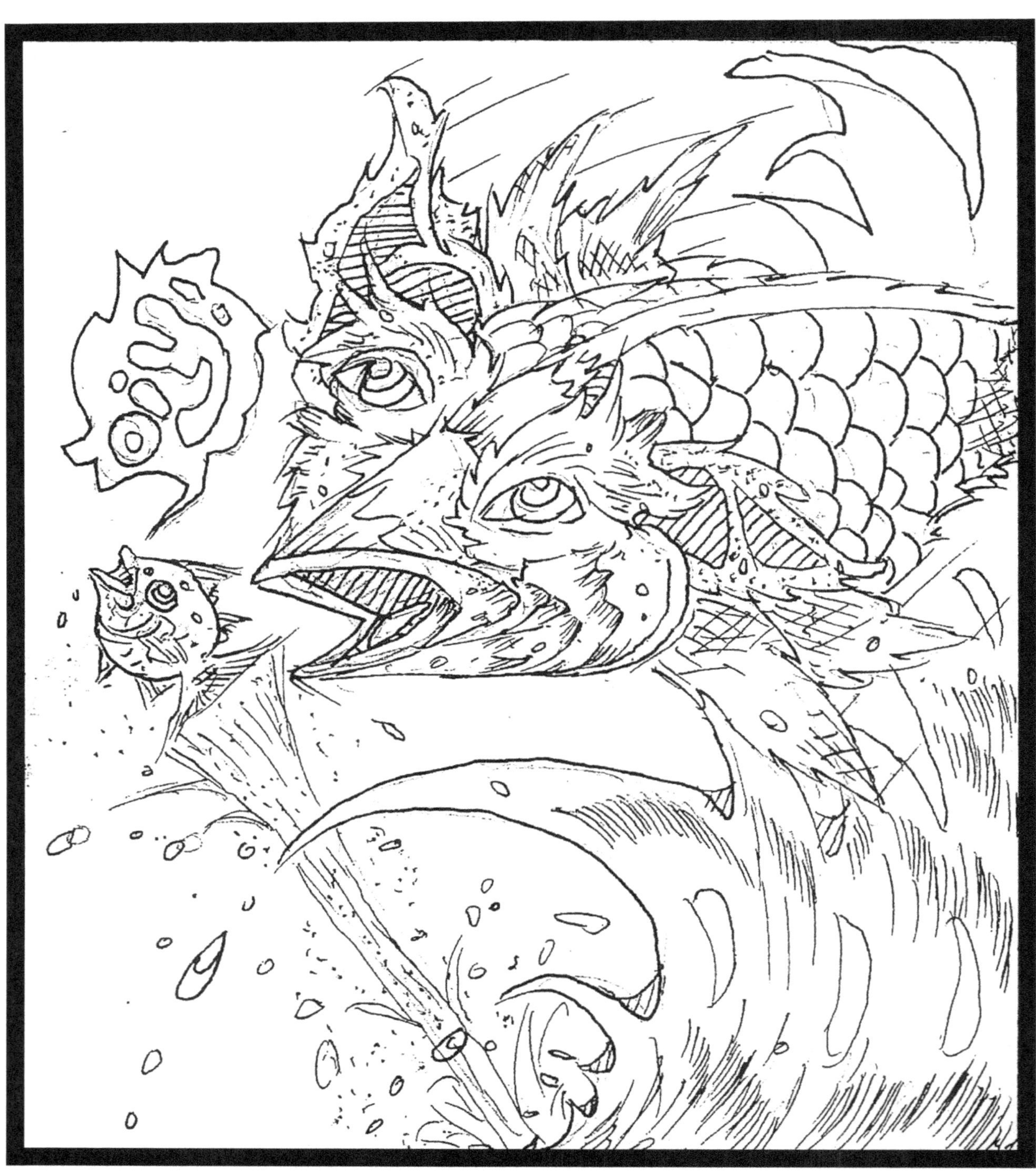

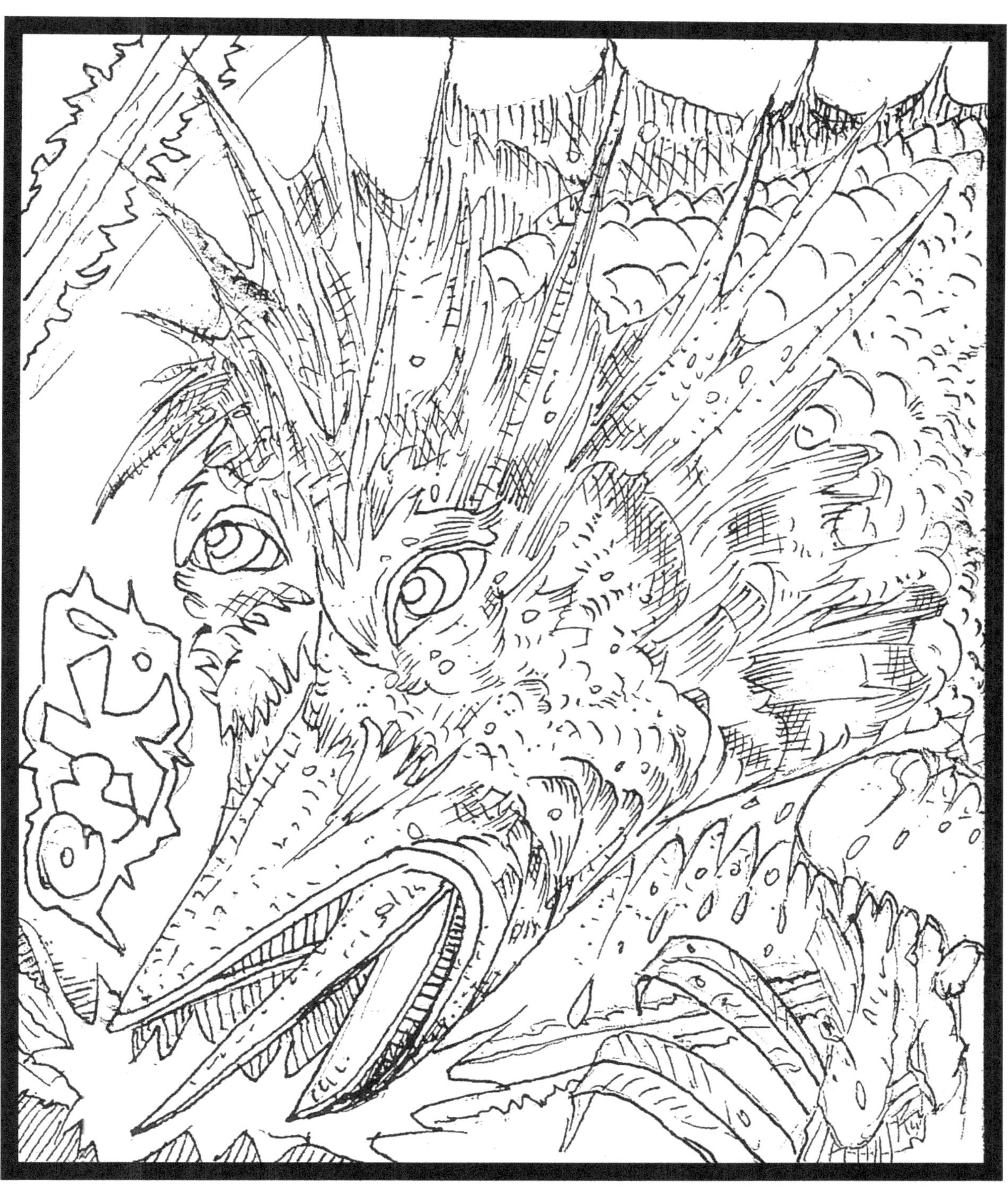

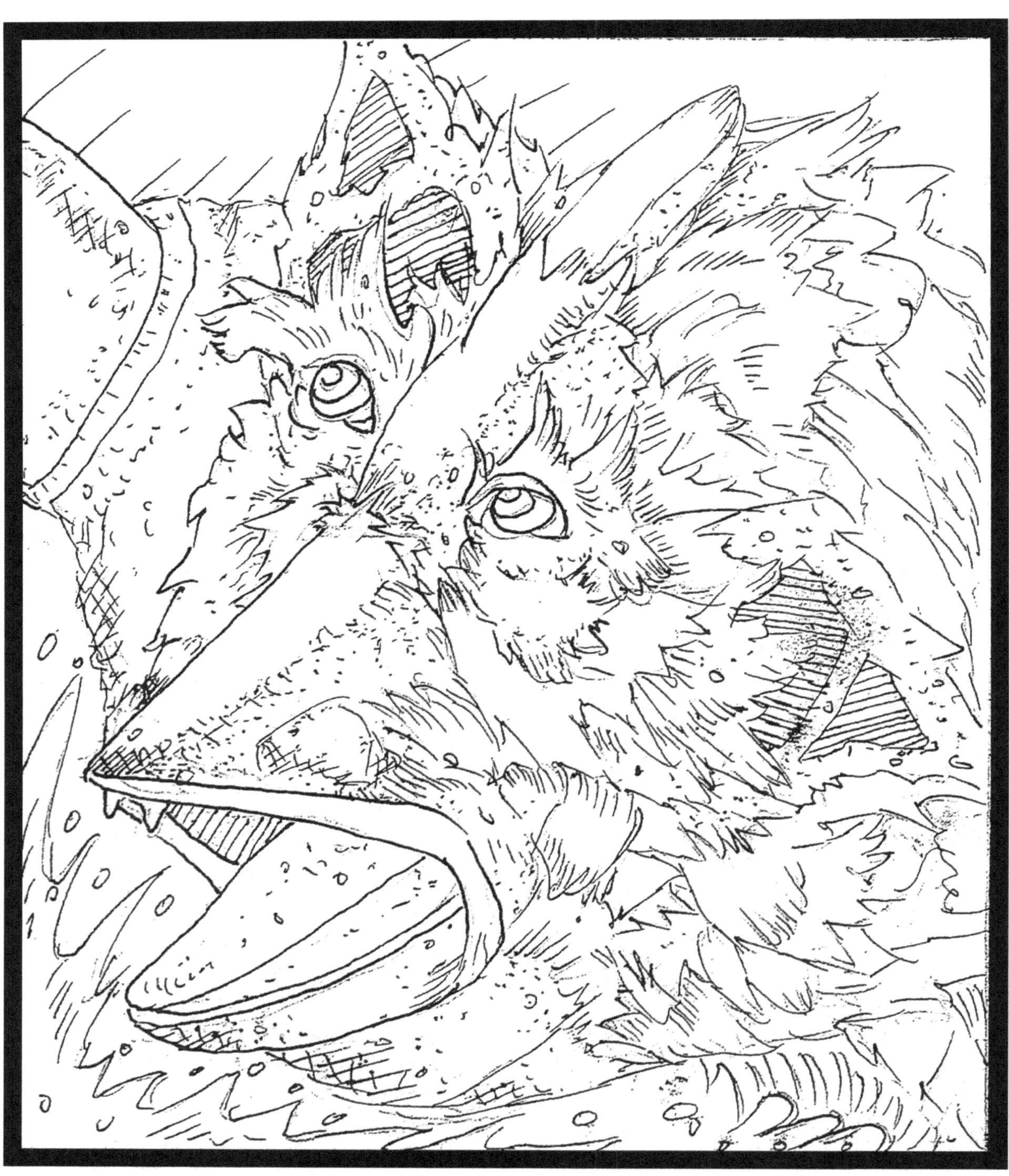

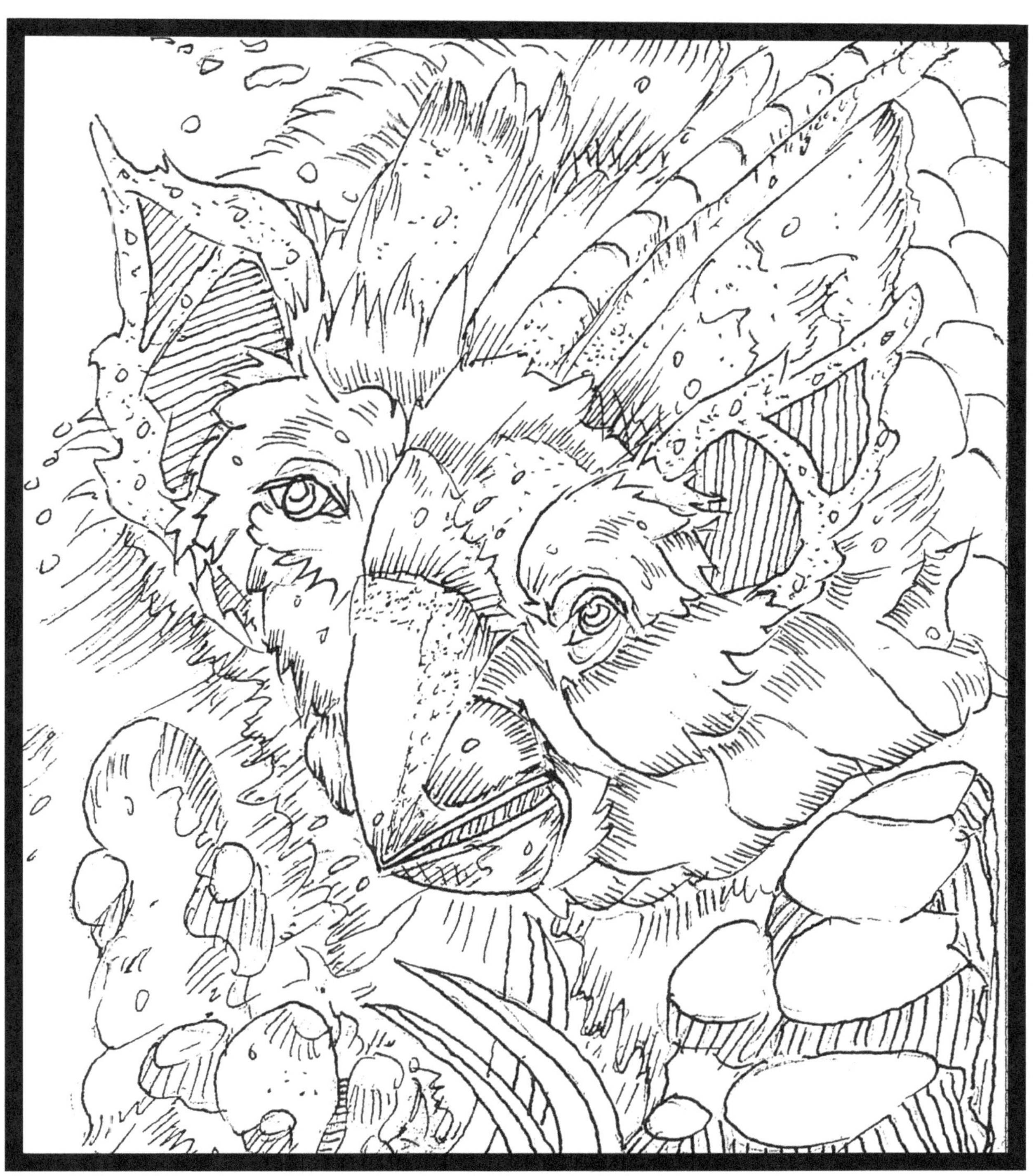

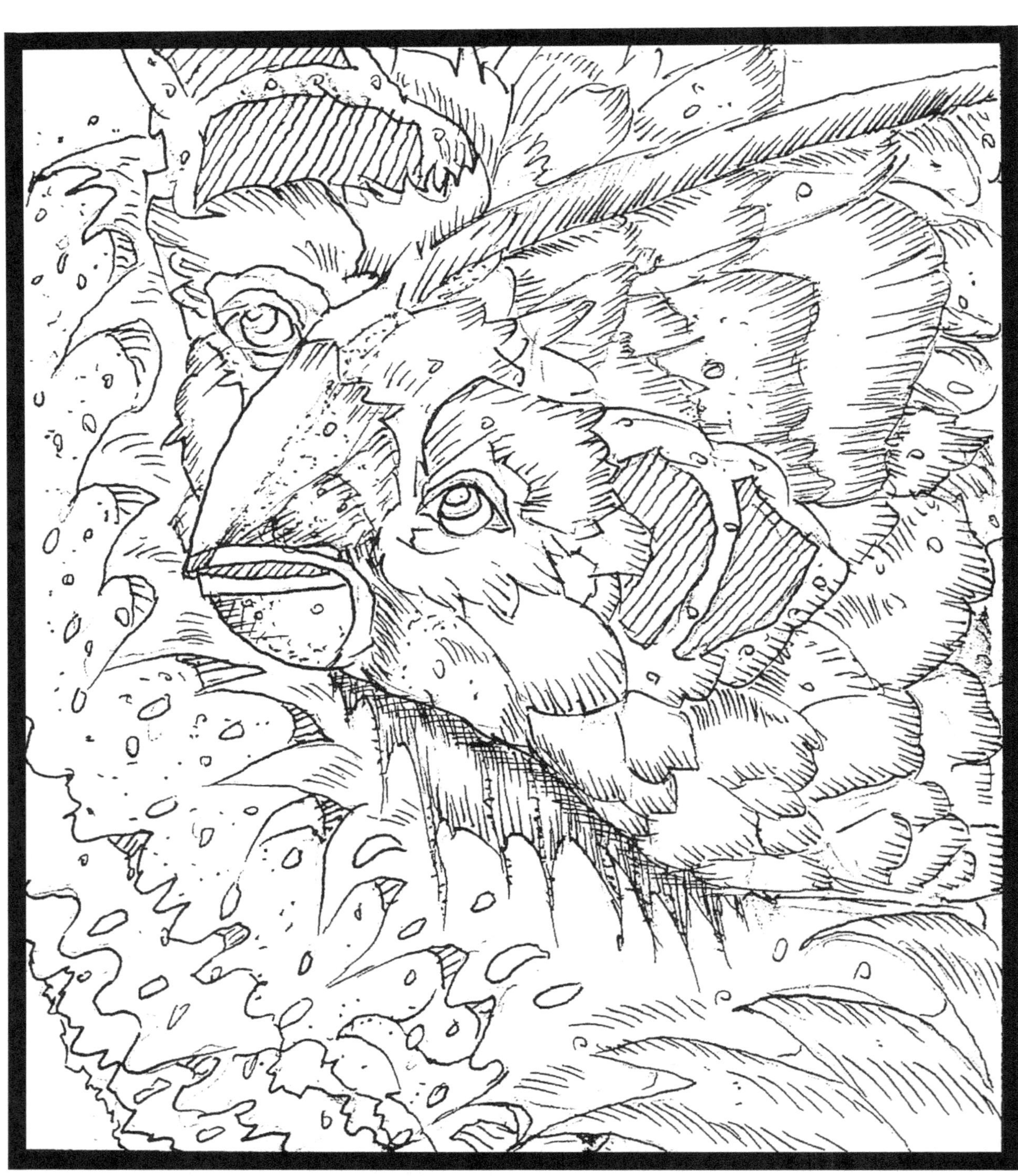

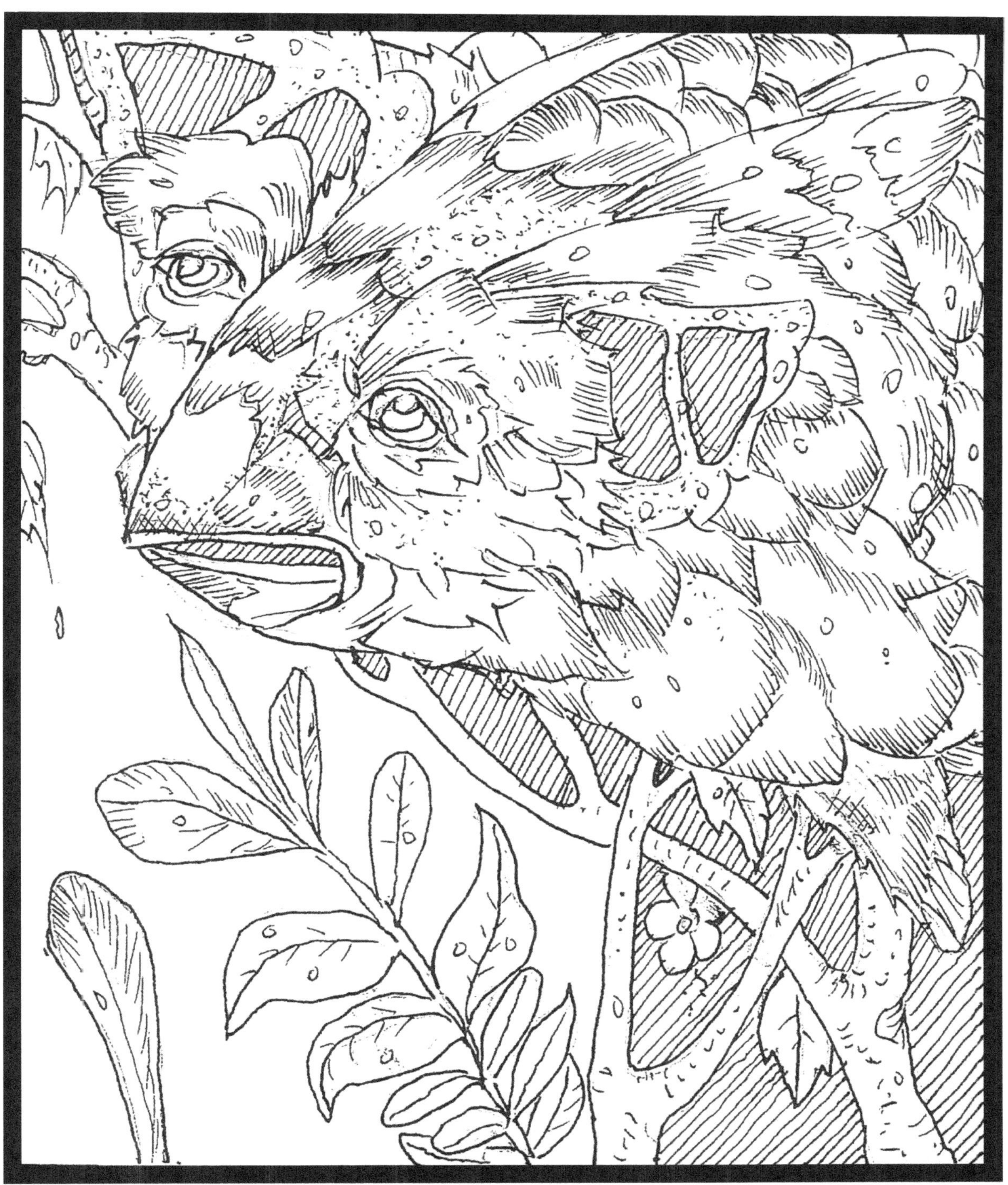

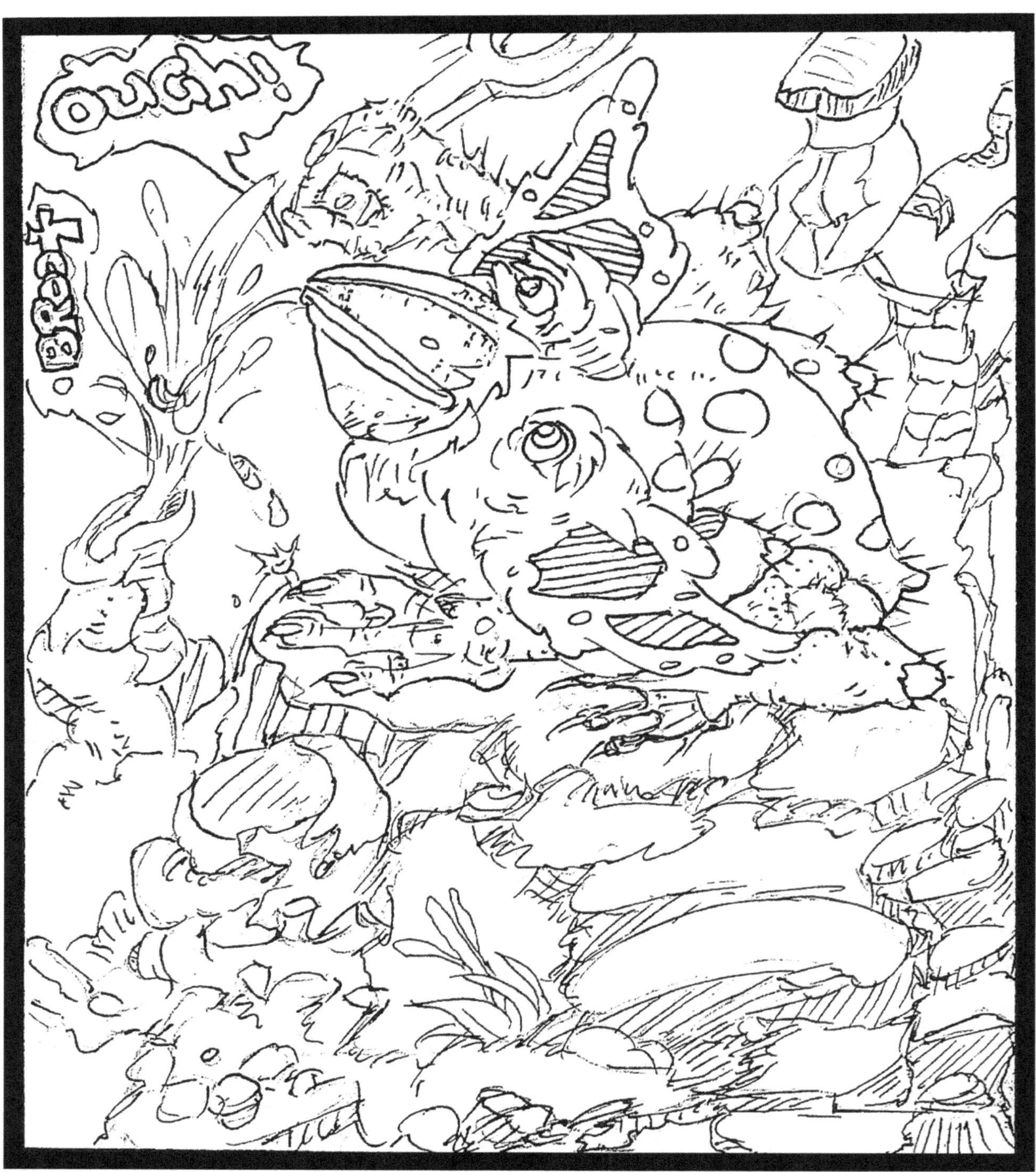

OUCH!
BRET

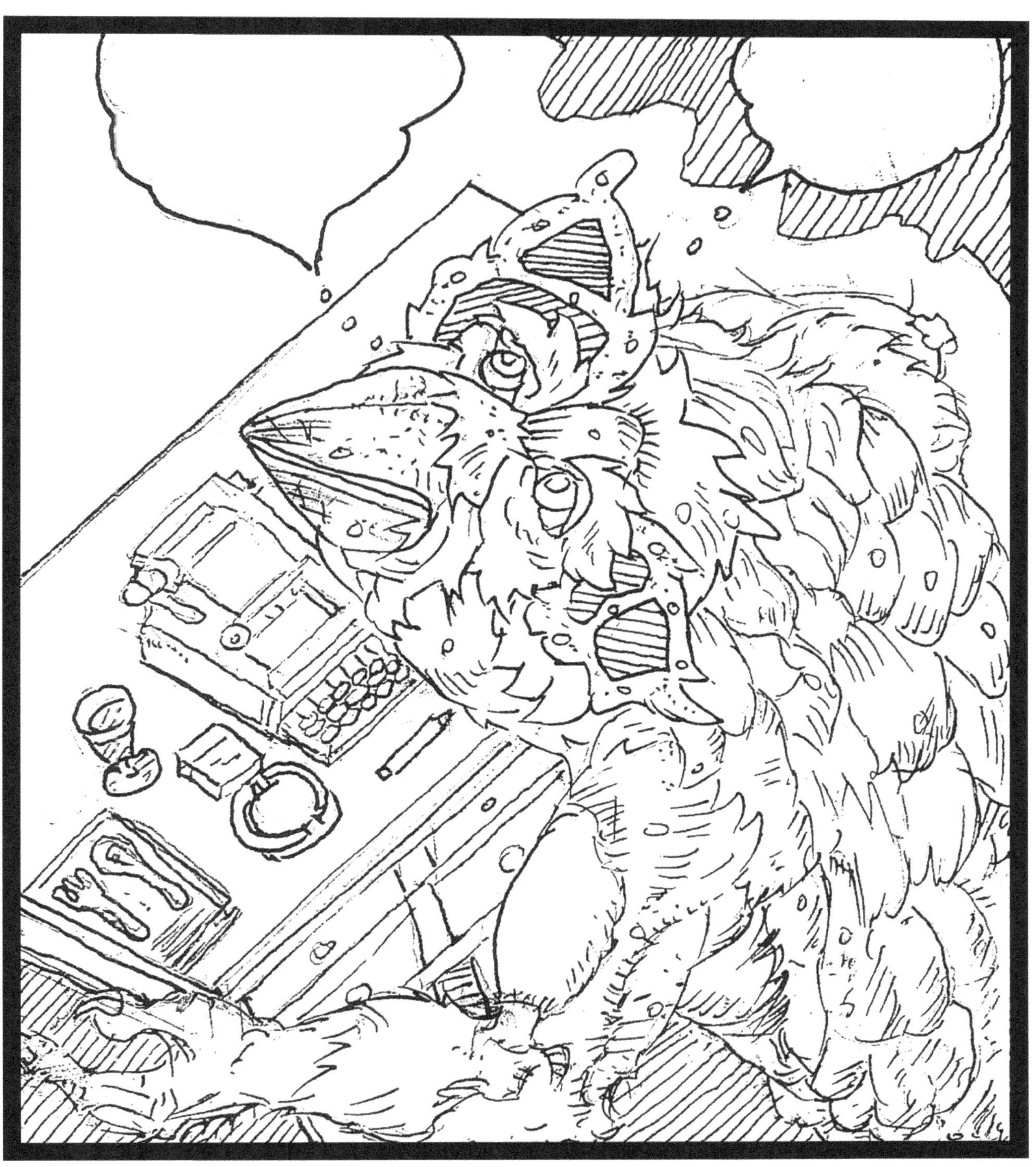

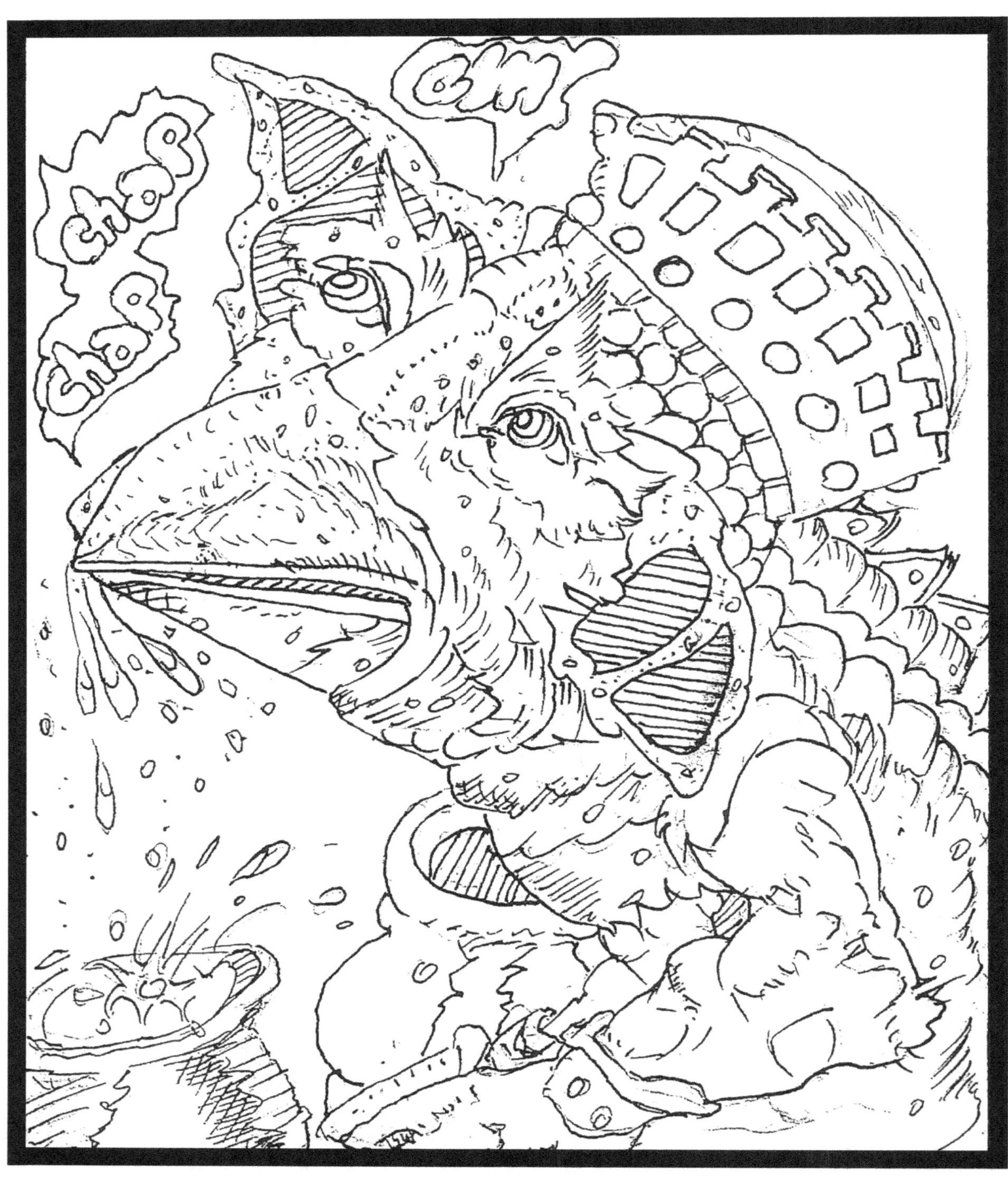

chop
chop
chop
CHOMP

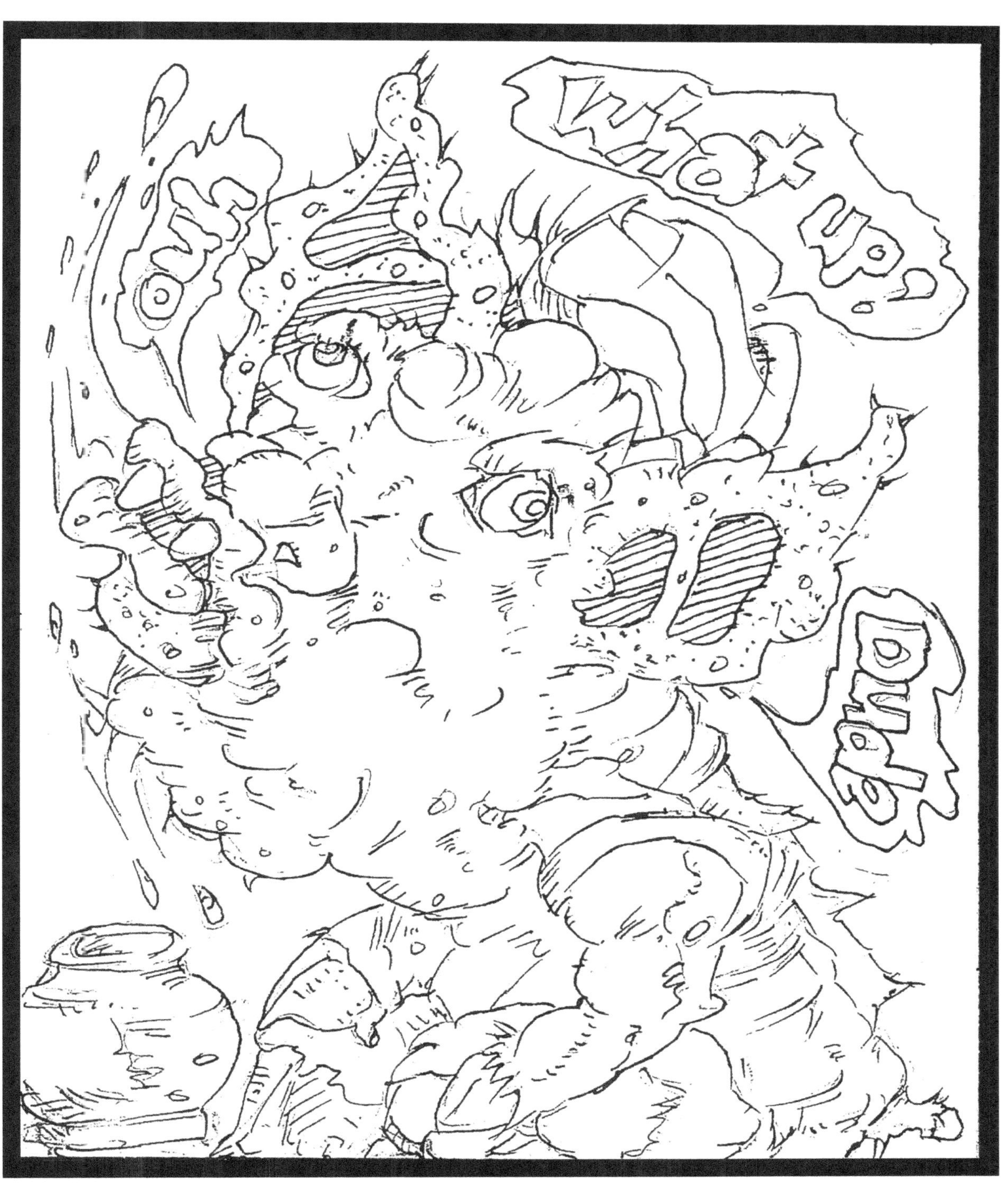
Yo!
What up?
Dude

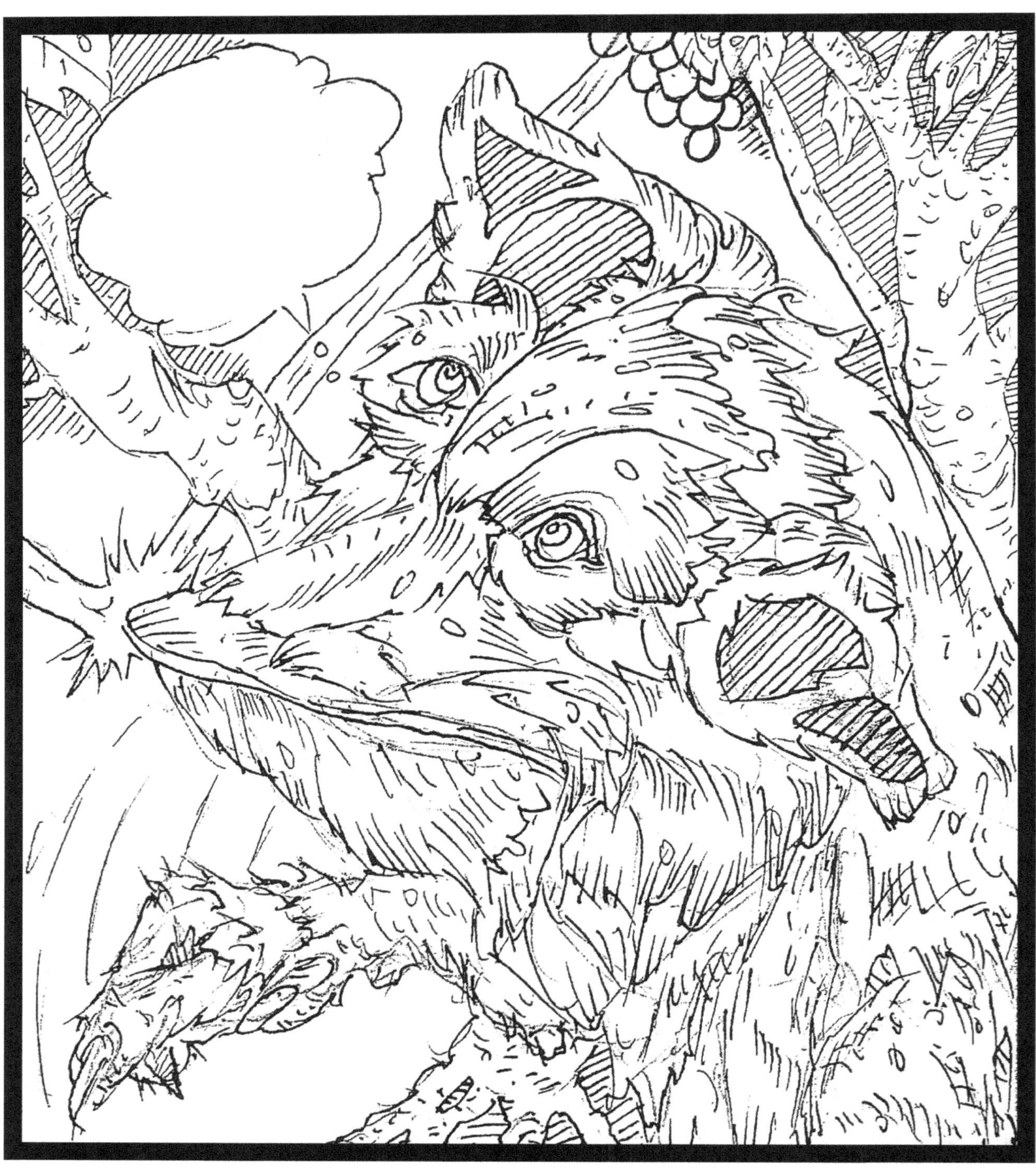

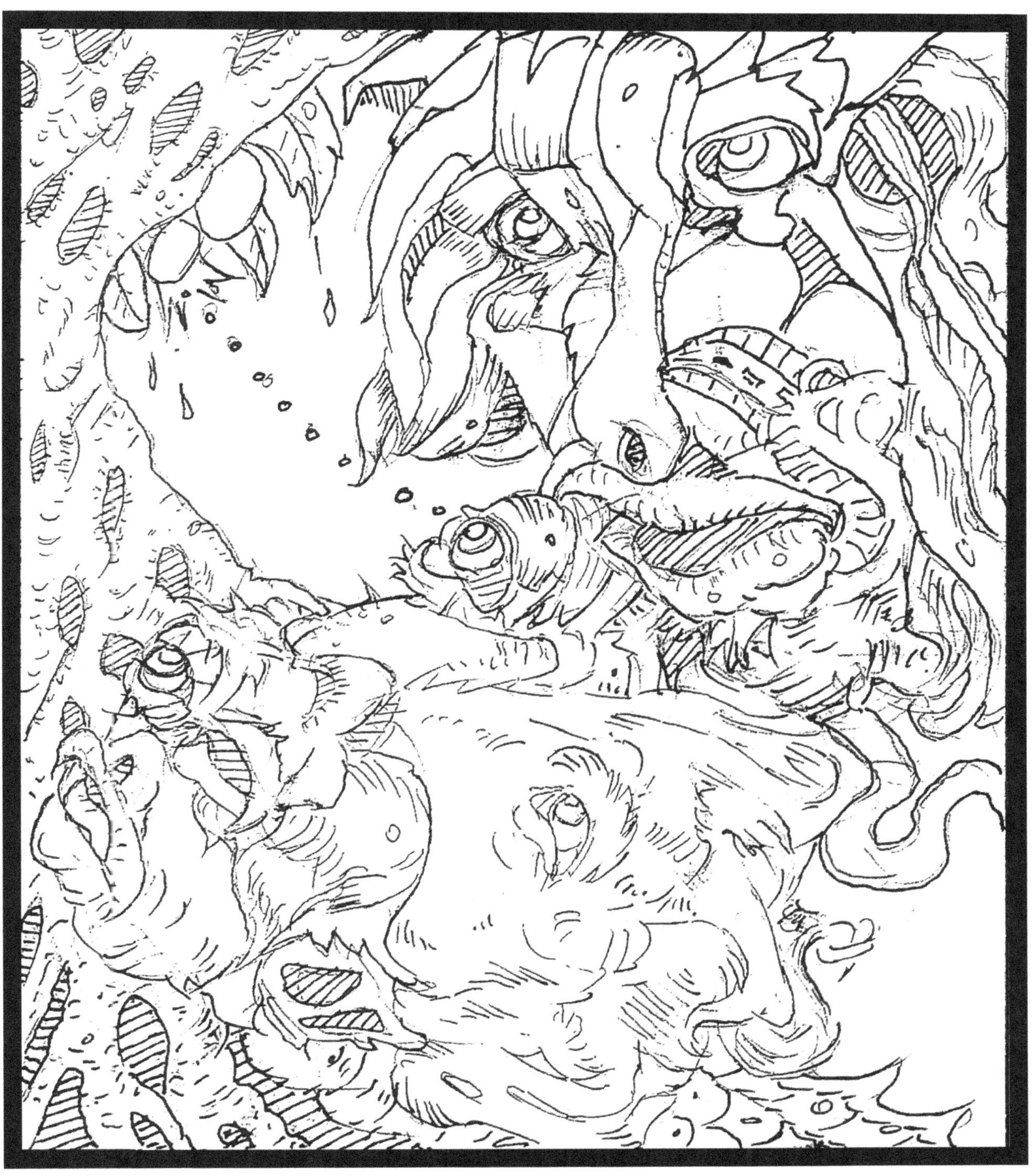

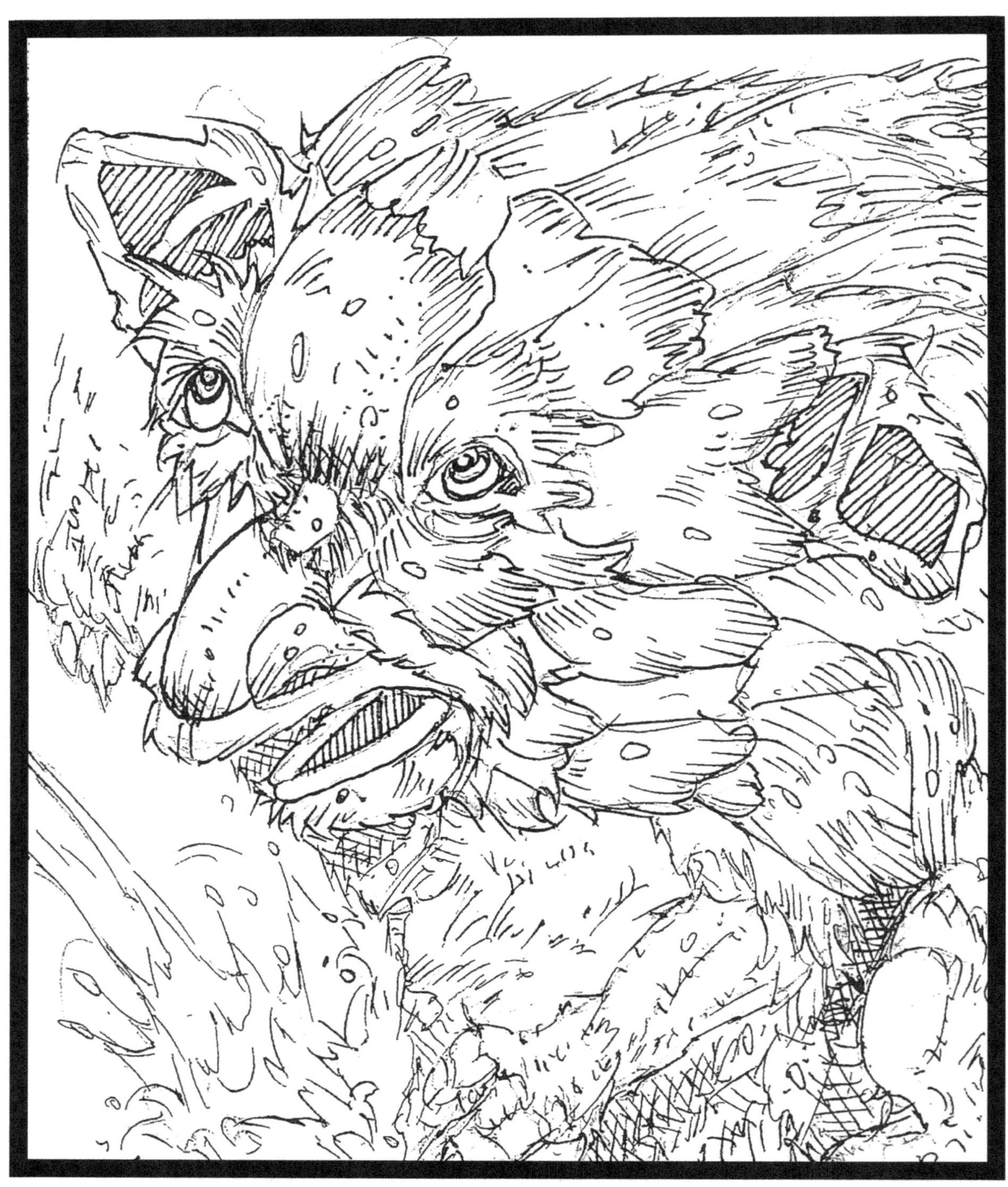

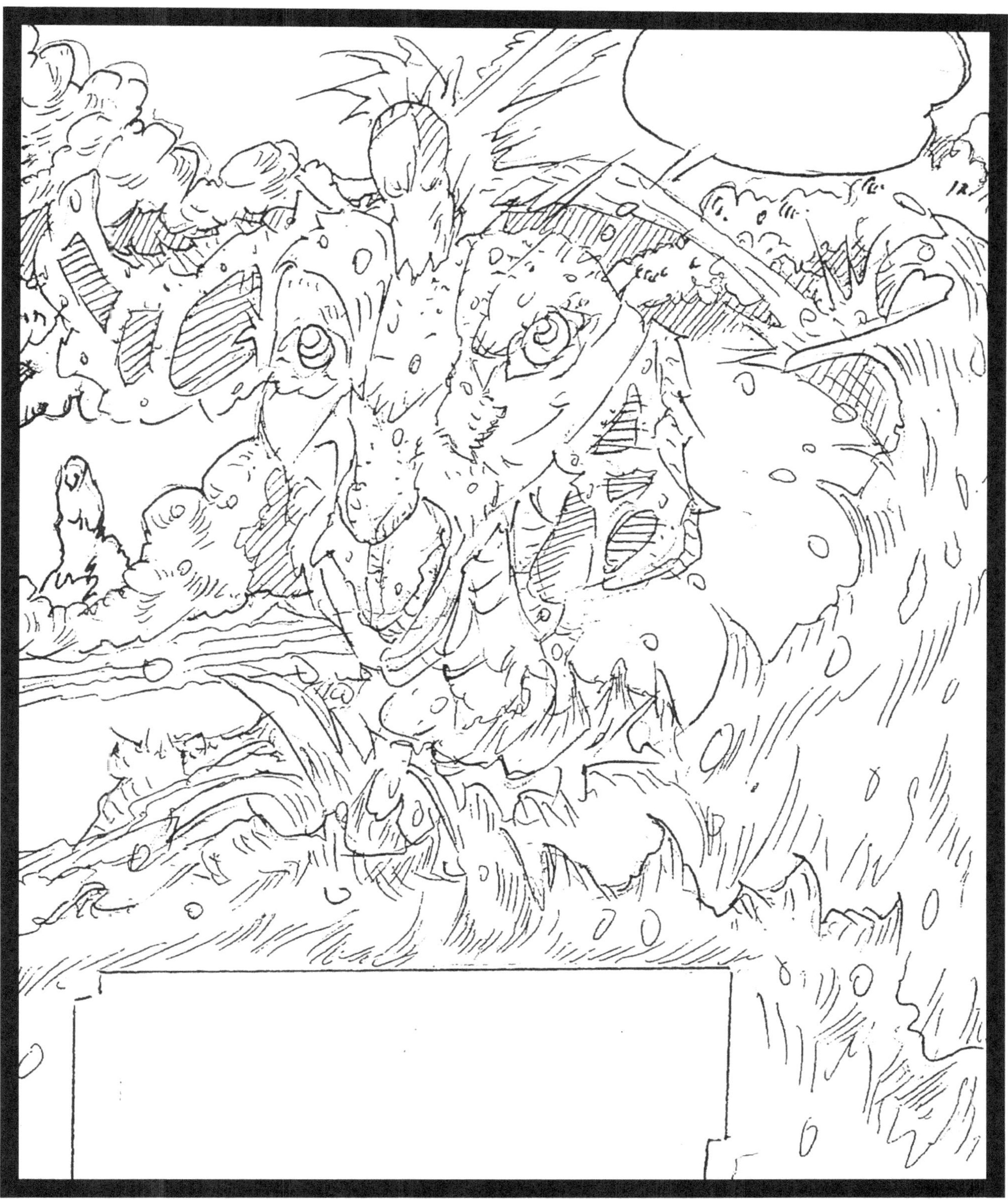

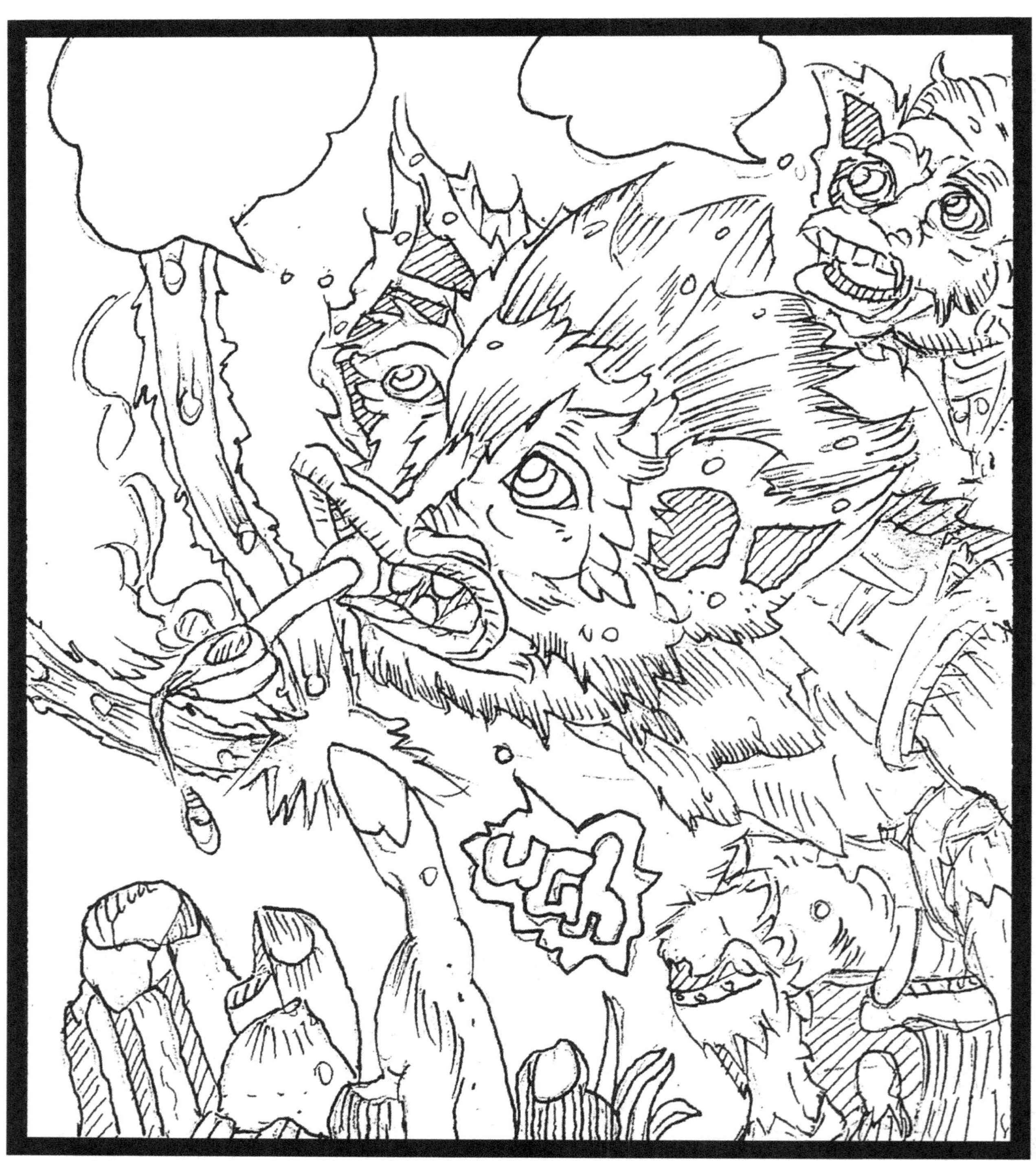
UGH

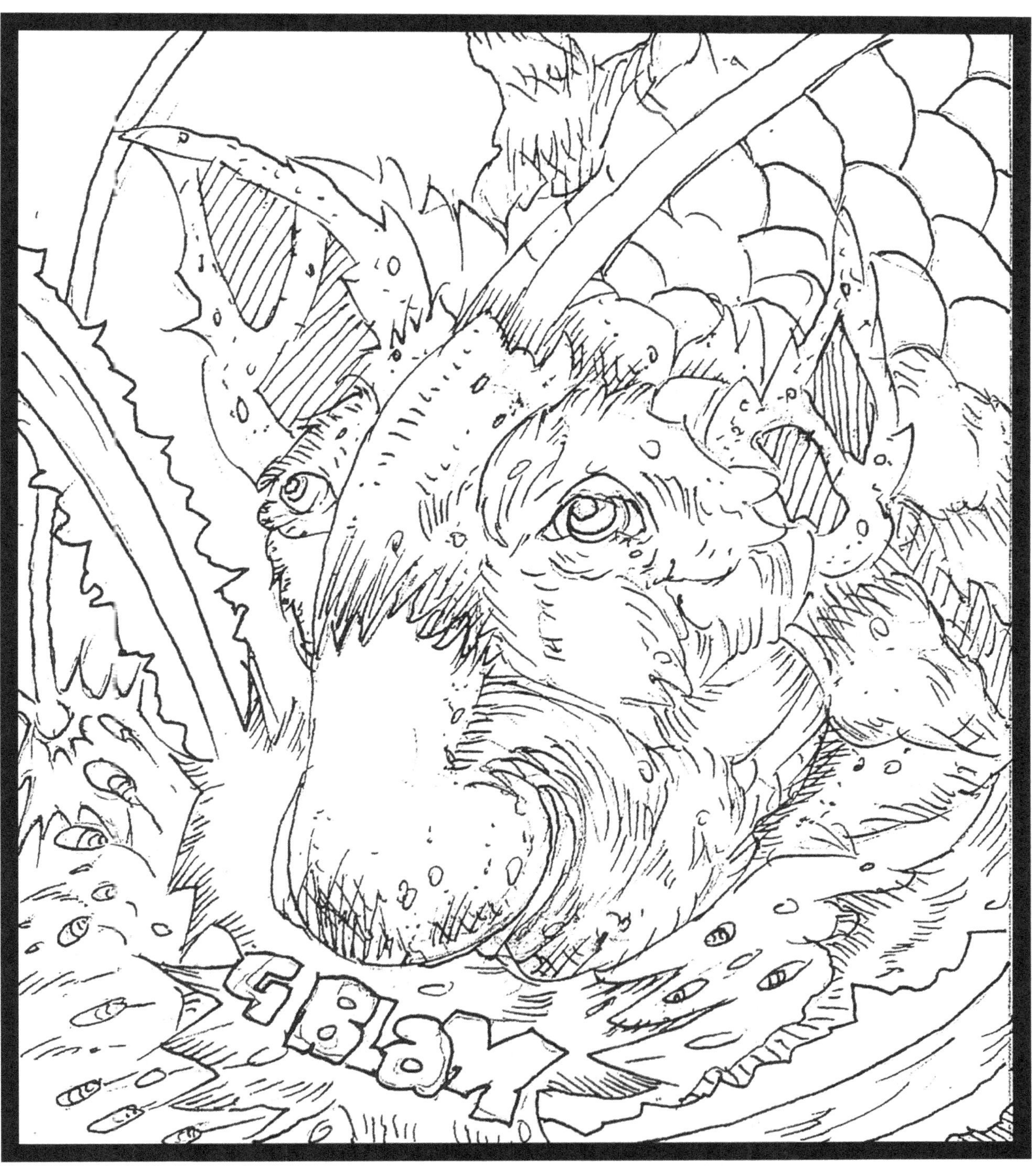
G'DAY

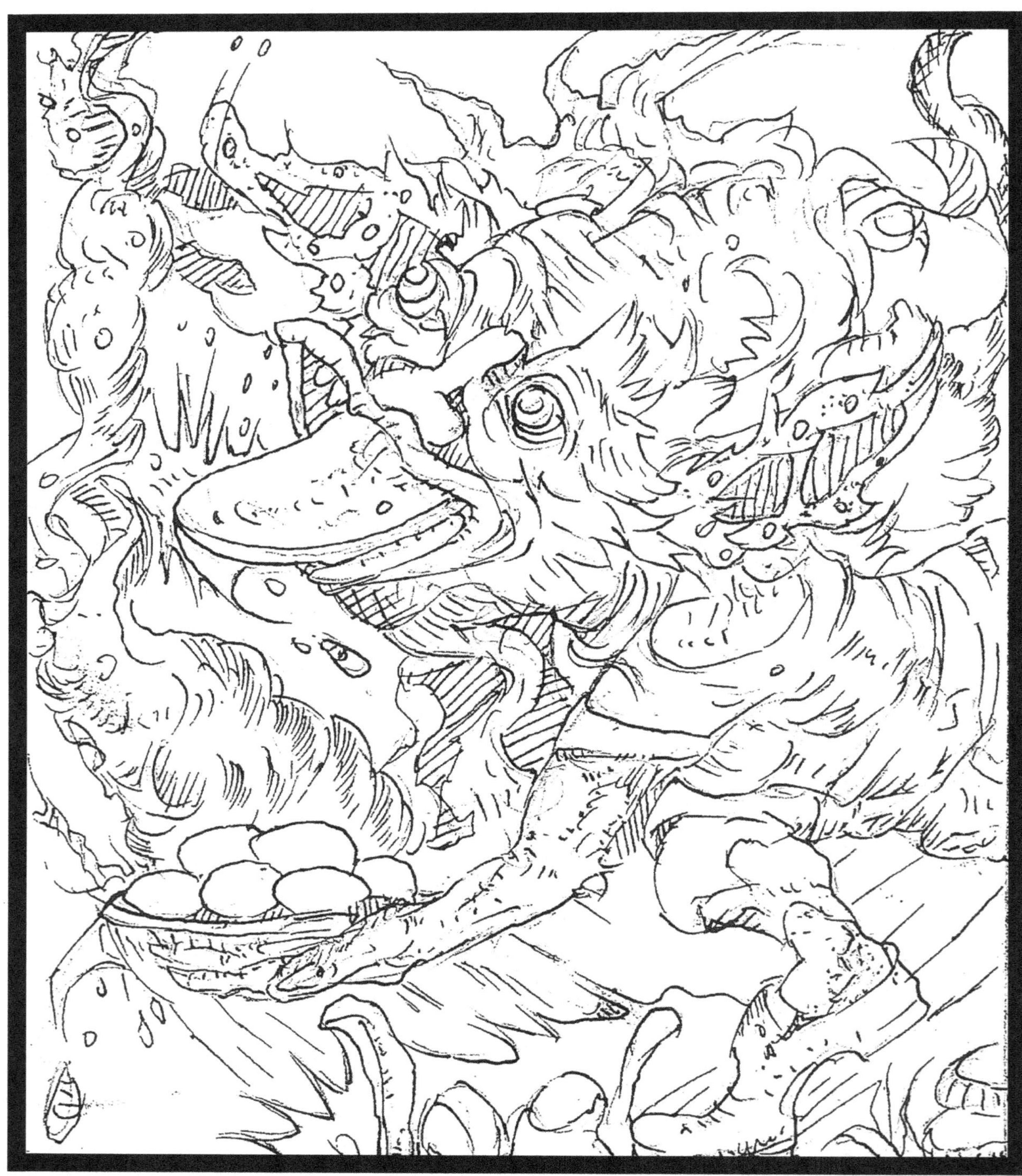

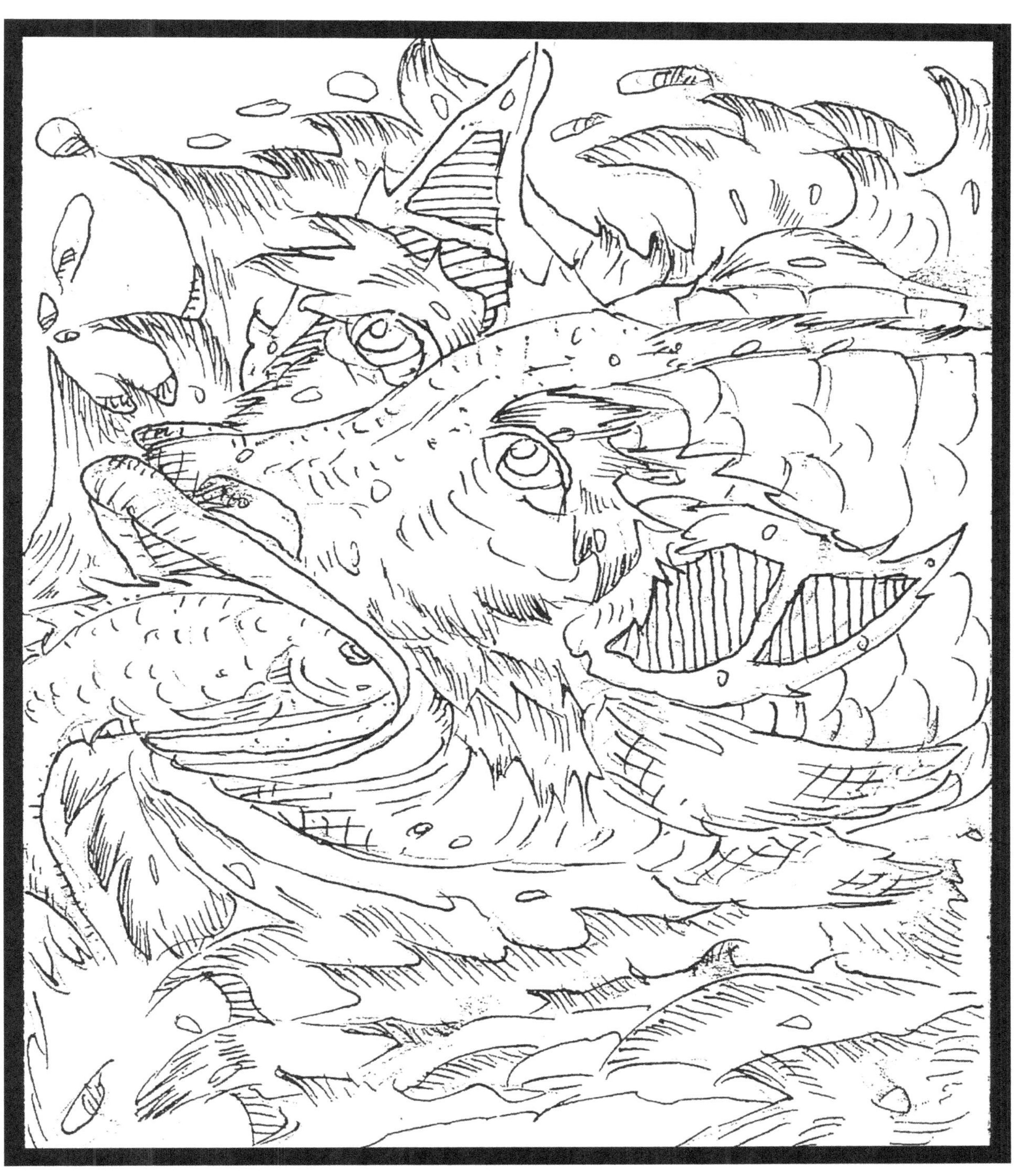

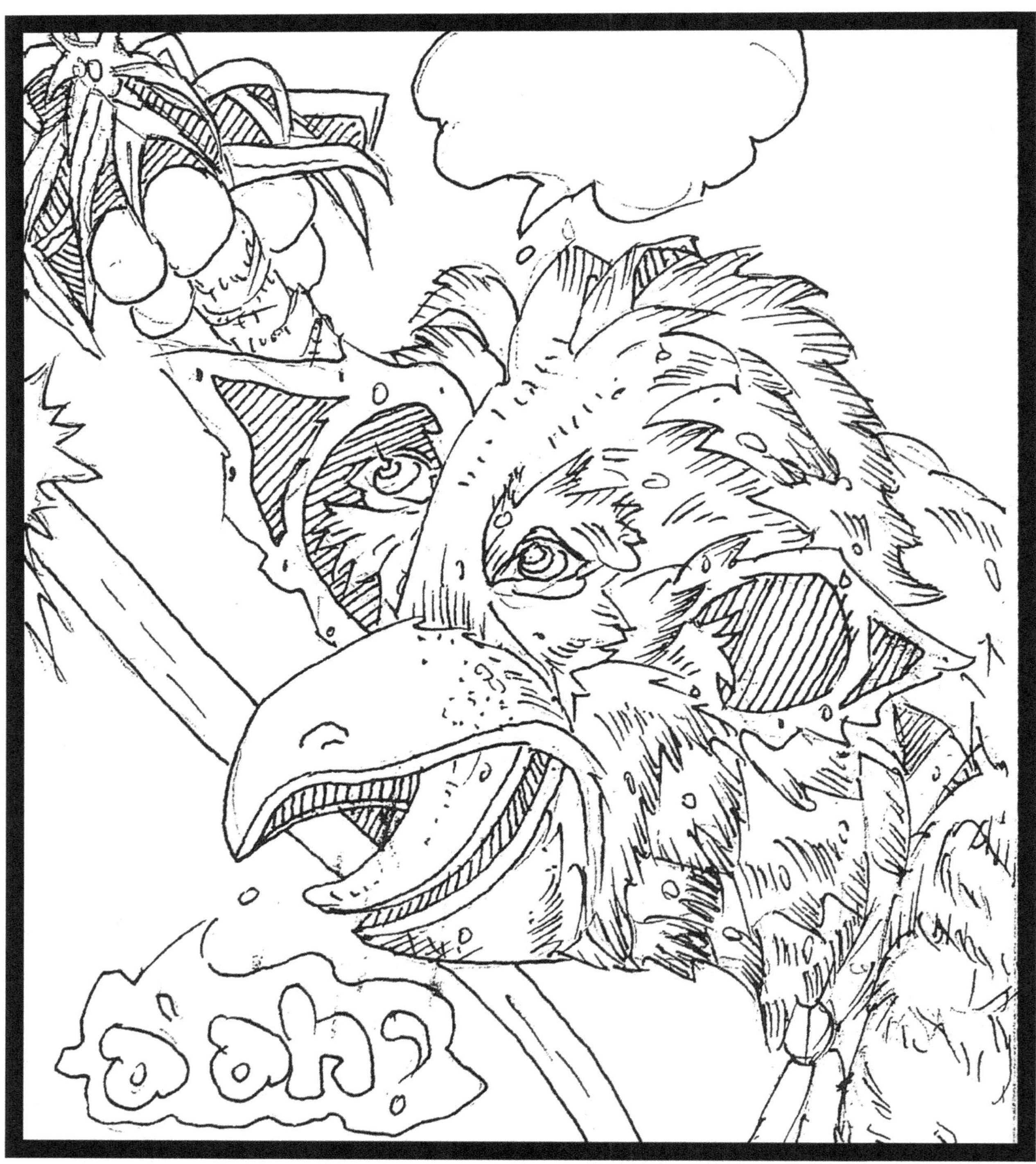
a'ah?

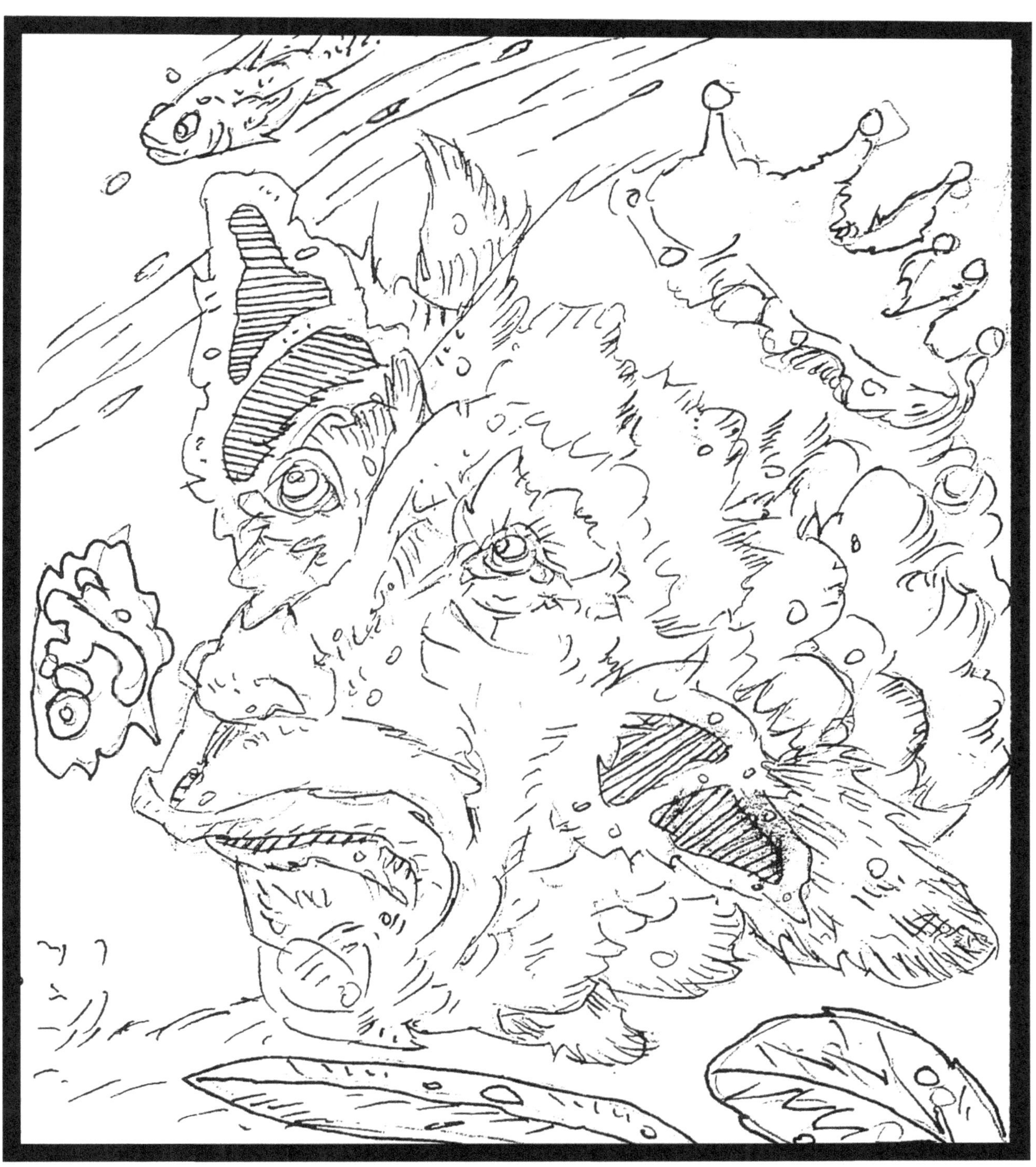

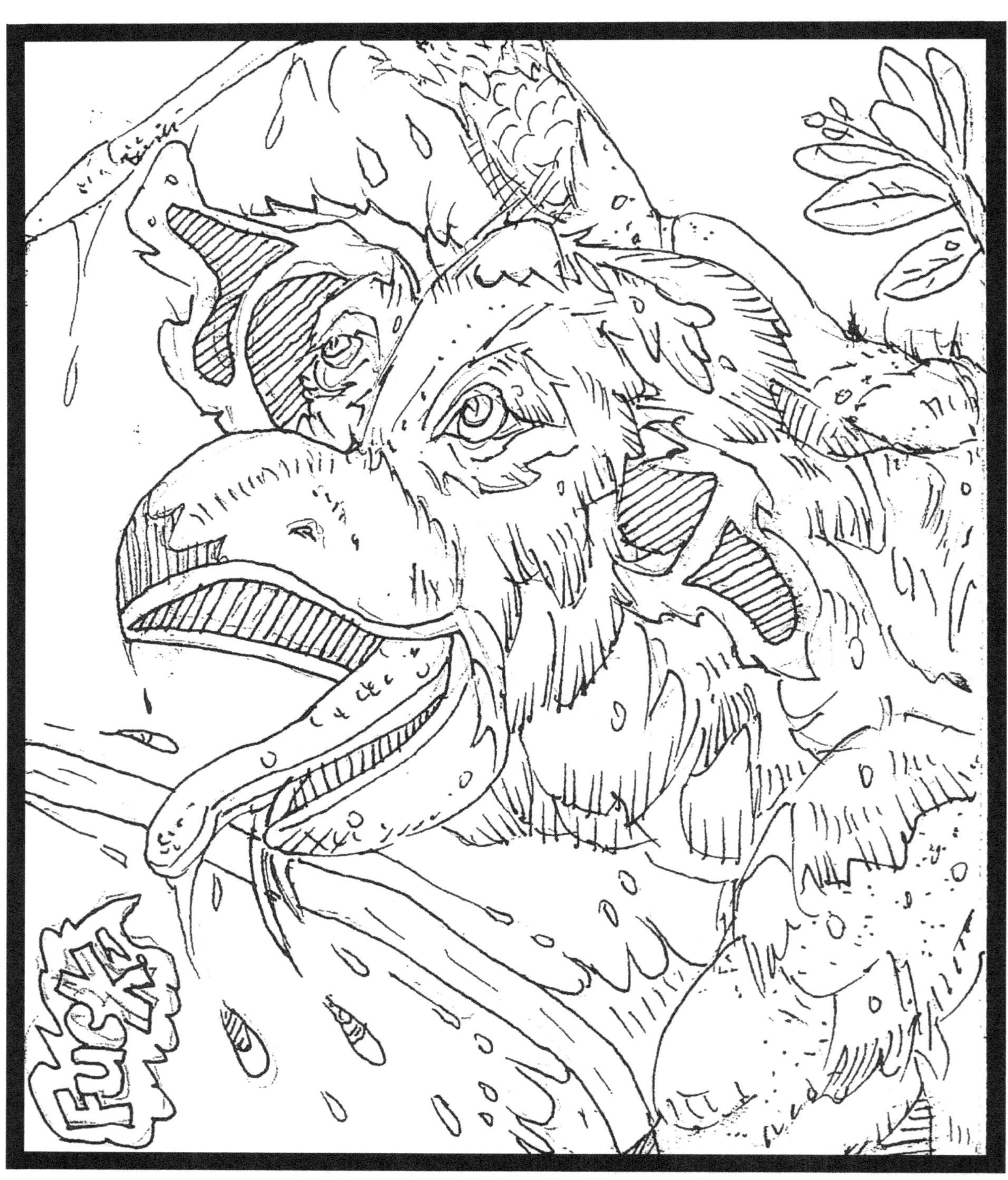

FUCK
YA

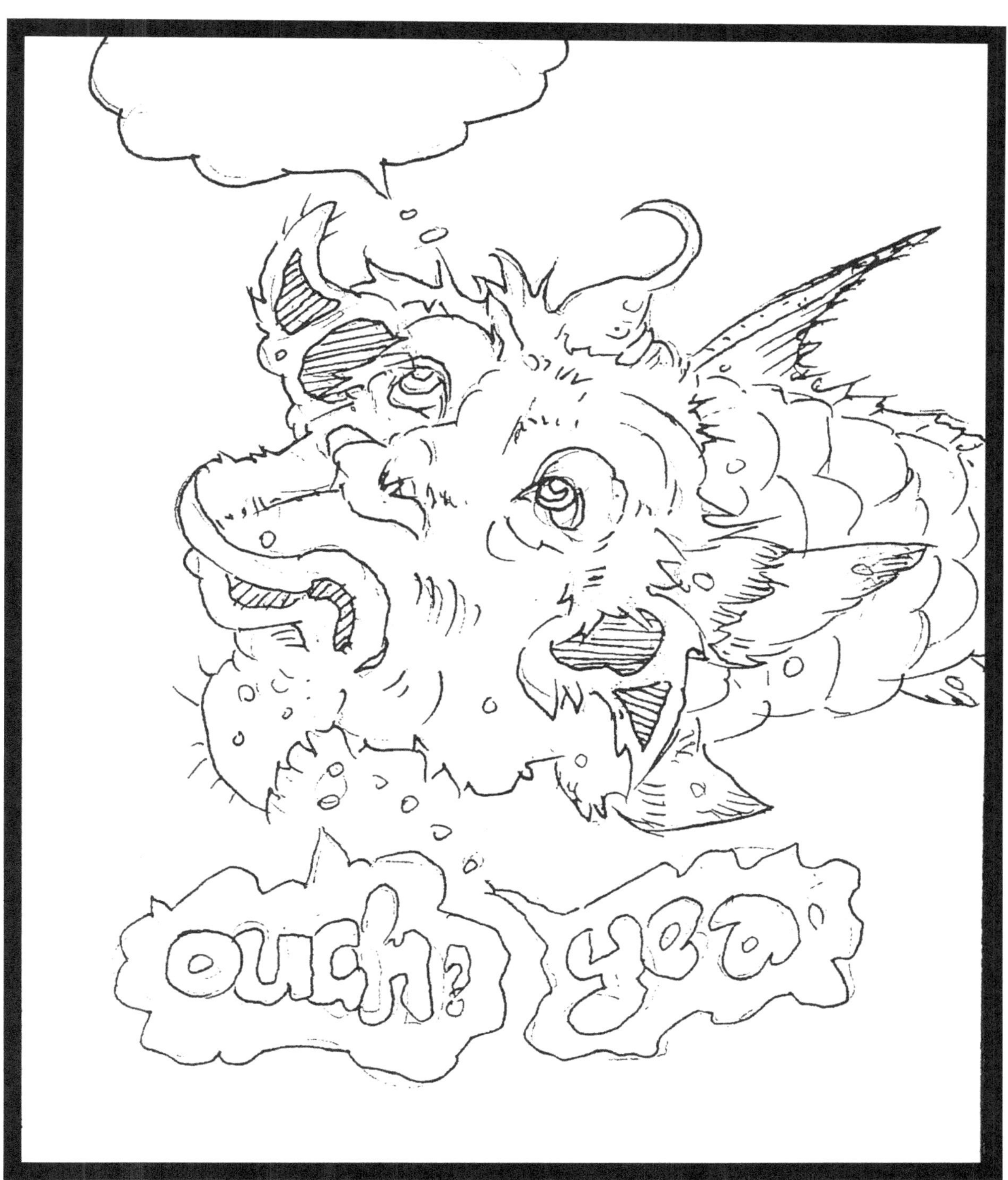

ouch?
yea

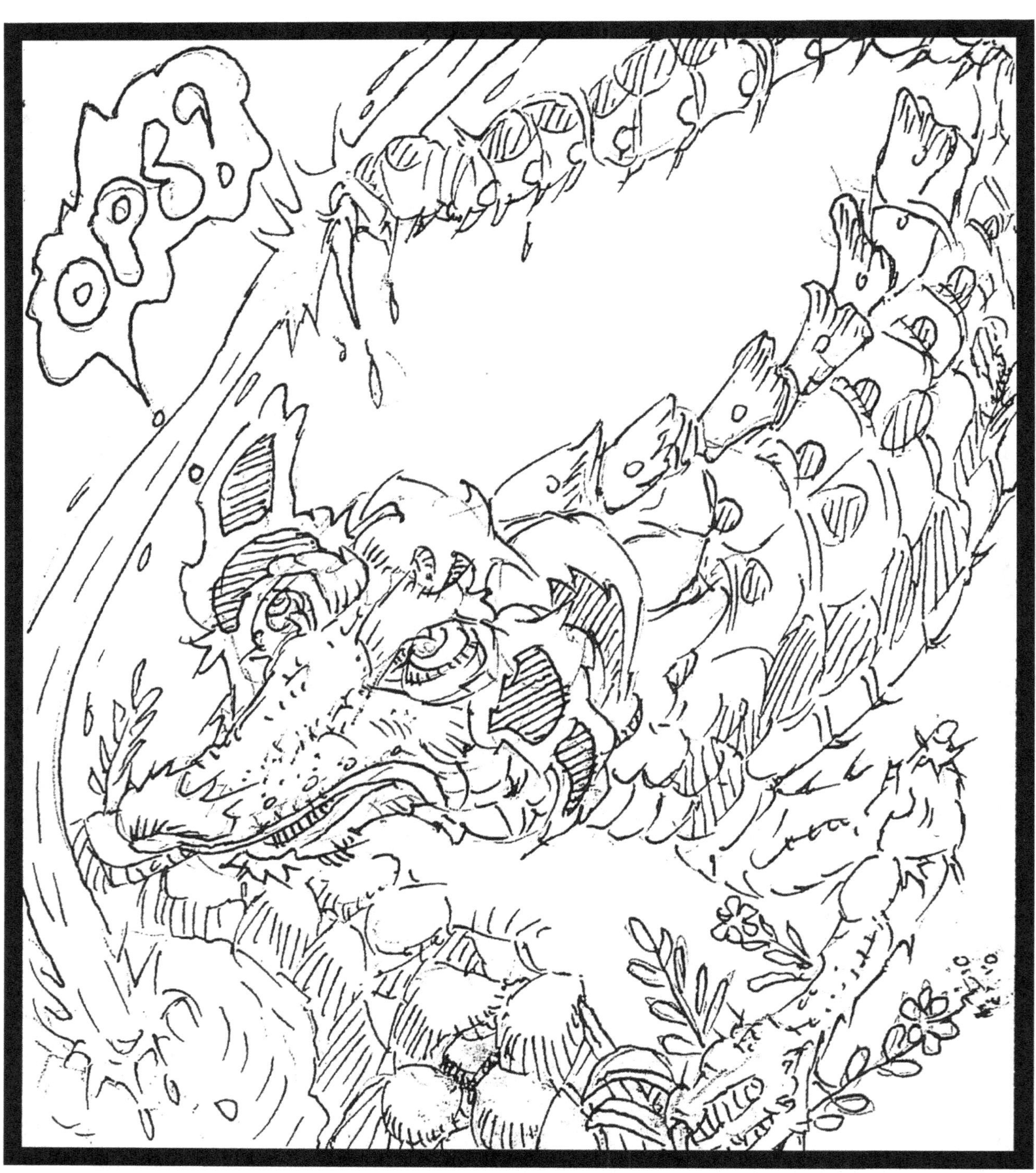
OOPS!

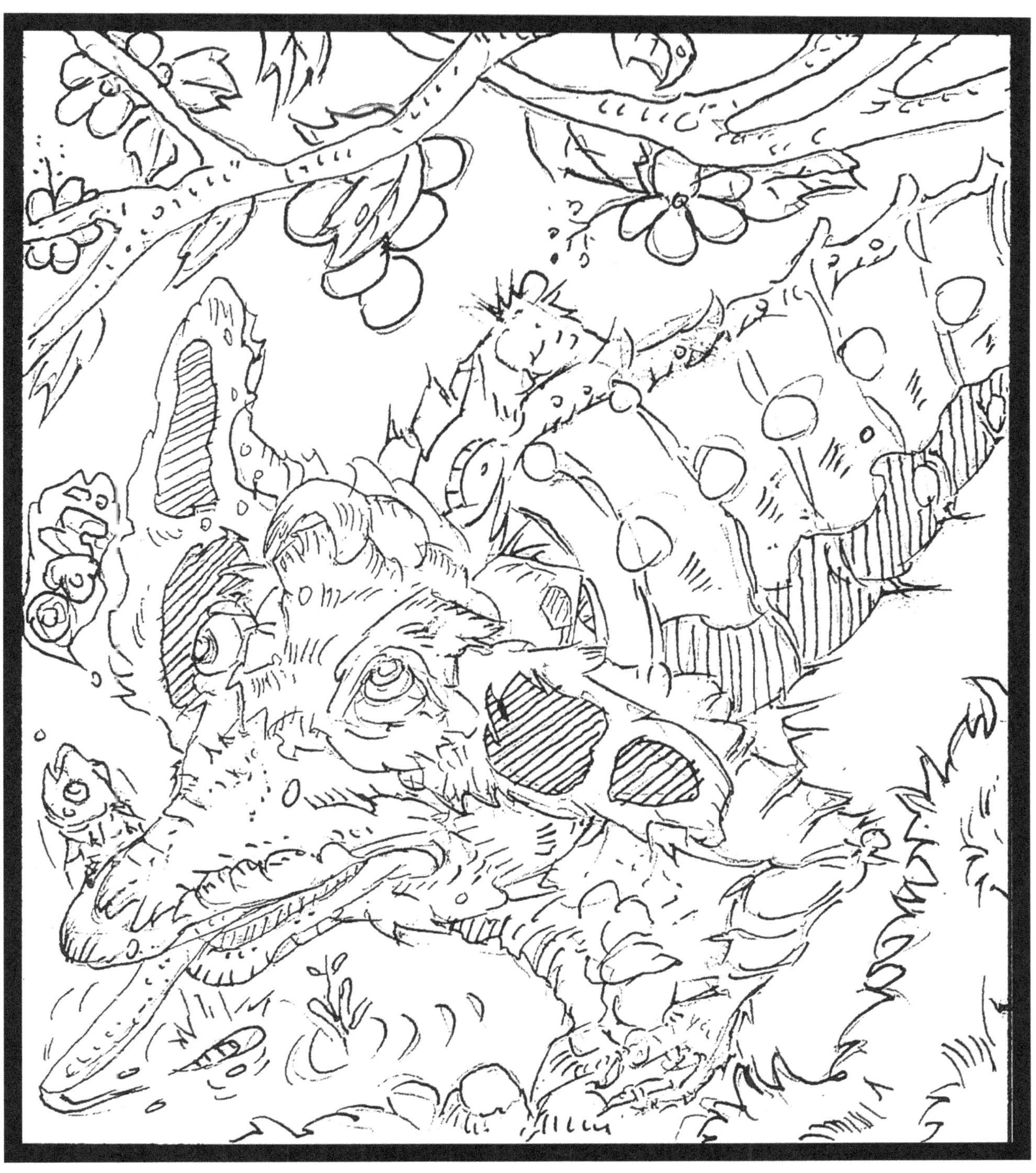

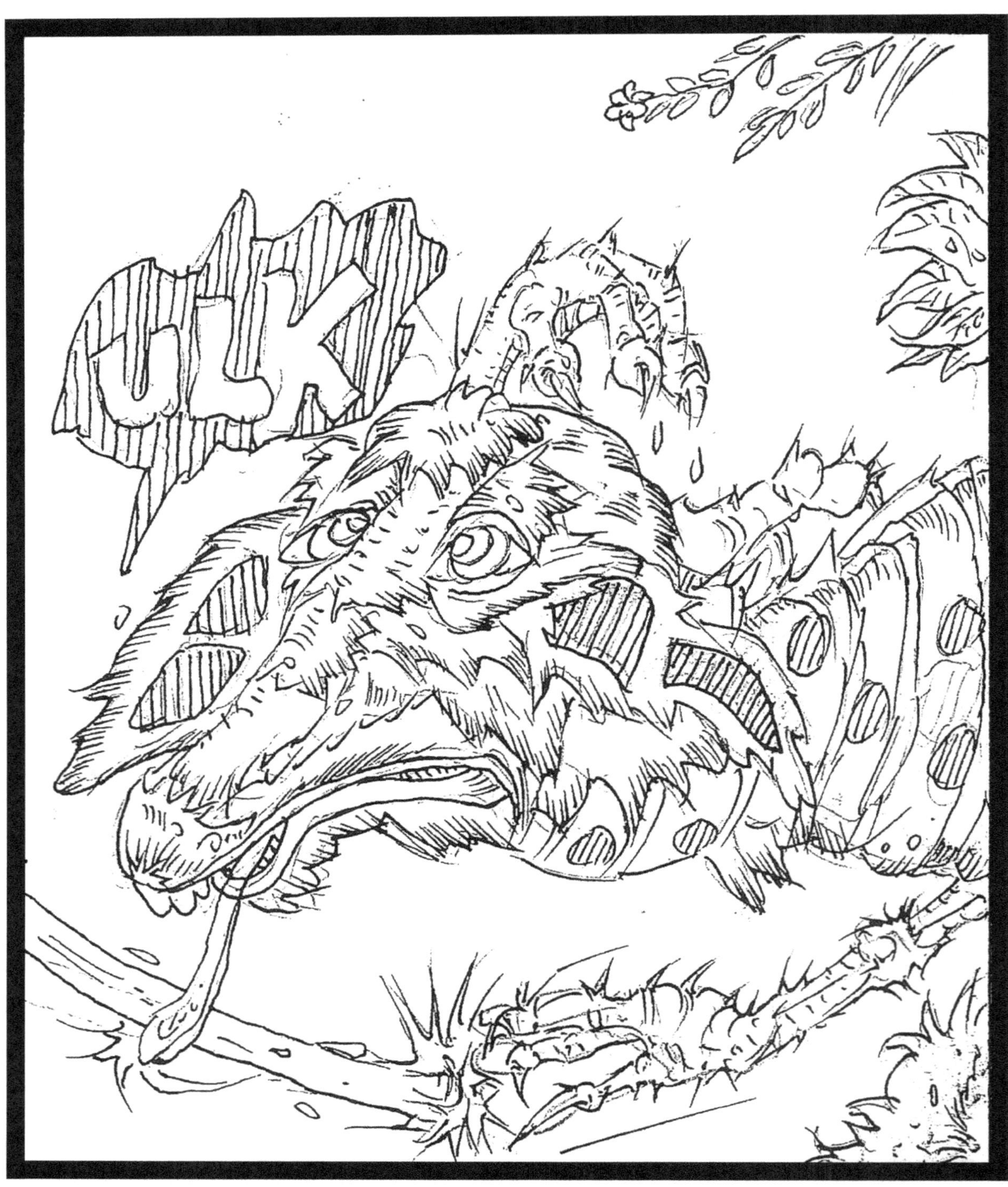
ULK!

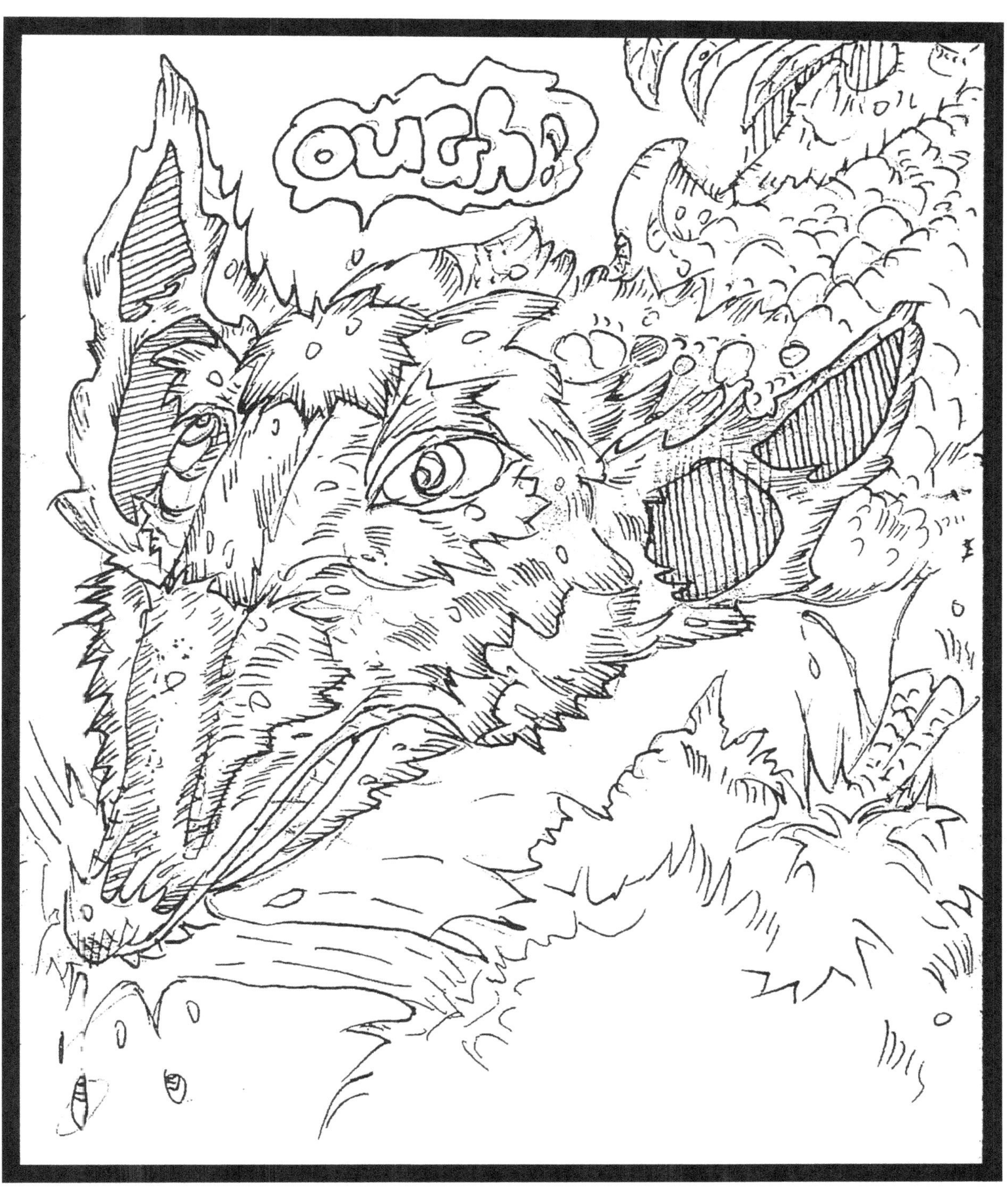

OUGH!

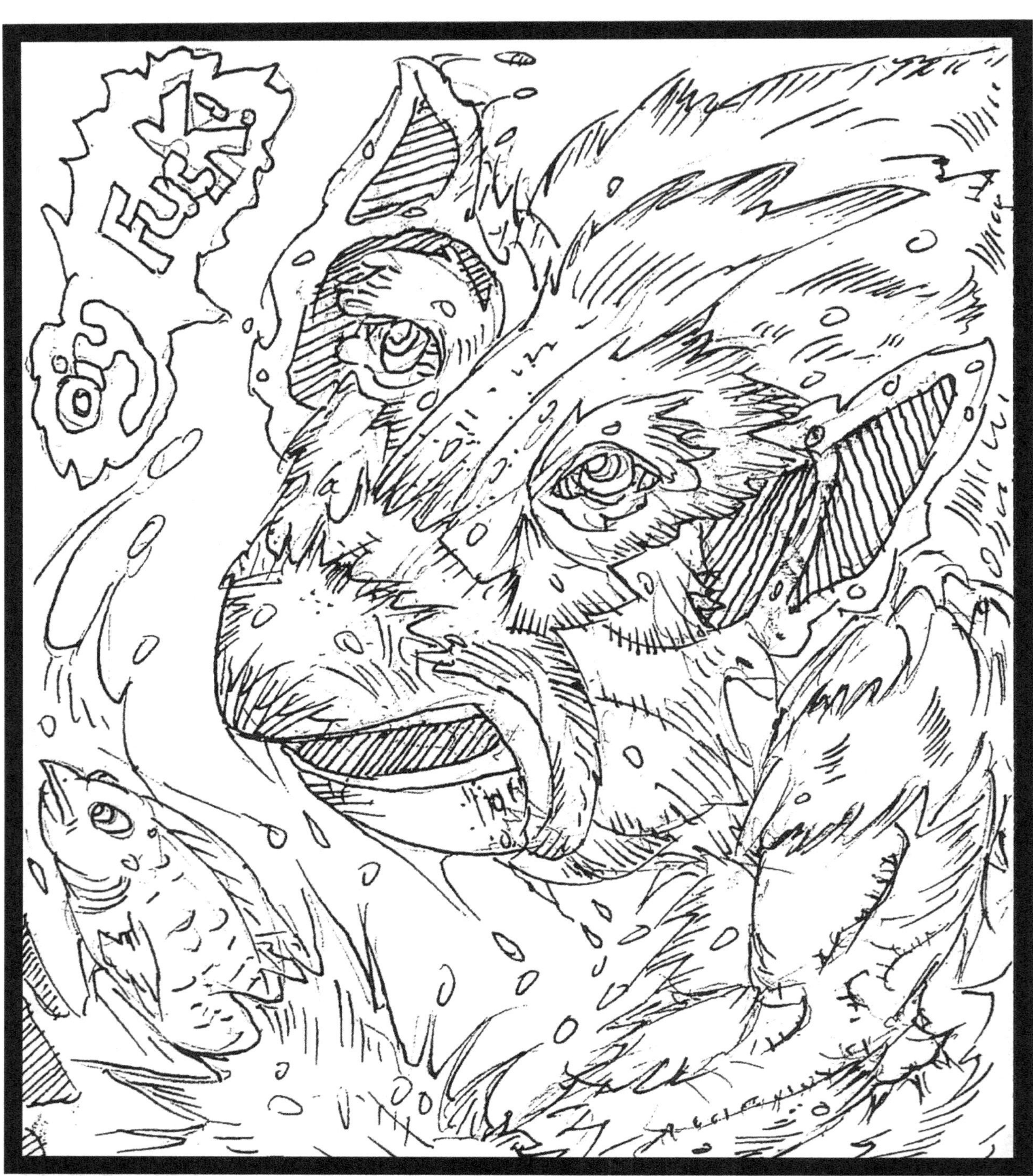

FUK!

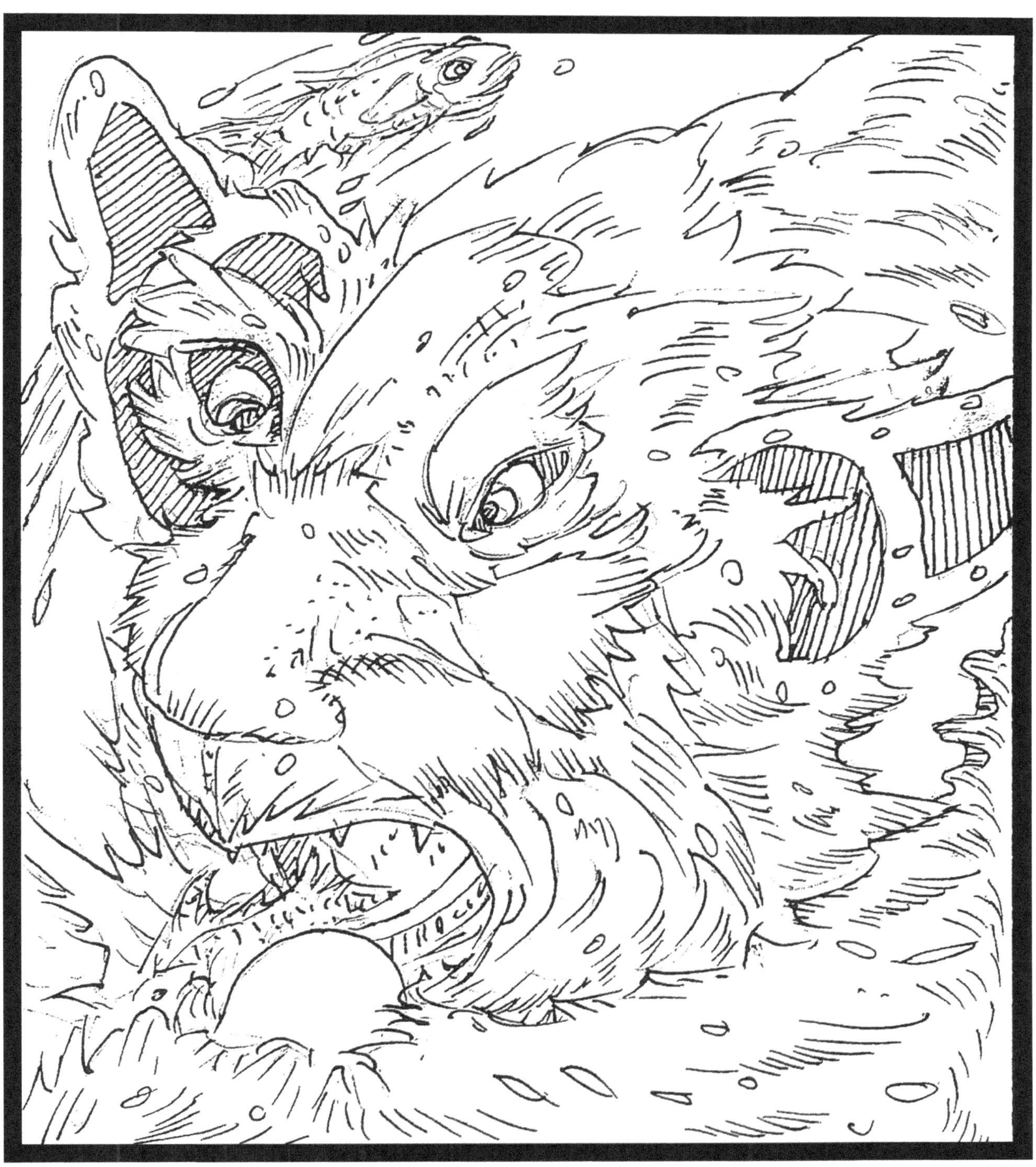

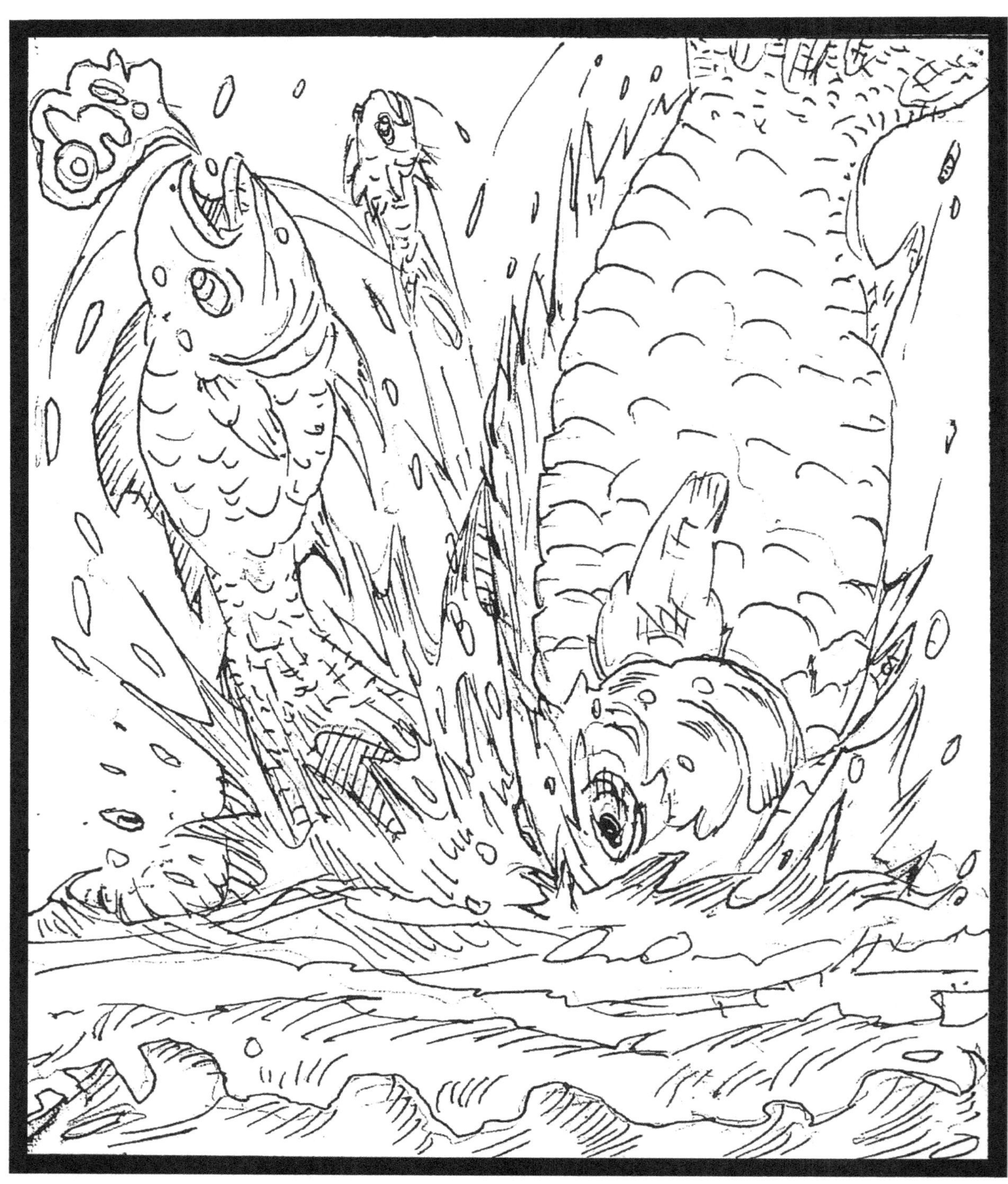

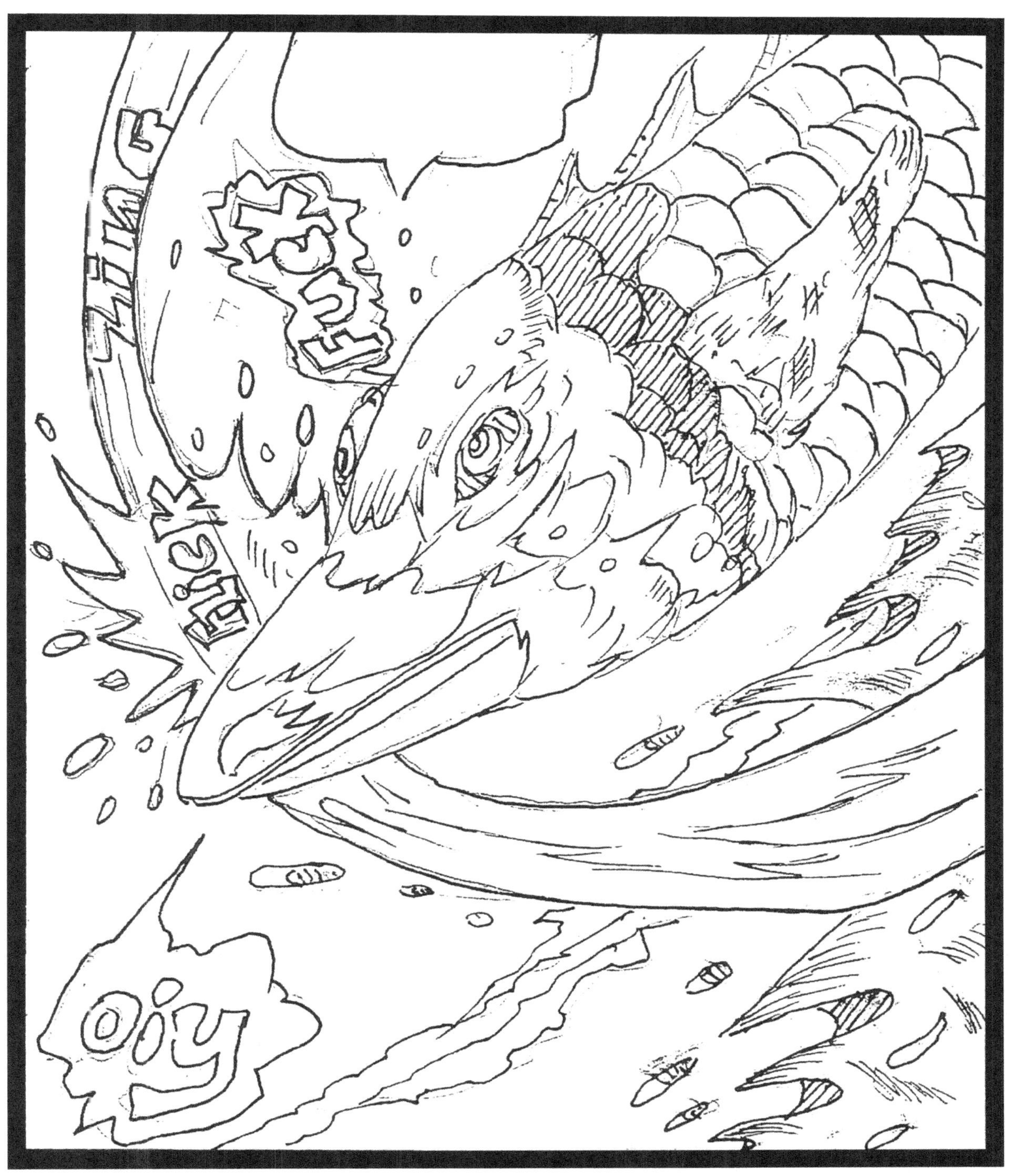

SWiiNG
FUCK
FliCK
oiy

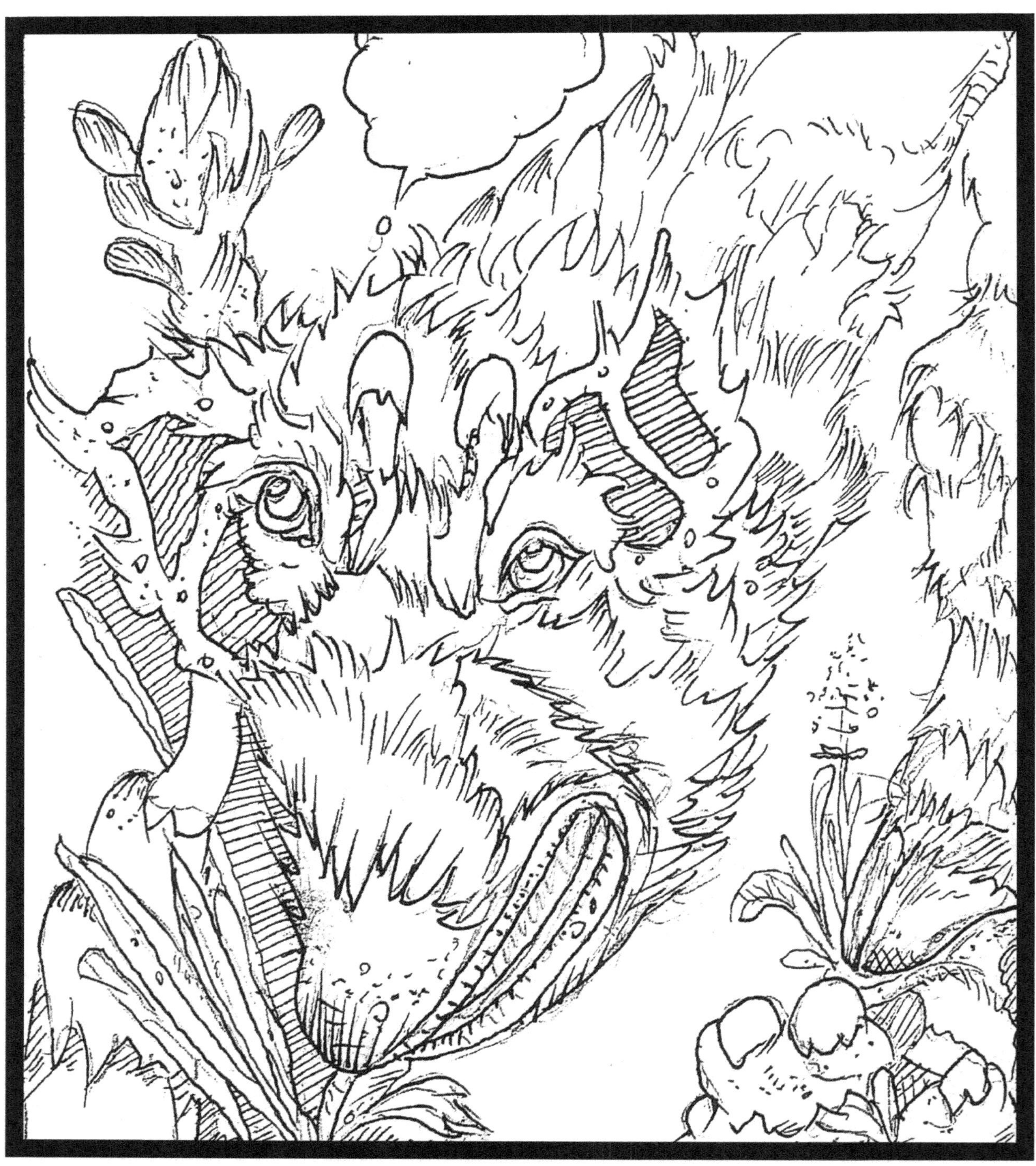

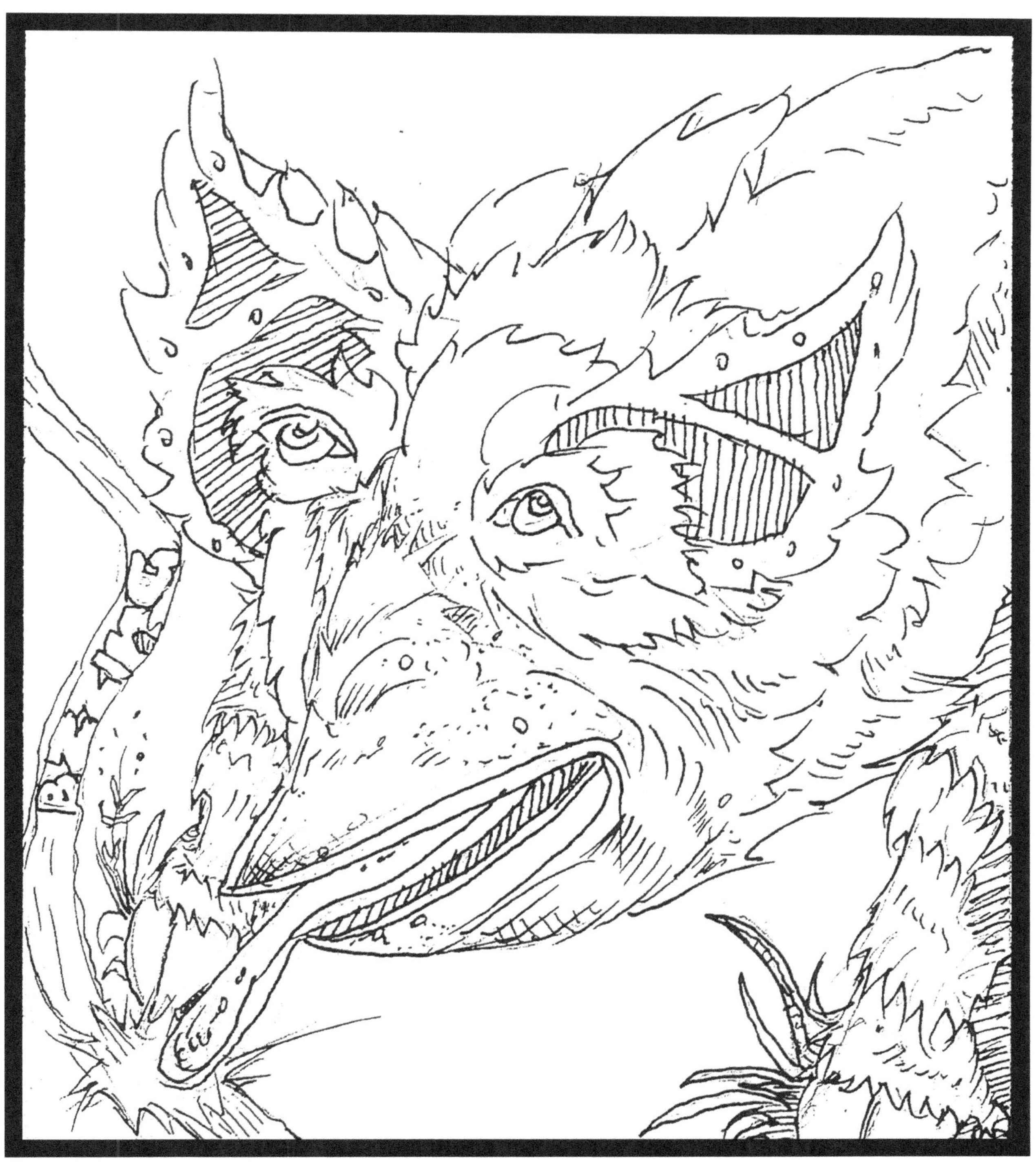

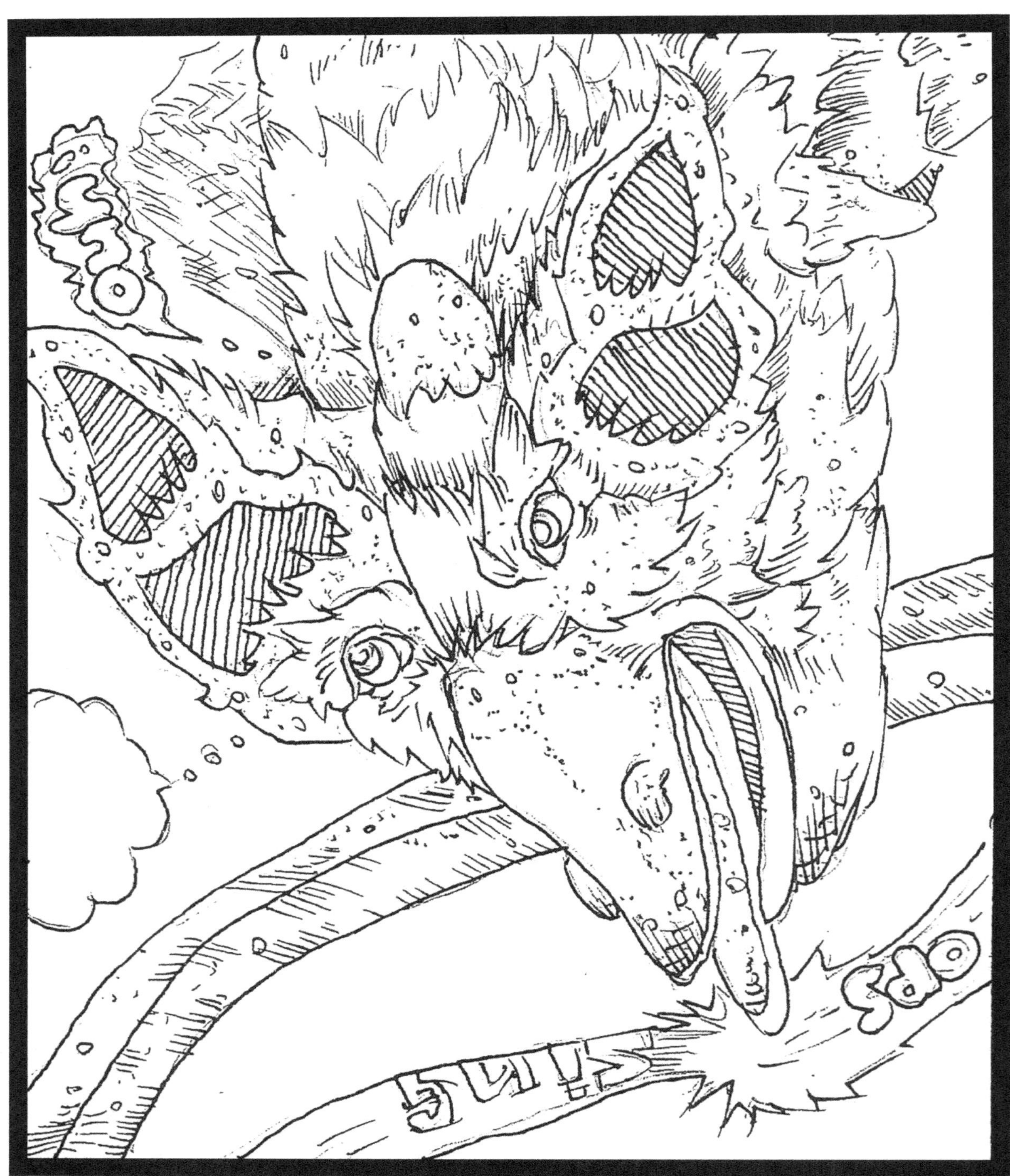
OOM
OPS
SHIS

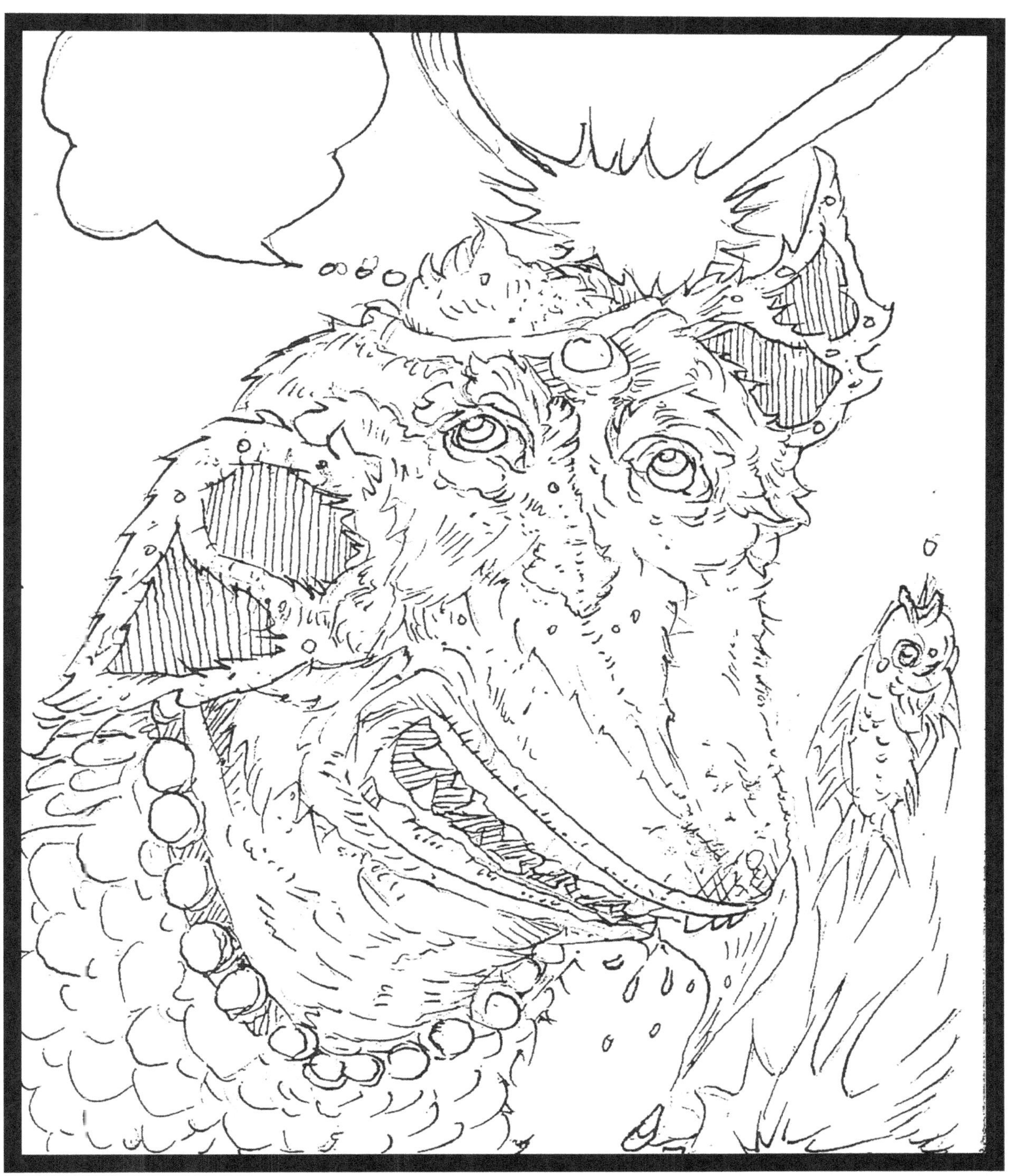

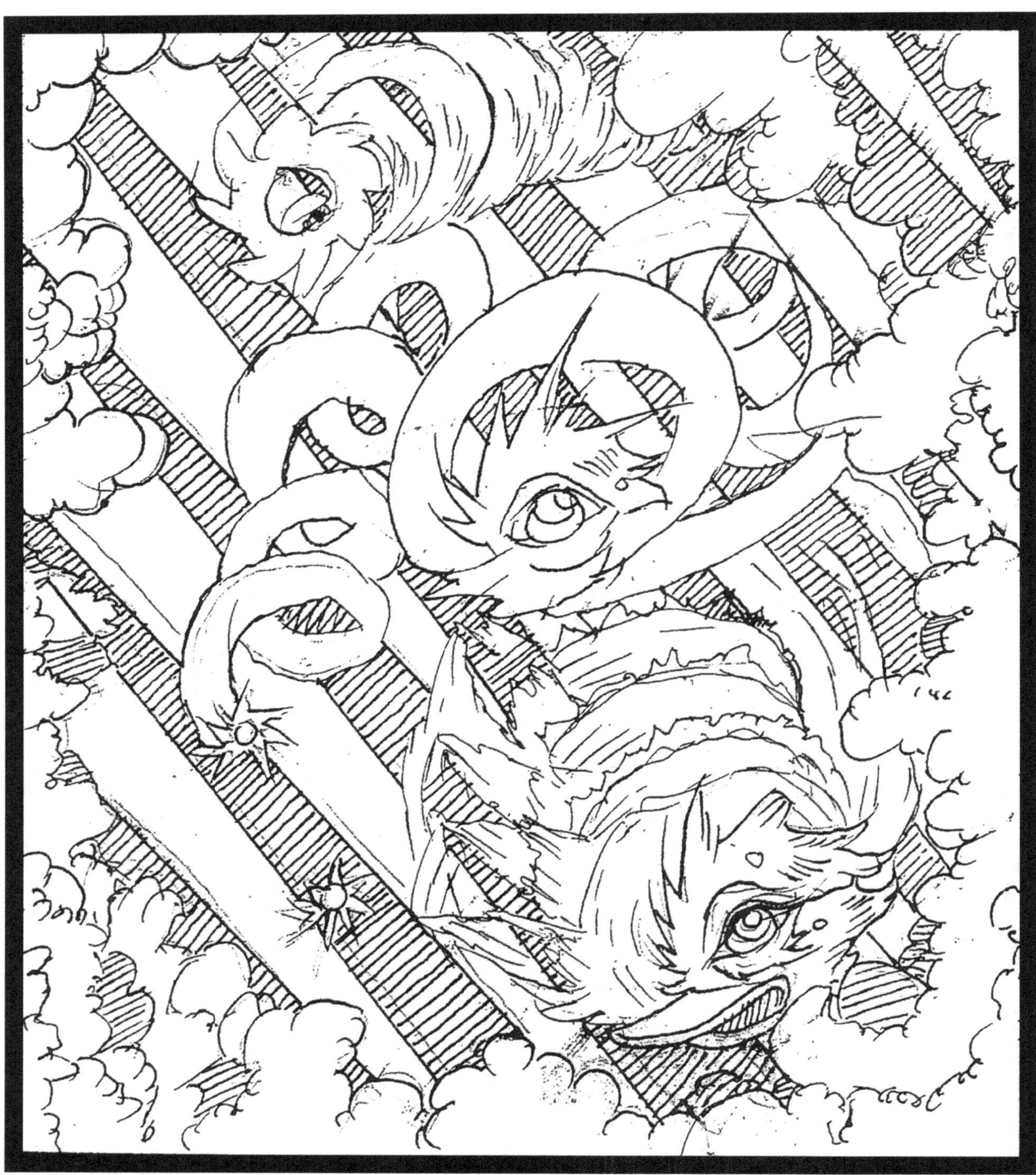

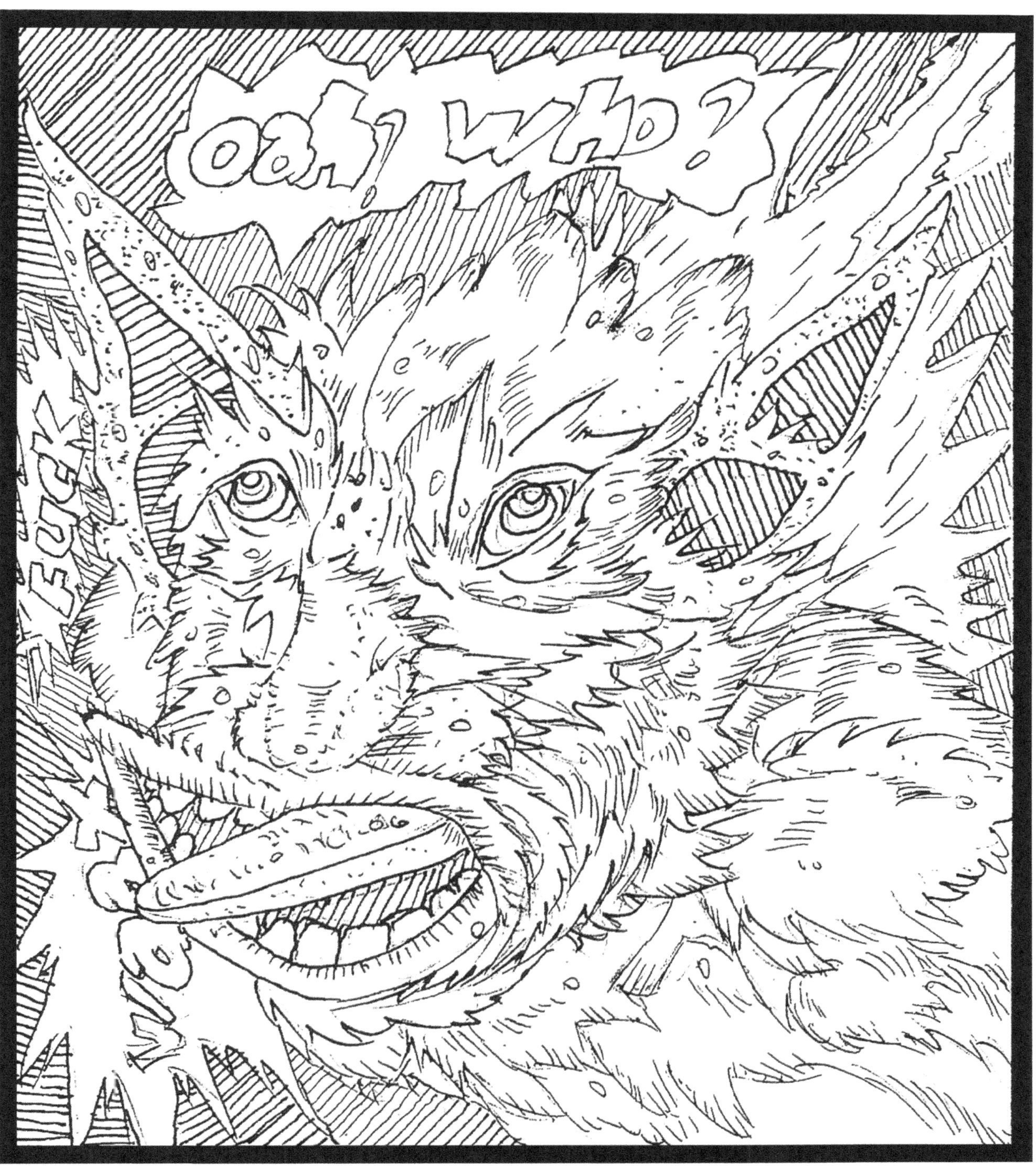

209

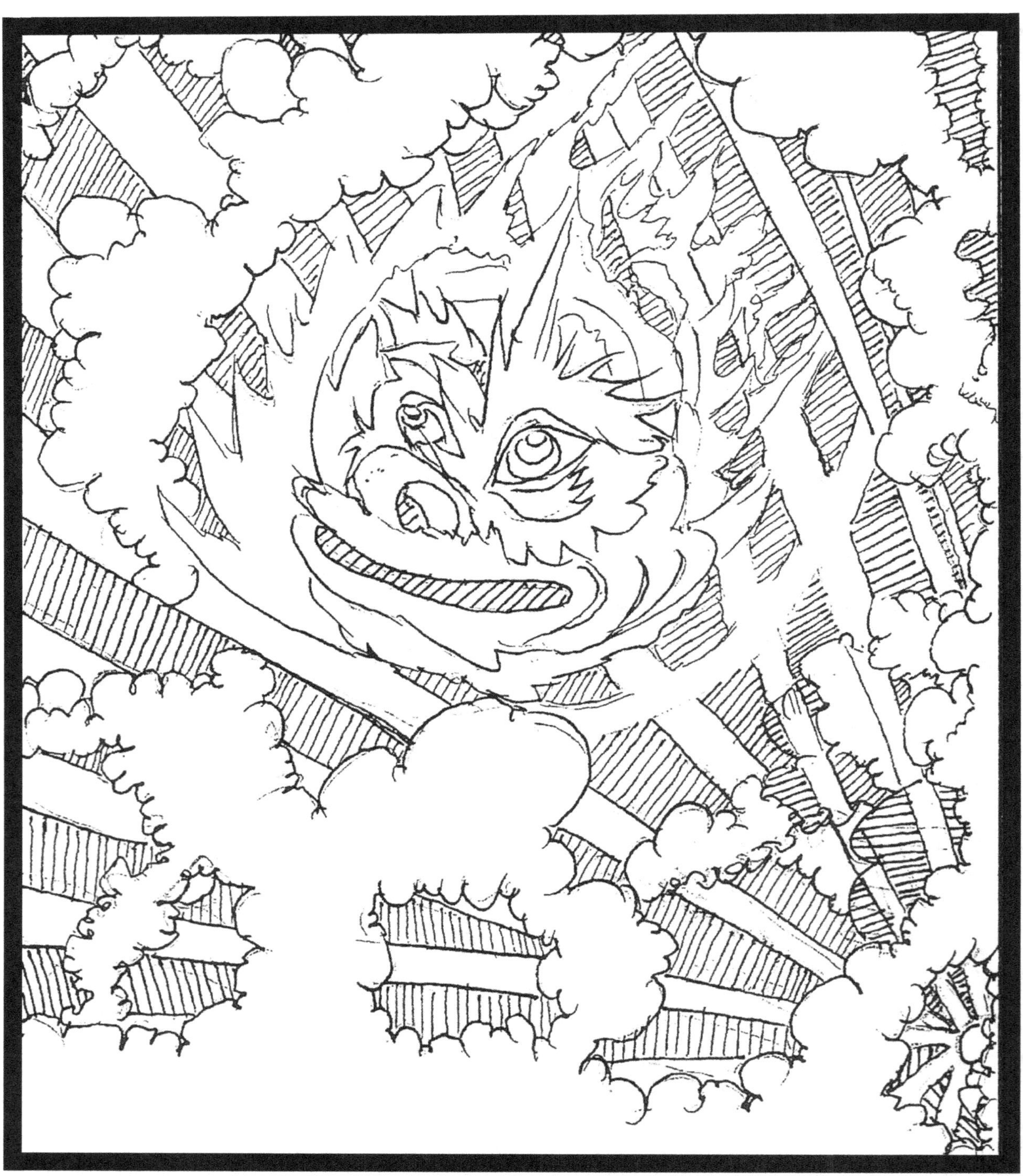

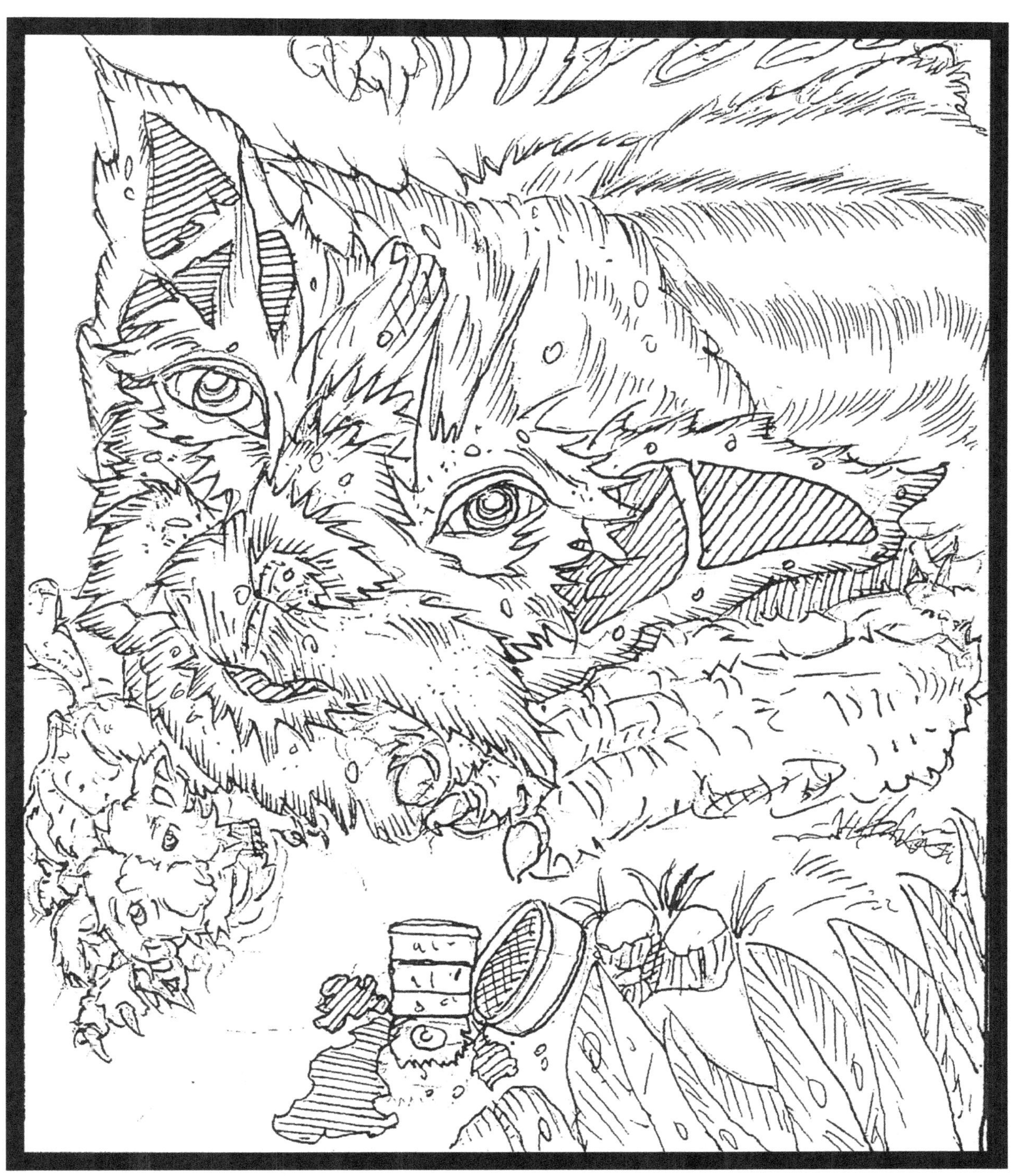

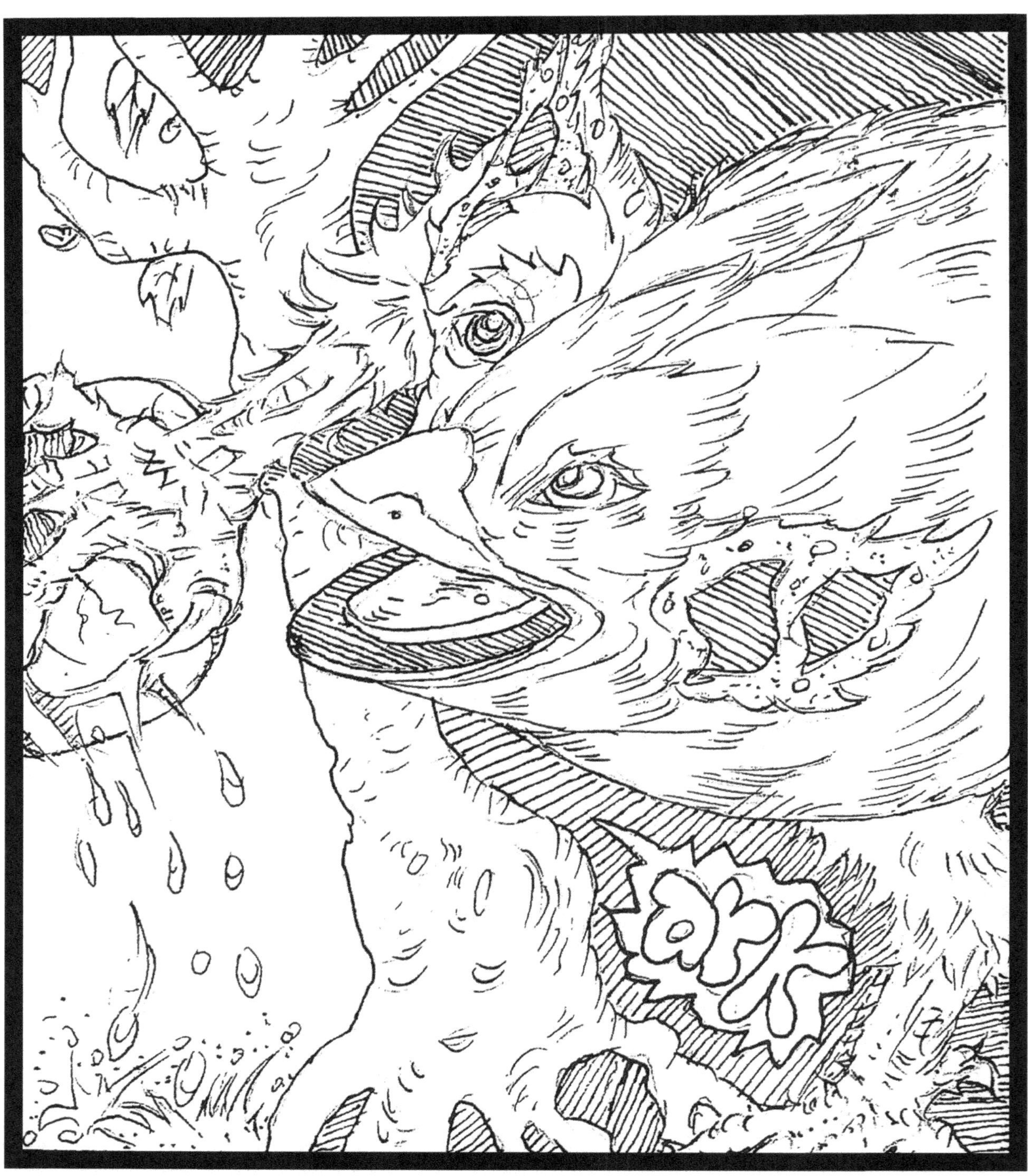

ark

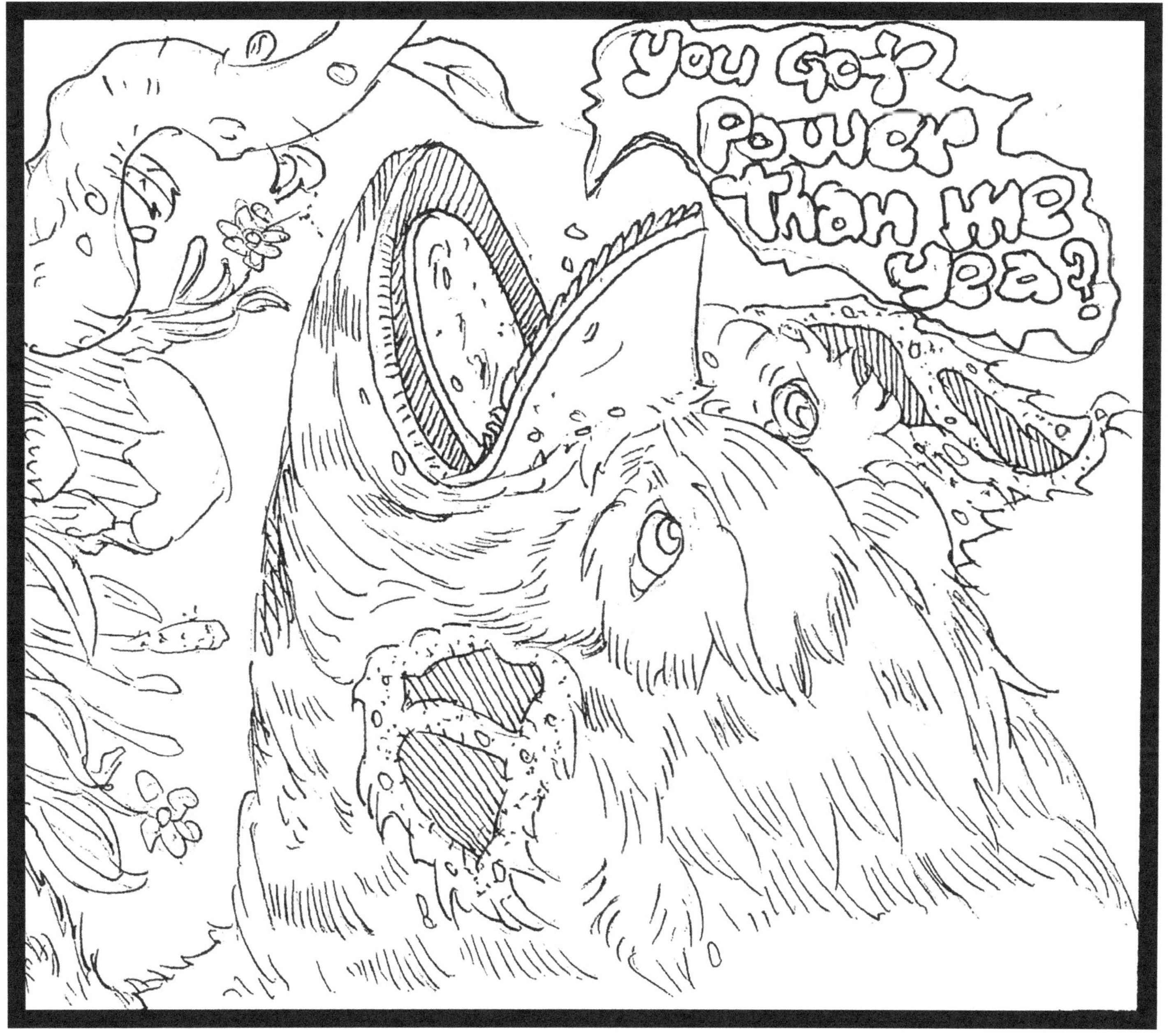

You Got
Power
Than me
yea?

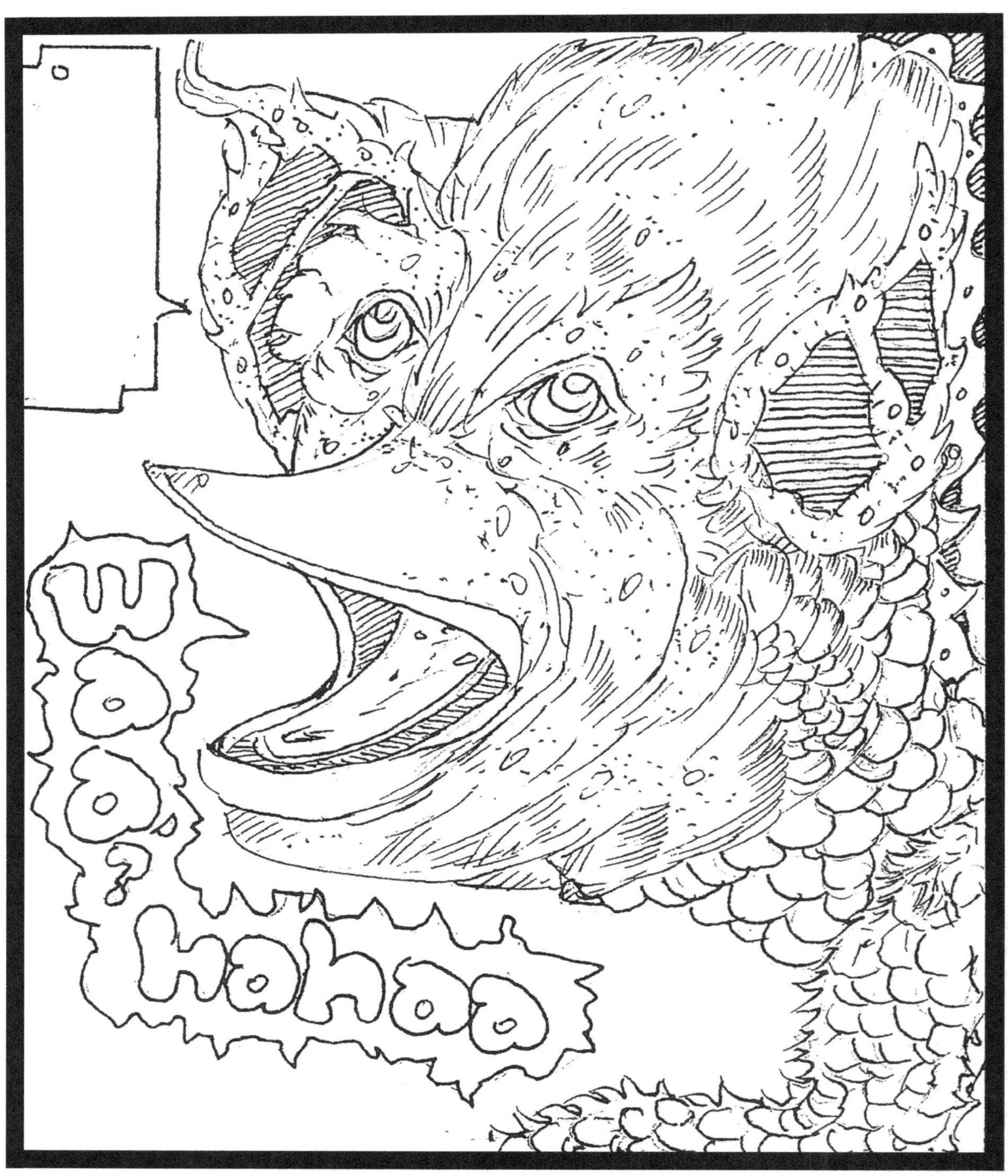

Waa,
hahaa

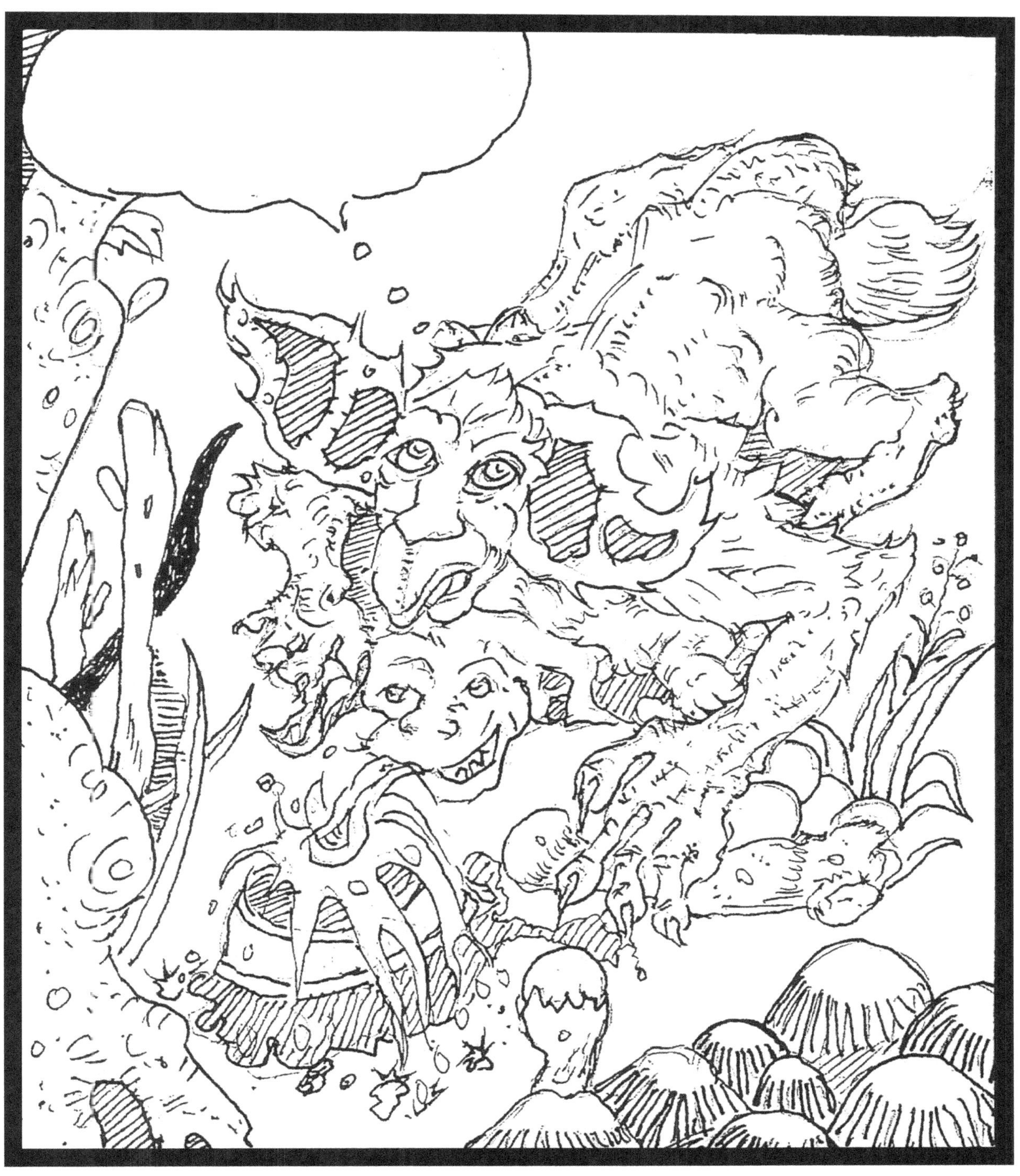

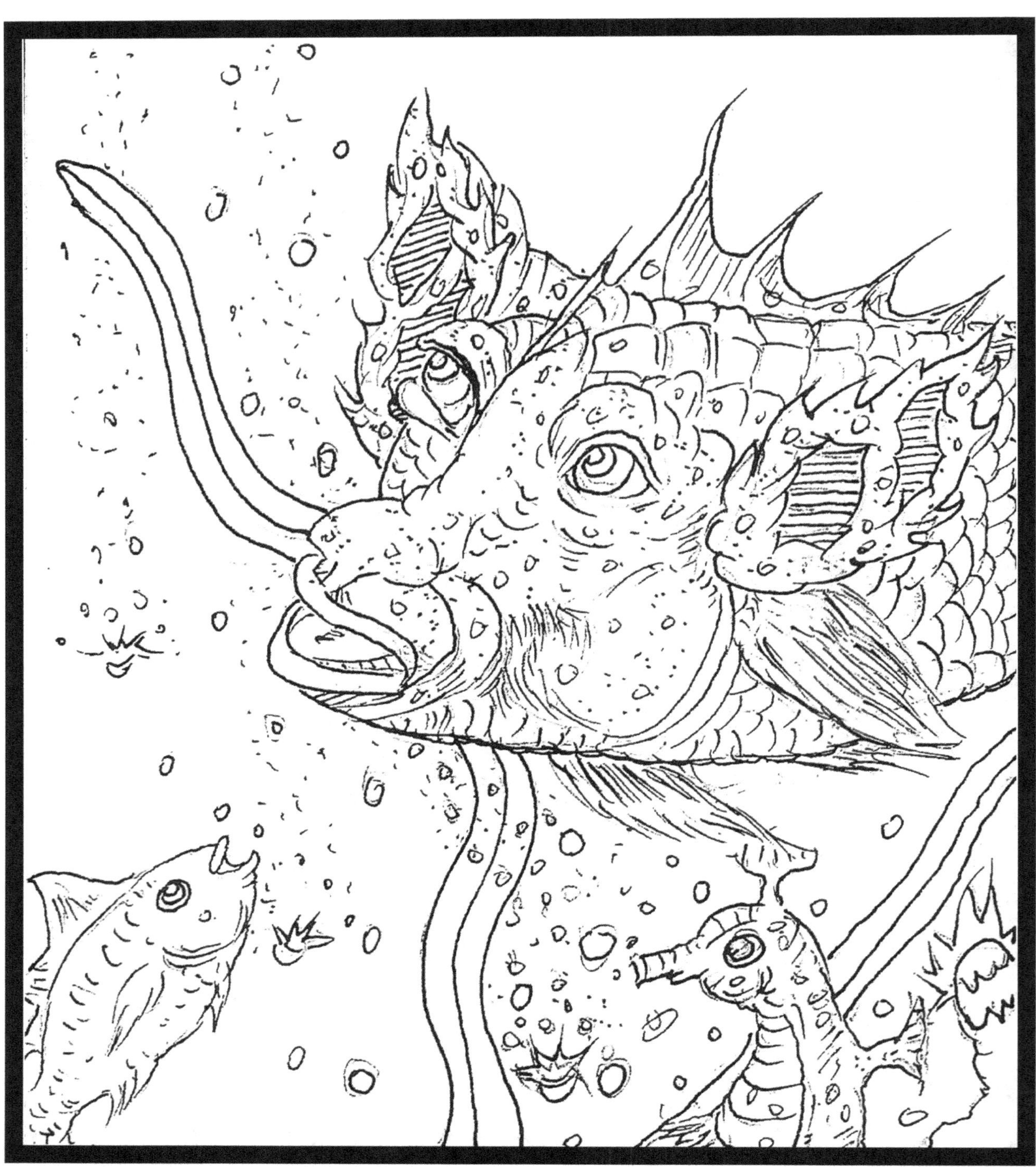

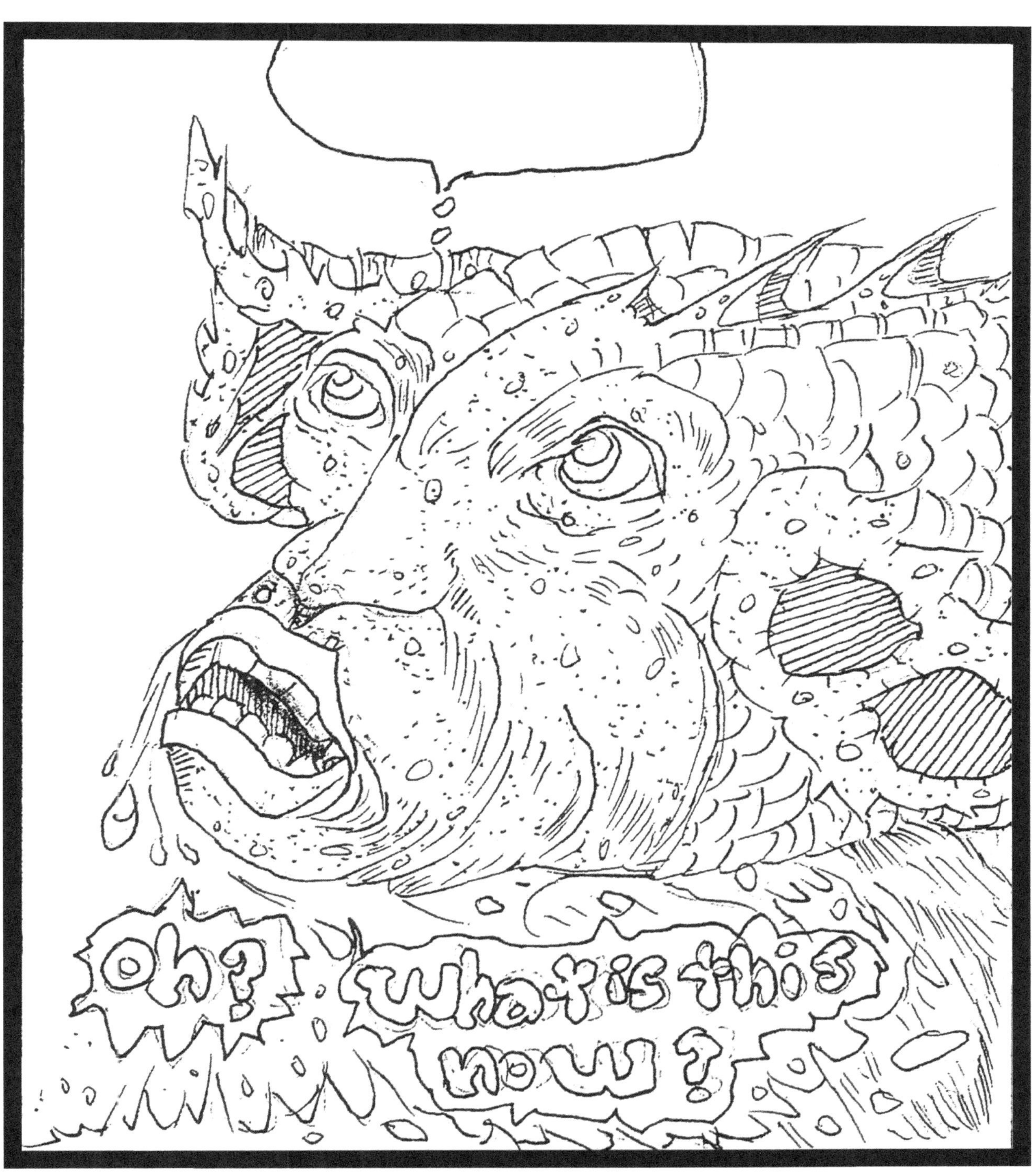

Oh? what is this now?

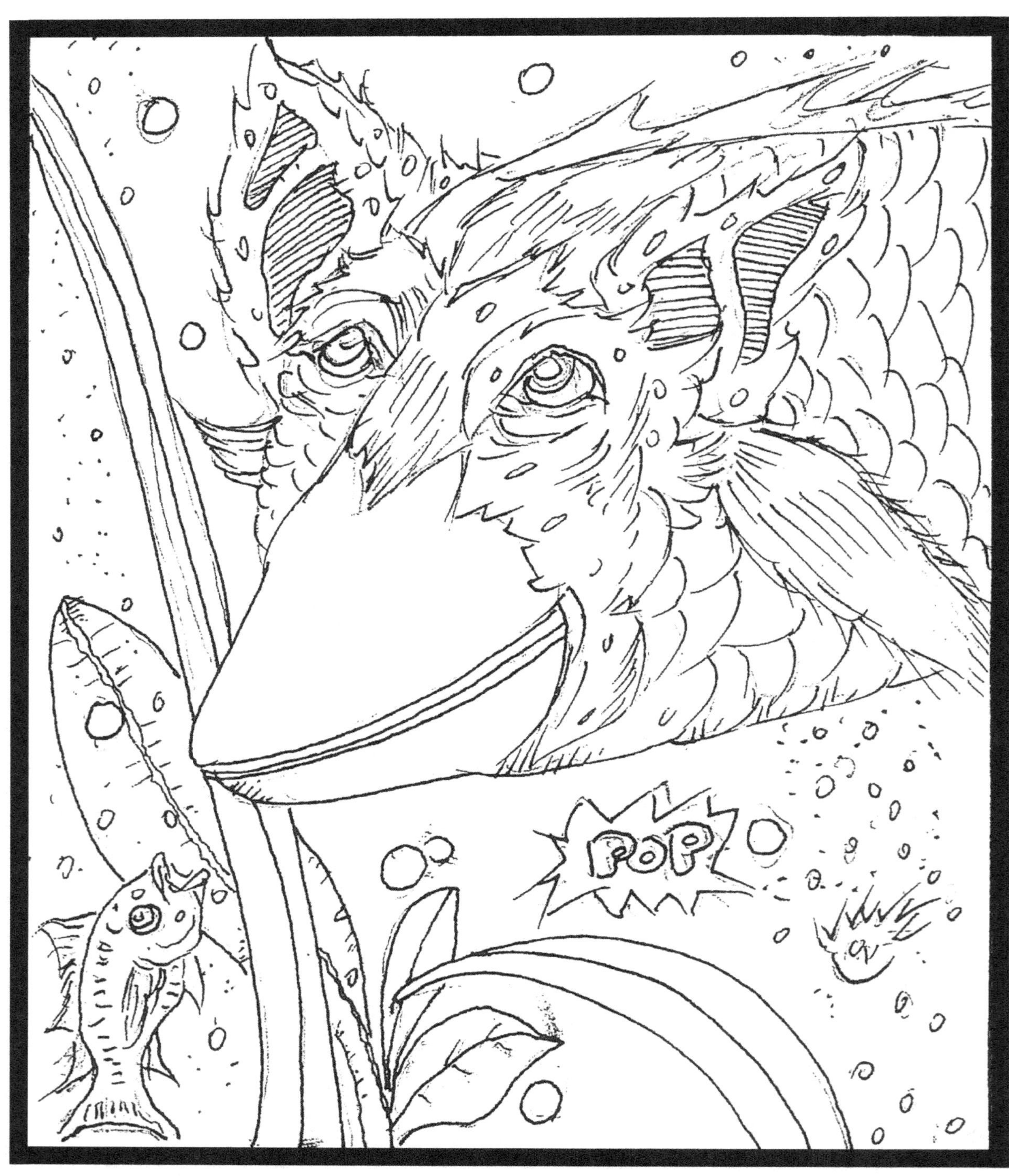

POP

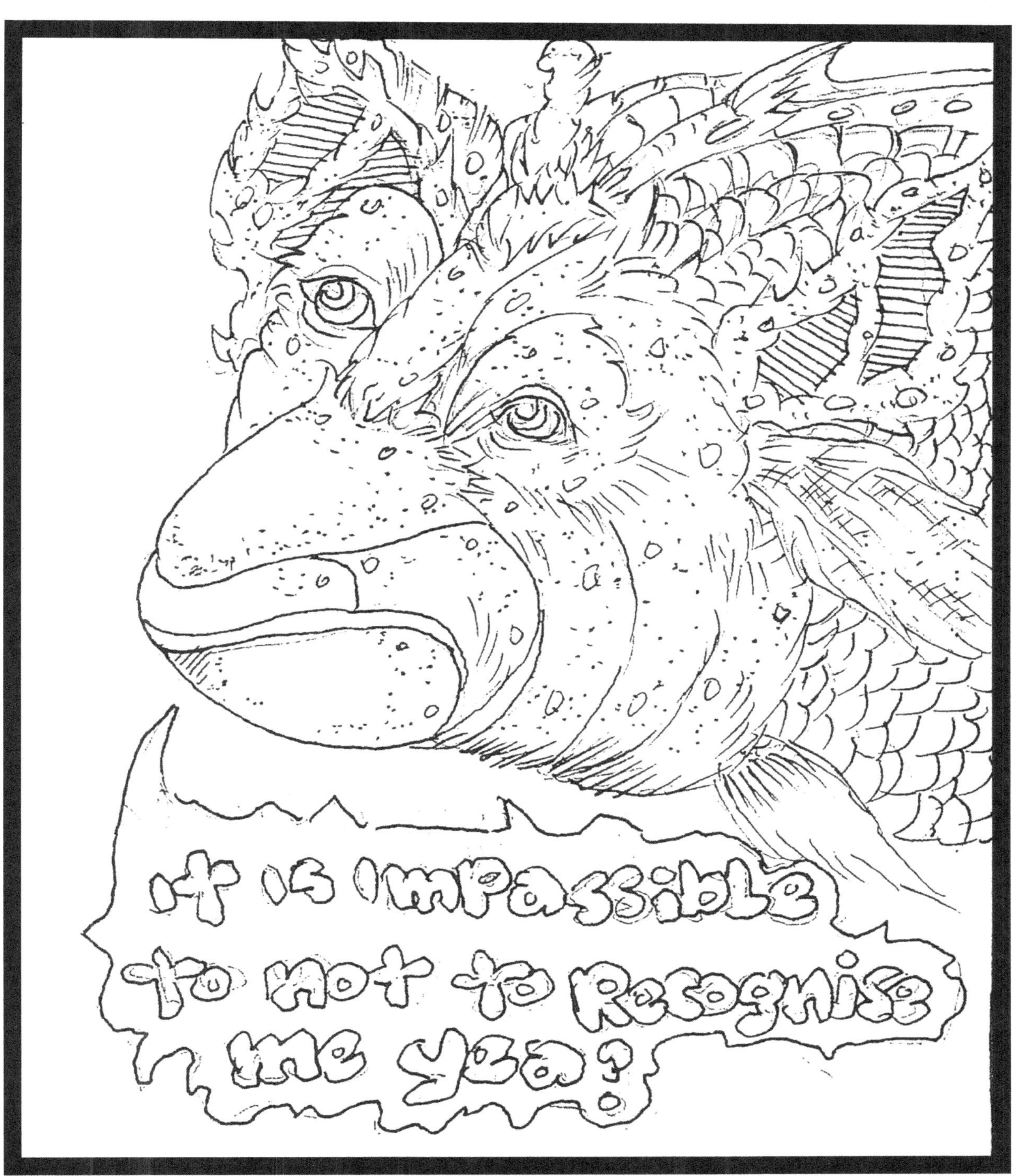
it is impossible
to not to Recognise
me yea?

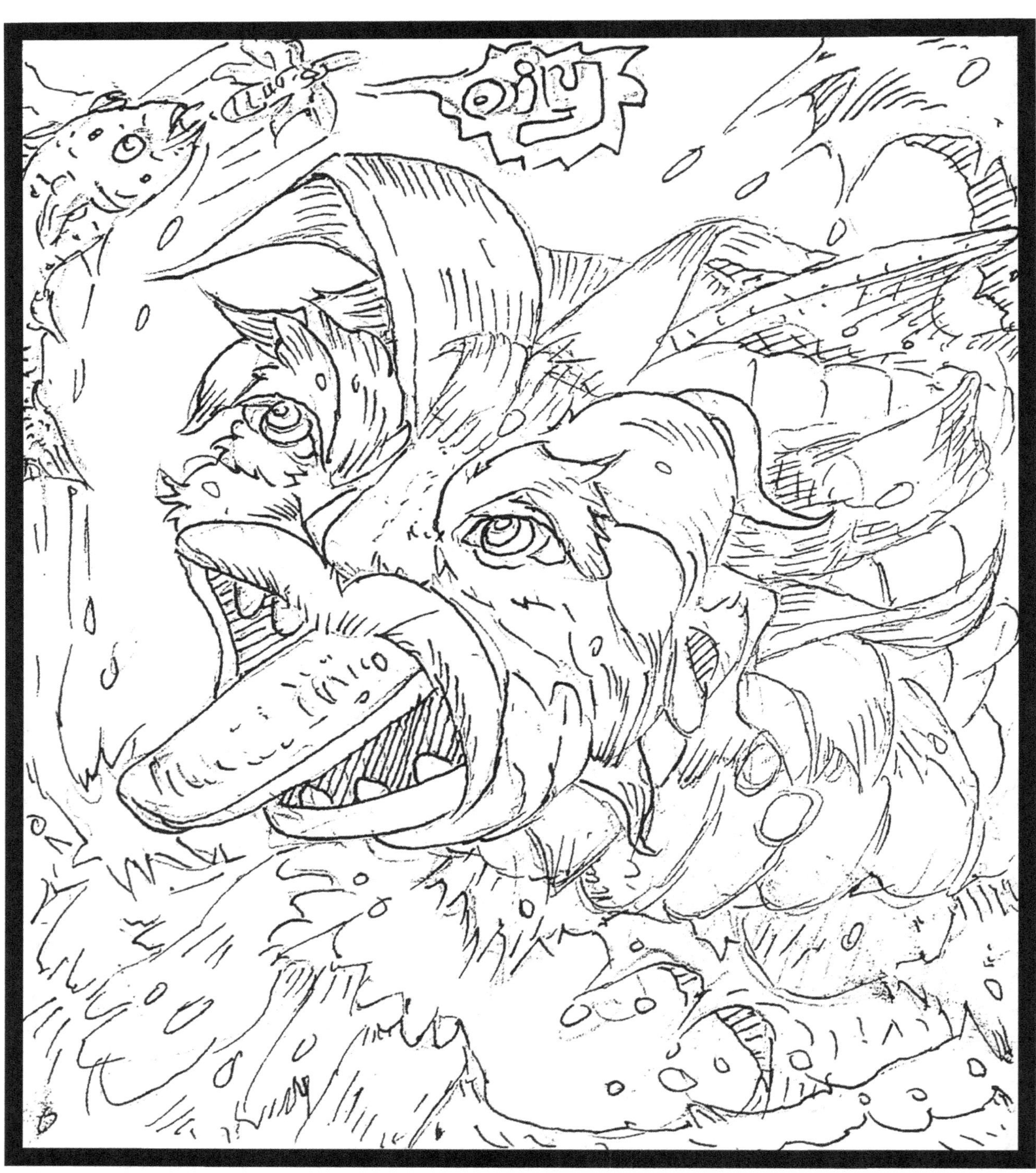

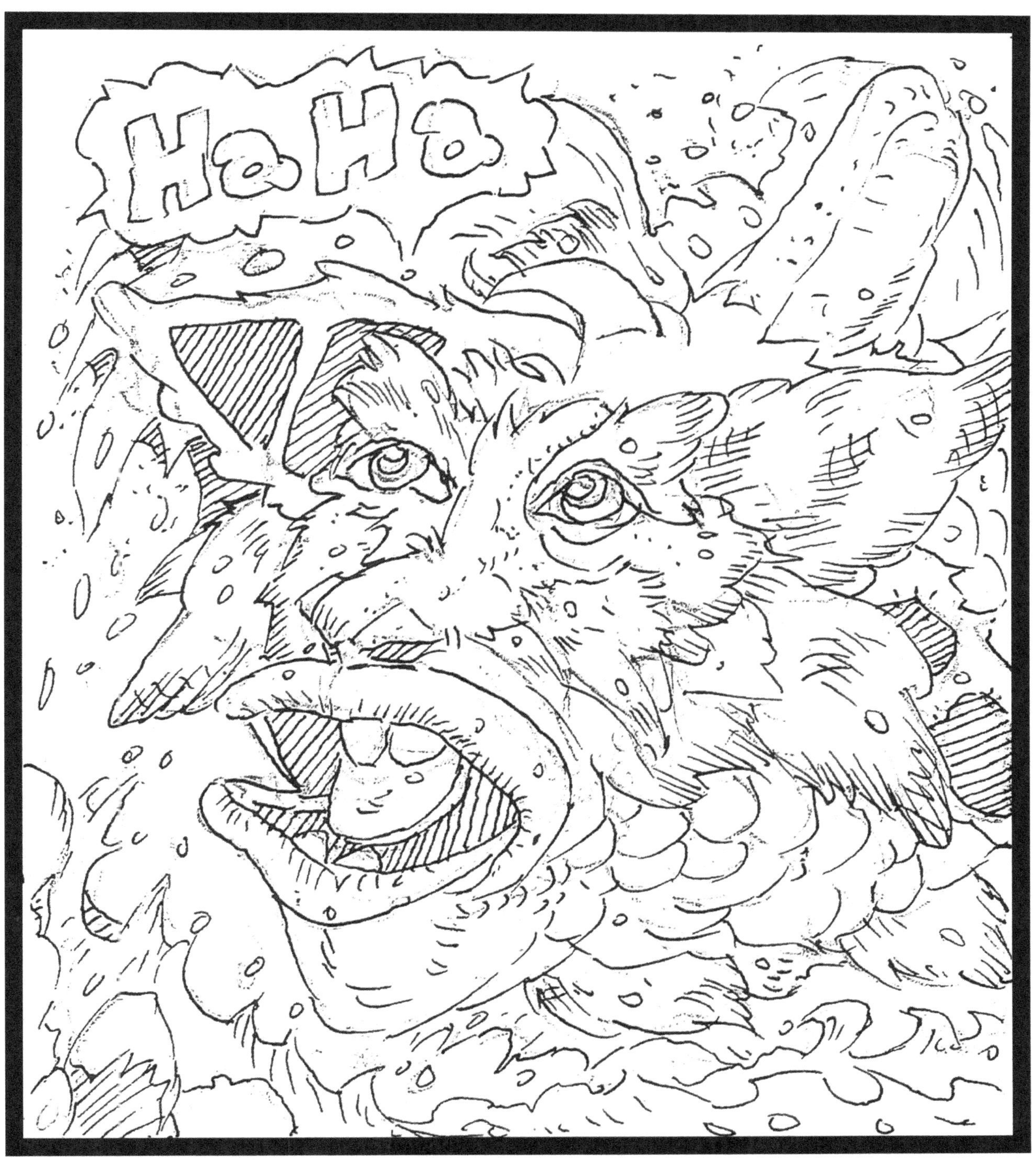

Ha Ha

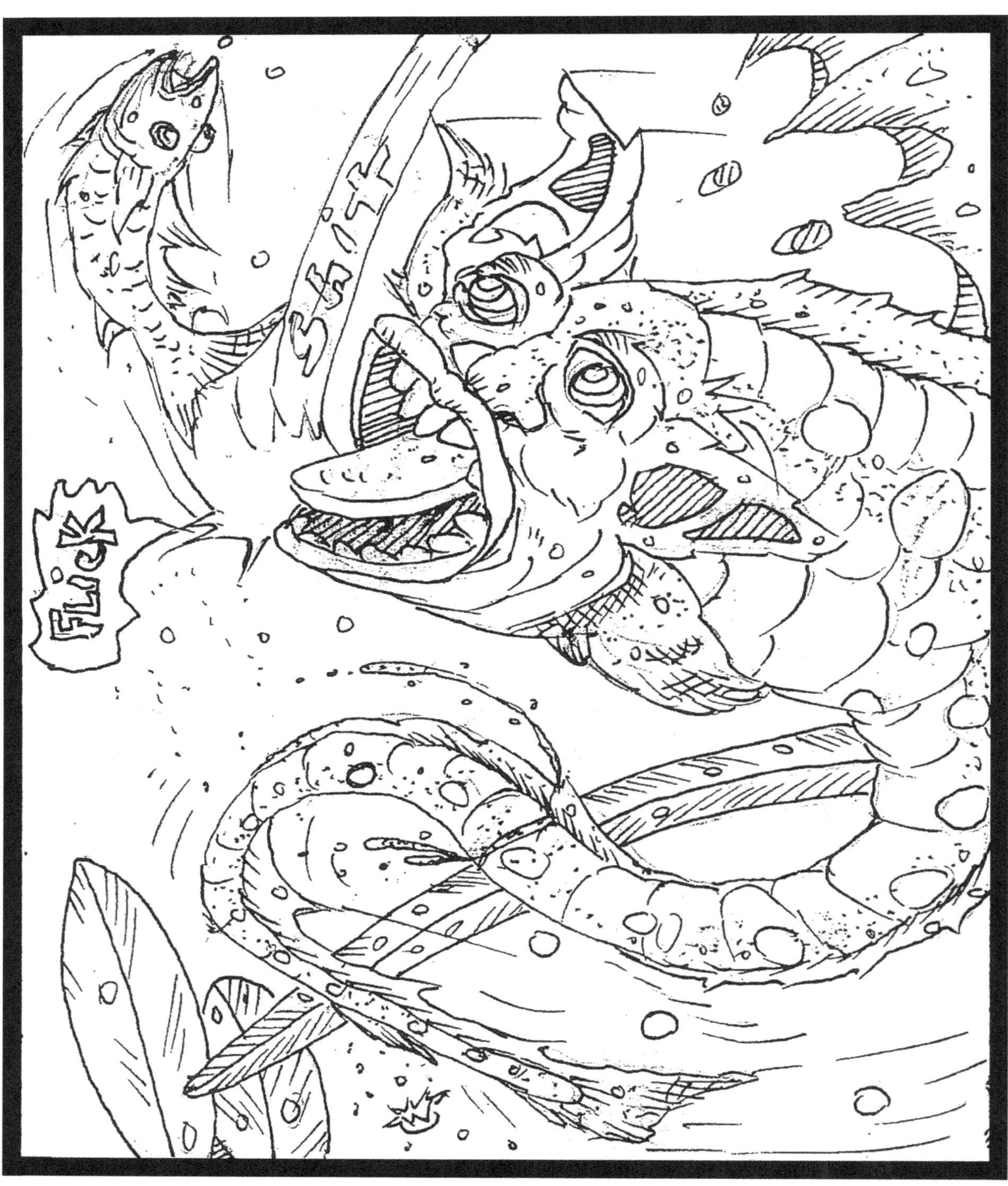

SHIFT
FLICK

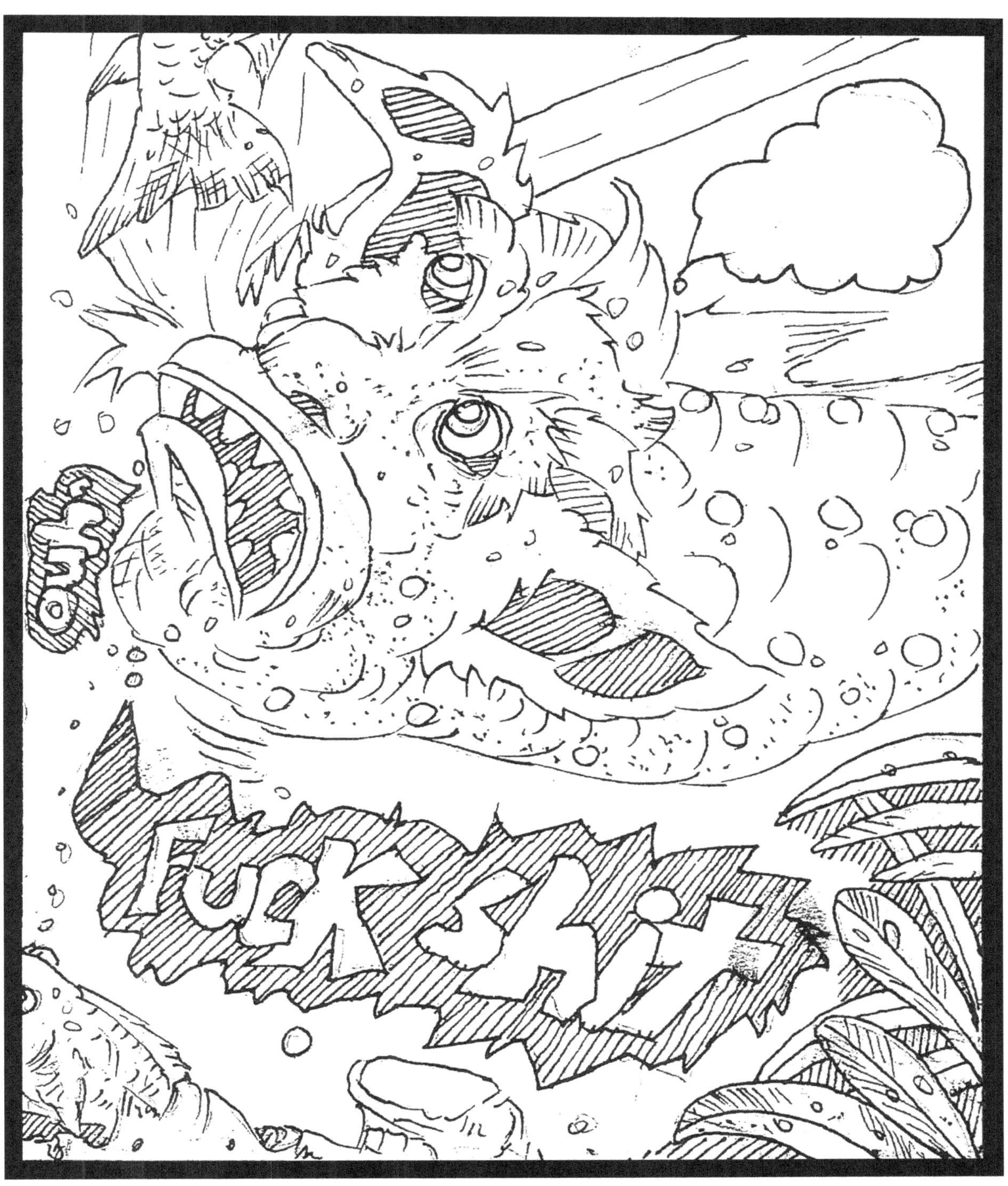
OH!
FUCK SHIT

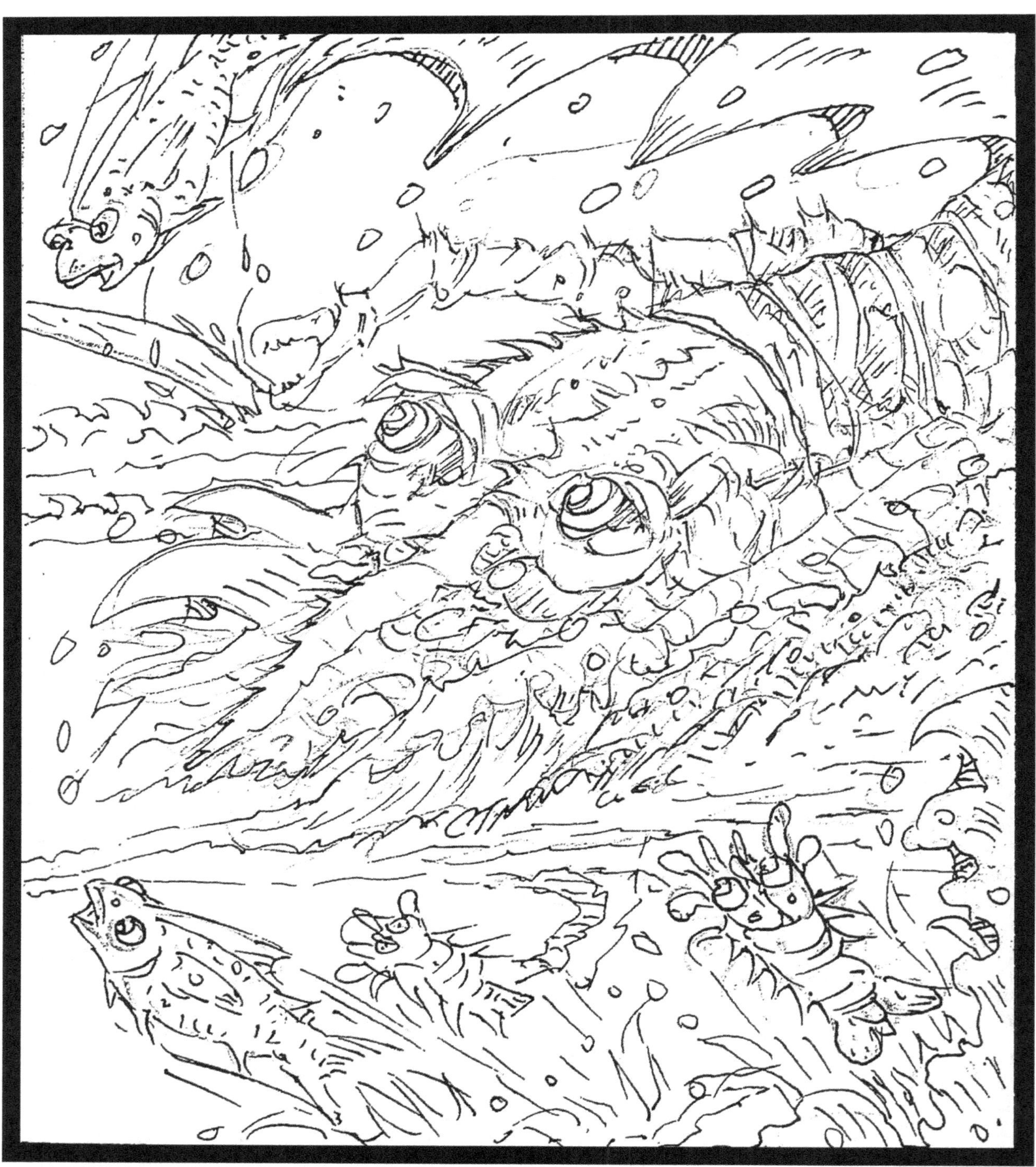

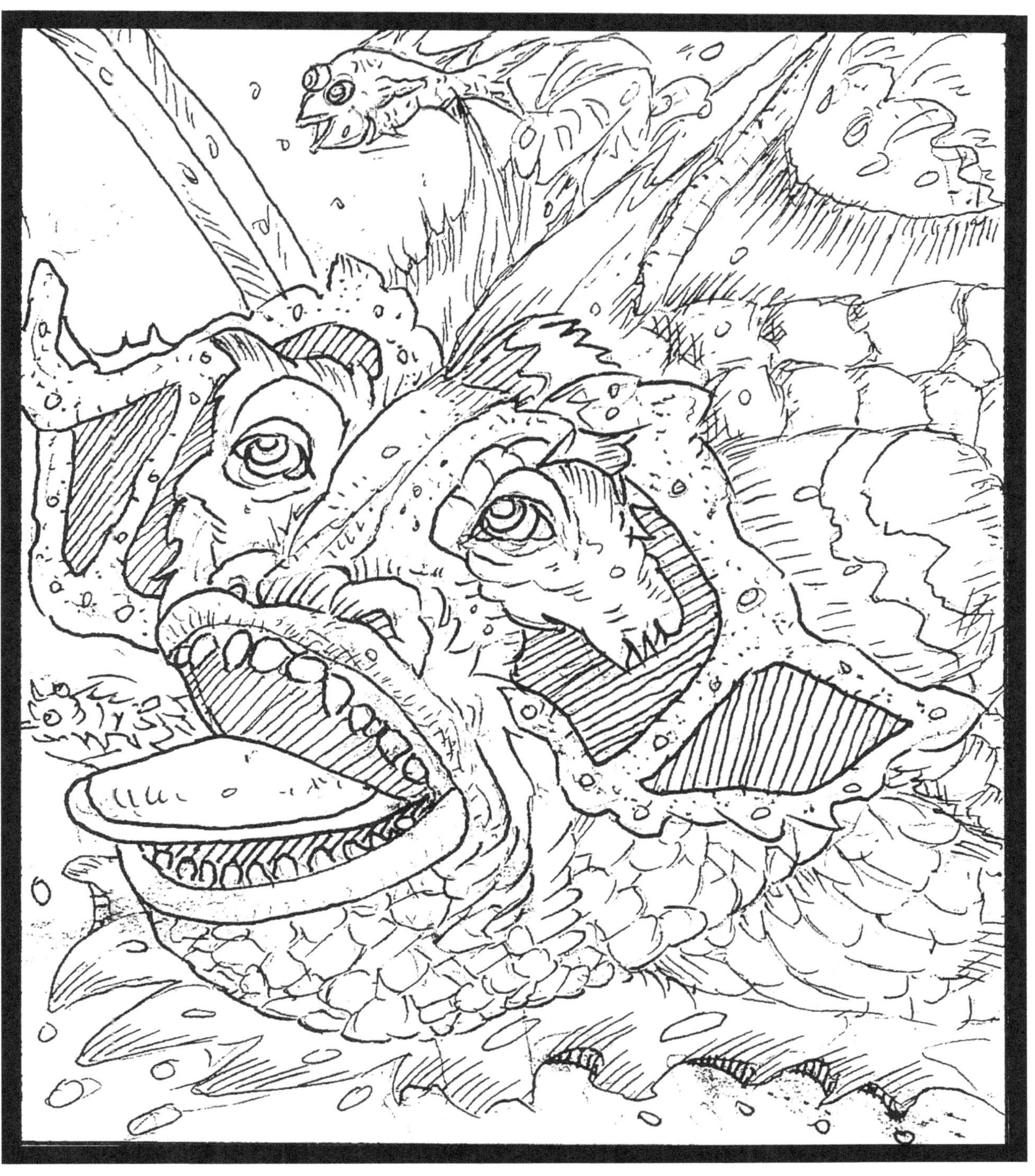

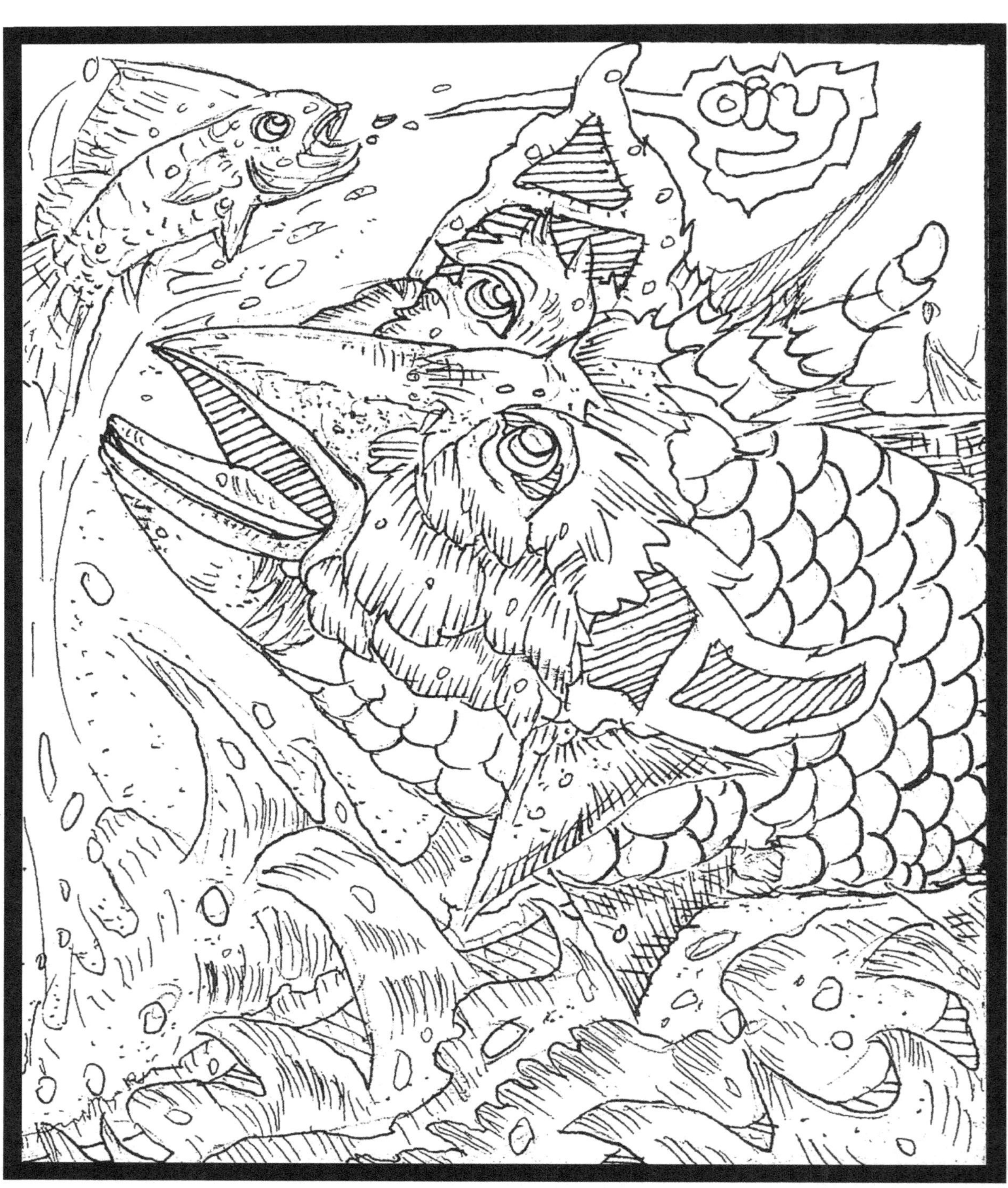

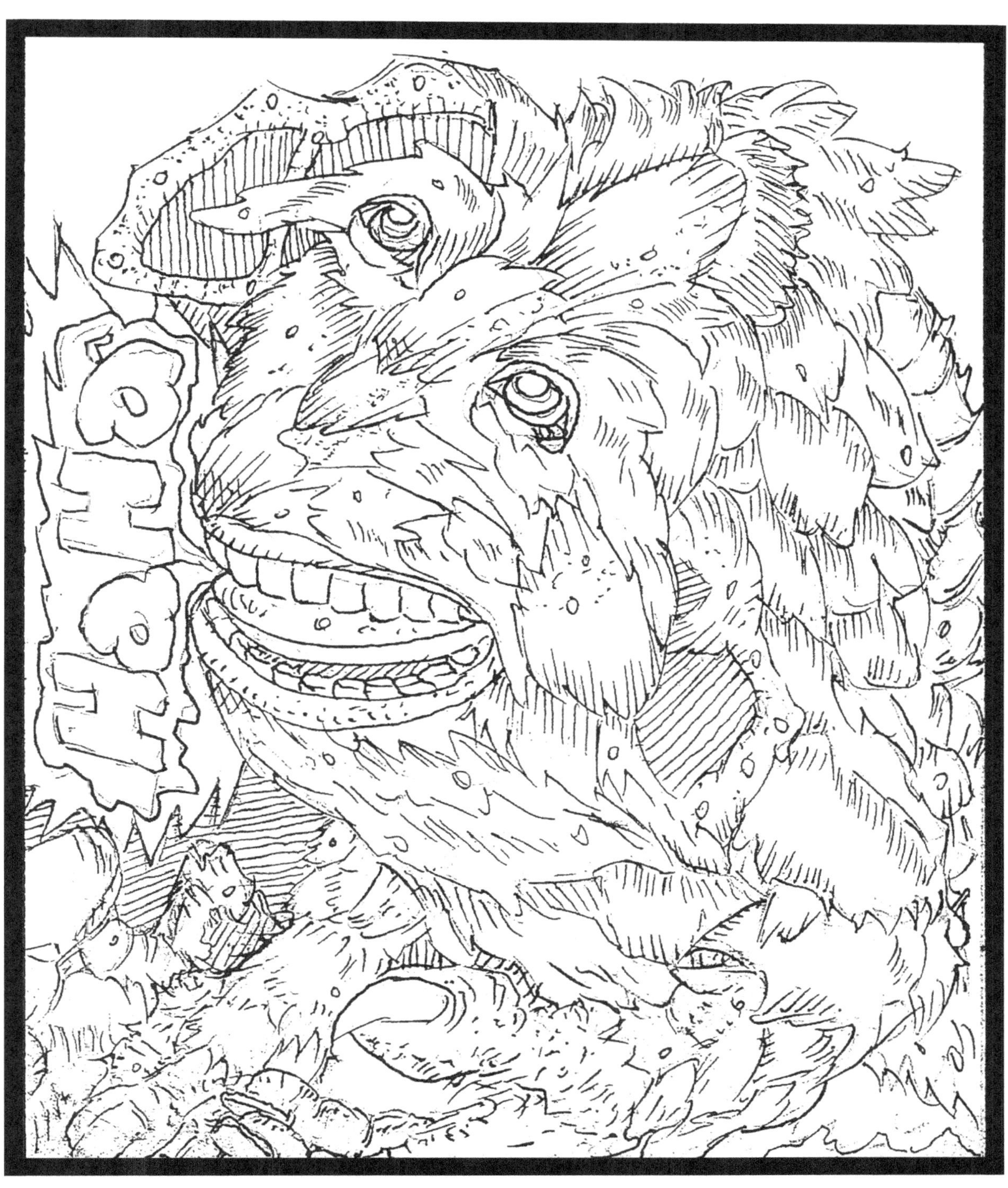

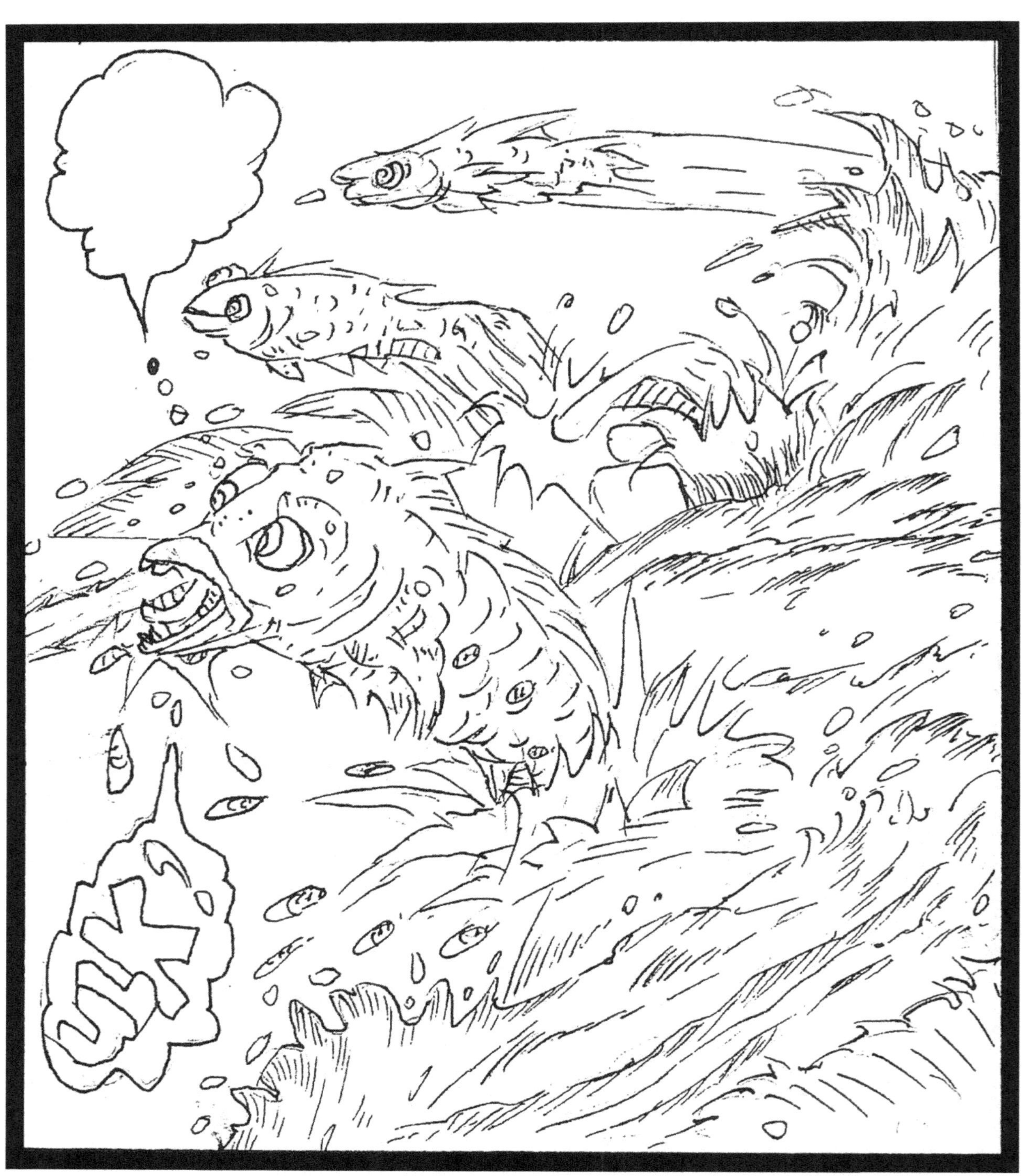
ゴボボ

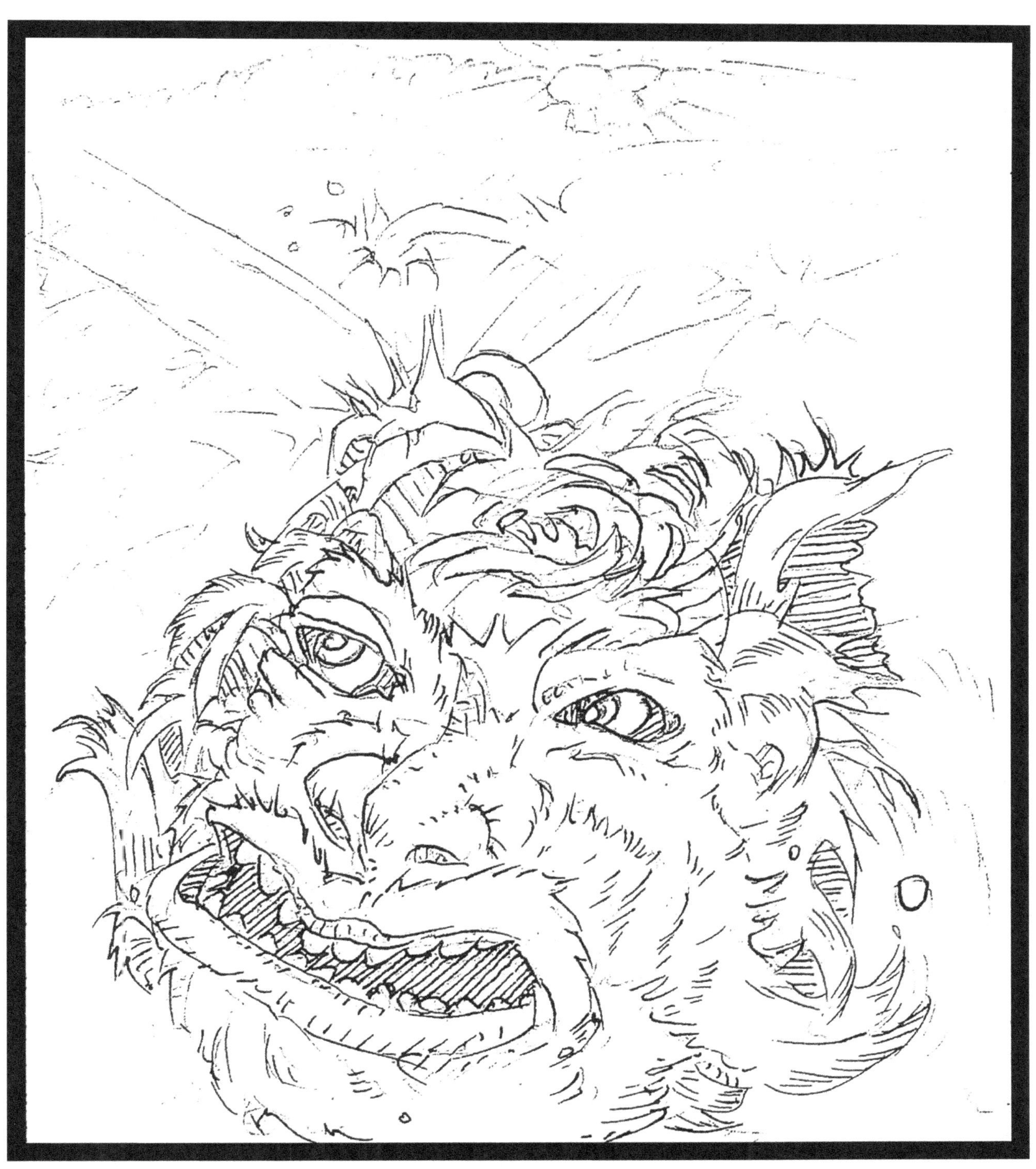

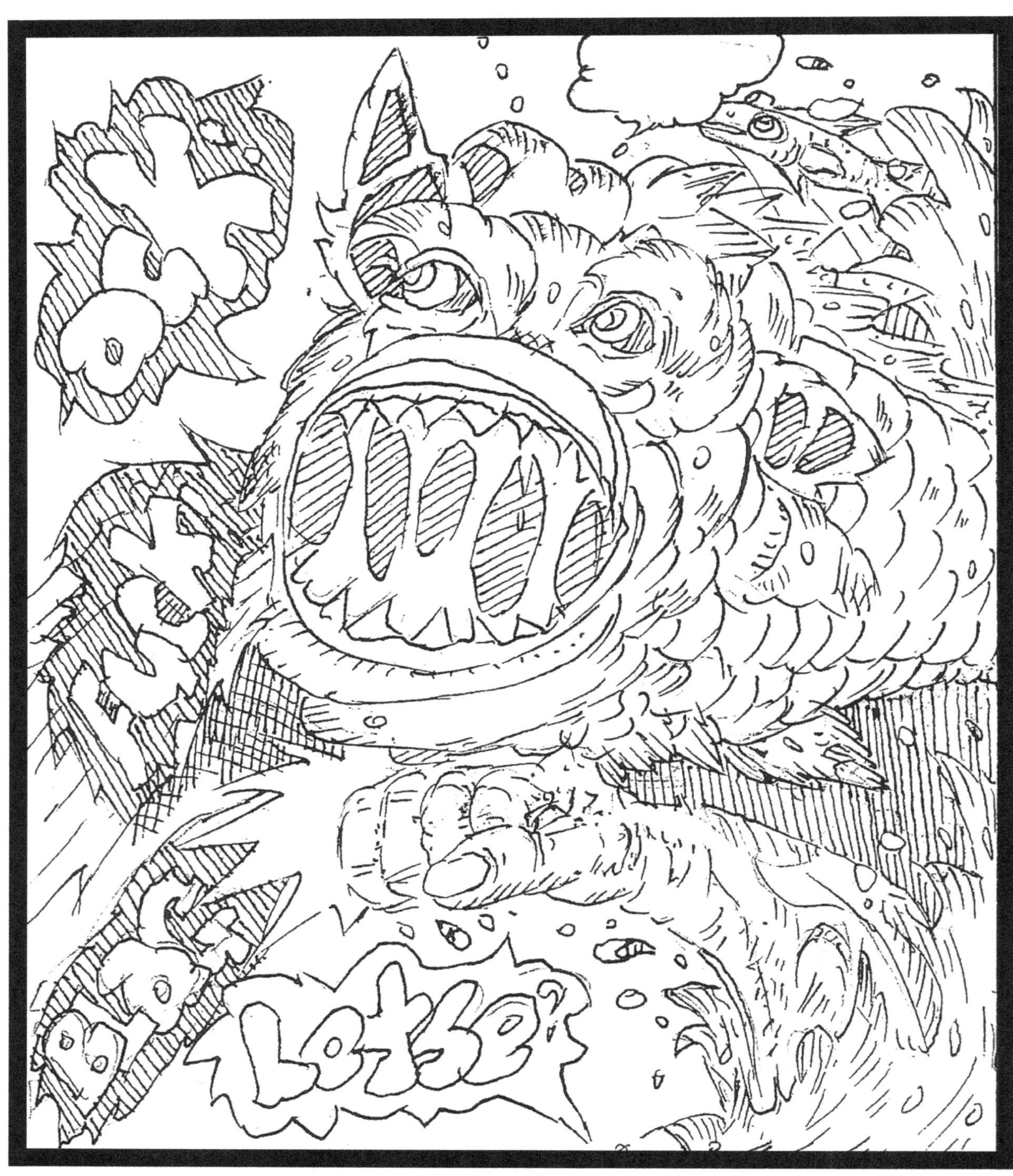
OH SH*
FU*K
BLACK
LOTUS?

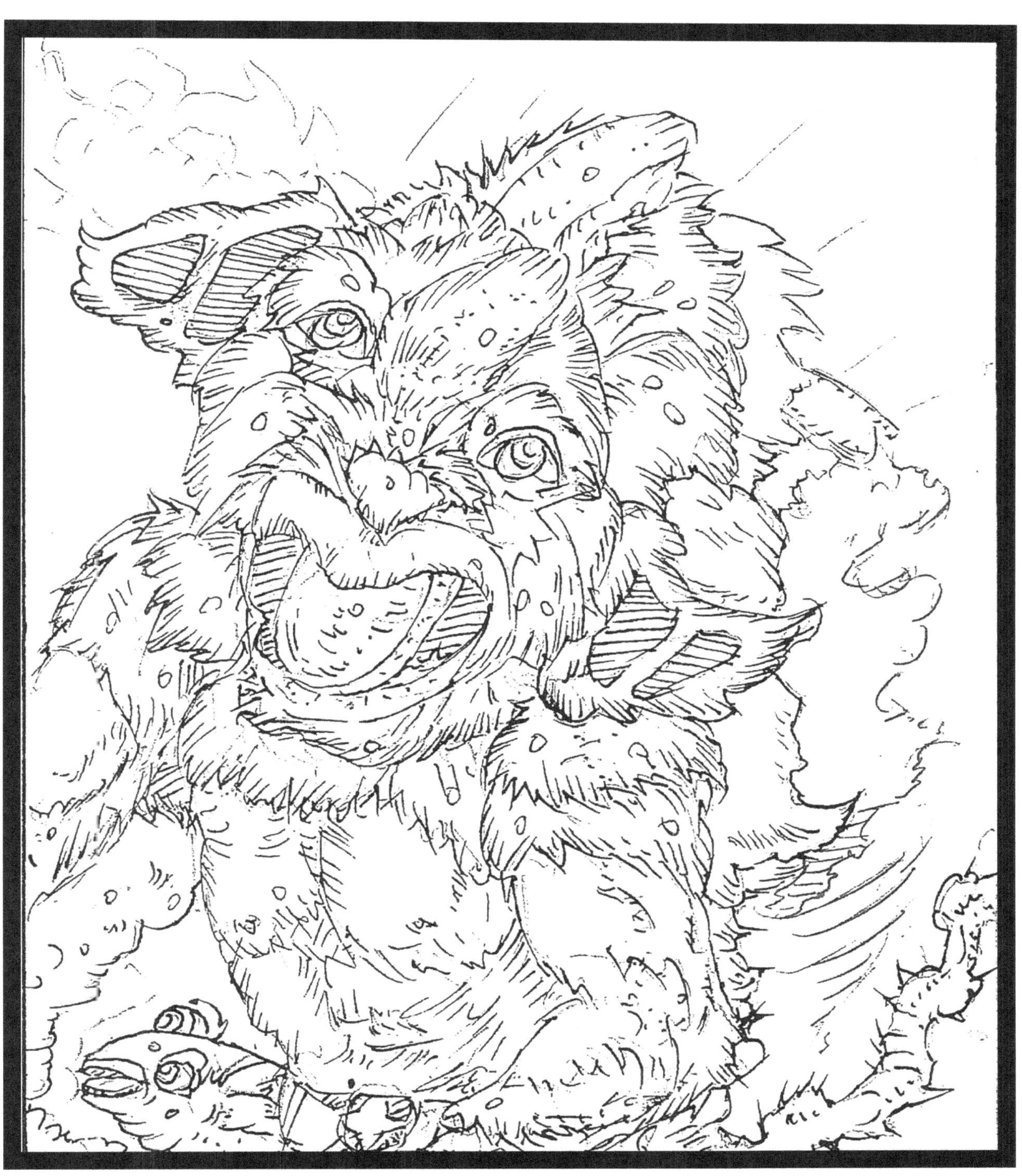

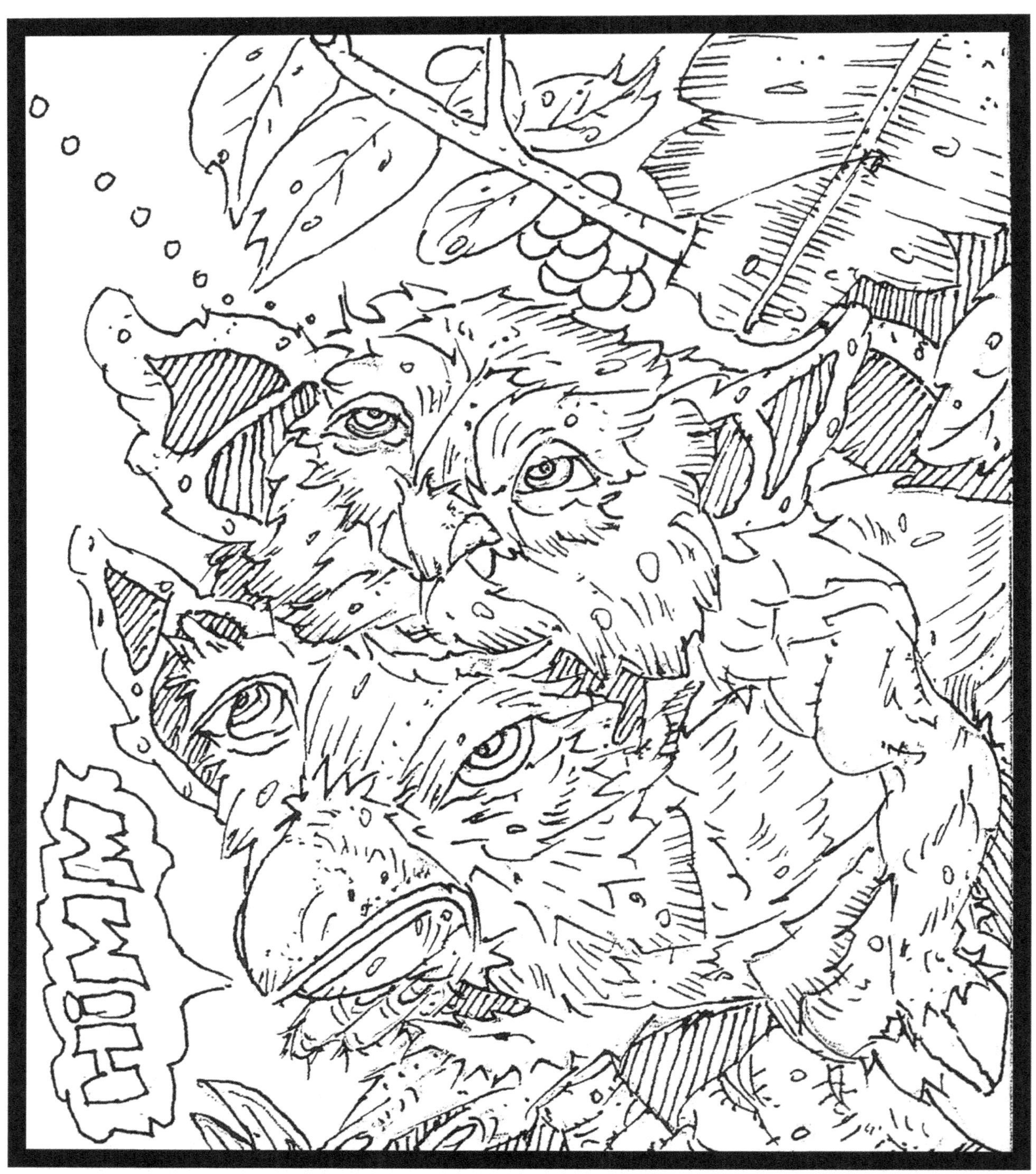

CHOMM!

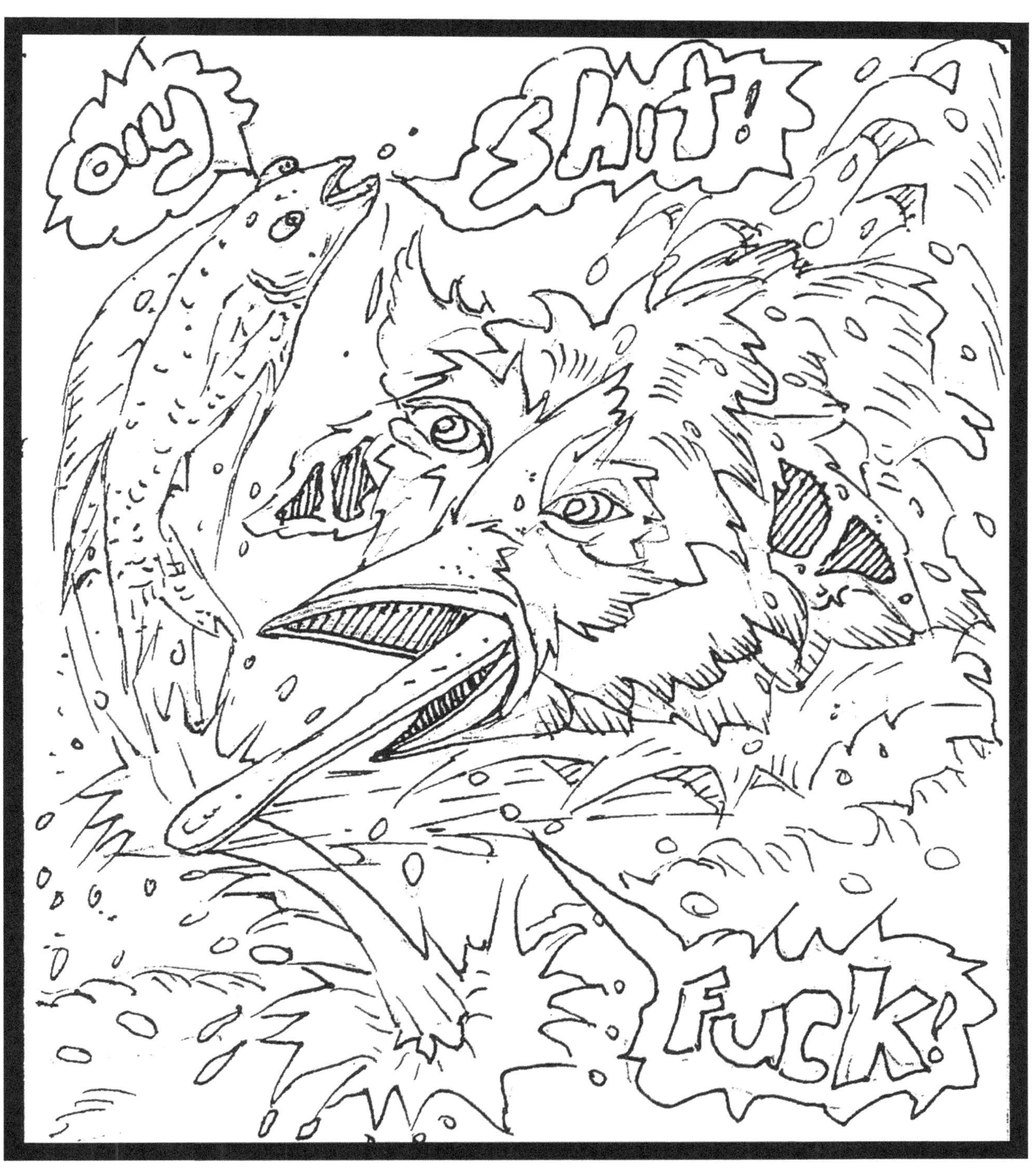

Oy!
Shit!
Fuck!

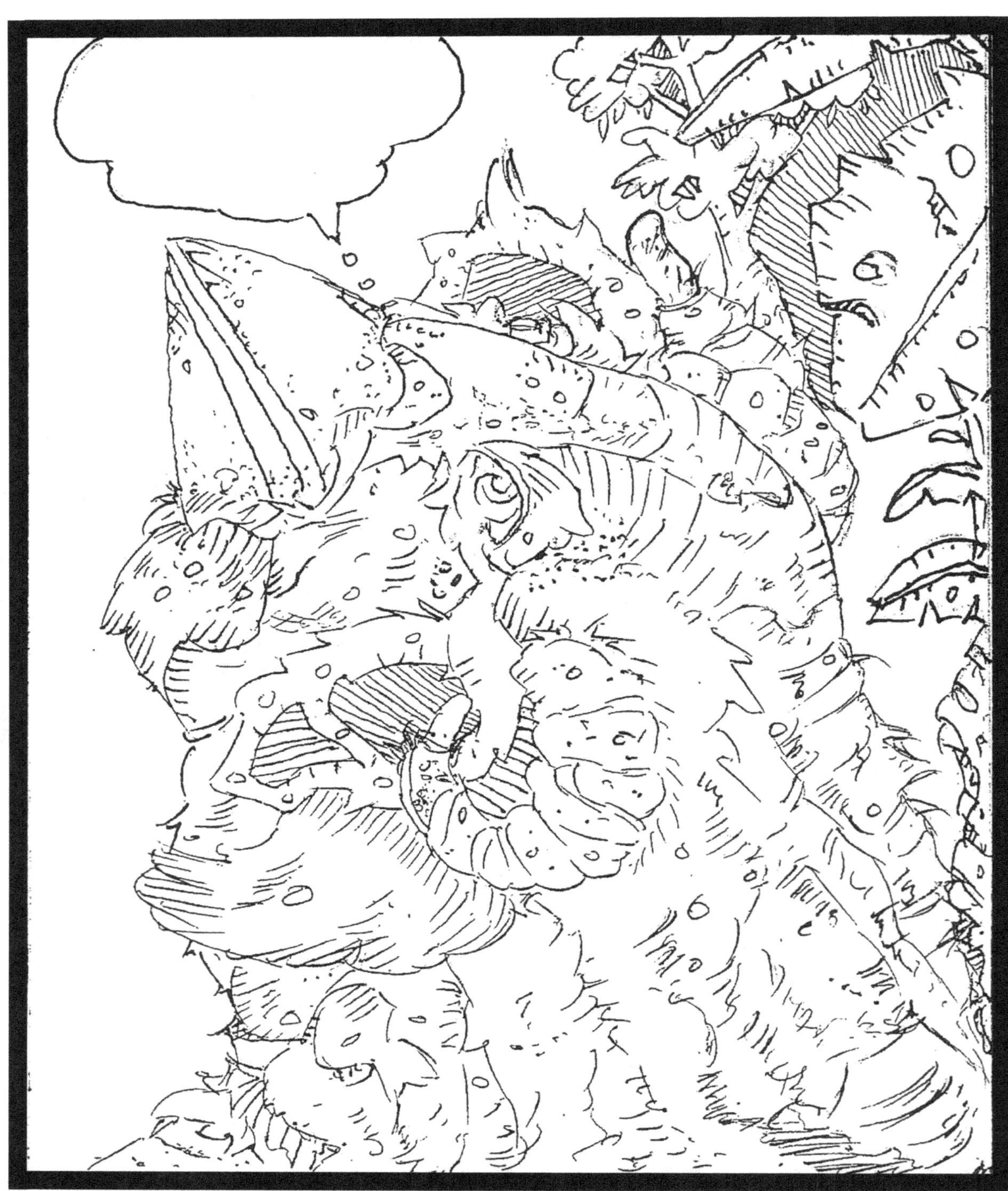

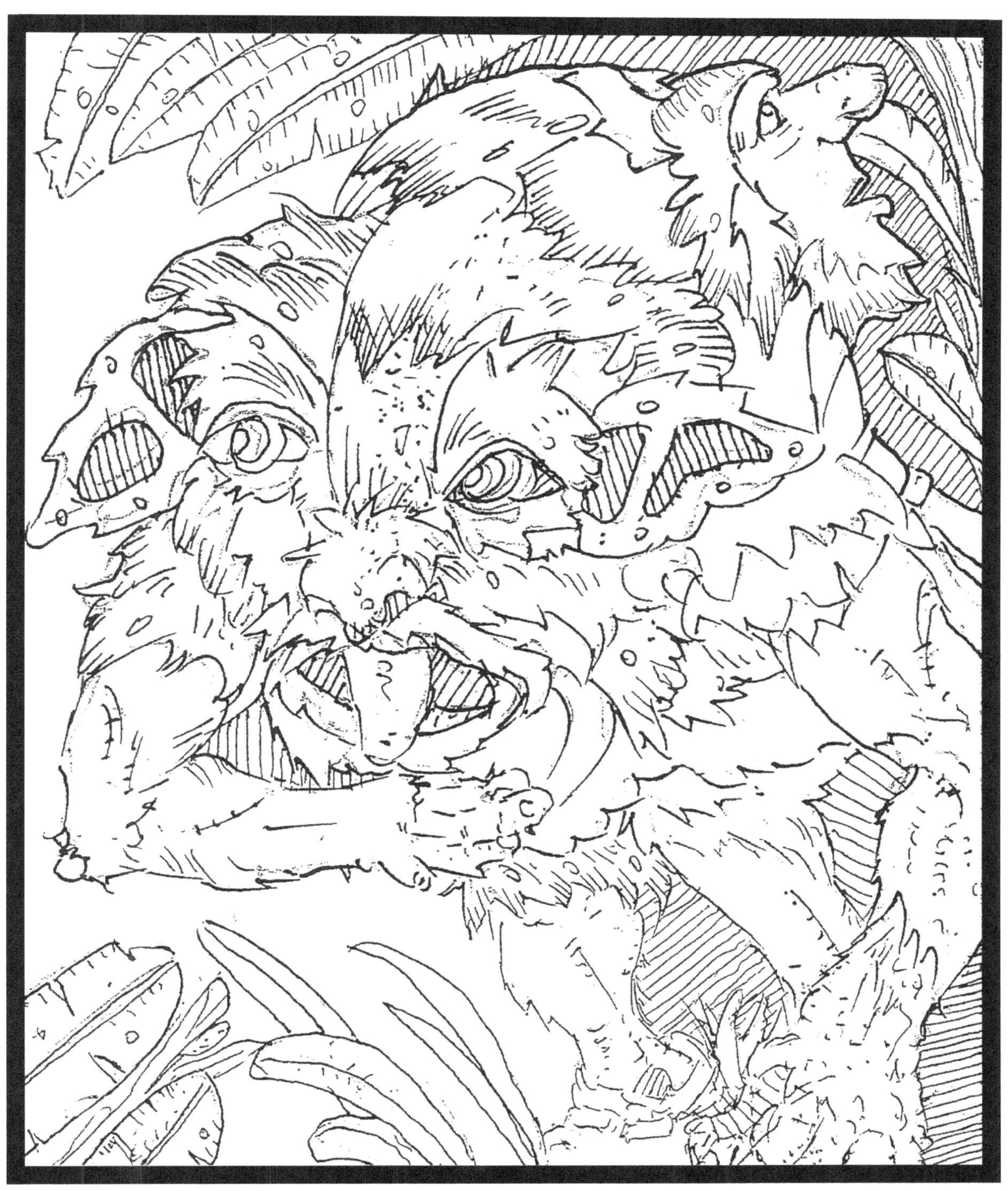

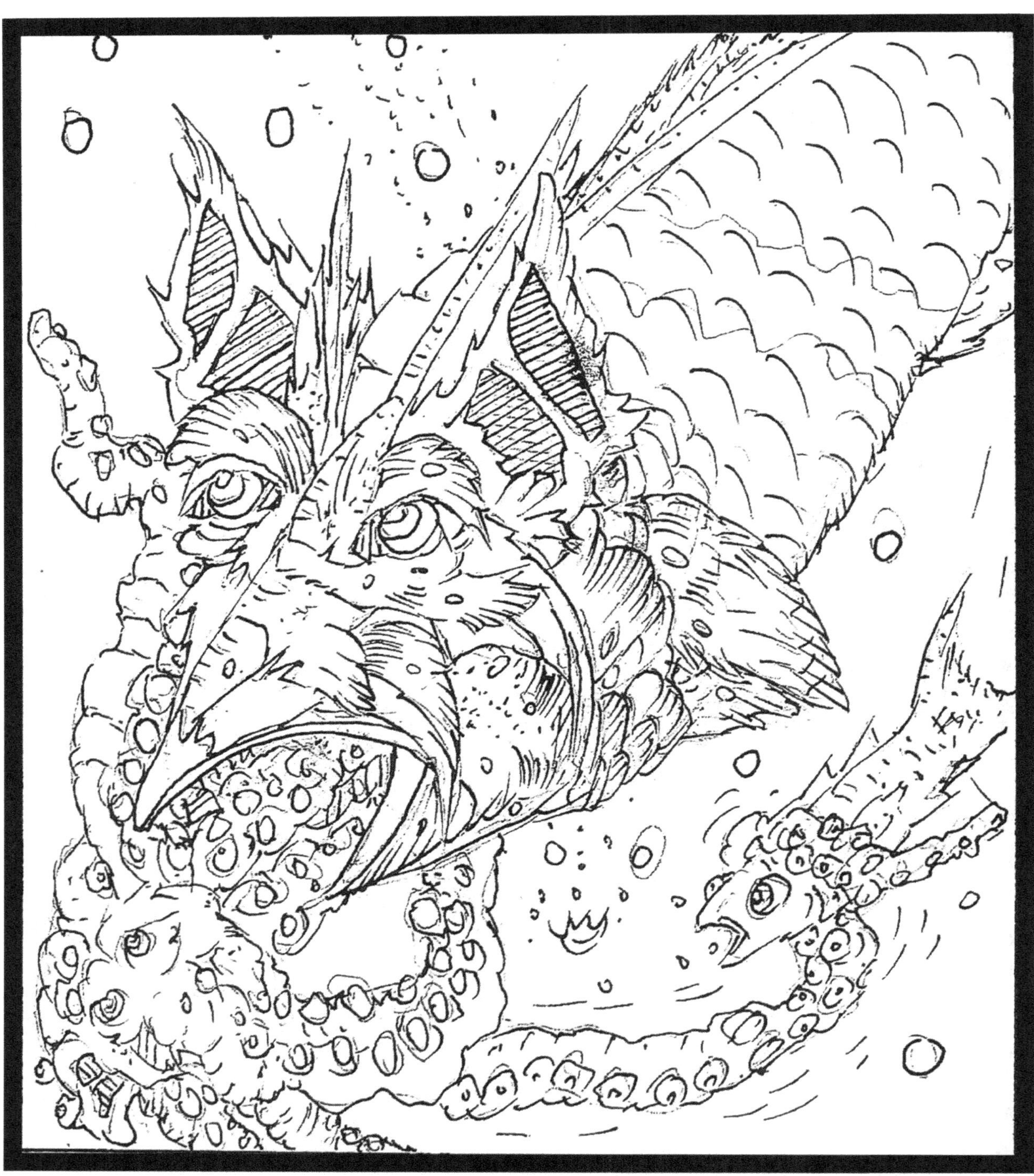

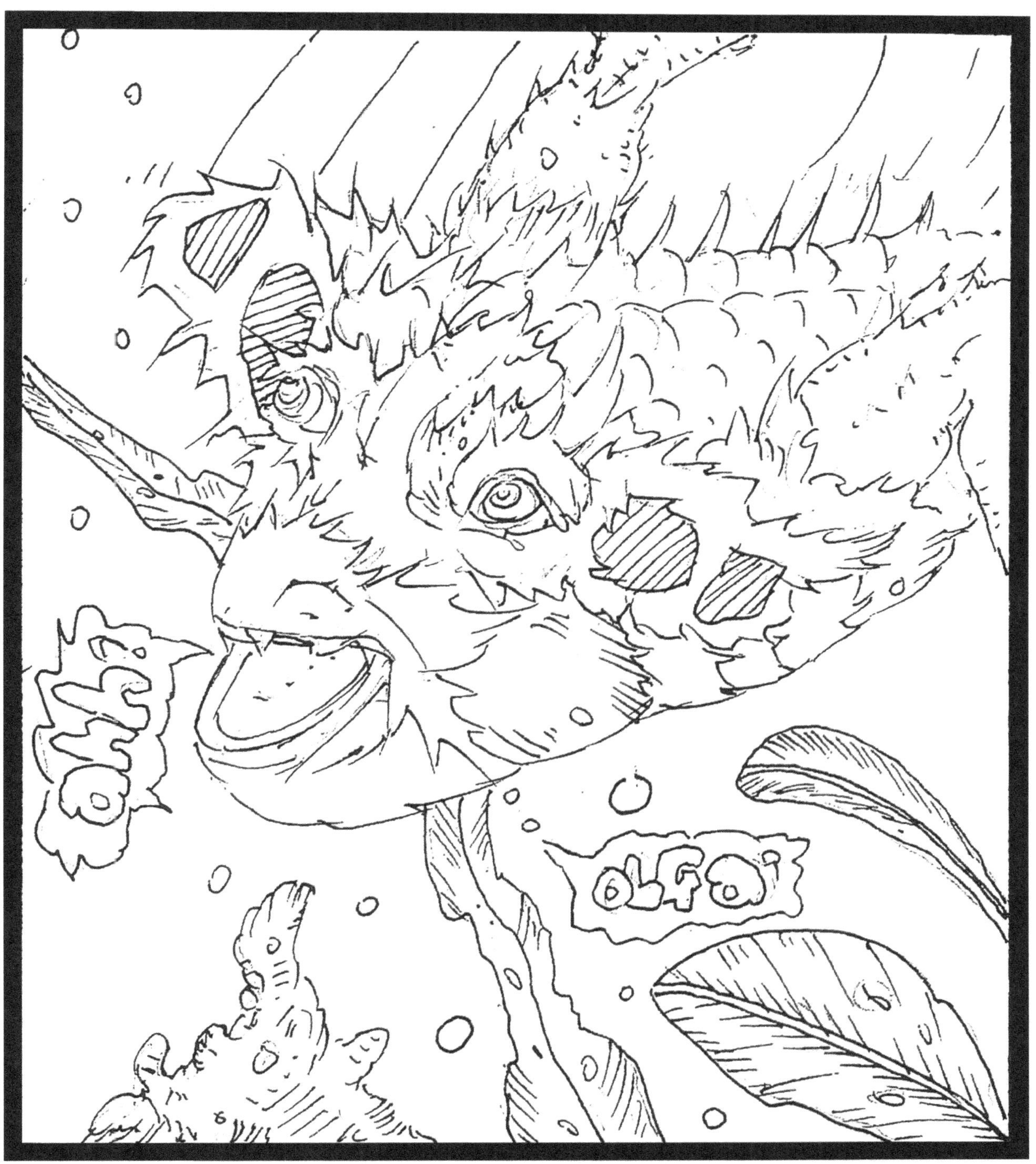

237

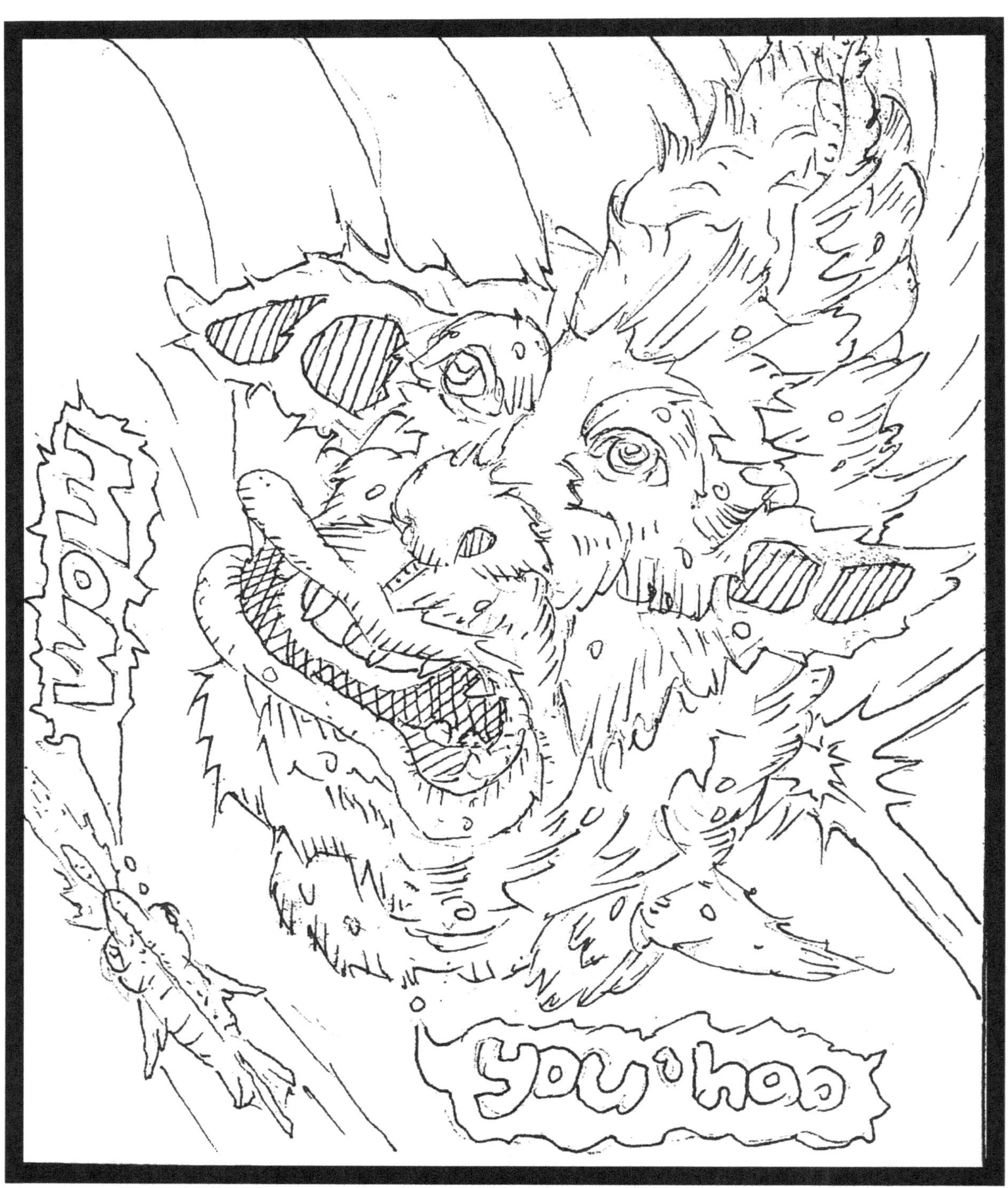

WOW
YOU'hoo

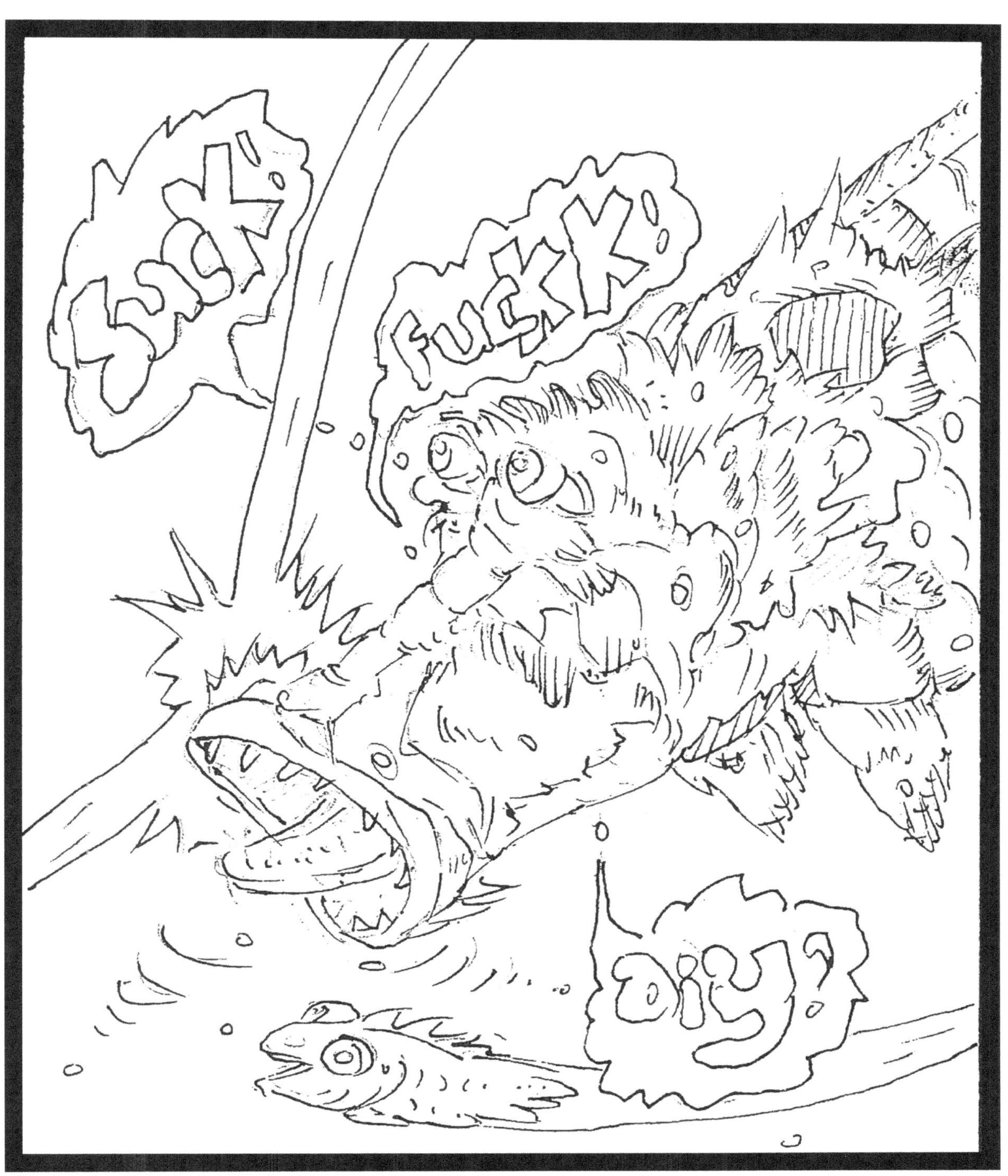

Suck!
FucKK!
DiY?

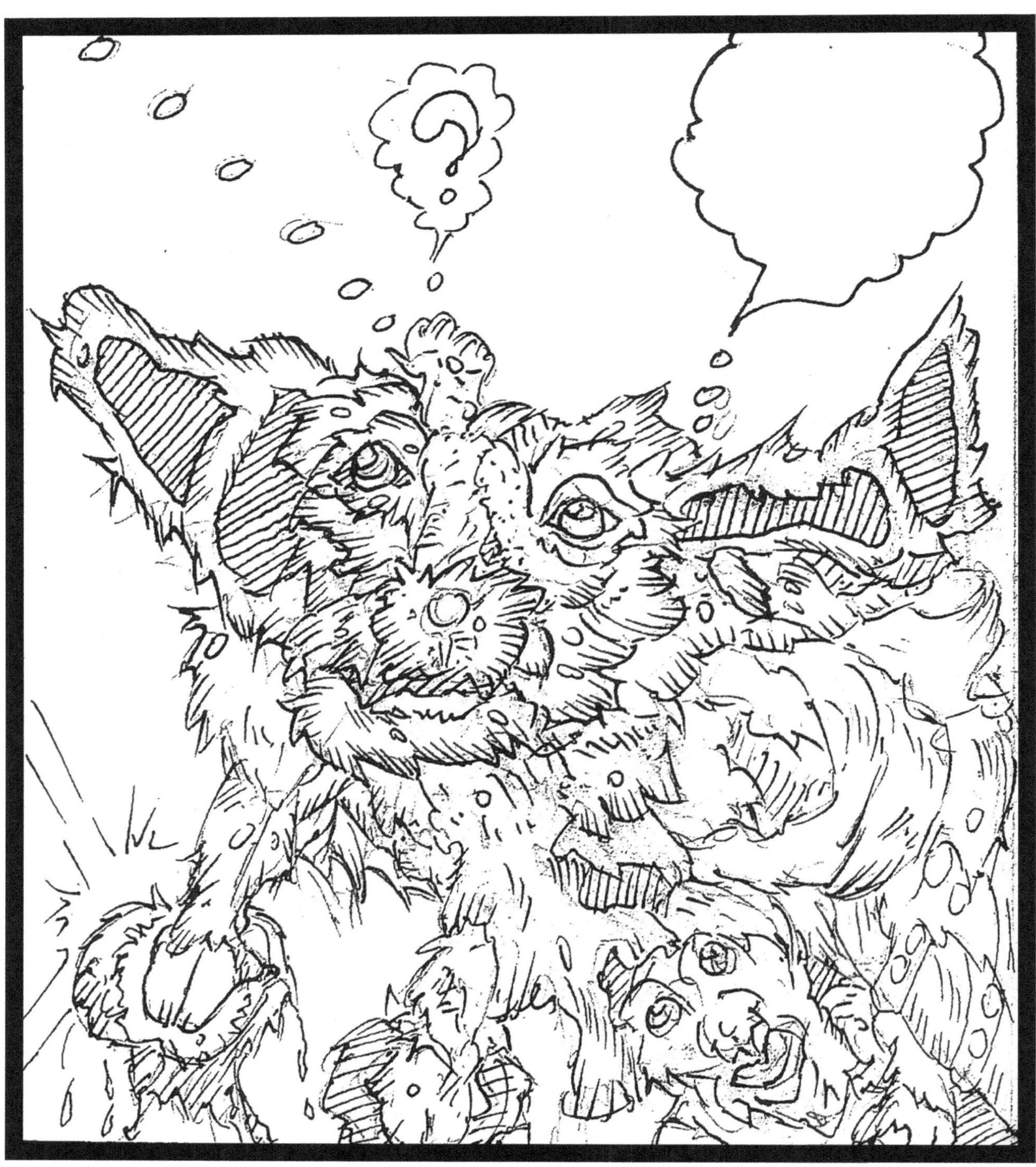

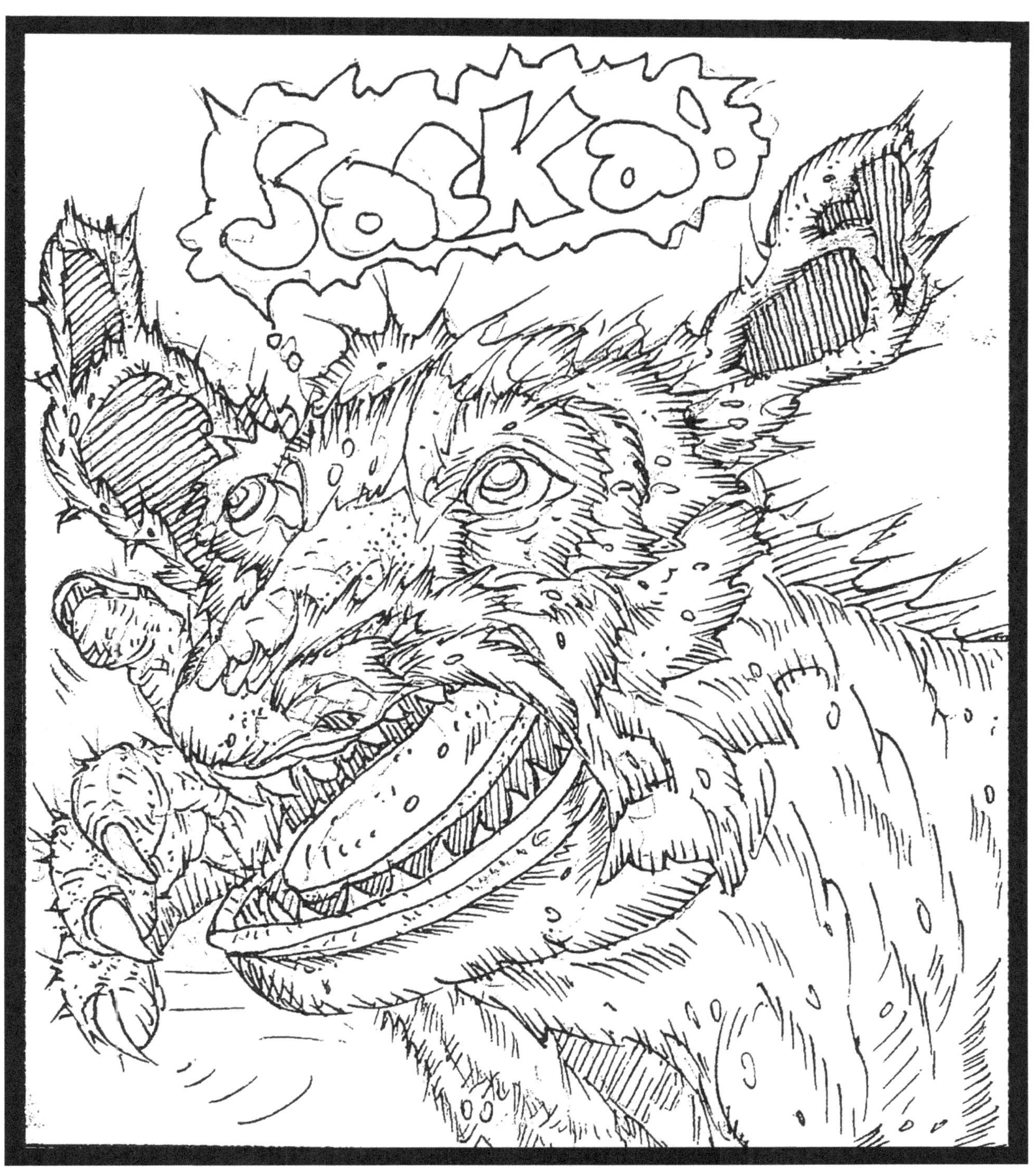

SaKa!

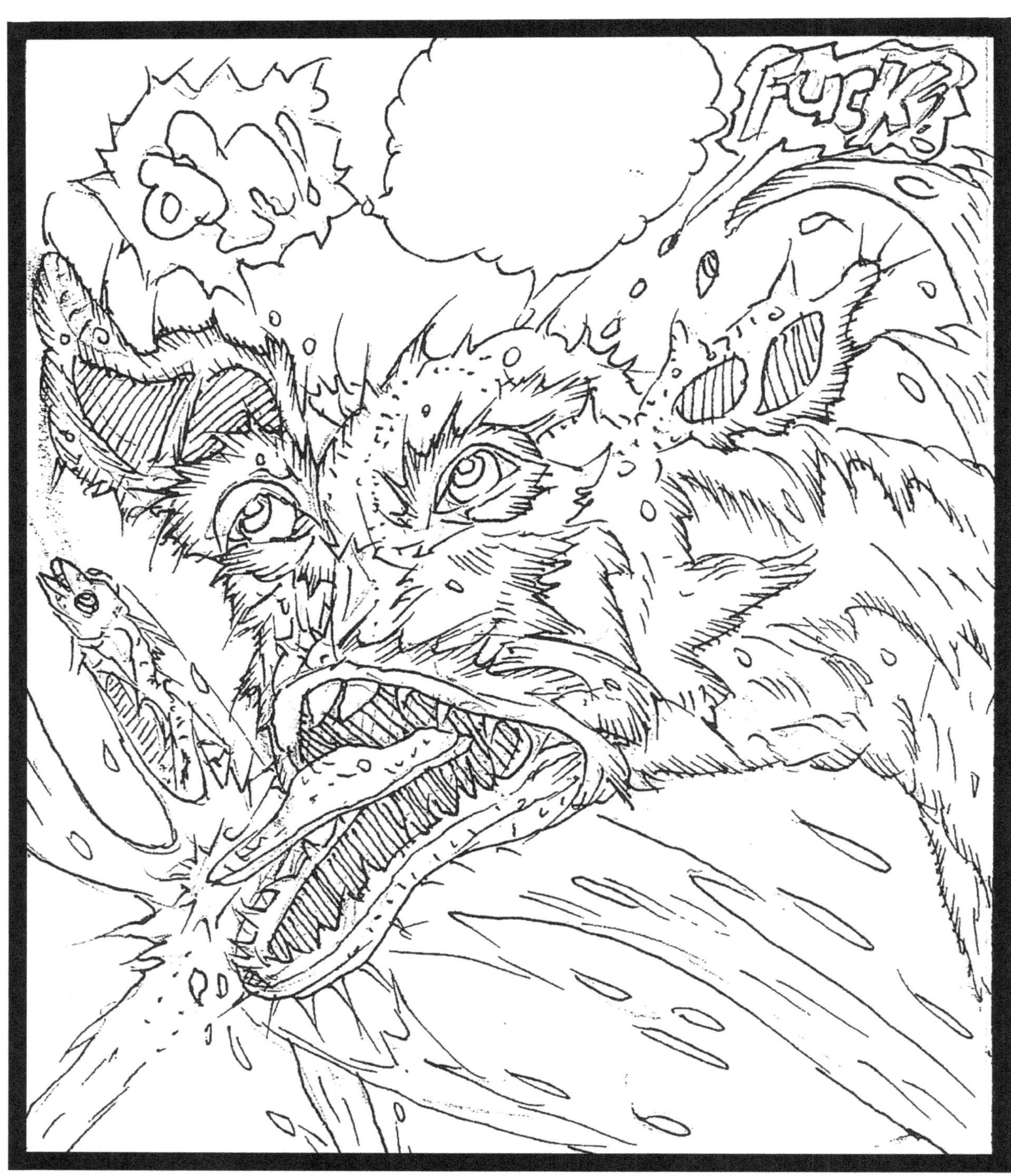
FUCK!

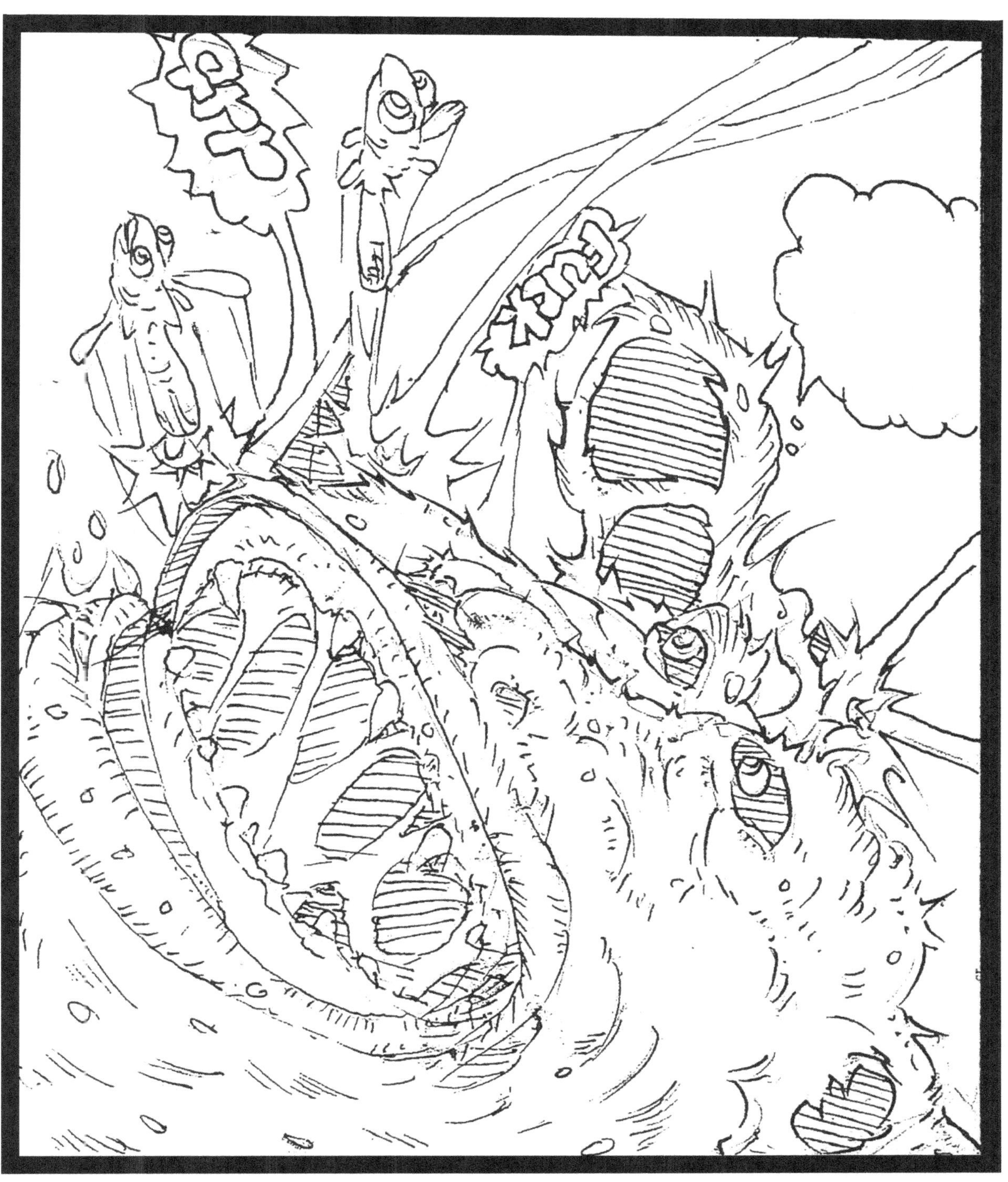
GRP
FUK

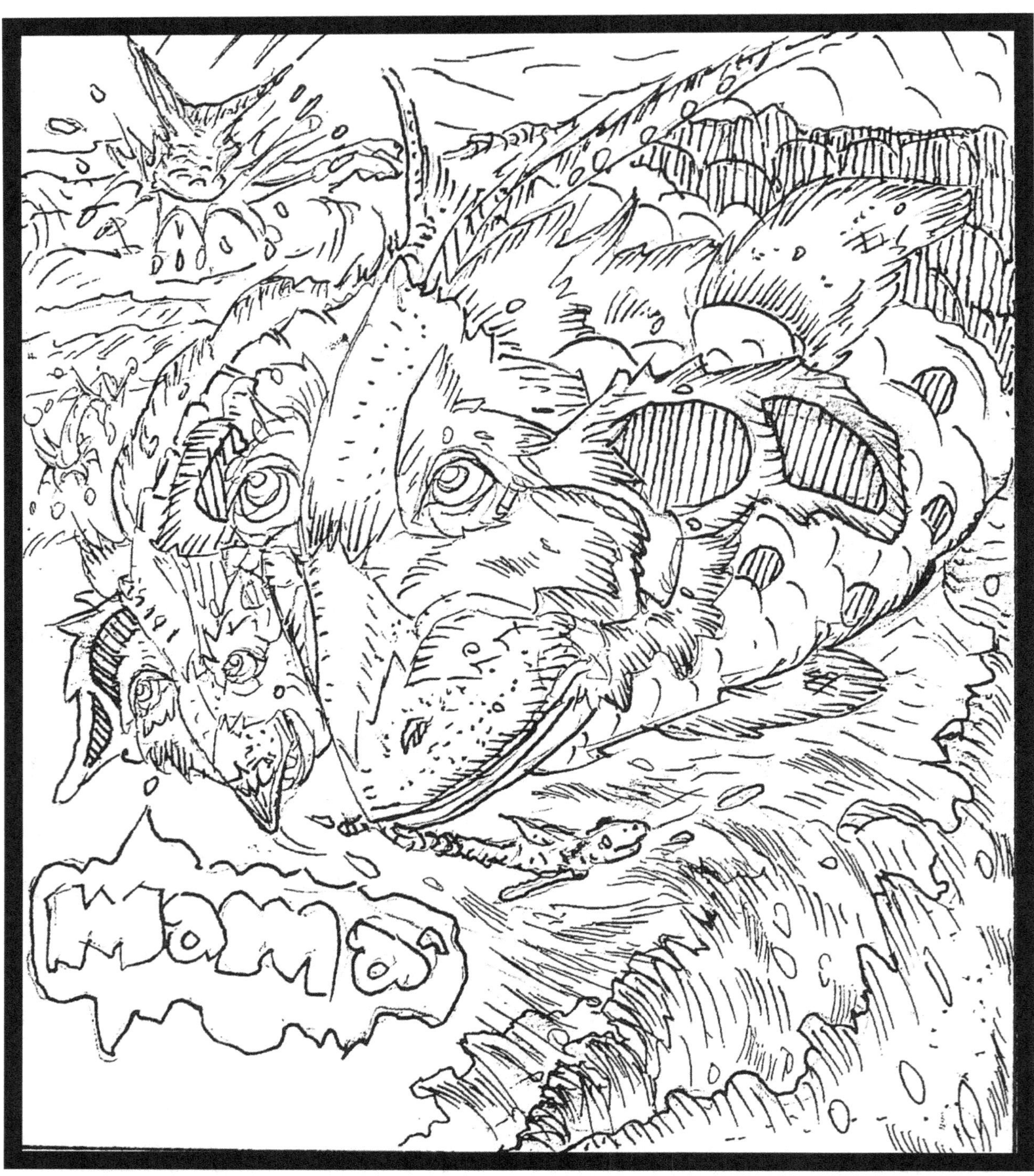

mama

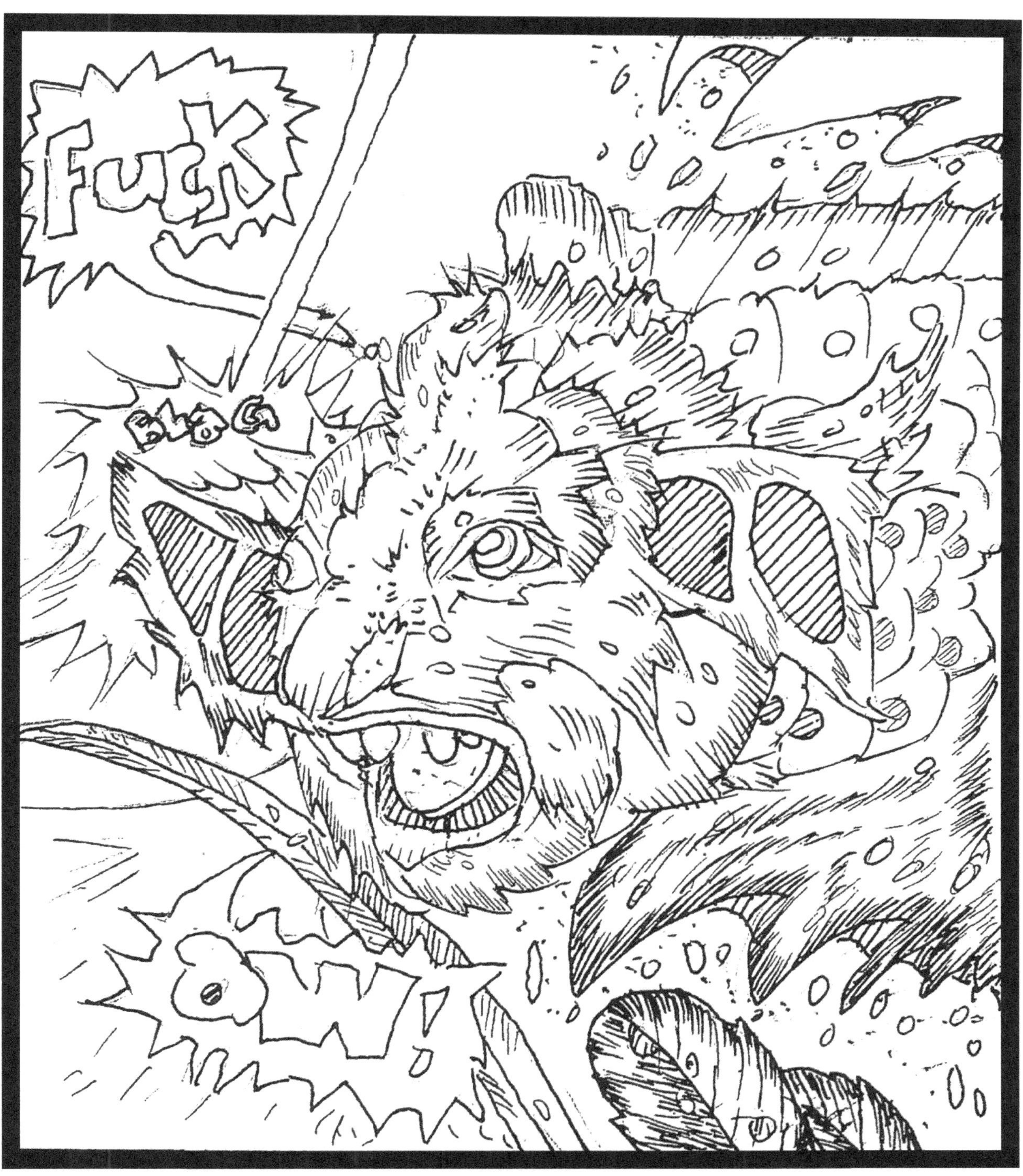

FucK
BLBG
OW!

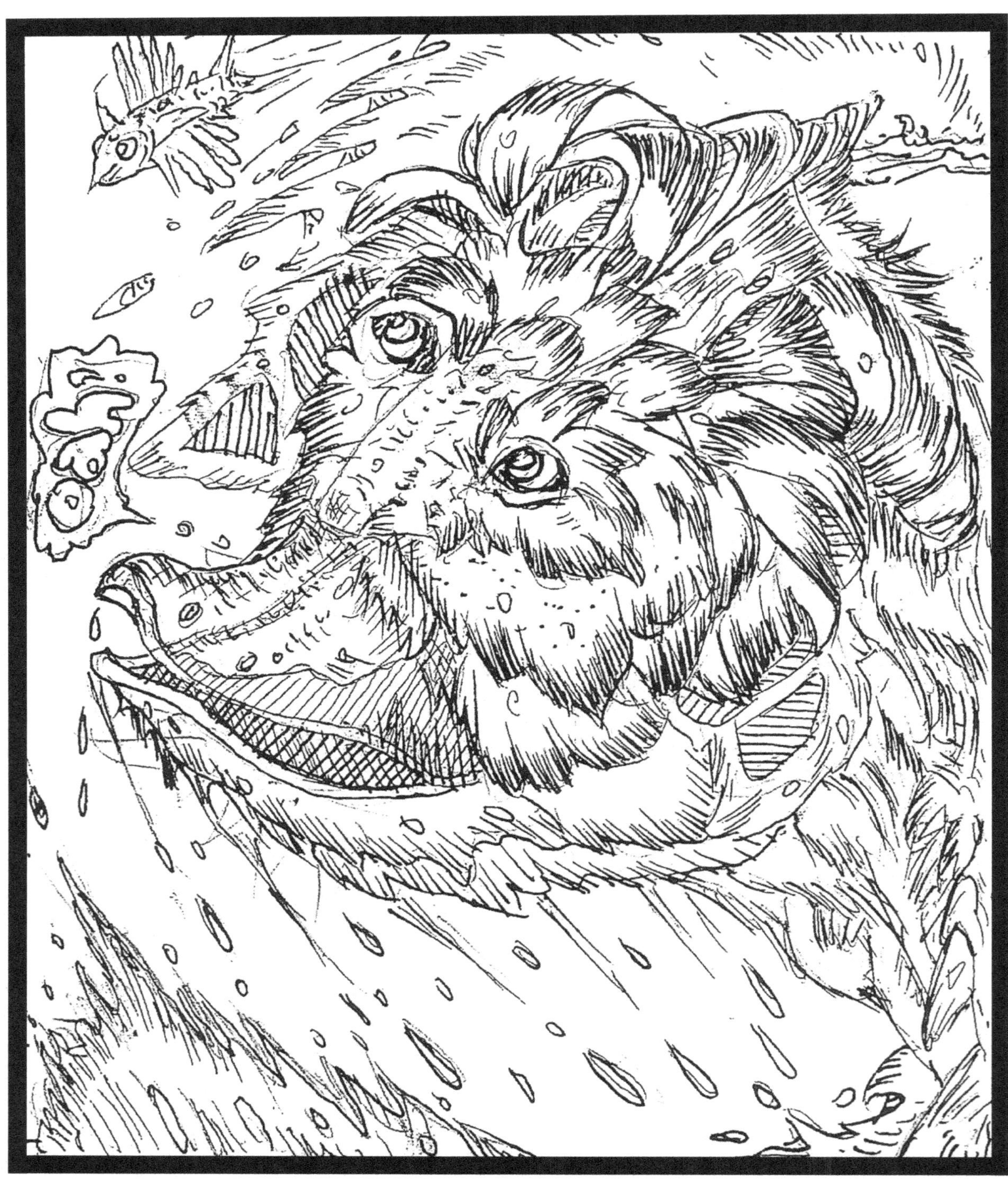

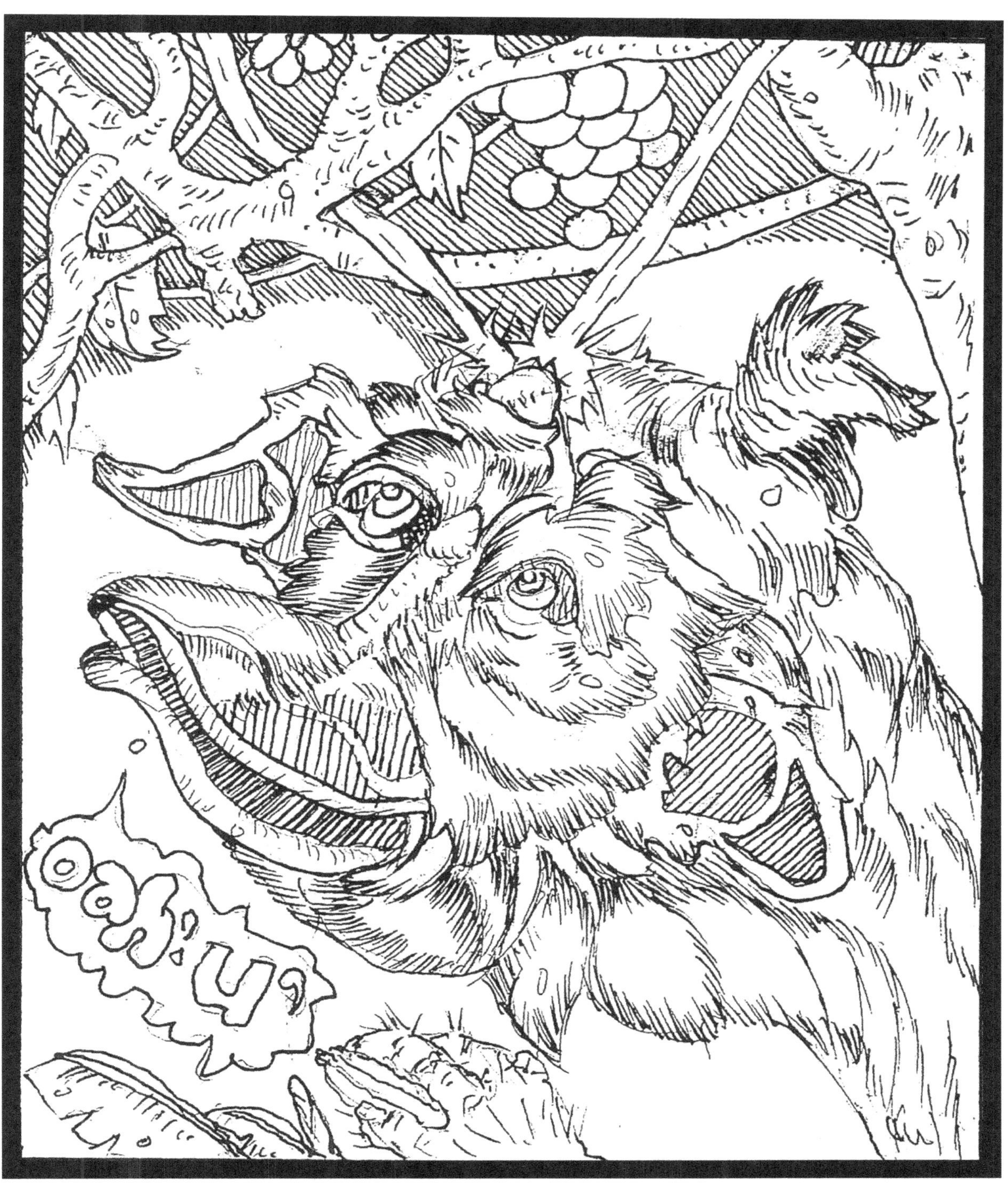
Oah'u?